ART THAT MOVES

ART THAT MOVES

the work of

LEN LYE

roger horrocks

AUCKLAND UNIVERSITY PRESS

in memory of Leigh Davis
poet / artist / innovator

First published 2009
This reprint 2015

Auckland University Press
University of Auckland
Private Bag 92019
Auckland 1142
New Zealand
www.press.auckland.ac.nz

ISBN 978 1 86940 422 2

National Library of New Zealand Cataloguing-in-Publication Data
Horrocks, Roger.
Art that moves : the work of Len Lye / Roger Horrocks.
Includes bibliographical references and index.
ISBN 978-1-86940-422-2
1. Lye, Len, 1901-1980. 2. Artists—New Zealand—Biography.
3. Kinetic sculpture—New Zealand. 4. Experimental films—New Zealand. I. Title.
709.2—dc 22

COVER DESIGN: Sarah Maxey
Printed in China by Everbest Printing Co. Ltd

contents

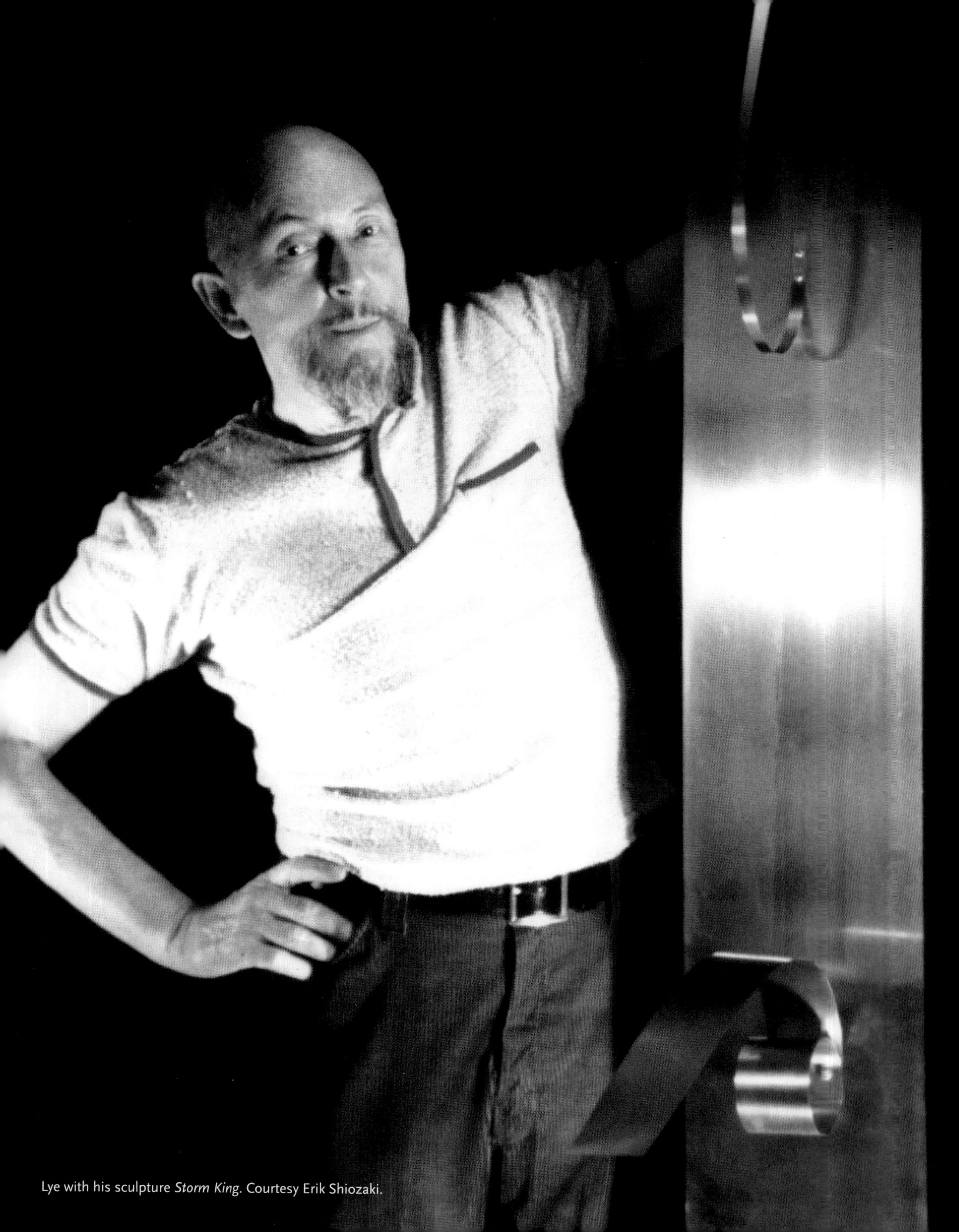

Lye with his sculpture *Storm King*. Courtesy Erik Shiozaki.

introduction

THIS BOOK IS BOTH ABOUT AN IMPORTANT ARTIST – LEN LYE – AND about a big idea: that movement (or motion) can be composed as art. Lye believed that only a few of the possibilities of the idea had so far been explored. His writings supplied the theory for a new kind of art, and his films and kinetic sculptures demonstrated the practice. To get to know them is to learn to look at movement from a new perspective. In a 1964 essay, 'The Art that Moves', Lye wrote:

> Kinetic art is the first new category of art since prehistory. Its cultural value rates with that of both painting and sculpture . . . . [but] it took until this century to discover the art that moves. Had we taken the aesthetic qualities of sound as much for granted as we have taken those of motion, we would not now have music. But now, in kinetic art, we have begun to compose motion.[1]

Artists' manifestos tend to overstate their case, but my book seeks to show that Lye could strongly support these claims by the power and originality of his films and sculptures. In addition, his essays represent a highly ambitious and coherent attempt to theorise an art of movement. By working in this area, he felt he could express his 'most poetical sense of being'.[2] My book aims to explore what the world of art – and the world in general – may have looked like through the eyes of an artist whose primary interest was 'the mystery of motion'.[3]

I was first drawn to Len Lye's work by the energy of his films. After corresponding with him for several years, I went to New York to meet him, and ended up working as his assistant for the last months of his life. His personality was as lively and surprising as his art. While helping to pack up his work and personal papers to be shipped to the Govett-Brewster Art Gallery in New Zealand, I was amazed to discover how wide-ranging his career had been. I went on to research and write a book about his life – *Len Lye: A Biography* – published in 2001.[4] I continued to derive great pleasure from his films and sculptures, and decided a couple of years ago to follow up with a book about his work. Public interest in Lye was increasing, and people kept asking me for information about how exactly he had made his art. Also, sensing the fact that his work was based on an unusual approach, they wanted to learn more about his ideas.

As I researched this book, I found myself coming to share Lye's obsession with 'the mystery of motion'. What exactly is an art of motion, and is it really as new as he claimed? There are studies of kinetic art, but I felt that none of them was persistent enough in seeking to analyse the aesthetics of literal movement. From Lye's perspective, the development of such an art called for new thinking about artistic form and a new approach to the training of artists. Like the related term 'energy', movement is ubiquitous in our lives, but we seldom analyse its meaning or its implications. We leave that to physicists and mathematicians, who provide impressive but highly technical formulas such as Newton's laws of motion or Einstein's $e=mc^2$. When I re-read Lye's own writings, both published and unpublished, I was struck by the care he had devoted to thinking about the human experience of movement and energy in personal and practical terms.[5]

Not that these were his only interests. His independent habits of mind led him to pursue experiments in many areas of art, and his other discoveries also deserve to be discussed and celebrated. But having come to see his theory and practice of 'the art that moves' as his most important contribution, I decided to make it the central focus of this book. Movement for Lye was all-pervasive – it was 'absolutely nothing or everything, ask any electron, atom or molecule, light, sound or any vibration mental or otherwise . . . . So movement needs all the insight possible . . .'[6] He was fascinated by what science was discovering about the flux of energies in nature, on both a microscopic and an astronomical scale, and he sought opportunities to discuss such matters with scientists. But his primary concern was to shape his own 'figures of motion' via the technologies at his disposal.

He was well aware of the attempts by traditional forms of art to imply motion – such as the Japanese prints of curling waves. And, 'since prehistory', dance had been exploring literal movement through the medium of the human body. He included dance as an important element in kinetic art, but he saw that technologies such as film and the electric motor produced new forms of motion which 'freed us from the restricted anatomical range of dance movements'.[7]

Today we have access to new forms of technology that can further enlarge the scope and potential of kinetic art. The powers of the computer can be used for many purposes, from the animation and circulation of images, to the production of large-scale versions of the sculptures that Lye designed but could not realise during his lifetime. His aesthetic continues to be just as relevant to the digital age as it was previously, as a guide to the dynamic ways by which artists can make best use of their resources to 'compose motion'.

Many critics and curators have recognised the originality of Lye's approach to movement. For example, when a new national art museum for Germany – the Kunst und Ausstellungshalle der Bundesrepublik Deutschland – held its opening exhibition in 1992, it presented its selection of the 100 most original artists of the 20th century. These were artists who had created 'masterpieces', 'extraordinary objects', 'seminal' works that had served to 'mark decisive points' in the history of art.[8] Lye was represented both by his sculpture *Universe* and his film *A Colour Box*. In explaining his inclusion alongside better-known artists such as Picasso, Dalí, Mondrian and Pollock, the catalogue quoted Lye's comments: 'Motion sculpture is a distinct form of modern art . . . . [My] sculpture, extending the infinite variety of fundamental patterns of movement, emphasizes the beauty of motion *per se*.'[9]

Pontus Hultén, the director of the museum and the main curator of this exhibition, was an enthusiast for kinetic art. But not everyone in the art world has shared that interest. While there have been other important museum appearances of Lye's work – such as a one-person exhibition of his films, sculptures, paintings and photograms at the Centre Pompidou in Paris in 2000, and a string of recent exhibitions in Australia (such as ACMI in Melbourne) – he has tended to remain better known to fellow practitioners than to the public at large.

His reputation has also suffered from the ups and downs of kinetic art in general. The art of motion had a great surge of popularity in the late 1950s and early 1960s, when the work of many artists was included in survey exhibitions.

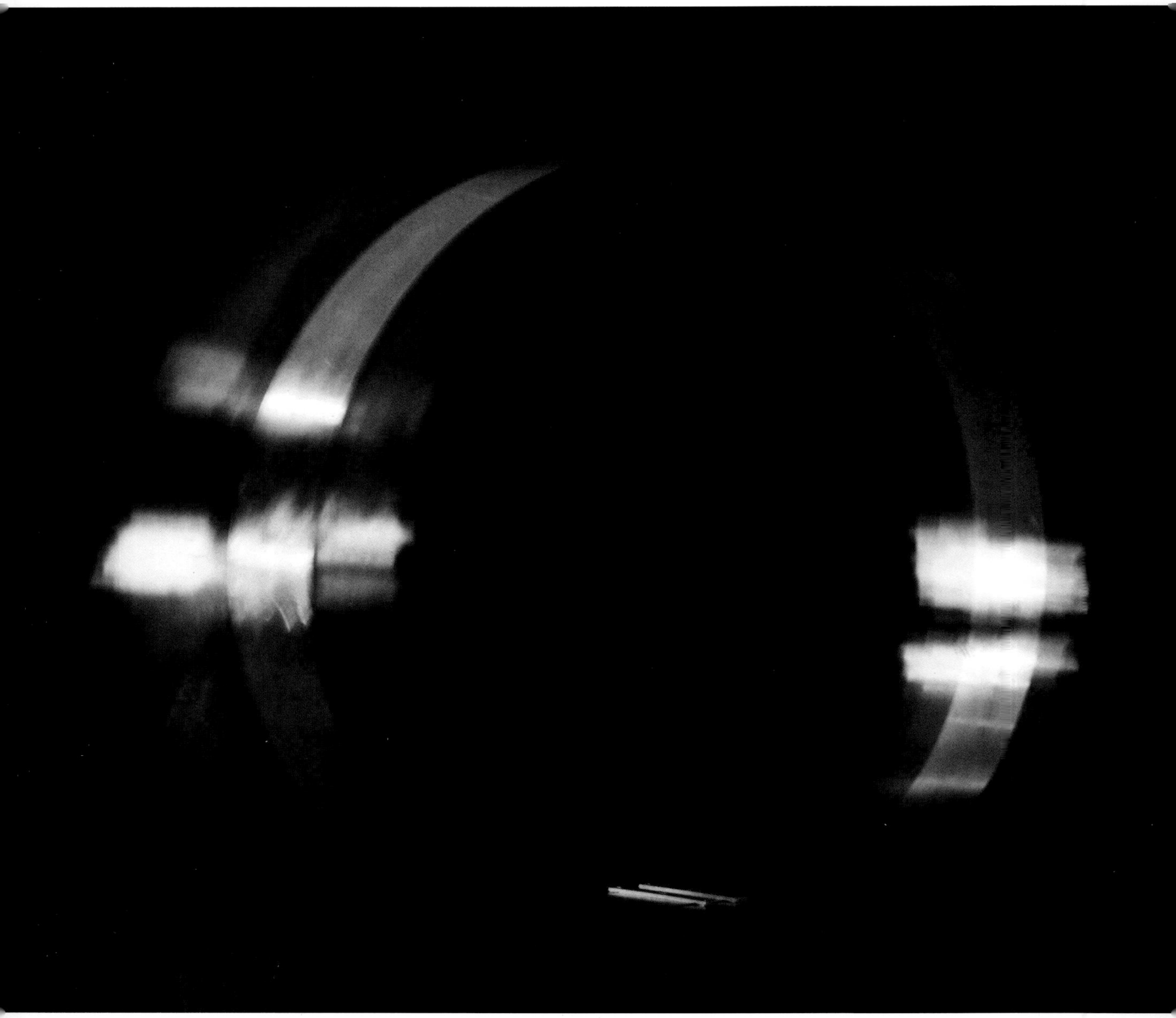

The sculpture *Universe* in motion. Courtesy Len Lye Foundation.

These shows drew large, enthusiastic crowds, but once the novelty had worn off, the category of kinetic art passed out of fashion. One of the problems was the uncritical, loose and all-inclusive way the concept of kinetic art was used, which made art critics impatient. While Lye's ideas were solid and specific, they were not heard in the midst of the hype. Kinetic art suffered not only from the art world's short attention span but also from the reluctance of many museums, dealers and auction houses to get involved in the maintenance and repair of motorised sculptures. It was more comfortable to return to the silence and stillness of traditional forms of art. Kinetic art was also not in tune with the cynical mood of post-modernism, which saw the genre as tainted by a naïve enthusiasm for science and technology. Individual artists such as Alexander Calder, Jean Tinguely, Vassilakis Takis and George Rickey continued to have exhibitions, as did Lye; and a few younger artists such as Rebecca Horn and Tim Hawkinson have gained international reputations through their innovative work with movement. But the idea that kineticism might represent a significant new 'category of art' has ceased to receive much attention.

Lye's deeply serious, manifesto-style advocacy of kinetic art looks back in some respects to 20th-century modernism, but that field of activity was more complex than we tend to acknowledge. Modernism opened up many new paths, and not all have become well-worn. Movement is a particularly clear example of business that remains incomplete because of 'the overwhelming technical and financial difficulties attending all kinetic experiments' (as Jack Burnham put it in 1968), and because of the problems of art-world politics described above.[10] Lye hoped that his work was 'going to be pretty good for the 21st century', and as Chapter 6 will document, his work and ideas are in fact having a delayed influence.[11]

This artist did important work in two media – film as well as sculpture – which gave him an unusually broad perspective on 'the art that moves'. Unfortunately, his major essays on the subject are either out of print or have never been published. My book aims to provide the first detailed account of his art of motion that covers both theory and practice. Many thoughtful critical essays have been written about particular aspects of Lye's work but there is not, to my knowledge, any text that focuses on what he regarded as his core concerns. This is not to imply that an artist's perspective on his or her own work should be regarded as the last word on the subject – but in Lye's case it seems useful as the starting point.

I will concentrate on his work in film and sculpture, but will also explore aspects of his painting, photography and writing that reflect an interest in movement.

The first chapter establishes historical contexts, starting with philosophers and photographers in the second half of the 19th century, and going on to trace the theme of movement in modernist art in the first decades of the 20th century. Lye enters at this point and draws ideas from the work of some of these forerunners. Chapter 2 traces the development of his art and thinking over his career. Having established a biographical context, Chapter 3 attempts to sum up his conception of 'the art that moves' as a theory relevant not only to Lye but also to any artist who works with motion. The subsequent chapters examine his practice as a filmmaker (Chapter 4) and as a kinetic sculptor (Chapter 5). In this way, the book seeks to provide the first systematic overview of Lye's achievement as a kinetic artist, looking at his most important works (such as *Free Radicals* and *Flip and Two Twisters*), and exploring interesting aspects of his other films and sculptures. The aim is to identify his distinctive idiom and to map out critical parameters.

The final chapter, 'Lye Today', uses problems of conservation to provide additional insights into his practice, besides telling the story of how and why large-scale versions of his sculpture came to be built posthumously in New Zealand. At times controversial, these activities highlight the need to develop new ways of thinking about restoration if future generations are to continue to have access to 20th-century kinetic art.

The book is accompanied by a DVD which contains some beautiful footage of Lye sculptures (directed by Shirley Horrocks). It also includes four of Lye's films, generously made available by the Len Lye Foundation. While his films can be fully appreciated only when they are projected in their original (celluloid) form, these digital copies should at least provide a useful introduction. The DVD begins with a new short film I wrote and directed, *Art that Moves* (produced by Shirley Horrocks, with camerawork by Leon Narbey). Within the constraints of a small budget, this film offers a creative reconstruction of Lye's early life and ideas. Its free-wheeling approach is intended to supplement the more scholarly, art-historical methods of the book.

A note on this reprint: I have updated the list of 'Resources' at the end of the book. Otherwise, its discussion of the principles of Lye's work as an artist remains relevant and has not been changed. In terms of Lye's legacy, however, I want to add one important piece of news: the establishment (in July 2015) of the Len Lye Centre in New Plymouth, a museum devoted to his work, with striking architecture by Andrew Patterson in the spirit of the artist.

one precedents

CHANGES IN HOW WE THINK ABOUT MOVEMENT HAVE FAR-REACHING implications, transforming the way we understand nature and the way we represent it in art. In the 60 years before Lye began his career as an artist, movement was an important and controversial theme, in science and philosophy as well as in painting and sculpture. To consider the theme from this broad perspective matches the spirit of Lye's own approach – he was always looking for connections between those fields. I shall focus not only on the work that directly influenced him but – at least briefly – also consider the general environment of ideas. The chapter starts with some innovative Victorian thinkers, then traces the development of photography, film and other new technologies, ending with the wave of radical thinking associated with art movements such as Futurism and Constructivism. Lye would be born into a society still dominated by Victorian assumptions but his art would be energised by new ideas about movement.

PHILOSOPHERS OF CHANGE

Charles Darwin's book *On the Origin of Species* (1859) had a huge, continuing influence on artists and philosophers as well as on scientists, and henceforth an interest in motion was often linked with the theory of evolution. Lye was no exception, and one of his favourite themes was 'the beginnings of organic life up to [the] development of an anxiety all human' (as he summed up the subject of his film *Tusalava*).[1] Darwin's theory stimulated widespread debate about the nature of the life-force that propelled evolution, and in the case of some philosophers and scientists this led to a general interest in energy and movement – from the workings of the human body to the secrets of 'heat, electricity, magnetism, light'.[2] Such speculations spread beyond the scope of Darwin's thinking, but the success of his work encouraged the search for other large theories that might reveal the overall patterns of nature.

One such attempt was Herbert Spencer's *First Principles*, first published in 1862. The author was 'lionised' and his book was read by 'most serious-minded Victorians'.[3] To Spencer, the world was full of 'motions, visible and invisible, of masses and of molecules'.[4] His chapter on 'The Rhythm of Motions' is full of vivid observation as he seeks to demonstrate that 'vibration' and 'rhythm' are fundamental to nature:

> When the pennant of a vessel lying becalmed shows the coming breeze, it does so by gentle undulations which travel from its fixed to its free end. Presently the sails begin to flap; and their blows against the mast increase in rapidity as the breeze rises. Even when, being fully bellied out, they are in great part steadied by the strain of the yards and cordage, their free edges tremble with each stronger gust. And should there come a gale, the jar that is felt on laying hold of the shrouds shows that the rigging vibrates . . . . Ashore the conflict between the current of air and the things it meets results in a like rhythmical action. The leaves all shiver in the blast; each branch oscillates; and every exposed tree sways to and fro. The blades of grass . . . , and still better the stalks in the neighbouring corn-fields, exhibit the same rising and falling movement . . .[5]

Spencer's description continues for sixteen pages, describing and analysing a multitude of other rhythmic movements – the patterns of movement in rivers, the quiver of violin strings, the vibration of a tuning fork, the sway of a railway train, the beating of the human heart, the rhythms of poetry, the pulsation of the Aurora Borealis, the rise and fall of the tides, the orbit of the moon, the rotation of spiral nebulae. 'Life, as it exists in every member of [every] species, is an extremely complex kind of movement . . . .'[6] For Spencer, 'all motion is rhythmical', and, 'Rhythm is very generally not simple but compound. There are usually at work various forces, causing undulations differing in rapidity; and hence beside the primary rhythms there arise secondary rhythms . . . double, triple, and even quadruple rhythms . . . .'[7]

Spencer's account is reminiscent of the work of many ancient writers who assumed that nature displayed an order and symmetry comparable to a work of art, and who took pleasure in revealing those underlying rhythms and patterns. For example, the early Greeks saw the workings of nature as a kind of universal dance in harmony with the music of the spheres; and Elizabethan writers such as Sir John Davies in *Orchestra* catalogued the rhythmic movements of flowers, stars and human beings.[8] Victorian readers of Spencer were reassured that despite the scientific discovery of evolution, they still lived in a universe that was 'meaningful and benign' as shown by the existence of rhythmic patterns that were 'as soothing as harmonics in music'.[9]

Lye may not have read Spencer, but, if he had, he would have enjoyed the exactness of his descriptions, particularly his interest in oscillation, a shapely form of movement that would play an important part in Lye's art. Spencer saw himself as a scientist rather than an artist, and inevitably he moved on from such small-scale observations to large hypotheses about nature and evolution. Had he been content to remain at the micro level, one could imagine his love of rhythmic patterns eventually giving birth to the idea of an art of motion.[10]

Another famous philosopher of movement was Henri Bergson whose *Creative Evolution* – first published in French in 1907 and translated into English in 1911 – provided a version of evolution that fired the imagination of artists. Bergson saw movement as central to evolution: 'Life in general is mobility itself.'[11] His thinking gained its remarkable impact from the fact that 19th-century philosophers and scientists (including Spencer) had taken it for granted that the flow of time could be measured – and therefore segmented – in a mechanical or mathematical way.[12] In contrast, reality for Bergson was 'a simple flux, a continuity of flowing'[13] or 'an infinite multiplicity of becomings variously coloured'.[14] He opened up new ways of thinking about form as a process of unfolding, which encouraged new modes of description such as the stream of consciousness in fiction, and a more fluid approach to form in music and painting.

He saw the ideal perspective as 'a mind placed alongside becoming, and adopting its movement'.[15] This could be interpreted as a call for kinetic artists, though that specific concept seems not to have occurred to the philosopher. To tune in to the flux, he saw the need for intuition to complement intellect, because the latter was too strongly attached to stable forms, geometrical shapes and scientific certainties. If we listened properly to intuition, 'it would give up to us the most intimate secrets of life'.[16] Lye would later speak in similar terms of what he called 'the old brain'.

Bergson's ideas were very much in the air during Lye's early years, and while it remains unclear whether the artist encountered them directly or indirectly, he was strongly drawn to the idea of unfolding form. There were, however, two areas in which he saw things differently. There was a characteristic blurring (or Impressionism) in Bergson's descriptions of movement that contrasted with Lye's love of precision. Bergson also had a negative attitude to the new medium of 'cinematography' because he regarded its basic method as the slicing up of time into separate frames – 'a series of snapshots'.[17] Lye saw that while this might apply to the mechanics, it would not be the experience of the viewer.[18]

Although he underestimated the potential of film, Bergson had much to say that was exciting to the artists of his day about the mysteries of time and movement, individuality and intuition. Also evocative were his speculations about consciousness as it developed from the primitive world of the amoeba, to the busy life of plants, to the complexity of the human mind. His ideas were rapidly picked up by avant-garde artists such as the Futurists. In 1935, Lye's first essay on movement would be in some respects a debate with Bergson.

THE CONCEPT OF EMPATHY

A type of thinking that would prove very important to Lye emerged in German art criticism around 1873 when Robert Vischer began talking about *Einfühlung* or how the viewer can 'feel into' a work of art. This term was translated into English in 1909 as 'empathy'.[19] Lye appears to have been unaware of most of the 19th-century writings on the subject, some of which were not translated into English until recently;[20] but having once encountered the idea in a contemporary context, he was persuaded that 'The whole business with any art is first, *empathy*' [his italics].[21]

The concept developed originally out of an inter-disciplinary dialogue between art and science, in particular, new developments in psychology and physiology. The aim was to study as closely as possible the way a spectator interacts with a work of art. Writers in this tradition saw the viewing of art as a highly active process involving many aspects of the individual – brain and body, feeling and intellect, the conscious and the unconscious. Since perception was complex and

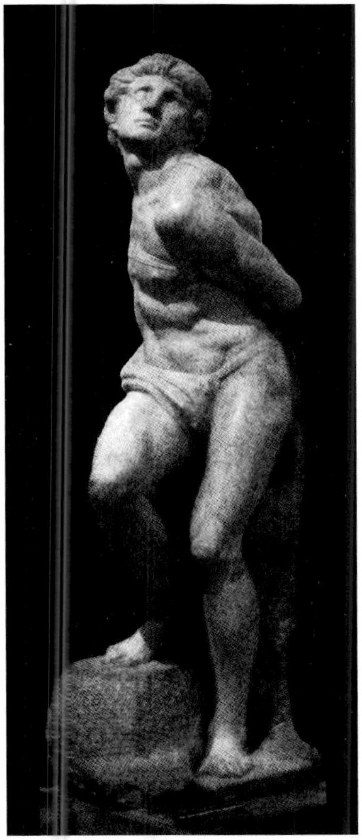

Vigorous representation of the body made Michelangelo Buonarroti an artist of particular interest to those writing in the empathy tradition. His *Rebellious Slave* strains against his bonds. Slightly larger than life size, the marble sculpture (now at the Louvre) was left unfinished in 1516.

multi-dimensional, criticism had to augment intellectual analysis by exploring the rich spectrum of physical and emotional responses. This tradition anticipated some of Freud's innovations through its insights into the unconscious; but what Lye would find particularly useful was its strong emphasis on the physical dimensions of art.[22]

The body with its 'motor-nerve' system was as important a perceiving mechanism as the eye. To quote Theodor Lipps, 'If I see a tree swaying in the breeze I carry out its movements in imaginative imitative activities.'[23] And for August Schmarsow, while 'the intuited form of three-dimensional space arises through the experiences of our sense of sight', it also 'consists of the residues of sensory experience to which the muscular sensations of our body, the sensitivity of our skin, and the structure of our body all contribute'.[24] When someone looks closely at a painting or sculpture, their body responds, consciously or not, to impressions of balance, mobility, tension, effort and weight. For example, viewers are stirred by the strongly physical feelings of movement, poise and muscular exertion in Michelangelo's sculptures.

The writers in this tradition were no less interested in intellectual aspects (such as symbolism), but they realised that any account of perception that overlooked the visceral and emotional aspects remained incomplete from both an artistic and a scientific viewpoint. While movement was only one of the elements brought into the foreground by this approach, the kinetic or kinesthetic aspects of art had never previously received so much attention.[25] Robert Vischer even proposed that 'The visual artist should enjoy motion for its own sake, completely apart from its motive.'[26] He was not advocating a pure kinetic art, however, but trying to emphasise the need for a painting to work fully as a 'sensory' experience, in addition to any emotional, intellectual or literary appeal it might have.

From 1894, the work of the art critic Bernard Berenson – born in Lithuania but brought up in the United States – popularised the idea of 'tactile values' in art. His work was not directly linked to the German empathy tradition but he introduced similar ideas into Anglo-American art criticism. He wrote:

> In our infancy, long before we are conscious of the process, the sense of touch, helped on by muscular sensations of movement, teaches us to appreciate depth, the third dimension, both in objects and in space . . . . His [the artist's] first business . . . is to rouse the tactile sense, for I must have the illusion of being able to touch a figure, I must have the illusion of varying muscular sensations inside my palm and fingers corresponding to the various projections of this figure, before I shall take it for granted as real . . . .[27]

Berenson enthused about 'movement values' as well as 'tactile values': 'Turning our attention . . . to movement . . . we find that we realise it just as we realise objects, by the stimulation of our tactile imagination, only that here touch retires to a second place before the muscular feelings of varying pressure and strain.'[28] Berenson, unlike later artists such as Lye, always brought the discussion back to issues of realism. Concentrating on the art of the Renaissance period, he valued implied movement and tactility in art because of what they contributed to the sense of reality. As modern art developed, his talk of reality and representation came to seem old-fashioned.

The empathy tradition passed out of favour in Germany partly through the impact of Wilhelm Worringer's book *Abstraction and Empathy: A Contribution to the Psychology of Style*. Published in 1910, 'this doctorate thesis of a young and unknown student' was perfectly timed to provide a rationale for the emergence of abstract art.[29] Worringer used 'empathy' as a shorthand term for 'naturalism' which he associated with 'imitation', 'materialism', and the conventional demand that images should be familiar and accessible. He also criticised 'modern experimental psychology', the area of science from which the empathy tradition had drawn, for being confined to the same 'European-Classical' paradigm.[30] The kind of 'abstraction' that Worringer favoured was 'geometrical' or 'pure' abstraction, which he linked with various non-European traditions of art (such as Oriental, Egyptian and 'primitive' art). The book provided an exciting introduction to these alternative artistic traditions.

The idea of empathy ceased to be fashionable during the first half of the 20th century, though it continued to have some currency in architecture, a field that naturally involved the experience of the body moving through space. Heinrich Wölfflin wrote about the ideas of Johannes Volkelt in his 'Prolegomena to a Psychology of Architecture': 'The spatial form is interpreted in terms of movement and the effect of forces . . . . To interpret the spatial form aesthetically we have to respond to this movement vicariously through our senses, share it with our body organization.'[31]

There were also a few American critics who kept this type of discussion going, such as Herbert S. Langfeld who wrote in 1920 in *The Aesthetic Attitude*:

> Probably one of the most vivid experiences of empathy that we can have is in perceiving an object that we realize is not well-balanced and may fall at any moment, as for instance, in witnessing one acrobat balancing another at the end of a long pole. As the acrobat in the air sways back and forth on the verge of plunging head first into the orchestra, the audience goes through at low tension all of his contortions.[32]

And when we perceive works of art, 'it is through the muscle sensations that we can, with practice, make the finest discrimination of line and shape, although the clue to such discriminations will appear to come directly through the eye'.[33]

There was also an impressive British art theorist, Violet Paget, who wrote under the pseudonym of 'Vernon Lee'. In books such as *The Beautiful: An Introduction to Psychological Aesthetics*, she combined the latest discoveries of psychology with an artist's sensitivity to lines as vectors of movement. For example, when she described a natural landscape, she saw it as a field of forces like a Cézanne painting. A mountain was a 'drama of two lines *striving* (one with more suddenness of energy and purpose than the other) to *arrive* at a particular imaginary point in the sky, *arresting* each other's *progress* as they *meet* in their *endeavour*'. (The italics are hers.) Her heightened perception turned the mountain into a kind of kinetic sculpture: 'this simplest empathic action of an irregular but by no means rectilinear triangle goes on repeating itself like the parabola of a steadily spurting fountain: for ever accomplishing itself anew and for ever accompanied by the same effect on the feelings of the beholder'.[34]

Although a few art theorists of this kind kept the idea of empathy in circulation, there were other attacks besides Worringer's. Bertolt Brecht associated empathy with the process of emotional identification demanded by theatre audiences brought up on orthodox forms of realism, and he sought to replace it by the alienation or estrangement effect.[35] Both Worringer and Brecht characterised the empathy tradition too narrowly, but it suited their polemical aims, for modernism was engaged in a battle with conventional realism in all the arts. Discussions of abstract art – particularly those versions associated with pure, neo-Platonic, geometrical forms – had no use for a tradition of criticism that emphasised physicality, touch and movement. Eventually, Lye would revive the tradition of empathy and develop it in new ways. In contrast to Worringer, he would see it as deeply relevant to 'primitive' art, and he would fully develop the hints it contained for a new type of art in which movement became the primary component. From his perspective, abstraction and empathy would be allies rather than rivals.

PHOTOGRAPHY AND MOVEMENT

The discovery of photography around 1839 created great excitement, but while this medium could magically conquer time by freezing a scene, it could not handle movement. By the 1870s, however, exposure time had been greatly reduced thanks to more sensitive plates and lenses, and two innovators became obsessed with the idea of photographing movement – Eadweard Muybridge, born in England in 1830 but working in the United States, and Étienne-Jules Marey, born in the same year in France. By the end of the century, both men would be famous as the pioneers of a new science of movement based on photography's ability to reveal subtleties that eluded the human eye.

Even today their names are usually the first to come to mind when people interested in the visual arts hear a term like 'patterns of motion'. But the primary concern of both men was not art but science. Marey was a physiologist who began by studying movement in the human body – the pulse, the beating of the heart, the circulation of blood, respiration and the working of the muscles – analysed in his 1868 book *Le Mouvement dans les Fonctions de la Vie.* A resourceful inventor, he worked to develop new recording and measuring instruments. Excited by the medium of high-speed photography, he expanded his research to cover movement of all kinds, including that of animals, insects and birds. How birds flew was an area currently receiving a great deal of attention because inventors were competing to develop the first aeroplane. Marey's photographs and analysis demonstrated that the flying methods of birds were so complex and specific that they could not easily be adapted to human machines.

Muybridge was a commercial photographer with an entrepreneurial streak who became involved with movement when he was hired by Leland Stanford, a railroad magnate who had become a breeder of horses, to see whether high-speed photography could reveal the secrets of how horses moved their legs. Experts had never been able to decide whether all the hooves of a horse could be in the air simultaneously as it ran. In 1872, Muybridge took a series of photographs that settled the matter. This made a fascinating story for the news media, and his photographs began to be circulated around the world. Painters who saw the images – such as Edgar Degas in France and Thomas Eakins in the United States – decided they had to rethink the way they had been painting horses. Muybridge came to see himself as a scientific investigator of movement, and he

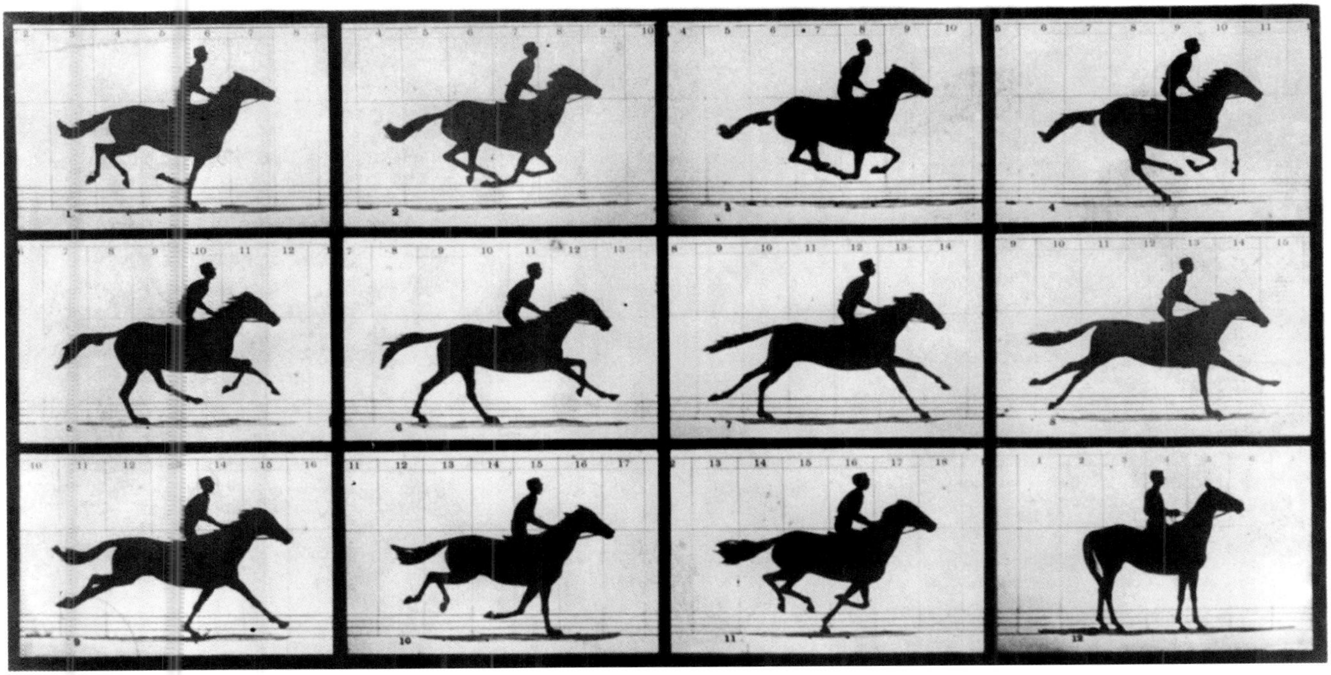

Eadweard Muybridge made these silhouette photographs of a 'Horse in Motion' in 1878. They were taken 1/25 second (or 27 inches) apart, and the exposure time for each image was 'less than the two-thousandth part of a second'. The public was shocked to learn from Muybridge's photographic series that at times all the legs of a horse left the ground, and the positions of the legs were less regular and symmetrical than artists had assumed. Library of Congress.

convinced two universities to sponsor his ambitious photographic projects as a form of cutting-edge research that would lay the foundations for a new branch of science.

Both Marey and Muybridge sought to analyse movement by taking sequences of photographs with exposure times as short as a thousandth of a second. Both men were highly ingenious in the way they adapted the latest types of camera and photographic material. Muybridge used a row of cameras, each activated in turn by an electromagnetic shutter system. In 1879, he increased his battery of cameras from twelve to 24, and in 1884 (assisted by dry-plate photography and a more precise clockwork shutter system) he expanded it to 36, sometimes arranging the cameras in three sets of twelve to record the same movement simultaneously from different angles. A journalist summed up his subject matter in this way:

> . . . out of the 781 plates he has now published, only 95 are devoted to the horse, and only 124 to other animals and birds, while the other 562 are devoted to men, women, and children, nude, semi-nude, and draped, walking, running, dancing, getting up and lying down, wrestling, boxing, leaping and playing athletic games – in short, acting before our eyes the animal life of man.[36]

Muybridge's largest collection was entitled *Animal Locomotion*.

Marey developed alternative methods that he called 'chronophotography'. In 1882, he introduced the 'photo gun', a camera in the form of a rifle with a disc-shaped magazine that was able to take twelve photographs per second. Such a camera enabled Marey to pan quickly to follow the subject, such as a bird in flight. He experimented with stereoscopic photographs of birds, and also converted at least one of his bird sequences into a bronze model. With a long line of flapping wings frozen, this object made a stunning sculpture, even though its purpose was scientific analysis and not art.

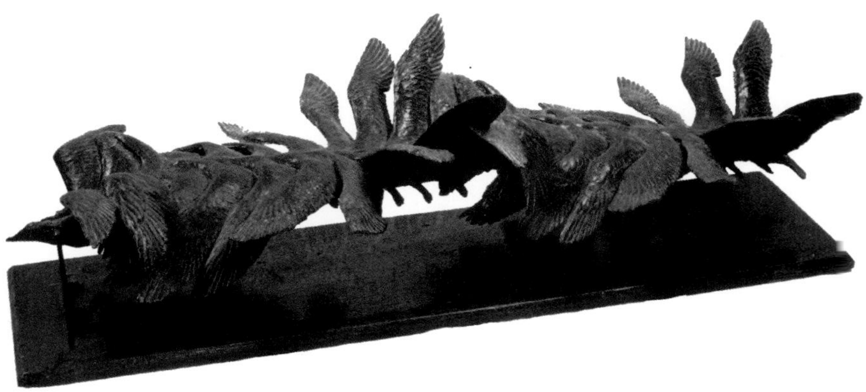

Marey's 1887 bronze sculpture *The Flight of a Gull* (now in the Musée Marey at Beaune).

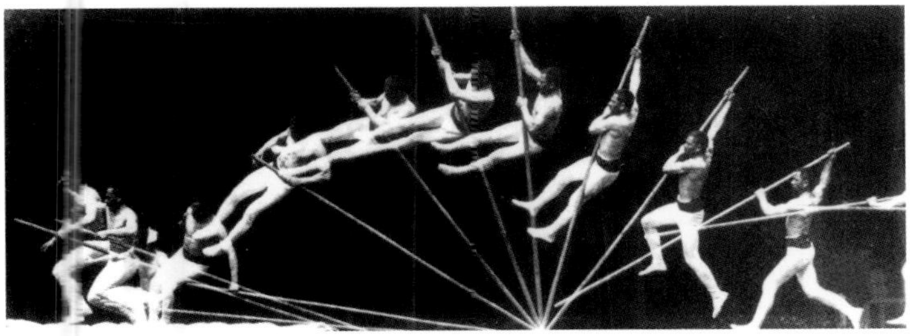

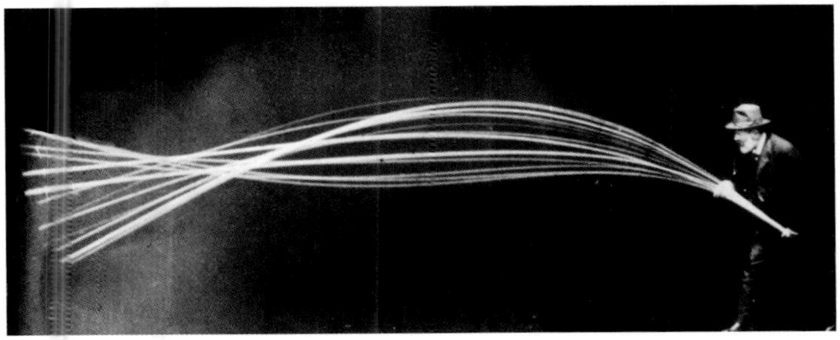

A 'chronophotograph' by Etienne-Jules Marey of a man pole-vaulting, and another that shows Marey shaking a long wooden rod.

When Marey began capturing the successive phases of a movement on a single photographic plate, he required his human subjects to wear black costumes marked with vertical white lines so that he could record the resulting linear patterns. This method of multiple exposure produced images with a strong sense of visual rhythm. The results caught the attention of many artists. Marcel Duchamp described his 1912 painting *Nude Descending a Staircase* (see colour section) as 'the convergence in my mind of various interests [including] the cinema, still in its infancy, and the separation of anatomical positions in the photochronographs of Marey'.[37] As the poet X. J. Kennedy later described Duchamp's painting:

> One-woman waterfall, she wears
> Her slow descent like a long cape
> And pausing, on the final stair
> Collects her motions into shape.[38]

When the painting was exhibited in New York in the Armory Show in 1913, it generated so much controversy that it became an icon of modern art, reproduced around the world, even in *The Sydney Mail* which remarked, 'if a drunken man

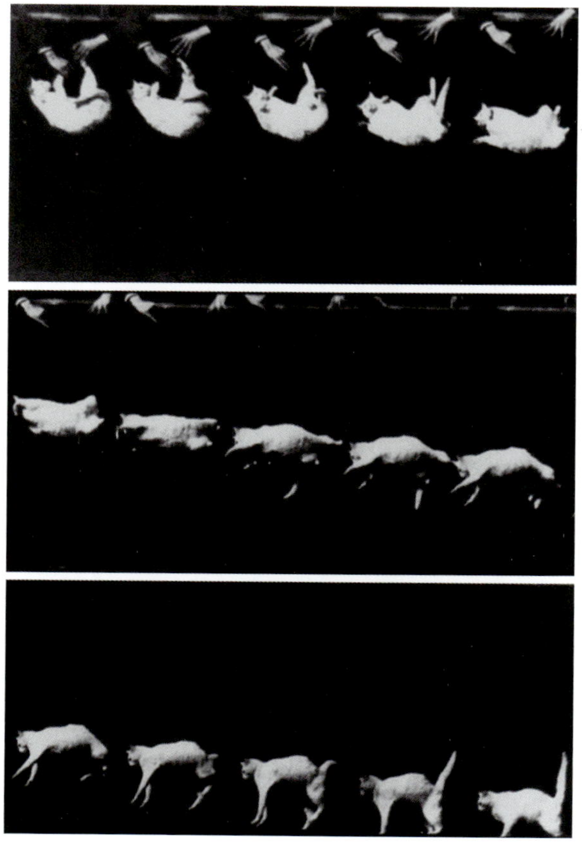

Marey's 1894 series of photographs to demonstrate how a falling cat always lands on its feet.

were watching a nude running swiftly downstairs he might get some such impression'.[39] Lye, influenced either directly or indirectly, created Duchamp- or Marey-like images in his 1936 film *Rainbow Dance*, when 'a man jumping through the air leaves successive images of himself behind' (see colour section).[40] One of the innovations of Lye's sequence was the way he gave each of the silhouette images a different colour.

Marey and Muybridge, who met in 1881, always respected each other's work, though the former was more of a pure scientist and Muybridge more of a showman. Marey spent his later years studying particular forms of motion such as waves, water currents, falling balls and smoke trails. For more than 20 years, the two researchers helped to awaken a serious interest in movement, encouraging closer study than ever before. Basically they focused on static photographs. Their high-speed exposures produced fascinating discoveries such as what drops of water looked like when suspended in mid-air. Such images were a dramatic extension of human eyesight, though they were frustrating for any viewer who wanted actual movement. As such, they were an obvious target for Bergson's attack on the mechanical slicing up of time. Marey's main aim was precise measurement, and the potential problems with this approach were soon demonstrated in the business world by the fashion for Taylorism, a method of measuring jobs in terms of 'time and motion'. This attempt to increase worker efficiency produced some striking analyses of movement, but its excesses were brilliantly parodied by Charlie Chaplin in *Modern Times*.[41]

From Lye's perspective, Marey and Muybridge did not add a great deal to the *aesthetics* of movement. But Marey did have an interest in what Lye would describe as 'figures of motion', such as his research into the fact that a bird's wings tended to describe a 'figure 8' as they flapped up and down. He showed that the flight of insects was a variation on this looping kind of forward movement. Marey's 1894 book *Le Mouvement* contains some intriguing flight diagrams, in addition to photographs of virtual volume (the illusion of bulk when an object such as a metal wire spins round rapidly).[42] He also speculated about the influence of photography on contemporary artists, though he wrongly assumed that they would be mostly interested in the realist implications.

Above all, what Marey's and Muybridge's work demonstrated was the fact that movement was a rich but largely unexplored subject. For that reason, their findings could be used in a number of different ways – as science, as art, as sports analysis, as a management tool and (by the public at large) as 'infotainment'. Marey's best-known experiment consisted of 60 photos of a falling cat taken in one second. Besides helping his scientific colleagues to understand for the first time how cats were always able to land on their feet, it aroused the curiosity of the public, as Muybridge's horse photographs had done. As an animation, the falling cat is still being viewed today on YouTube.

A number of other photographers and inventors were drawn to this area of experiment,[43] but despite the interest that such work held for artists, and despite all the talk of a *science* of movement, no one up to 1904, when Marey and Muybridge died, had articulated an *art* of movement.

MOVING IMAGES

When 'movies' arrived in 1895 – the year of the first public film screening, presented by Louis and Auguste Lumière in Paris – the 'science of motion' lost its

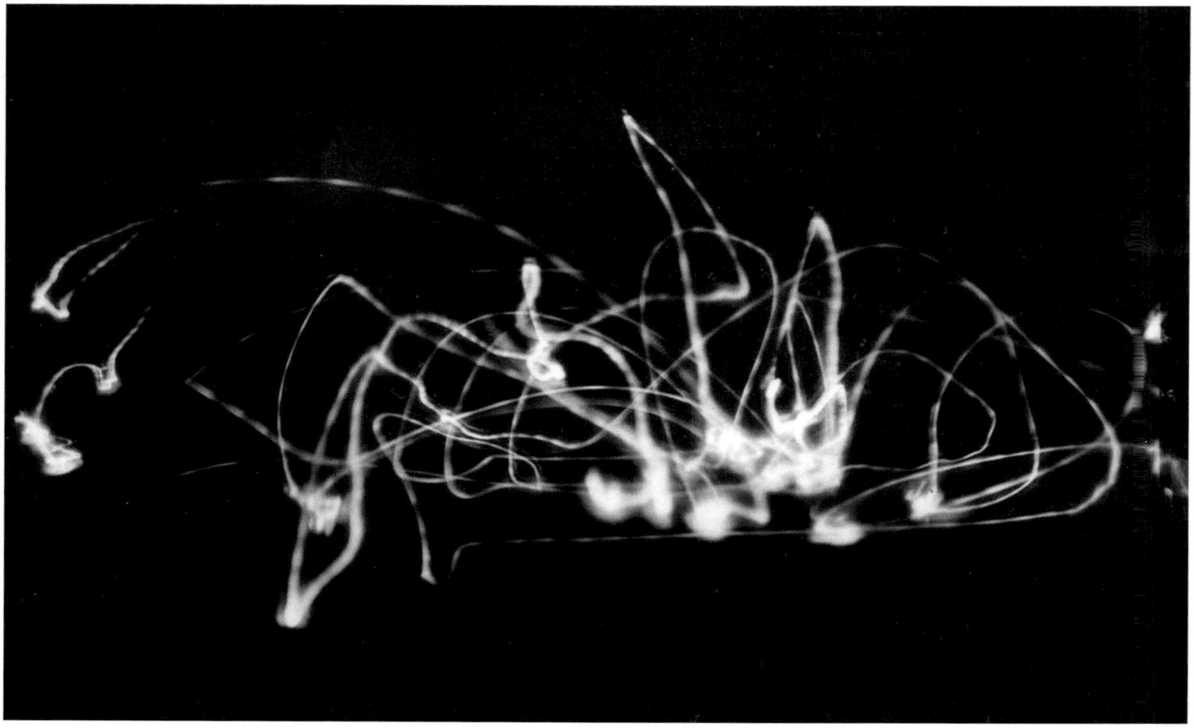

ABOVE Frank and Lillian Gilbreth were among those who researched work habits in the USA. Around 1913 they attached ligh bulbs to the fingers of 'Miss McPhail' in a darkened room and took this time-lapse photograph of her folding a handkerchief Unlike other followers of Taylorism, the Gilbreths took a serious interest in patterns of motion. Courtesy Purdue University Libraries, Archives and Special Collections: Frank Gilbreth Archives. BELOW Stereoscopic photographs by Marey showing the pattern of movement made by a man walking slowly. The test subject wore a light near the base of his spine.

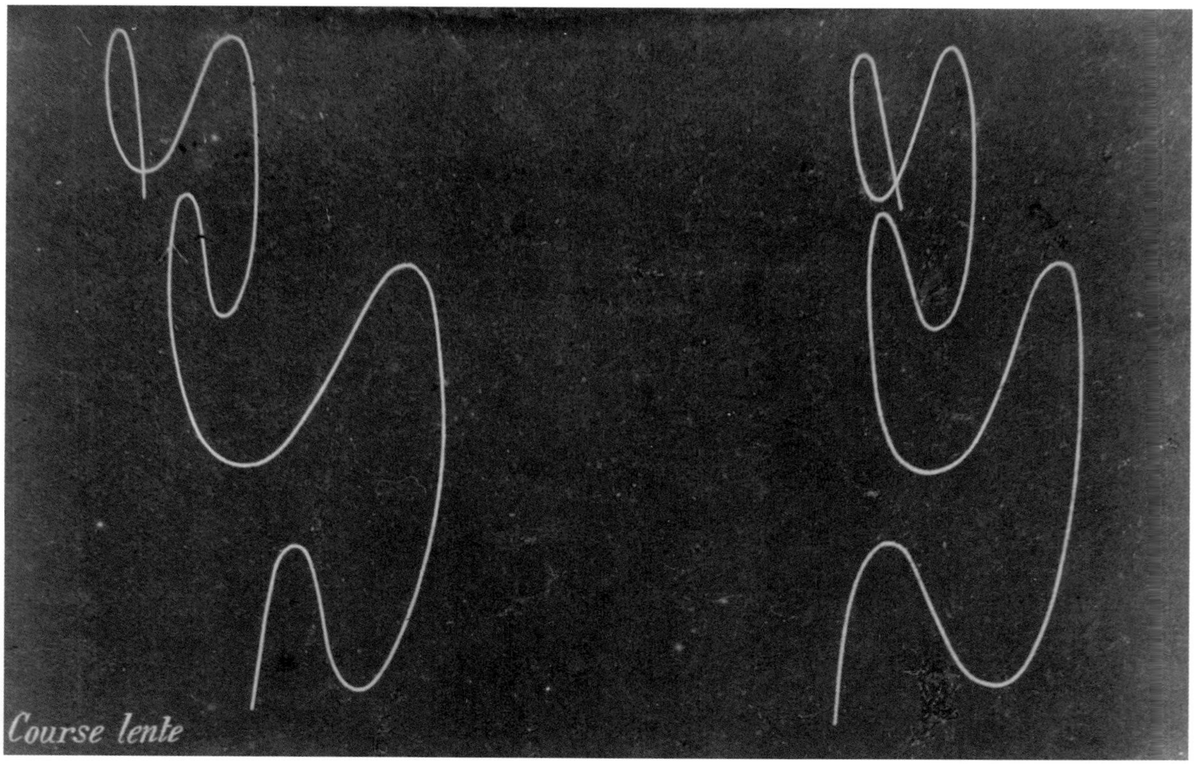

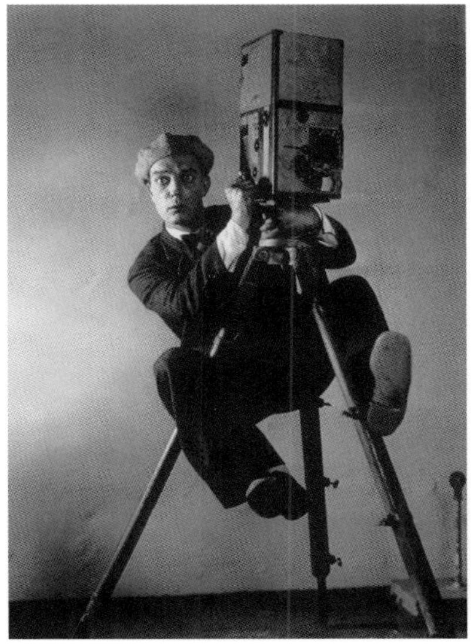

Actor and director Buster Keaton (seen here in *The Cameraman*) was one of the masters of visual slapstick comedy. Licensed by Austral-International Press Agency Pty Ltd.

novelty value and the new medium appeared to offer the perfect vehicle for an art of movement. The 'cinema' took its name from the Greek word for motion (spelled with a 'k' in Britain in the early days, like the word 'kinetic'). But though it was based on movement, the new medium also served as a platform for a number of other elements. For many people, it was primarily a source of entertainment. In that sense, it was the culmination of more than a century of 'motion toys', such as the Zoetrope which appeared in the 1860s as a spinning bowl with slots for viewing, or 'flick books', patented in 1868. Muybridge had contributed to that tradition by developing the Zoöpraxiscope which combined a spinning disc of sequential images with a projector. Unfortunately, his animations only lasted for a second or two.

Early films were initially very short, taking the form of coin-in-the-slot peep shows and fairground attractions, until storefront theatres ('nickelodeons' in the United States) began to be established around 1905. Films became one-reelers, running for 10 to 15 minutes. Cameramen experimented with a range of possibilities such as speeding up or slowing down motion – effects easy to produce, as cameras were cranked by hand. A genre of outrageous, ultra-fast, slapstick comedy developed. Artists loved the energy of the new medium, and the French avant-garde monthly magazine *Les Soirées de Paris* included reviews of the latest Keystone comedies. But was film yet an art? The avant-garde had no desire for the medium to be 'rescued' by champions of middle-class culture (such as the Film d'Art group in France which sought to bring classic plays to the screen). What was required was not up-market subject matter but more questioning of the medium, more emphasis on aspects that were uniquely 'filmic'.

By the time Len Lye became a film-maker, he felt that little progress had been made, at least within the mainstream cinema tradition. In 1935, he and Laura Riding declared in their essay 'Film-making': 'The language of the cinema is movement. When it attempts to make of movement a literary language the result is a physical-intellectual caricature-language . . . . people have been trained to go to the cinema to enjoy respectable hysteria . . . .'[44] These comments were deliberately provocative in the manner of a manifesto, but there was a serious idea underlying them. The film industry regarded motion as only one of many ingredients, and most viewers would consider it strange and reductive to pay too much attention to that single ingredient rather than to the characters, dialogue, stories, themes, stars, clothes, settings, special effects or the other subjects that film-goers talked about. For 'fine art' film-makers such as Lye, specialisation was essential if the artistic use of motion were to progress. This principle had been demonstrated by abstract artists who had revitalised painting when they turned away from representation and focused solely on colour and form.

By 1935, a number of innovative film-makers had grappled with the question of what 'the language of the cinema' should be, but only a handful had chosen movement as their primary answer. Lye would join that small tradition and make original contributions to it. Before looking at his film work, however, we need to go back 30 years to the beginnings of 'modern art' and the context out of which it arose, to understand some of the other foundations of Lye's thinking about art and movement.

MODERNISM AND MOVEMENT

All periods are periods of change but some upheavals are greater than others. Today we are living through an exceptional period of change, driven primarily by the computer and the Internet. The first two decades of the 20th century were also a period of profound change, not only in war and politics but also in technology. During those years, new forms of transport modified the human sense of movement. Since the 1830s, trains had familiarised passengers with window views blurred by speed, but that experience was intensified by the mass production from the 1900s of gasoline-powered cars and motorcycles, and the first aeroplane flight in 1903 by the Wright Brothers (although some would argue that Richard Pearse beat them to it). This new freedom of movement was matched by the power of radio, telephones and motion pictures to reconfigure the human sense of space and time.

Simultaneously, the arts were going through a period of transformation, especially after 1905 when Picasso and his associates began developing Cubism. As 'modernism' undertook a total re-evaluation of art, it was inevitable that the theme of movement would crop up.[45] Granted, other issues tended to attract more discussion, such as new forms of representation, the concept of abstract art, the imagery of the unconscious mind, the use of chance, and the struggle against the political or cultural establishments of the day. More attention was paid to visual qualities such as light, colour and shape than to movement. Nevertheless, this period laid the groundwork for what would become kinetic art.

The Futurists

Futurism was the first area in which the theme of movement became prominent. The Futurists (who emerged in Italy in 1909) were such energetic publicists that journalists came to use the name of their group as a generic label for any far-out form of modern art. (For example, Lye was described as 'the Futurist New Zealander' when he began exhibiting in London in 1928.)[46] One of the group's favourite genres was the manifesto, as a vehicle for provocative speculations and for attacks on all whose eyes were 'warped by routine'.[47] The Futurists had many exciting new ideas but were inclined to smother them in hype and macho posturing, and they also had a habit of boasting about ambitious experiments that were yet to leave the drawing board. Their favourite themes included 'energy', 'speed', 'rebellion', 'power', 'dynamism' and 'violence', and two that Lye would share – opposition to 'the literary' in art and the pursuit of direct 'sensation'.

In the first 'Manifesto of Futurism' in 1909, F. T. Marinetti wrote: 'We affirm that the world's magnificence has been enriched by a new beauty: the beauty of speed. A racing car whose hood is adorned with great pipes, like serpents of explosive breath . . . is more beautiful than the *Victory of Samothrace.*' And: 'We want to hymn the man at the wheel, who hurls the lance of his spirit across the Earth, along the circle of its orbit.'[48] Marinetti constantly drew attention to movement but tended to conflate it with speed. (An artist such as Lye would be equally interested in slow speed – in a film such as *Tusalava* – or in non-mechanical movement.) The Futurists' obsession with modernity also led to a sweeping rejection of 'archaic' art – such as the work of 'the primitives or the savages'[49] – artists whom Lye would later value more highly than the Futurists.

Marinetti was at his best in talking about the transformation of modern life by new technology:

> An ordinary man can in a day's time travel by train from a little dead town of empty squares, where the sun, the dust, and the wind amuse themselves in silence, to a great capital city bristling with lights, gestures, and street cries. By reading a newspaper the inhabitant of a mountain village can tremble each day with anxiety, following insurrection in China, the London and New York suffragettes, . . . and

the heroic dog-sleds of the polar explorers. The timid, sedentary inhabitant of any provincial town can indulge in the intoxication of danger by going to the movies and watching a great hunt in the Congo.[50]

His interest in the way the new media were reshaping consciousness anticipated the much later development of media studies.

While Marinetti tended to concentrate on issues such as speed and simultaneity, less prominent Futurists such as the film-maker and photographer Anton Giulio Bragaglia referred directly to movement. In his 1911 manifesto 'Futurist Photodynamism', Bragaglia discussed how to 'trace the shape of movement' in photography, film and painting.[51] Marey's work was obviously an important starting point for him. (Spencer, Bergson and Muybridge also turned up in Futurist manifestoes, but Marey was the key figure.) Bragaglia saw Futurism as transcending the 'precise, mechanical' methods of chronophotography by seeking to reveal the 'essence' of a movement. The artist could represent movement in a more 'ideal and lyrical' way by focusing on the viewer's subjective experience of it. The images might seem 'distorted' but they were true to human experience. Unfortunately, his explanation of what this 'vertiginous lyrical expression of life' might mean in practice was far from clear: 'We will endeavour to extract not only the aesthetic expression of the motives [of a movement], but also the inner, sensorial, cerebral and psychic emotions that we feel when an action leaves its superb, unbroken trace.'[52] In the course of the manifesto he criticised film-making to date for lacking an 'aesthetic concern for rhythm'. The second half of his 70-minute film *Thaïs* has survived, but it is a fairly conventional melodramatic narrative, distinguished only by its stylised sets.[53]

There are Futurist paintings that more effectively illustrate Bragaglia's ideas. Giacomo Balla's *Study of Ongoing Lines (Swallows)* (1913) was based directly on one of Marey's photographs. *Little Girl Running on a Balcony* (see colour section), *Dynamism of a Dog on a Leash* and *The Violinist's Hands* (all 1912) are structured like chronophotographs but are 'distorted' in a painterly fashion, and given a lively visual rhythm like Duchamp's *Nude Descending a Staircase*. The 'Futurist Painting: Technical Manifesto', which Balla had written in 1910 along with Umberto Boccioni, Carlo Carra, Luigi Russolo and Gino Severini, offered this rationale: 'On account of the persistency of an image upon the retina, moving objects constantly multiply themselves; their form changes like rapid vibrations, in their mad career. Thus a running horse has not four legs but 20, and their

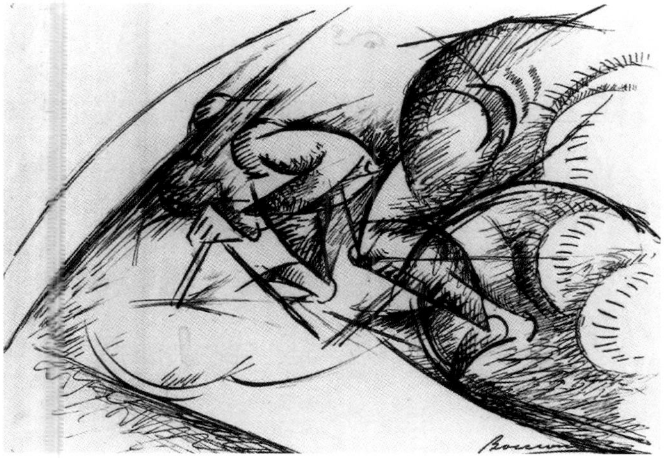

Umberto Boccioni's *Dynamism of a Cyclist*, 1913.

movements are triangular.'[54] In 1912, these painters criticised the Cubists and the rest of the French avant-garde because they 'obstinately continue to paint objects motionless [and] frozen'. In contrast, the Futurist painters 'seek for a style of motion, a thing which has never been attempted before'.[55]

For all its high claims to originality, Futurist painting was – as its rivals were quick to point out – still linked to the Impressionists who had been fascinated by the subjective experience of change. Monet, for example, had made a series of paintings of haystacks in 1890–91 focusing on subtle shifts of light and colour. The Futurist painters went one step further in directly evoking movement, but their work was still confined to static canvases. Their art tended to concentrate purely on visual impressions, without taking into account the physical responses to movement that had been so important within the empathy tradition. Also, while there was a remarkable energy to their ideas, some artists felt that their paintings lacked precision. The Futurists sought to produce 'a sensation of chaotic excitement' that reflected the 'fast and fragmented' nature of 'modern life'.[56] They seldom presented a clear, complete pattern of movement (or what Lye would call a 'figure of motion') because they liked to add contrasting or 'intersecting' movements, so the scene became a crowded field of forces. Futurist music pursued a similar emphasis on 'simultaneity' – 'not merely variety, but chaos and clashing of rhythms, totally opposed to one another'.[57]

Despite its scatter-shot approach, Futurism made some important contributions. One was Boccioni's memorable bronze sculpture, *Unique Forms of Continuity in Space* (1913, see colour section). This stylised, striding figure, which evoked movement as strongly as any static sculpture could, was a worthy, three-dimensional counterpart to the *Nude Descending a Staircase*. Boccioni, a compelling advocate of movement (and an enthusiast for Bergson), wrote in 1912:

> We cannot forget that the swing of a pendulum or the moving hands of a clock, the in-and-out motion of a piston inside a cylinder, the engaging and disengaging of two cog-wheels, the fury of a fly-wheel or the whirling of a propeller, are all plastic and pictorial elements, which any Futurist work of sculpture should take advantage of. The opening and closing of a valve creates a rhythm which is just as beautiful to look at as the movements of an eyelid, and infinitely more modern.[58]

In 'Plastic Dynamism' (1913) he wrote, 'We Futurists have discovered form in movement, and the movement of form.'[59] He articulated what would become a basic principle of kinetic art: 'A body in movement . . . is not simply an immobile body subsequently set in motion, but a *truly mobile object*, which is a reality quite new and original.'[60] In 'Absolute Motion + Relative Motion = Dynamism' (1914), he discussed 'the vantage-point of speed': 'Until today men have observed changes produced by the wind in the trees, the countryside, drapes, etc. They have not so far looked at the way that trains, cars, bicycles and aeroplanes have upset the contemplative concept of the landscape.'[61] He lamented the fact that 'The concept of motion in the study and representation of life has always remained outside art proper', and he spoke of 'the search to find a new form' that could convey 'the heartbeat' of movement.[62] Boccioni had not yet developed these ideas fully when he died in 1916 at the age of 33, after falling from a horse during a cavalry training exercise.

Other Futurists speculated about a shift from sculpture to 'plastic complexes that we will set in motion'.[63] Giacomo Balla and Fortunato Depero, in their 1915 manifesto 'Futurist Reconstruction of the Universe', proposed the making of 'complexes' that would produce noises, change shape, fly, explode or behave like 'mechanical animals'. While similar ideas are being realised today by research laboratories, the tone of this manifesto was too extravagant for it to provide a practical plan of action in its own time. A more important manifesto was Bruno Corra's 'Abstract Cinema – Chromatic Music' (1912) which announced that he and his brother, Arnaldo Ginna, had made films painted directly on celluloid, like abstract paintings in movement, entitled *The Rainbow* and *The Dance*.[64] The films were 'colour symphonies', silent but inspired by music.[65] One included 'a whirling of catherine-wheels' and 'an agile pirouetting of spinning tops'.

Unfortunately, no trace of the films has survived. The essay clearly suggests that Corra and Ginna were the first to come up with the idea of 'direct' (or camera-less) film-making, but, as always with Futurist writings, it is necessary to treat the elaborate descriptions of the films with a measure of scepticism. Corra and Ginna also seem to have focused their thinking more on patterns of colour than on patterns of movement.

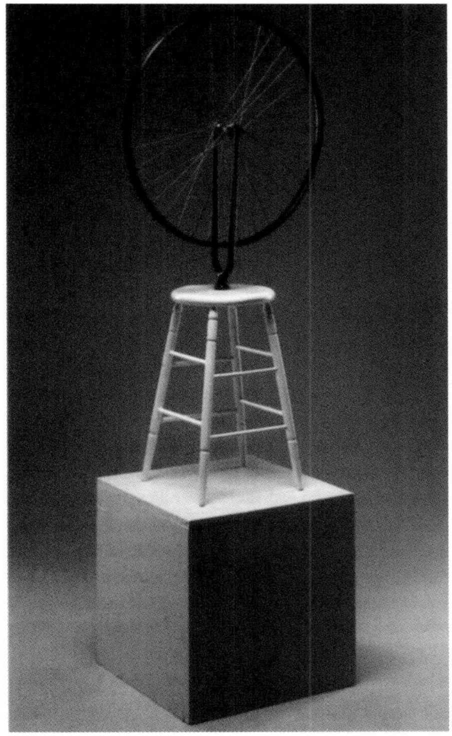

Marcel Duchamp's *Bicycle Wheel* 1913. Licensed By Viscopy, Australia.

Marcel Duchamp

When French artist Marcel Duchamp turns up in popular art books today, he is often characterised as the person who invented two genres: 'kinetic art' and 'ready-mades'. He is said to have done so in 1913 with the same work, *Bicycle Wheel*, a wheel mounted on a kitchen chair, which critics have described as the first work of art made from 'found objects' and also as the first 'kinetic sculpture'.

Although Duchamp himself did not use any of these terms at the time – not even claiming the work as 'art' – he is certainly a prestigious figure for kineticism to claim as its father. Since the development of conceptual art in the 1960s, his reputation has grown to eclipse Picasso's. After a phase of making canvases with implied movement such as *Coffee Mill* (1911) and *Nude Descending a Staircase* (1912), Duchamp rejected the medium of painting and turned instead to 'ready-mades' (manufactured objects found by the artist and applied to his own purpose) and to devices that produced optical illusions. His closest link with kineticism was the series of works he created in the 1920s involving spinning circles and spirals that gave the impression of three-dimensional shapes. He found that a hand-cranked gramophone turntable was the easiest way to set his circular forms in motion. He took a serious interest in science, and his optical experiments appear to have preceded the scientific discovery of what is called 'the stereo-kinetic effect'.[66] The difficulty he encountered in manufacturing these objects – having to struggle with financial, technical and safety problems – anticipated the experience of later kinetic artists. On one occasion, while testing *Rotary Demisphere (Precision Optics)*, Duchamp and his collaborator Man Ray were almost killed by flying glass.

Nevertheless, later artists of motion have tended to see Duchamp not as the father of their genre but as a more distant relative – an eccentric uncle, say. According to the sculptor George Rickey, 'Duchamp showed, by deferring his work with movement for years and confining it to optical phenomena, that his concern therein was dadaist and superficial.'[67] Although the *Bicycle Wheel* was capable of being spun, and museum visitors contrive to spin it when guards are not watching, the artist was not drawing attention to an interesting pattern of movement; his primary concern was to challenge conventional definitions of art.

Duchamp also engaged in film-making. His 1920 attempt to make a stereoscopic film in collaboration with Man Ray ended with a processing disaster, but in 1926 he managed to complete *Anémic Cinéma*, which consisted of nine sayings based on elaborate word-play, alternating with abstract spiral patterns, spun this way and that on a gramophone turntable. Duchamp's optical experiments and his film could be seen as anticipations of what became known as 'op art'. When this tendency was at the height of its influence in the 1960s, it was often grouped with kinetic art because it made use of literal or implied movement, but artists such as Lye insisted that it had a different basis. Duchamp's approach was strongly conceptual, and his aim was less to explore particular visual patterns than to illustrate the unstable and problematic nature of human perception. *Anémic Cinéma*'s treatment of language was similarly ambiguous, witty and subversive. Duchamp's work opened up rich possibilities for later artists to develop, and would prove to be very much in tune with the skeptical mood of post-modernism. But other artists of his period would contribute more directly to the development of an art of motion.

Naum Gabo

For Lye, the first kinetic artist was not Duchamp but Naum Gabo. In 1961 Lye was startled to see for the first time a photograph of Gabo's 1920 sculpture *Kinetic Construction (Standing Wave)*, employing the same kind of movement as a work he had made in 1959.[68]

What Lye did not know is that the Russian artist had also written a manifesto which provided a theoretical basis for kinetic art. This 'Realistic Manifesto' (1920) was written by Gabo though it was co-signed by his older brother, Anton Pevsner.[69] (Naum had changed his surname to Gabo to avoid being confused with his artist brother.) They handed out thousands of copies of the manifesto all over Moscow.

Their context was the seething ferment of modernist art in Russia in the years just before and after the Bolshevik Revolution.[70] In addition to Russian versions of Futurism and Cubism, important new movements arose such as Suprematism (concerned with geometric, abstract forms) and Constructivism (with which the 'Realistic Manifesto' was associated). This last movement rejected traditional art in favour of a more technological approach allied with engineering, architecture and industrial design. Gabo had a personal background in science and engineering that would prove useful to his kinetic art. He borrowed the term 'kinetic' from those areas, and appears to have been the first to use it to describe a genre of art.[71]

The title of the 'Realistic Manifesto' referred not to old-fashioned forms of realism but to Gabo's vision of what the contemporary world was actually like. For him, the modernist belief that new times called for a new art had been made even more urgent by the 1917 Revolution. Influenced by Bergson's philosophy, Gabo saw movement as the key issue: 'We renounce the thousand-year-old delusion in art that held the static rhythms as the only elements of the plastic and pictorial arts. We affirm in these arts a new element . . . kinetic rhythms as the basic forms of our perception of real time.'[72] The manifesto emphasised rhythm, 'force' and 'space–time' as ingredients of art. Colour and volume were distractions, and lines were only useful when they indicated the 'direction' of forces. Gabo dismissed the Futurists' claim to have already created an art of motion because their approach was merely a repackaged version of Impressionism, combined with Marey's chronophotography: 'It is obvious now . . . that by the simple representation of a row of momentarily arrested movements, one cannot re-create movement itself.'[73]

Gabo's manifesto was the passionate expression of a concept – kinetic art – but it offered little in the way of practical details. The artist's one great achievement in putting his theory into practice was *Kinetic Construction (Standing Wave)*, a thin, vertical, metal rod approximately 60 cm in height, attached via springs to an electric motor at its base. When the motor caused it to vibrate, the rod seemed to dissolve into pure energy. Lye would later describe the tense but elegant form it assumed as 'the elliptical shape of a harmonic curve'.[74] Vibration produced the illusion of 'virtual volume'. The work was so concentrated and had so few parts that it looked simple, but, as Gabo explained, the process of testing and manufacturing such a device had been an exhausting business that took nearly nine months, even with the technical support he had received: 'I had to change a great many springs. I had to choose the length, strength and elasticity

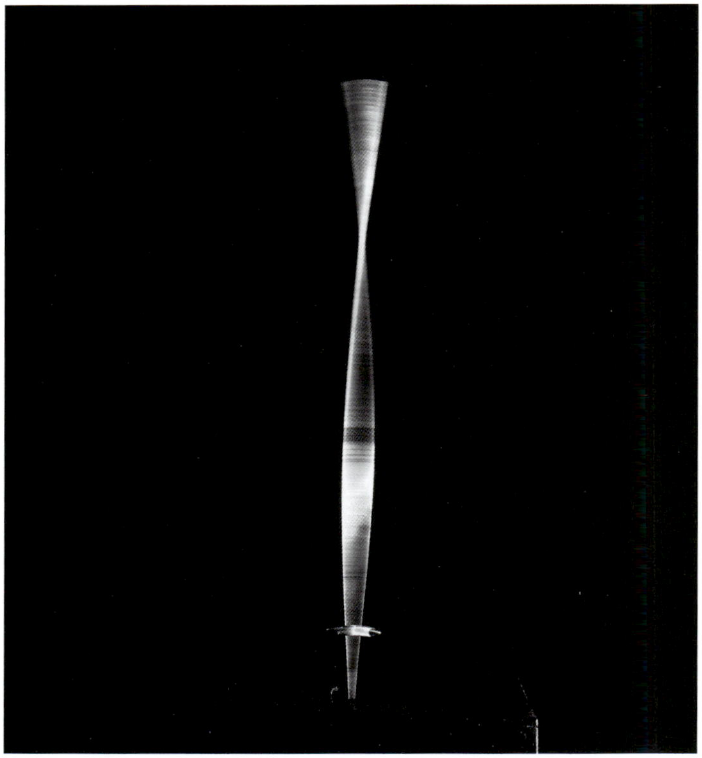

Naum Gabo's *Kinetic Construction (Standing Wave)* 1920 (replica 1985). © Tate (London 2008) and Nina Williams.

of each one; I had to attach a kind of brake to the main spring . . . .'[75] And there were complicated issues of vibration and balance. The scarcity of engineering materials in post-revolutionary Russia made the project extremely difficult.

After its completion, the work was exhibited in Moscow, then in several other European countries. As the first 'kinetic sculpture', it challenged reviewers to assess it in a new way. As the manifesto had recommended, this was art that sidelined colour and line and foregrounded energy and rhythm. Some spectators saw it merely as a gimmick, or as a kind of 'demonstration model', and some disapproved of the idea of machinery encroaching upon art. One person who clearly understood that this 'vibrating shimmer of a frantic vortex of movement' was an 'audacious and perfect conception' was the Hungarian critic Ernö Kállai.[76] In 1922 he wrote, 'In Gabo's kinetic sculpture the formal conception is deliberately based on the idea of movement. Consequently, the sculpture not only conveys movement, but also is produced by it.'[77] Kállai recognised that this approach put previous simulations of movement in art in their place 'as an inadequate and make-shift substitute'.[78]

Gabo had created (in Lye's words) a 'classical example of composed energy', but the subsequent history of the sculpture, and of the artist, demonstrates the difficulties associated with the genre.[79] The work was to have been part of an exhibition of Gabo and Pevsner's art in Paris in 1924, but there were mechanical problems. It performed successfully in several shows between 1926 and 1930, but appears then to have been retired. Fortunately, it was able to be restored in 1964. As for the artist, he had found the creation of this work so difficult that he would never make anything like it again. He produced a few small models such as *Rotating Fountain* (1925), but in 1929 he said that he had run 'into almost insuperable difficulties of a purely technical nature'. Kinetic sculpture was so dependent on mechanics that he found it 'impossible to create complex configurations'. He added: 'my initial hopes that the application of the new constructive sculpture to kinetics would reveal boundless possibilities were destroyed'. The 'way out of this difficulty' would have to wait for future developments in technology.[80] In the same year, he wrote in his diary: 'My whole anxiety now is to obtain money . . . . Damned sculpture. It is the most expensive branch of art and the least lucrative.'[81]

Gabo turned to film as an alternative way of presenting his 'kinetic constructions', and was excited that sound had recently become part of the medium since 'rhythm must be emphasized musically'.[82] Unfortunately, he found the medium of film as prohibitively expensive as sculpture. Gabo's experience was shared by many modern artists who were fascinated by the film medium, or by the idea of combining art with other forms of technology, but lacked the necessary skills or finance to realise their dreams. For example, the Russian-born Léopold Sauvage had painted several hundred frames between 1912 and 1914 for a film to be called *Coloured Rhythm*. Sauvage wrote in 1914: 'Painting, having liberated itself from the conventional forms of objects in the exterior world, has conquered the terrain of abstract forms. It must get rid of its last and principal shackle – immobility . . . . I will animate my painting . . . my instrument will be the cinematographic film.'[83] But lack of money and technical problems had prevented the completion of his project.

Gabo experimented with the new possibilities that electric light technology opened up for designing synchronised displays of light and colour. He created avant-garde sets and costumes for dance (most notably for the 1927 Ballets Russes production of Henri Sauguet's *La Chatte*). He also consolidated his reputation for static forms of sculpture. When a Cubist or Constructivist artist made something three-dimensional, critics often spoke of a sense of movement created by the way the shapes changed as a spectator walked round the object.[84] Gabo worked in this tradition and liked to heighten the complexity by using transparent materials for some of the surfaces. There was much implied motion in his sculptures ('I want your consciousness to be aware of the . . . dynamic forces')[85] and he continued to use the term 'kinetic', applying it even to a stone carving. He built a major reputation in the United States, but if we recall Kállai's comments about his earlier achievement, it is hard not to see the later work as a step backwards, a 'make-shift substitute' for true kinetic art.

ABSTRACT FILMS AND THE ART OF MOTION

In 1921, a year after Gabo made the first sculpture that 'not only conveys movement, but also is produced by it', the German artist Walther Ruttmann created the first film of that kind.[86] Ruttmann had a very clear theoretical understanding of his new approach. He had announced in a 1917 statement that he was 'in love with the flickering muse' [the film medium], but 'people have gotten stuck in the wrong direction . . . instead of creating something self-contained by proceeding from its essence'.[87] Film needed to focus on 'movement' and all the 'possibilities of changes between light and dark, between motionlessness and movement'. And: 'The creator of films must work with this material as if it were brush and palette.'[88] By 1919, when he wrote his manifesto 'Film as an Independent Art Form', he had developed his ideas about motion still further. He acknowledged that 'speediness' had become more pronounced in everyday life, as the Futurists kept insisting but speed was merely a superficial aspect of something more profound – the need for art to develop its awareness of time. This would produce 'An art meant for our eyes [but] differing from painting in that it has a temporal dimension (like music), . . . in the temporal unfolding of its form.' Also, 'This new art form will give rise to a totally new kind of artist, one whose existence has been only latent up to now, one who will more or less occupy a middle ground between painting and music.'[89] This was another thoughtful manifesto for the art of motion, but once again it had limited circulation and appears not to have been combined with its Futurist or Constructivist counterparts. Even today these writings about motion remain isolated in odd corners of art history.

Ruttmann's first film, *Lichtspiel* [Play of Light] *Opus 1*, gave a dazzling demonstration of what it meant to use movement as 'brush and palette'. The shapes were painted on glass plates and filmed one frame at a time, and Ruttmann then

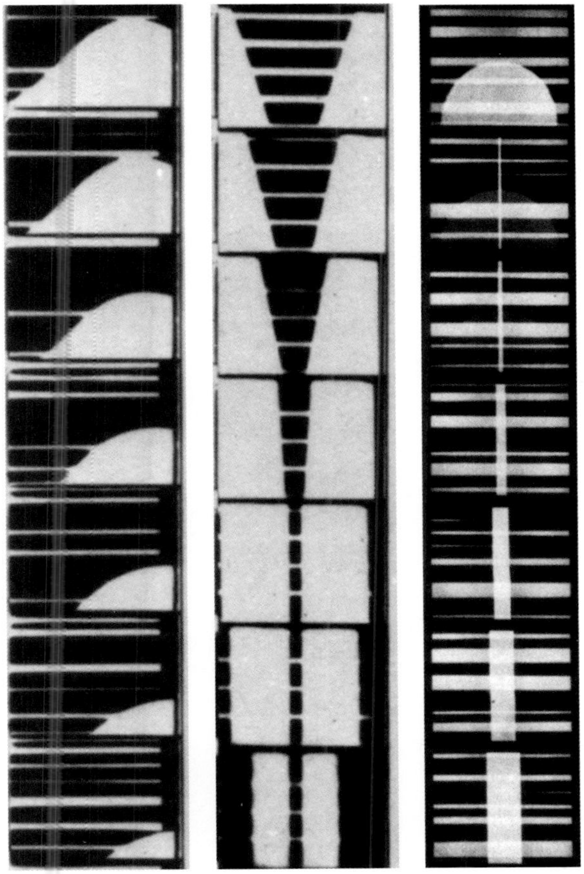

Three sequences (each consisting of seven frames) from Walther Ruttmann's *Lightplay Opus 4*, 1924.

applied colour to the 35mm film print. The ten minutes of animation displayed both a sure grasp of the medium and a subtle sense of movement. The forms were abstract and geometrical but they had the ability to stretch (like a balloon inflating or deflating) or to move in quirky ways, like cartoon characters. Sharp triangles made prodding and stabbing motions, curving shapes rippled and swam, bars of colour swung from side to side like searchlight beams. The one representational sequence was a beautifully animated wave breaking. Rhythm was an important ingredient of the film, and there was a great deal of repetition and symmetry. Ruttmann persuaded Max Butting to compose a complex piece of music, modern for its time, which was played live by a string quartet to accompany screenings of the film. (The film-maker himself played the cello part.)[90]

Ruttmann had been a painter, but after being seriously injured in the war, he had decided to give up this traditional medium to devote his energies to film.

Clearly the 'brush and palette' of *Lichtspiel* still had links with painting, and colour and geometrical form continued to play an important part; but the film also contained patterns of motion that unfolded with great kinetic energy. His work had emerged not from the film industry but from the visual arts – in particular, the energetic avant-garde scene in Berlin, with its emphasis on geometrical abstract art. Soon he was joined by other film-makers with a similar approach. Hans Richter and Viking Eggeling (born in Sweden) started out by making scroll paintings with sequential images, an idea borrowed from the ancient art of China, before moving on to films. Richter made three *Rhythm* films between 1921 and 1925, later claiming that he had completed an abstract film before Ruttmann. Eggeling made two films, of which only one (*Diagonal-Sinfonie*) has survived. These film-makers used geometrical forms in a more austere way, and while they produced some wonderful moments, they had not mastered the medium quite as thoroughly as Ruttmann.

Richter wrote a prophetic manifesto, 'The Badly Trained Soul' (1924), which argued that those who wanted to appreciate this new genre of films needed to overhaul their viewing habits and to cultivate a particular area of their mind: 'this ability was provided for in the construction of the psyche, but it now lies fallow, unused'.[91] (Science would reveal in our own time that there is indeed a region of the brain that specialises in movement.) Richter's manifesto sketched out an abstract film aesthetic, based on his and Eggeling's films, but its talk of 'contrasts' (or opposed shapes) and 'affinities' (or rhymed shapes) was too generalised to offer much guidance.

This upsurge in abstract film-making reached its climax in a legendary screening on 3 May 1925 at the UFA theatre in Berlin under the title of 'The Absolute Film'. This was a multi-media happening that included a performance of three *Colour Sonatinas* by Ludwig Hirschfeld-Mack of the Bauhaus (an art school that was becoming famous as a centre of modernism), who played them on the 'color-organ' he had invented. There were films by Viking Eggeling, Hans Richter, and the second, third and fourth films in Walther Ruttmann's *Lichtspiel* series.[92] (Like *Opus 1*, each film offered a series of kinetic variations on a set of geometrical shapes.) The programme was completed by two French avant-garde films, *Entr'acte* by René Clair from ideas by Francis Picabia, and *Images Mobiles* – later known as *Ballet Mécanique* – made by Fernand Léger and Dudley Murphy, with the help of Man Ray.

According to Christine Noll Brinckmann, the programme 'caused a sensation and a scandal, was repeated for a much larger public and was intensely discussed and reviewed'.[93] It may seem surprising therefore that there were almost no sequels in Germany. But Eggeling died shortly after the screening, and technical and financial problems had exhausted the other German film-makers. The impact of Sergei Eisenstein's film *Battleship Potemkin* in the same year redirected the attention of the vanguard film audience to editing and new styles of narrative. Both Ruttmann and Richter went on to make representational films influenced by Eisenstein.[94] There was also much interest in sound when that technology was introduced at the end of the 1920s. The tradition of the 'absolute film' was, however, brilliantly sustained and extended by a slightly younger film-maker, Oskar Fischinger, who would develop his own kinds of abstract imagery in the late 1920s by a variety of methods, including the slicing of wax and the use of multiple projectors.[95] His subsequent film-making career would run parallel to Lye's, and the men came to know and admire each other's work. Lye would also have film-making connections with Richter in London and New York. He appears never to have met Ruttmann, but that is hardly surprising as the German artist abandoned avant-garde activity in the 1930s and joined the Nazis to make propaganda films.

In summing up the first phase of kinetic film-making, we can see how strongly it reflected the European interest in geometrical abstraction. The films can be linked with the static art being produced by groups such as De Stijl and the Constructivists, or the work emerging from the Bauhaus. These modernists tended to concentrate on geometrical forms which they saw as the foundations of visual experience; and some expressed a utopian optimism that geometry might serve as a universal language for art, architecture and design. Many took a serious interest in the classical tradition of music and saw their abstract art linked closely with it.[96] Some even associated geometrical forms with a kind of mystical resonance. These ways of thinking would remain strongly present in the arts, influencing later kinetic sculpture and experimental film, such as the work of the Hungarian film-maker and photographer Laszlo Moholy-Nagy, author of the important book *Vision in Motion* (published posthumously in 1947).[97]

A different kind of artist was Man Ray, an American based in Paris, who revived the very early photographic method of directly exposing film without a camera and combined it with his avant-garde interests. Ray embarked on this 'rayogram' method around 1920 and two years later adapted it to film-making.[98] Contributing a short film to a Dadaist evening, with the ironic title *Return to*

Reason, he sprinkled 'salt and pepper [and] pins and thumbtacks at random' on strips of film stock. He added, 'I had no idea what this would give me on the screen.'[99] The results were startling and dynamic. Lye would be influenced by his rayogram method, and a similar spirit of playful anarchism would inform later kinetic sculpture by artists such as Jean Tinguely.

Meanwhile, there was a range of experiments in the broader field of live action films, with stylised sets and costumes (such as *The Cabinet of Dr Caligari*) and non-linear narrative and complex editing (such as Eisenstein's use of 'intellectual montage'). The main movements of modern art – such as Expressionism, Futurism, Dadaism and Surrealism – had established a foothold in the film medium, with each pursuing its own specialised set of priorities. These innovations added to the excitement that surrounded the medium of film in the 1910s and 1920s, but they did not necessarily contribute to the development of a specialised art of motion. Lye's own approach would differ from all of the tendencies described in this chapter – from geometrical abstraction, optical art, Dadaist chance and Russian montage – but he would be aware of those artists and grateful for their pioneer work.

The first quarter of the 20th century laid the foundations for an art of motion, but unfortunately this development was then slowed down by a combination of causes. Technological changes such as the coming of sound and improved colour processes opened up exciting possibilities but they also increased the costs and technical complexities so that few artists could afford to make experimental films during the early sound era. In painting and music, the energies of the avant-garde began to ebb as Picasso and Stravinsky led a return to Neo-Classicism, and the idea of an art of movement persisted in only a few corners of the avant-garde. Above all, there were demoralising social changes, starting with the devastating impact of the Great Depression from 1929. Fascism ruthlessly suppressed modernist art in Germany and Italy, and Stalinism destroyed its energies in the USSR.

This is the wider context in which Lye would come to maturity as an artist. Describing his early years in New Zealand, the next chapter also makes clear why he approached these European traditions from an unusual angle.

two Len Lye

a kinetic biography

NEW ZEALAND AT THE START OF THE 20TH CENTURY WAS AN UNLIKELY place for a future avant-garde artist to be born – a small, remote country, dominated by a slow way of life and a down-to-earth, pioneer culture of farmers and traders. Leonard Charles Huia Lye (or 'Len Lye' as he later preferred to sign his paintings) was born in 1901 in the southern city of Christchurch. With a population of only around 60,000, this was the second largest city in a country based on agriculture and primary production. Over the next decade, if the Futurists' excited talk about new technologies and the speed of urban life had reached New Zealand, few artists would have found their themes relevant.

Local artists with a taste for modernity made their escape to Europe, including the painter Frances Hodgkins in 1901 at the age of 31, and the writer 'Katherine Mansfield' (Kathleen Beauchamp) in 1908 at the age of 19. Lye followed in their footsteps at the age of 25, and he often speculated in his later years about how growing up in New Zealand had left a deep 'imprint' on his art.[1] While the country could have used some more culture, there was no shortage of nature. Outdoor activities such as tramping, running, rugby and riding horses were important to Lye. His later art of motion had a distinctive physicality, always involving the body as well as the mind. And he kept drawing on images of nature such as sea creatures and wave patterns. As a young artist he was also strongly drawn to the indigenous cultures of New Zealand and the South Pacific.

A personality can never be entirely explained by circumstances, but some of the dramatic events of his early life must have influenced him. On the darker side, the death of his father just after his third birthday made it necessary for him to be sent to a series of foster homes, and to live most of his childhood in poverty. His mother Rose was a warm, loving person, but there was no support from the state in those days, and the only jobs available to her were housekeeping and cleaning, and employers did not want small children around.

His earliest childhood memory curiously anticipated the powerful effects of light and sound in his later steel sculptures. When his father was dying, the adults sent the boy outside into the yard. Thoroughly upset, the three-year-old flew into a tantrum. When he spotted a kerosene can, he ran over and with all the power in his small legs began to kick it. The effect was vastly more dramatic than he had imagined: 'I can still feel the impact of my kicks on that can and hear an echo of tinny clashes. What is most clear is a great flash of quivering sunlight that came from the can. I stood stock still at it. I don't know what I did next. I think I went over and sat on a log and looked at the can. We're all stopped short by wonder sometime, and that's when it first stopped me in my tracks.'[2] This 'great flash' was soon followed by another mystery as the adults brought him news that his father had died. 'I couldn't figure out where he had gone. How could someone living and moving simply vanish?'[3] But in later years Lye could never think back to the shock of his father's death without also remembering the excitement of the flash – the astonishment of a three-year-old discovering that he could summon up his own thunder and lightning.

His other most intense early memories concerned the period he spent, three years later, at the Cape Campbell lighthouse at the north-east tip of the South Island. His mother had just married a man named Ford Powell who was the assistant lighthouse keeper. Lye would lie in bed at night and watch the lamp at the top of the 22-metre (73-foot) lighthouse flash on and off, like a giant kinetic sculpture, creating complex reflections of light on the windows. The six-year-old was also fascinated by the wild coastal landscape with its rockpools and mysterious sea creatures. But, after a year, his step-father suffered a mental breakdown, became violent and had to be permanently committed to hospital, so it was necessary for Lye and his brother to leave Cape Campbell and resume the circuit of foster homes.

All these misfortunes could have left him insecure and troubled, but instead he emerged from them with great self-reliance and confidence. As a child, he was

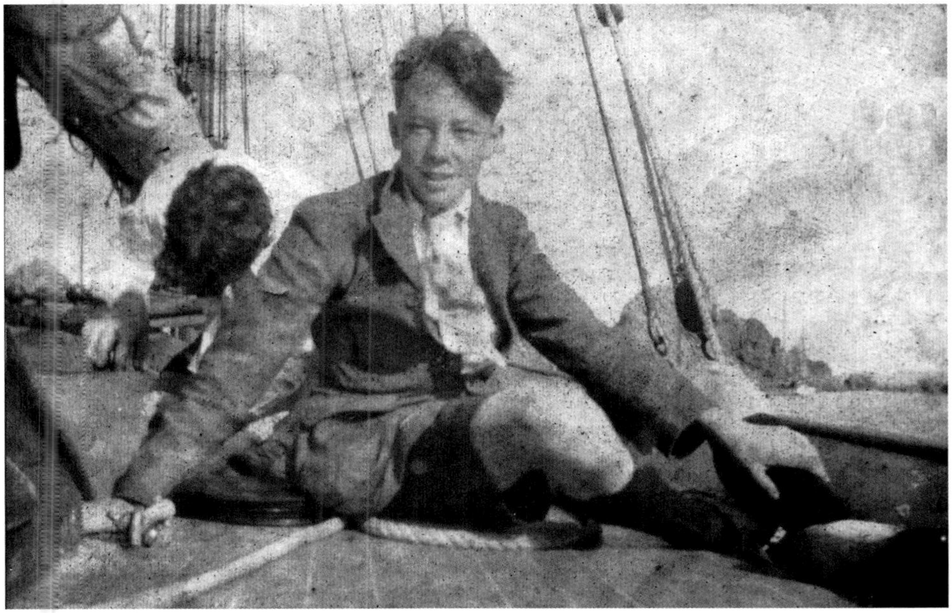

Len Lye at the age of fourteen on a yacht.

an exceptionally independent thinker. Anecdotes abound, such as the story of how he informed his Catholic mother at the age of eleven that he 'didn't believe in God' and refused to be swayed by the arguments of the local priest. (In Lye's words, 'My brain lit up – I knew he didn't know.')[4] Often isolated, he developed his own amusements, such as a game that involved trying to recall in detail the most vivid sensations of the day, including movements observed or actions performed. (This game kept him entertained on occasions when he was sent to bed early as punishment.) He was a natural leader with a quick wit and a strong appetite for experience. The fact that he grew up as a tough kid from the wrong side of the tracks can help to explain the vehemence with which he later rejected the hidebound, snobbish attitudes he sometimes encountered in the arts. Though he was a very good student, he had to leave school at the age of thirteen because he needed to help support his family. His development was a remarkable case of self-education, and he believed passionately in the importance of free public libraries ('You've just got to have them if you want social evolution').[5]

As a teenager, his interest in movement was strong but still unfocused. His brother Philip remembered him enthusing about Frans Hals's *Gipsy Girl*, a well-

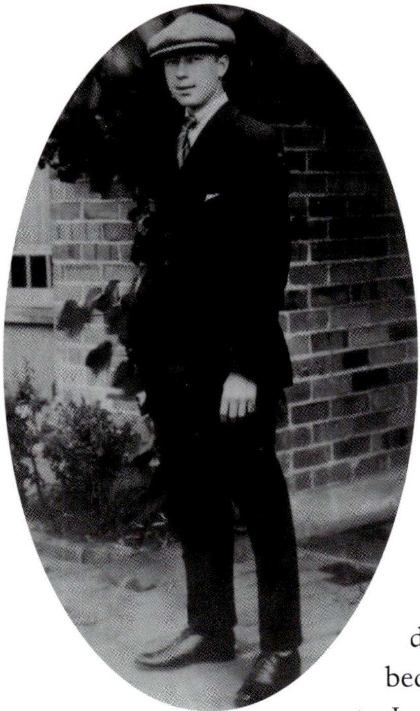

known 17th-century Dutch painting of a young woman with a mischievous laugh.[6] Lye said, 'What a pity that picture can't move!' In 1918, when he was living in Wellington, he started taking part-time art classes at the Technical College. The approach was very traditional – students were taught to revere and imitate the great artists of the past, and there was no discussion of modern developments. Nevertheless, Lye found art classes a pleasant change from his day job in a warehouse. He was happy to acquire traditional craft skills and was soon winning prizes for drawing from the New Zealand Academy of Fine Arts.

At that time, the cutting edge of modern art in New Zealand was Impressionism. Local painters who worked outdoors and depicted transient effects of colour and light horrified local reviewers because of the apparent looseness of their technique. Lye gravitated to Impressionism, starting with the work of two British forerunners who had created images with a strong sense of implied movement – John Constable in his oil sketches of clouds, and J. M. W. Turner in his use of light and colour.[7] Around 1920, Lye was inspired by a stray comment from his favourite teacher, the talented but traditional painter Harry Linley Richardson. Richardson never talked about modern art but he was supportive of his unusual student. On this occasion, Lye heard him praise an artist for having developed his own distinctive approach to art. In the context of the art education of the period, this was a radical idea and Lye was immediately seized by it.

Lye in Sydney, circa 1922 (above) and circa 1925 (opposite, photographed by his girlfriend Mary Brown). Courtesy Joe Davis and Len Lye Foundation.

He remembered the precise moment, months later, when he succeeded in formulating his own approach. On his early morning job delivering newspapers, he was at the top of a hill in the kind of windy weather that Wellington is known for. As he later described the scene:

> It had been raining all night, and there were these marvellous fast little skuddy clouds in the blue sky. As I was looking at those clouds I was thinking, wasn't it Constable who sketched clouds to try to convey their motions? Well, I thought, why clouds, why not just motion? Why pretend they are moving, why not just move something? All of a sudden it hit me – if there was such a thing as composing music, there could be such a thing as composing motion. After all, there are melodic figures, why can't there be figures of motion?[8]

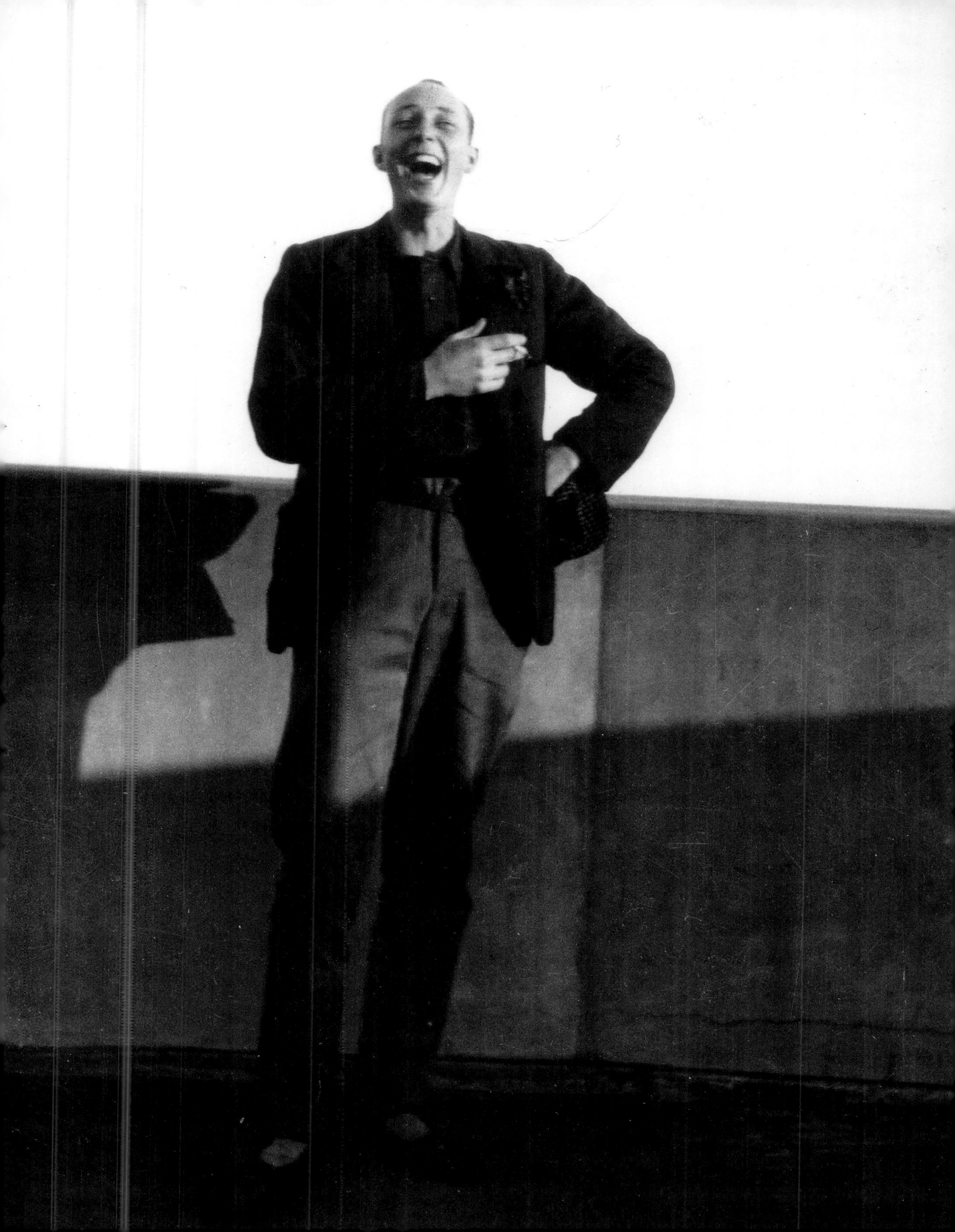

Lye felt he had just had 'the best idea of his life',[9] though he would need time to work out its implications. While the above description makes the 'figures of motion' concept clearer than it probably was at the time, this experience was certainly a revelation for him.[10] His idea linked up with the Impressionists and their interest in the changing patterns of light and the uniqueness of every moment; and it could also be related back to English Romantic writers such as Wordsworth with their sense of 'a motion and a spirit' that permeated nature. But Lye's approach went a step further by focusing on specific patterns of movement.

While he had always been interested in movement, he was now committed to bringing it directly into art. First he sketched a range of everyday activities in an attempt to develop a form of movement notation.[11] Sitting on the back of a horse-drawn cart, he tried over and over to draw the changing folds in the clothes of pedestrians: 'I stared at such things as the diagonal lines in their flapping overcoats as they swung along, or criss-crossed lines formed on a skirt by the owner's walking motion.' The people he drew 'would be wondering what the hell was going on'.[12] Each night, when he looked over his drawings, he would try to remember what they represented, and whether the creases and folds he had drawn had come from faster or slower movements.[13] He then turned to a more stylised form of 'repetitive movement marks'[14] to match his interest in cyclic motions, such as the 'dancing' of a mast as an anchored boat bobbed back and forth.[15] If he had ever come across Herbert Spencer's descriptions, he would have been excited to recognise a similar interest in rhythmic patterns.

Lye had almost no audience for his drawings: 'My work [looked] crazy unless people were given some explanation, so I quit bothering to show it. The explanations were far more difficult to make than the sketches.' He was himself dissatisfied with his 'spaghetti-looking sketches'.[16] The flight of a seagull 'came out looking like a tangle of fishing lines'.[17] He felt he had not yet solved the basic problem of how to transfer movement to the static page: 'What the hell do I *compose* motion with? What's going to carry the motion? Well, that problem knocked me bandy.'[18] While he continued to study movement in nature, he also turned to books. It was clear to him now that the 'realism' he had been taught was only one way to represent the world.

In the library he discovered modernism and was hugely excited by it. Today, in the Internet age, it is important to realise how slowly information about modern forms of art circulated during the first decades of the 20th century. An artist in a small, marginal country like New Zealand had only a few fragments of the jigsaw. There were no modern paintings on display, and only a few black and white reproductions in print. Many of the newspaper and magazine stories about modern art were scornful, but Lye became adept at reading between the lines. He developed such extraordinary library skills that by the mid-1920s he was probably better informed about modern art than anyone else in the country. Most of the examples he found were not concerned with movement but they did help to open up the whole issue of representation.

Very occasionally he would locate a source that contained first-hand information, such as Ezra Pound's *Gaudier-Brzeska: A Memoir.*[19] This book was a catalyst for many young artists – such as Henry Moore in England – and it became Lye's bible. Henri Gaudier-Brzeska made compelling connections between modern art and tribal art. For Lye, the book was a treasure-trove of information about 'Cubism, Expressionism, everything that was going on'.[20] He was fascinated by the translation of a *haiku* (a short Japanese poem) quoted by Pound – 'The fallen blossom flies back to its branch: A butterfly'[21] – and he often returned to it when musing about his own art of motion. He painstakingly copied out by hand the text and illustrations from library books. (It would be over 40 years before photocopiers appeared in public libraries.) Throughout these years, he kept his research mostly to himself, and his continued involvement in sport and outdoor

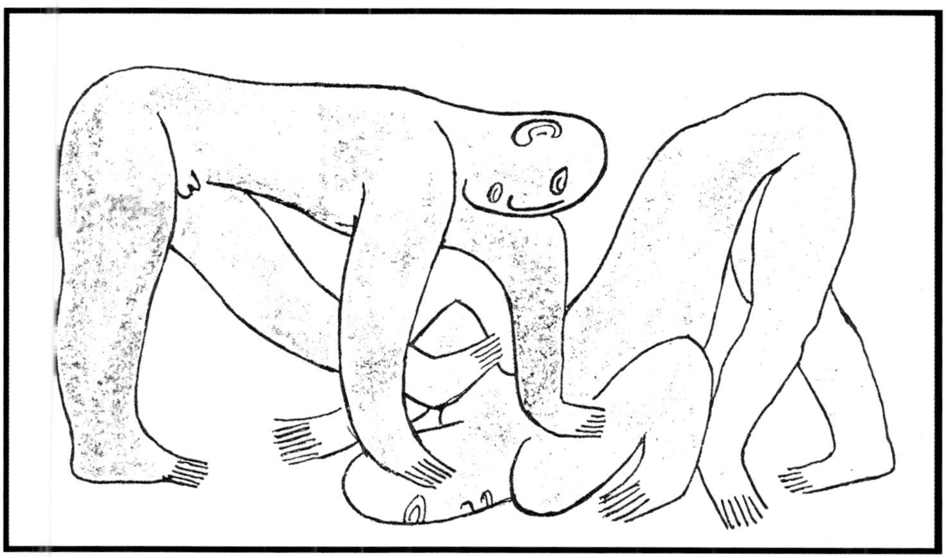

Gaudier-Brzeska's 1913 pen-and-ink drawing *Wrestlers* was included in Ezra Pound's book *Gaudier-Brzeska: A Memoir.* Lye made this copy of the drawing in his sketchbook. Courtesy Len Lye Foundation.

activities helped shield him from the stereotypes routinely applied by the macho culture of his peers to any young man perceived as arty or intellectual.

Apart from some examples of Futurism – a movement rejected by Pound and Gaudier-Brzeska as old-fashioned Impressionism attempting to seem modern – Lye still 'hadn't ever come across anybody talking about motion in art'.[22] When he finally saw an illustration of Lyubov Popov's stage set for the Meyerhold Theatre's 1922 production of *The Magnificent Cuckold* (see colour section), he was so impressed by this kinetic construction with wheels and a propeller that he made it his long-term goal to travel to Moscow. It was one of his main motives for becoming a seaman in 1926. He never succeeded in reaching Moscow, however, but in the meantime the USSR lost its avant-garde energies as Stalin consolidated his power.

Since modernism was an explosion of many ideas besides movement, Lye's reading sent him in many new directions. The most important theme was one he would later call 'the old brain' (a term borrowed from science). His starting-point was the unconscious, a concept he first encountered in Freud's *Totem and Taboo*, but he was soon aware that his perspective on the subject was different from that of psychoanalysis. The Surrealists were fascinated by Freudian dream symbolism, but for Lye the most important aspect of the unconscious was the overlap between mind and body. This reflected his concern with movement since the activities of our bodies – from breathing to running, from swimming to love-making, from the pumping of the heart to the coordination of fingers in guiding a paintbrush – all depend on complex processes that are to some extent unconscious. Lye's interest in this area of 'proprioception' reflected his strongly physical approach to life and drew him towards organic or biological imagery rather than geometrical abstraction or machine shapes (though he did pass through an early phase of 'mechanical art').[23] It also attracted him to the new genre of jazz music which he saw as body-oriented in its rhythms. Jazz displayed (in Lye's phrase) 'the personal tonal quality of breathing' in the individual sound of a trumpet or saxophone player.[24] He saw the old brain most strongly represented in modern artists such as Brancusi and Gaudier-Brzeska whose sculpture had physical resonance and a vivid sense of implied motion.

Another reason he sought physicality in art was as an antidote to the Victorian squeamishness about sex that still dominated the local culture. He found a healthier attitude to the body reflected in the art of ancient and tribal traditions – not only African (which Lye had read about in discussions of Cubist art) but also Maori, Aboriginal and South Pacific art. This was a major discovery for him because he was living in the vicinity of those traditions. He wrote, 'I knew I was not a chip off the Western art block, I knew it in my bones.'[25] He liked the frank treatment of sexuality in some of the carved figures he saw on Maori marae.[26] He also admired those figures as the work of artists acutely sensitive to stance and gesture, and therefore rich in suggestions of movement. Another way he sought to link his work on movement with his interest in ancient and tribal cultures was by finding out as much as he could about their dance rituals.

As part of the modernists' challenge to mainstream values, they redefined 'primitive' as a positive term and celebrated 'primitive art' as superior to much of the art of Western civilisation. While 'modernist primitivism' has in recent years been accused of appropriation and naïve forms of romanticism, it is important to take historical contexts into account. In Lye's case, he was one of the first artists of European descent to engage seriously with Maori and Aboriginal forms of art. Throughout his life, he continued to study tribal traditions in various parts of the world, and they were still an influence when he was making his final films. The link with tribal art was always one of the distinctive features of his kineticism. It is possible to find problematic aspects in every version of 'modernist primitivism', and Lye can be seen as having relied too much upon museums and anthropological literature (though he did criticise their limitations).[27] His view of the subject certainly contained a romantic streak. Nevertheless, his 'primitivism'

These images from the 1920s illustrate Lye's phase of interest in machine shapes. The first image (on the left) is one of various drawings of machinery he made in his sketchbook. The second is a bookplate he designed for the pianist Nigel Pearson in Sydney. The third image was the photograph in Edwin J. Kempf's book *Psychopathology* that inspired Lye to start making kinetic sculpture. Kempf's caption described the object as a 'copulation fetish by [an] impotent negro paranoic' instructed by God to build the 'first church of perpetual motion'. The final image (on the right) was a metal sculpture by Lye entitled *Construction*. Approximately 600mm high, this was included in the Seven and Five Society's 1928 exhibition in London. Courtesy Len Lye Foundation.

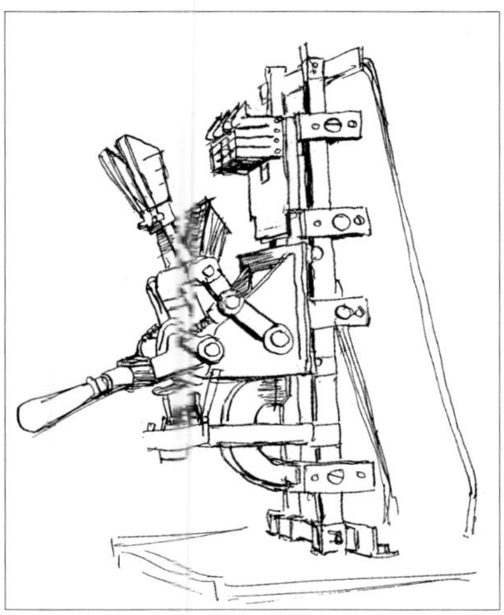

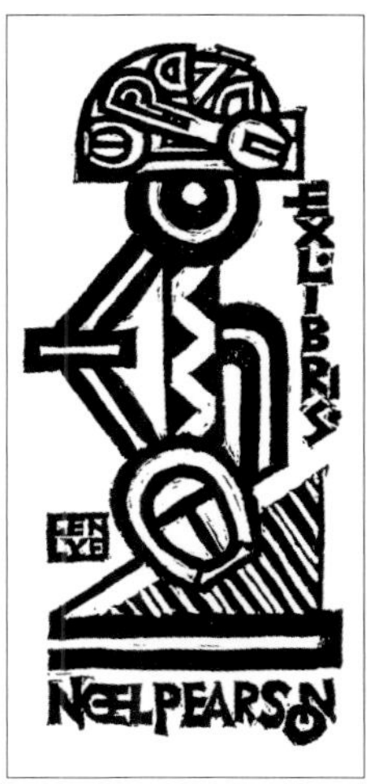

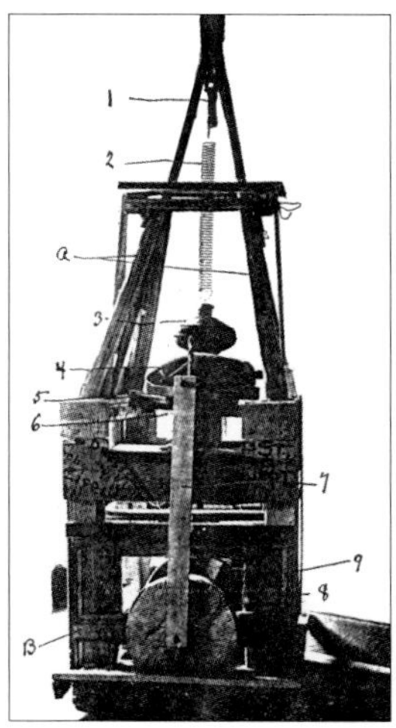

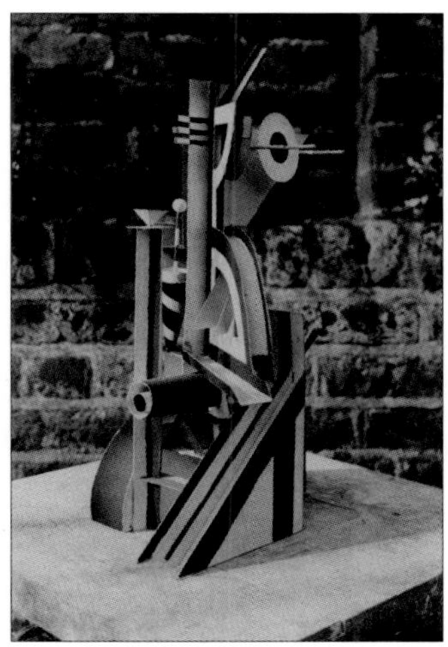

can be defended more strongly than most versions, for it was far from superficial. He was concerned about the specific contexts and social uses of the art, and he visited some communities – his study was not merely a fashionable interest in the exotic surfaces of objects from faraway places.

In 1923, Lye encountered an example of kinetic sculpture. He went to Australia to find out more about Aboriginal art and to check out the art scene in Sydney. In a library, he came across a recent American psychoanalytical book, Edwin J. Kempf's *Psychopathology*, which included the case study of a 'Negro paranoic' who believed that God had directed him to build 'the first church' of 'perpetual motion'. He had constructed a shrine about five feet high using pieces of boxes, a broomstick, ropes, a metal container and a number of cast-off spiral springs.[28] A sense of perpetual motion was created by the springs that allowed parts of the machine to continue rocking for a long time after receiving an initial push. The broomstick was kept spinning by a rope winding and unwinding, and there were pieces of a colourful barber's pole turned by levers. The maker sent photographs to a newspaper and attempted to have his design patented. Kempf accepted that the object could be regarded as a work of art, but he preferred to see it in Freudian terms as a phallic symbol. He interpreted its up-and-down motion as the patient's compensation for his own impotence.[29] Lye ignored Kempf's diagnosis – what excited him was the photograph of the pulley-belt construction. Here was a work that literally moved; and even if it was about sex, it deserved respect as a modern, kinetic version of the fertility objects in tribal art.

The photograph inspired Lye to build his first kinetic sculpture. This was a wooden box with a series of shafts connected to pulley belts and wheels, turned by handles from hand-wound phonographs. (Lye was not aware that around the same time Duchamp was making similar use of phonograph mechanisms.) Attached to the shafts were geometrical shapes and motifs from Aboriginal art, such as boomerangs, patterned shields and concentric circles. Wheels of different sizes made the shapes revolve at various speeds. Since Lye had to stand at the back to turn the handles, he needed to set up a mirror in front to view the results. After spending a great deal of time fine-tuning the results, he came independently to the same conclusion as other early experimenters such as Gabo, that making art of this kind was too difficult without engineering help. He left the sculpture behind in Sydney and it was subsequently lost.[30]

Soon he was seized with a new idea – that the medium with the greatest potential to compose motion was film. He had seen films before but had not

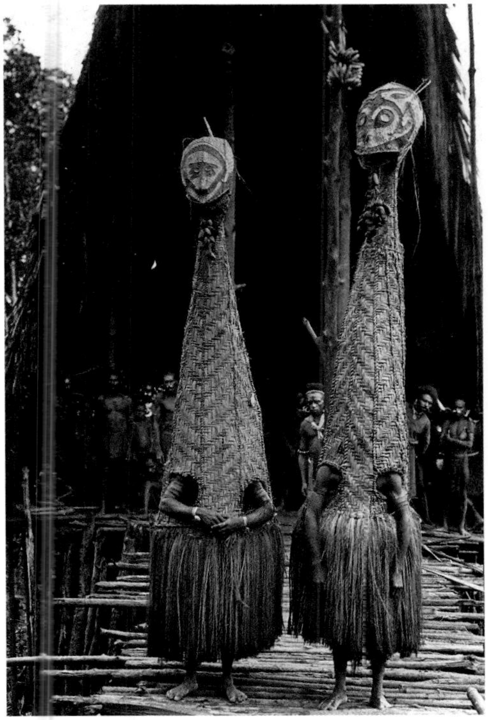

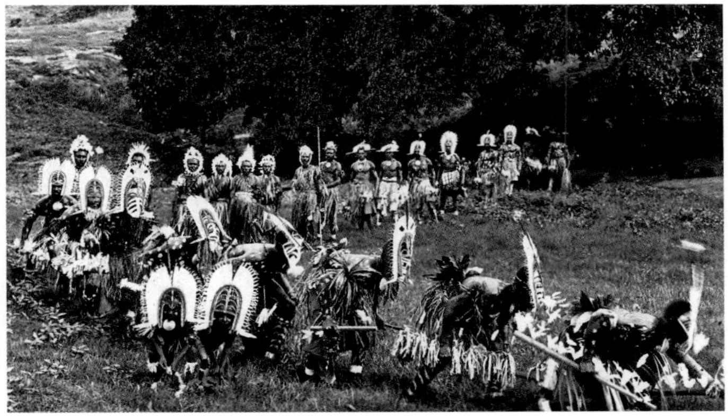

Two photographs taken by Frank Hurley while he was making *Pearls and Savages*. He described the two Papuan dancers with tall masks as 'the taboo goblins of Urama' who were 'regarded with great terror'. The dancers on the right were said to be performing a 'death dance'. ('The performers wear rattles on their elbows which make a sound instantly suggestive of the rattling of a skeleton.') Courtesy Pictures Branch, National Library of Australia, Canberra (NLA.PIC-VN3314275 and 3313864).

experienced anything like Frank Hurley's *Pearls and Savages*, a feature-length documentary about the indigenous people of Papua whose art Lye had been studying. He was scornful of Hurley's ethnographic commentary but very impressed by the scenes of ritual dancing. The film medium infused these scenes with a kinetic energy that had been absent from all the text and photographs he had found in books. *Pearls and Savages* was another occasion when Lye's approach to movement was linked with his interest in tribal art.

To learn the basics of film-making, he obtained a job in Sydney at Filmads, one of the few Australian companies that produced animated advertisements. He wrote, 'I suddenly realised that films had cuts and sequences.'[31] In his spare time, he made flip books containing a series of abstract shapes. His access to the film equipment was limited but he experimented with strips of black leader (blank film) by scratching 'doodles' onto them and staying behind after work to project the results. Unfortunately, he failed to complete what would have been the first abstract, experimental film made in the southern hemisphere. At this stage of his life, he was very restless and never confident that he had found the answer to his search for imagery that could 'carry the motion'.

After a brief return visit to New Zealand, he spent a year in a small village in Samoa where he learned the indigenous method of making *siapo* (tapa cloth), applying patterns by painting or by pressing an inked board to cloth made from the bark of the mulberry tree. This bold, rhythmic style of design would later inform his approach to the hand-painting of films. Lye's village life came to an end when the local governor ordered him to leave because he insisted on living with Samoans rather than with the white, colonial community. (A year later, Samoans would launch the Mau independence movement, in protest against New Zealand's heavy-handed administration.) Sent back to Sydney, Lye made friends with some talented artists such as the sculptor G. Rayner Hoff and the composer Jack Ellitt; but he decided the time had come to visit one of the centres of modern art. Accustomed to physical labouring jobs, he bought ship's papers from a drunken stoker, and stoked his way under the seaman's name to London.

LONDON

At first he had tried to find a ship going to Moscow, but for an artist from New Zealand there was a kind of ironic inevitability about ending up in London, centre of the British Empire. Twenty-five years old when he arrived, Lye saw himself as a late developer in comparison with his precocious heroes, the sculptor Gaudier-Brzeska and the poet Arthur Rimbaud. But any delay was partly a consequence of growing up so far from Europe. Fully developing his idea of kinetic art depended upon modern technology that was still beyond his means, and so far he had focused mostly on ancient, hand-made forms of art. His last works before leaving New Zealand and Australia had been a *Tiki* carved in wood and a marble sculpture of a couple making love (*Unit*). Both works were influenced by Maori art but also reminiscent of Gaudier-Brzeska and (in the case of the sculpture) Brancusi. They were striking but static old brain images.

In London, he was immediately accepted into an avant-garde group of artists, the Seven and Five Society. He impressed them as a 'stoker-sculptor' with a working-class manner and a unique personality, who had appeared out of the blue with some extraordinary works.[32] He was unpretentious and totally committed to art, and in the South Pacific he had somehow developed his own version of modernism. He struck the art world as an exotic Crocodile Dundee sort of figure. To the painter Julian Trevelyan, Lye was 'like a man from Mars who saw everything from a very different viewpoint, and it was this that made him original'.[33]

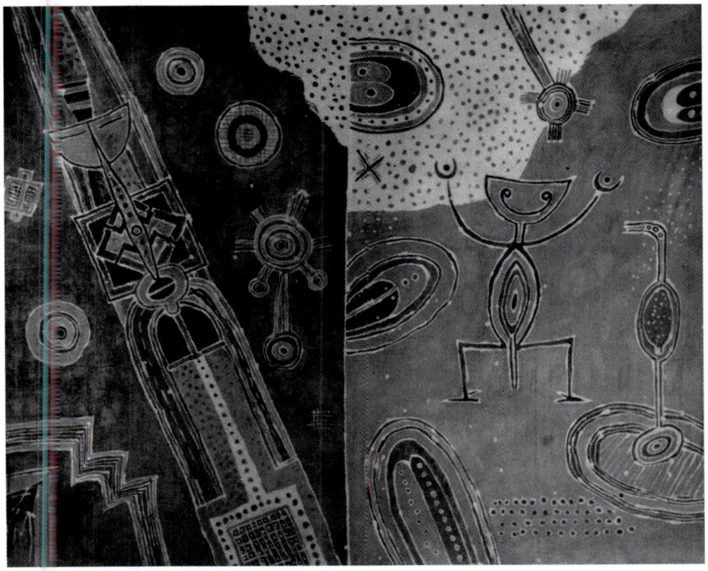

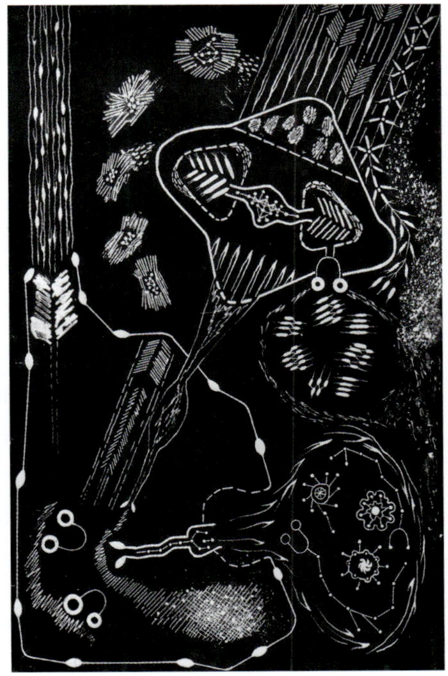

Living on a barge on the Thames (provided by Eric Kennington and A. P. Herbert), he produced paintings and batiks based on old brain imagery that looked like an unknown form of tribal art. Poets Robert Graves and Laura Riding commissioned a series of them as book covers for their Seizin Press. Riding later said of Lye's imagery, 'There gradually crystallised in his mind a system of imagery for the description of nature processes in terms of human drama.'[34] This imagery at first seemed static but it was full of allusions to 'processes' – storms and volcanoes, evolutionary change, struggles for survival and strange forms of reproduction.[35] Creatures were poised to move in odd ways (such as the 1933 painting *Cagn, who Made Things*, a figure with long legs like a folding gate).[36] But they were not based on any 'system' of symbolism, and even for the artist they remained ultimately mysterious.

Lye knew it was high time he introduced literal movement into his work. To gain access to film equipment, he obtained a part-time job in a London animation company similar to Filmads – the Hopkins and Weir studio, which produced cartoon commercials for beer and toothpaste. While working there as a 'filler-in', he studied the use of the rostrum camera and was given access after hours. He bought his own drawing table and learned the traditional process of animation by trial and error. Once he got into the swing of it, he could produce one second of

Abo Imp (left), a batik Lye made in the late 1920s, combined the ancient with the modern and the natural with the mechanical. The subject of rockets was topical around 1926 as Robert Goddard had just demonstrated the first liquid fuel rocket, encouraging speculation about space travel. The circle and dot motifs reflected Lye's strong interest in Aboriginal art. The dynamic image on the right was his design for the back cover of *Laura and Francisca*, a volume of poetry by Laura Riding published by the Seizin Press in 1931. It was printed white on clear blue. Courtesy Len Lye Foundation.

black and white film per day. He devoted much of the next two years to creating approximately 4400 drawings for a nine-minute film.[37] The laborious process of animation was a very effective, hands-on way for him to learn to compose and control movement. His only collaborator was his Australian friend Jack Ellitt, who had followed Lye to London. He wrote rhythmic piano music to accompany Lye's film. This was for live performance, since they could not afford a soundtrack, although the technology had recently become available. Ellitt, a highly innovative composer, a pioneer of electronic music and later a film director in his own right, would continue to work with Lye for a decade, supervising his music.[38]

The film was given a Samoan title, *Tusalava* (which Lye translated as 'Everything eventually goes full cycle'), and its images were influenced by Aboriginal art.[39] This was the first animation film based on 'modernist primitivism'. At the same time, it drew upon Lye's 'imagery for the description of nature processes in terms of human drama'. The film was not entirely abstract since it told a story of conflict, though its protagonists belonged to unknown species (like mysterious forms of life seen through the microscope). When the British Board of Film Censors was asked to approve *Tusalava* for screening, they told Lye they were completely baffled by it. Their suspicions aroused, they required him to explain what was really going on. He sent back a detailed account of how the film 'represented a self-shape annihilating an agonistic element'. In the end, the censors threw in the towel and gave the film a certificate.[40]

Tusalava has a very physical (albeit leisurely) sense of movement. Creatures rise like snakes and move in unison; muscular shapes push and pull; a monster like an octopus squirts ink and spins a 'core shape' like a top. The action grows more vigorous in the last third of the film, which anticipates the push-and-pull of Lye's later kinetic sculptures. The spinning of Aboriginal-style circles and ovals may echo his first attempt at kinetic sculpture. Much of the movement in the film seems derived from the energies of evolution – its creatures keep changing as they engage in the struggle for survival of the fittest.

The film was premiered at the end of 1929 by the London Film Society which covered the cost of the print. The Society screened it again in 1930 and 1932. Filmmaker Oswell Blakeston and critic Roger Fry praised it for its unique sense of movement.[41] A copy went to Paris to the Studio des Ursulines, and then toured other avant-garde venues in Europe where it made a strong impression on filmmakers such as Hans Richter. Films seriously influenced by modern art were still a rarity, and though viewers were intrigued, they were not sure how to talk about

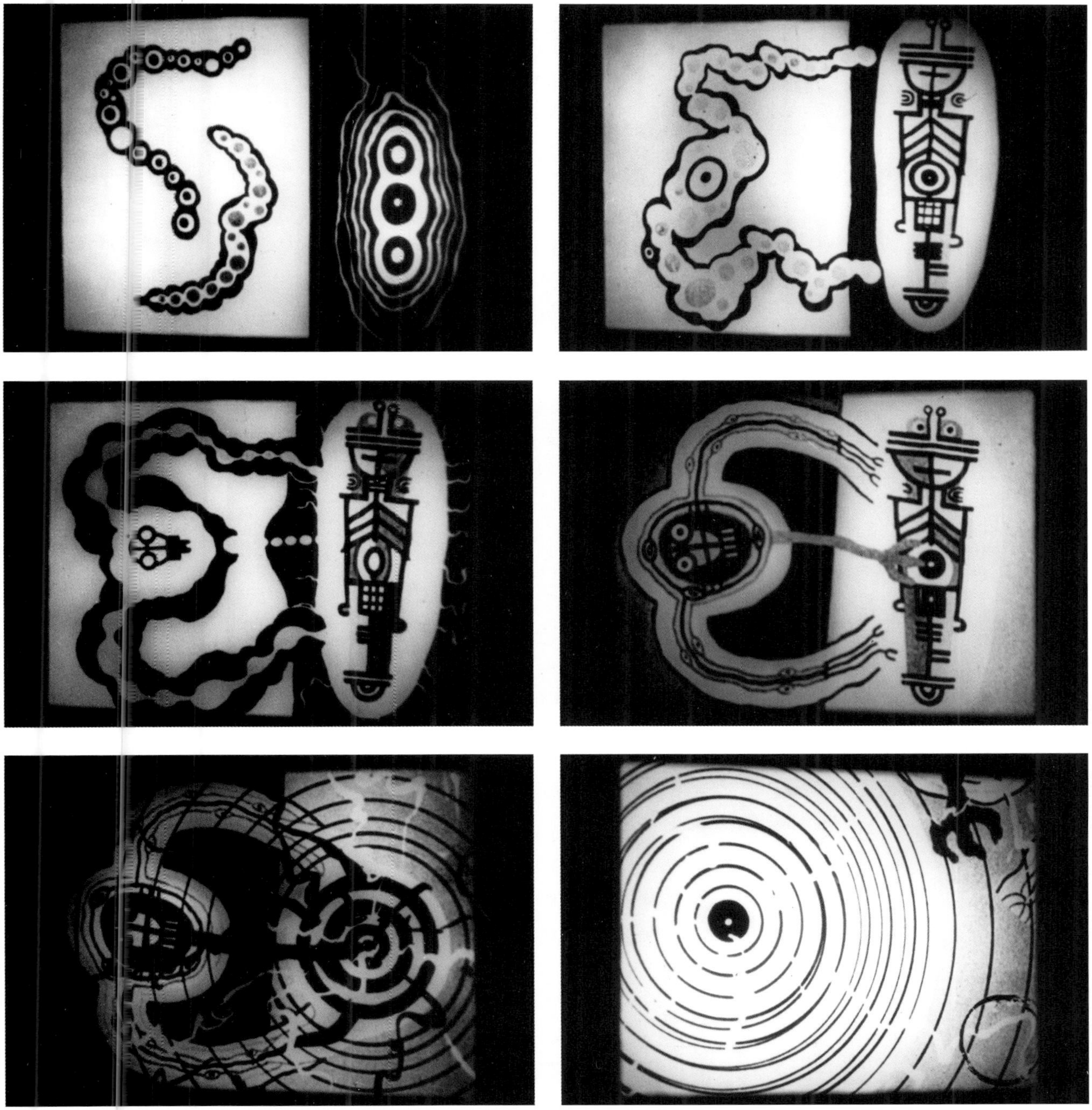

Six frames from *Tusalava*, 1929. The sequence reads from left to right. Courtesy Len Lye Foundation.

this unique film or how to contextualise it. Other films could be linked with groups such as the Dadaists, the Surrealists or the Bauhaus. Their images tended to be urban, contemporary, geometrical or machine-like, or based on intellectual concepts and word-play, whereas Lye's work evoked nature, ancient traditions of art and organic forms of life, with a strong sense of physicality and no words. He also drew upon the relatively unfamiliar indigenous cultures of the South Pacific. As the only film of its kind, *Tusalava* lapsed into obscurity.

Eager to expand his animation methods, Lye began work on the second and third parts of a *Tusalava* trilogy, to follow the process of evolution through to 'more humanized shapes' involving the use of 'marionette models'. He made detailed preparations for the trilogy which he expected to take 'about ten years'.[42] Ellitt planned to make innovative use of new recording technology to create a soundtrack of what would later be called electro-acoustic music or *musique concrète*. But the film world was going through big changes. The economic Depression initiated by the Wall Street crash of October 1929 complicated the search for sponsorship. Sound made the process of film-making more expensive, and the arrival of colour would soon add a further increase. Meanwhile, early sound equipment had such limited mobility that films in general became more static, dialogue-oriented and narrative-based. It was not the best time to seek sponsorship for an obscure experiment in movement.

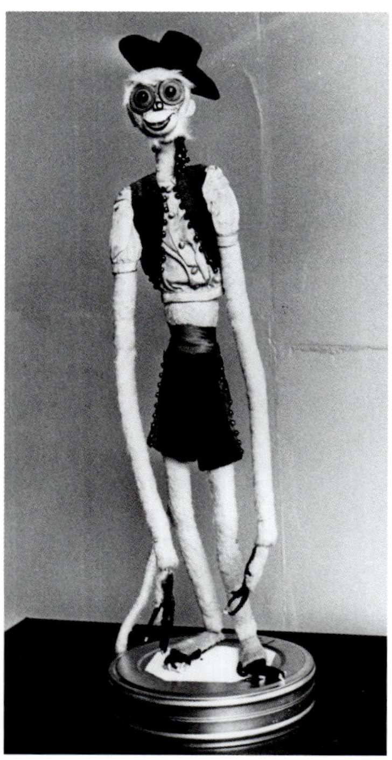

Lye made this monkey in 1934 for his puppet animation film *Peanut Vendor*. Courtesy Len Lye Foundation.

Lye exhibited images from the trilogy and Oswell Blakeston published a supportive essay, but no funding could be found.[43] Lye then tried to conceive of a film project that might appeal to investors. One encouraging precedent was the Diaghilev Ballet Company (formerly the *Ballets Russes*) which employed avant-garde composers and designers yet still attracted a large London audience.[44] Lye and his friends proposed a dance film called 'Quicksilver' as a British equivalent. He also planned a series of quirky puppet films synchronised to popular dance music, since this was one of the few areas of animation not yet dominated by Walt Disney. A three-minute demonstration film, *Peanut Vendor* (or *Experimental Animation*), was actually made, with a monkey puppet dancing to jazz by Red Nichols and his Five Pennies. None of Lye's proposals attracted a sponsor, so he took a job as cleaner in a film studio to earn a little money and to have the opportunity to watch how conventional feature films

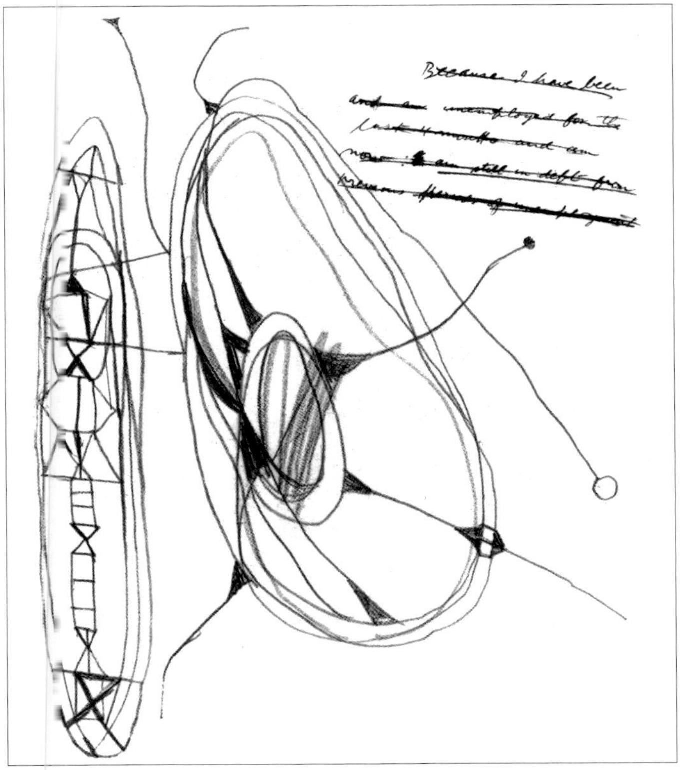

A doodle circa 1934, reminiscent of the 'octopus-spider death-figure' in *Tusalava*. Lye wrote 'Because I have been unemployed for the last 4 months and am still in debt from previous period of unemployment', then crossed out the words. Courtesy Len Lye Foundation.

were made.[45] These were difficult years but they did help him to extend his skills, such as learning how to synchronise images to music. Dance had always played a part in his thinking about movement, and his concept of dance greatly expanded during this period. An important source of information was the dance instructor Jane Thompson, who became his partner in 1927 and his wife in 1934.

DIRECT FILMS

During these years, Lye kept up his links with the avant-garde, writing pieces of experimental prose in the form of letters, which were published by the Seizin Press in 1930 as *No Trouble*. The paintings he exhibited with the Seven and Five Society became freer, more painterly and more abstract. As Riding noted, Lye had become dissatisfied with his 'system of imagery for . . . nature processes'

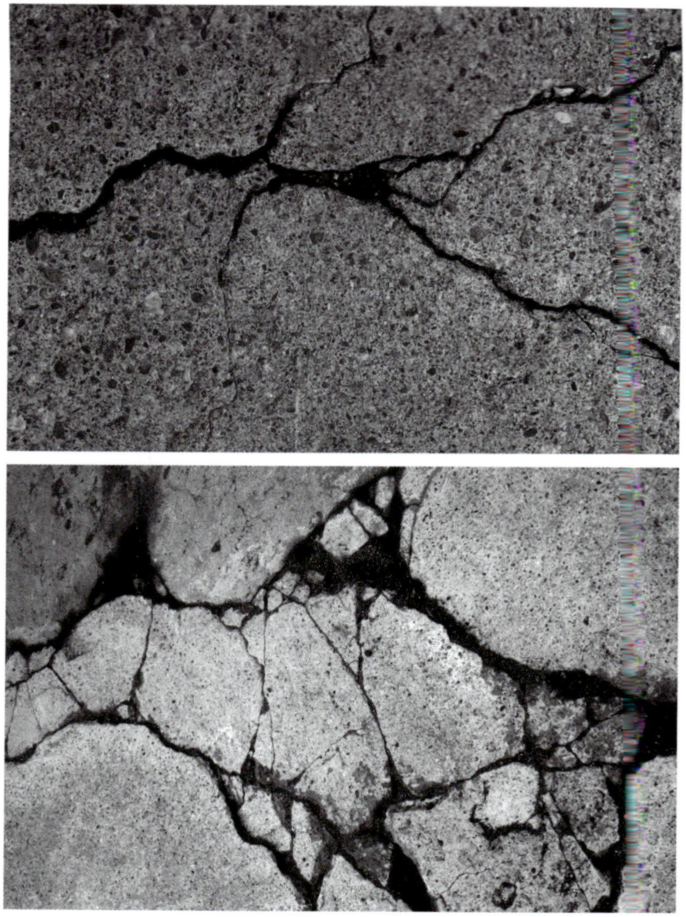

Two of Lye's many photographs of cracks. Such fractures interested him as patterns created by subterranean energies. These were among the examples he discussed in his slide-tape programme *Living Energy*. Courtesy Len Lye Foundation.

and 'abandoned [it] as too conventionalized in the totemistic sense'. Instead, he 'evolved a method of colour notation in oils that enabled him to record the actual activity of sensation in pictorial form'.[46] Lye was distancing himself from the hard-edge style of *Tusalava* and Aboriginal art, not to mention his previous years of drawing. 'Sensation' became a key word, as he saw his art as an attempt to stimulate the senses before the intellect could impose its usual preconceptions or closed forms. His new approach involved an increased use of 'doodling', or 'automatic drawing' as the Surrealists called it, seeking to make images by impulse and intuition. He became fascinated by the implied movement in lines and brushstrokes. He made copies of children's art, abstract graffiti, and the patterns created by cracks, peeling paint, stains and tyre tracks. Such marks were a 'visual contact with moving life'[47] or the evidence of subterranean energies.

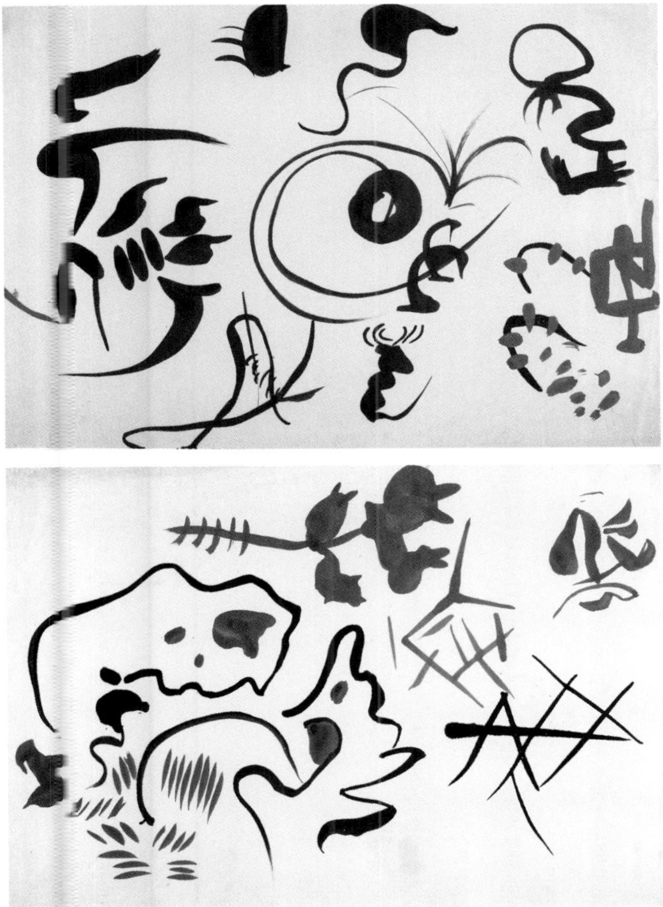

These 1930s sketches illustrate Lye's interest in 'doodling' and in cave art. Courtesy Len Lye Foundation.

Doodling for Lye was a very exploratory but also painstaking activity, with the devil lurking in the details. A literal example was the long process of doodling by which he sought to capture a 'devil figure' for his 1934 painting *Fire Devil*: 'I had a nag in my head not to let the devil escape me but to put salt on his tail . . . . I sketched many wild-looking figures over many months, sometimes wondering why I was persevering.'[48] This was typical of his approach to every medium – an exhaustive, trial-and-error process in search of 'a particular form . . . which fascinates me because I can't make out why'.[49]

Around this time, he expanded his study of tribal art to include the most ancient forms of cave art. These attracted him because he saw a great deal of implied movement and because they were the ultimate example of artistic innovation. He also started to align himself with the Surrealists, though not with the 'literary' tendencies of Salvador Dalí and René Magritte (whom he associated with Freud's dream symbolism), but rather with the abstract approach of painters such as Joan Miró (whom he saw as a great advocate of the old brain). All these new interests informed his painting and drawing and helped to prepare him for the major breakthrough that was about to occur in his film-making.

This was based on a flash of lateral thinking, or what New Zealanders call 'No. 8 fence wire ingenuity' (the discovery of a cheap, ingenious way of using everyday materials).[50] Unable to afford to rent a camera or to pay for processing, Lye began to collect unwanted scraps of film from editing rooms and to experiment with them by painting, scratching or stencilling abstract images onto the celluloid. He would then get access to an editing bench to assess the results. This harked back to his scratching of film in Sydney. What had deterred other animators from drawing images directly onto film was the jittery effect caused by the inevitable difference between one frame and the next, and it took a special kind of artist to regard this as an advantage, as a way to heighten the sense of physical energy or to match the resonance of musical instruments. Lye's love of doodling and his interest in movement (going back to his 'spaghetti-looking sketches') made him open to these vibrating images. Animators of all kinds from Walt Disney to the German abstract artists had emphasised precise shapes and smooth movements; and similarly, the long tradition of tinting films and adding hand-painted areas of colour by brush and stencil had emphasised neatness. Now the slow, wriggling creatures of *Tusalava* were replaced by bold, abstract brushmarks that scurried and quivered in a tense, muscular way. Lye still sought precision, but he saw that working with energy and movement involved a different kind of 'physical accuracy'.[51]

A strip of film was only 35mm in width, a tiny surface on which to paint patterns that would later be blown up to fill a cinema screen. To discover the best figures of motion was a time-consuming business but at least it was cheap – there was no need for a camera or film crew. Lye was also delighted to transform the high-tech medium of film into something hand-made, like tapa cloth. One of the other interesting features of 'direct film-making' (his preferred term) was its status as the only type of film-making that literally qualified for the 'auteur theory', the critical tradition that spoke of films as the work of an individual creator.[52] Only in a direct film is the touch or 'signature' of the maker physically present in every frame. Yet even Lye needed some help in combining his visual ideas with music. Ellitt took over this task, looking after the sound editing and helping to synchronise the images. The use of popular, jazz-influenced dance music increased the chances

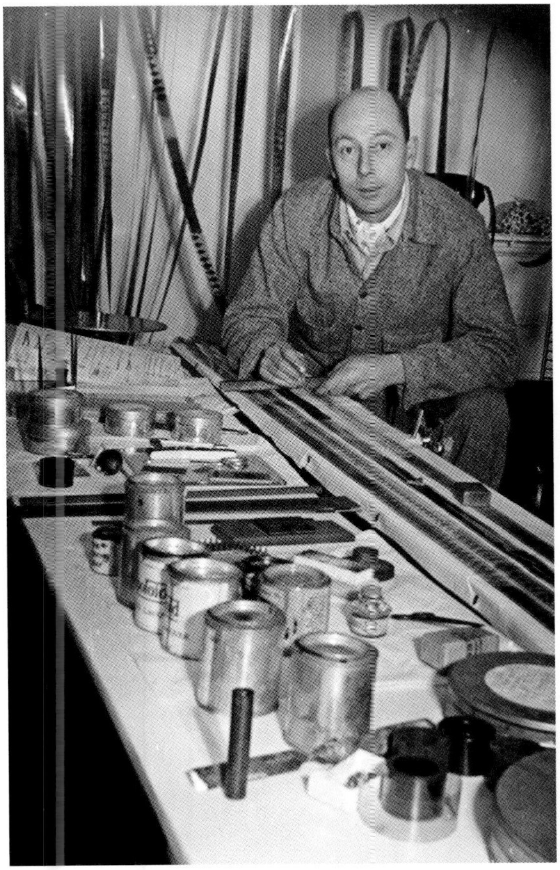

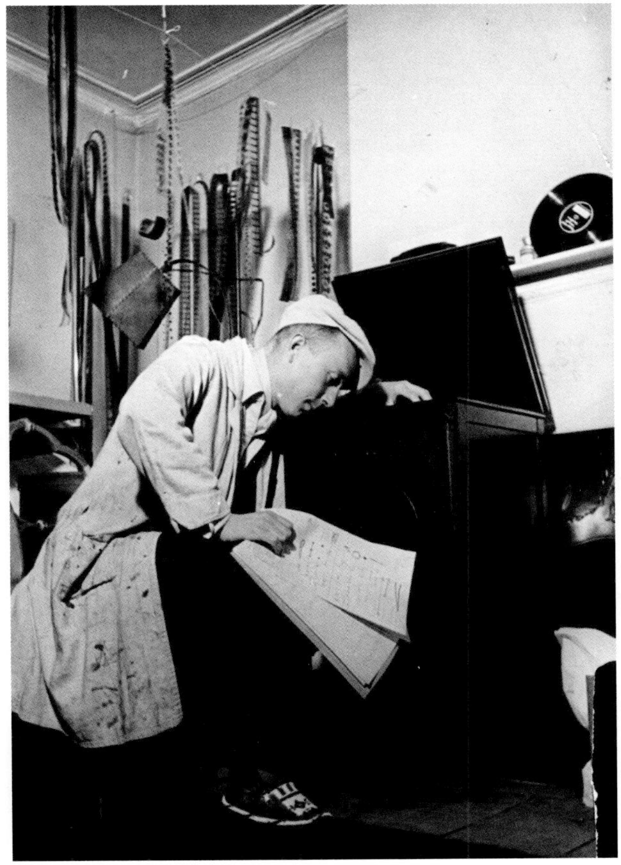

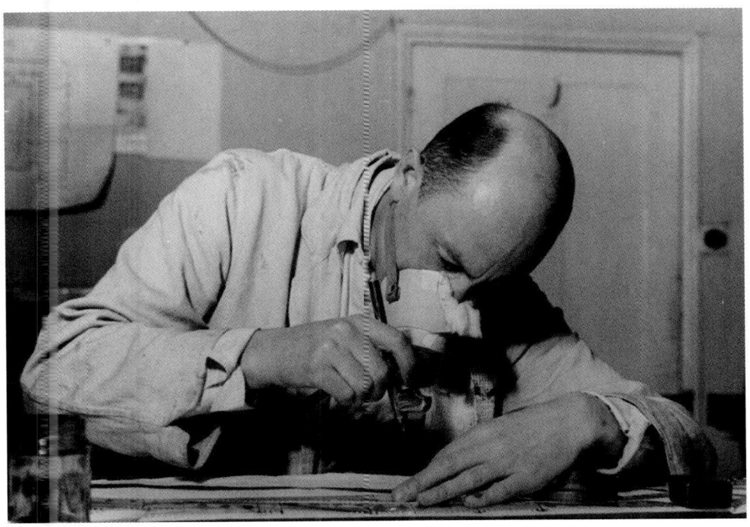

Lye at work on *Colour Flight* in 1938. He is shown painting film strips (which were hung up to dry), selecting gramophone records for the soundtrack and wearing a mask as he worked with an airbrush. Photos John Phillips. Courtesy Len Lye Foundation.

of finding a sponsor, and this was music that Lye genuinely enjoyed and respected for its physical vitality. He accepted rhythm and dance as natural ingredients of the art of movement, and his interest in popular music would help to make him one of the fathers of the 'music video'. His aim was not simply to translate music but also to develop visual ideas in counterpoint – with enough synchronisation to keep the images in step, but enough independence to ensure that the images retained the primary focus. This syncopation matched his own way of dancing at parties – he moved in an idiosyncratic style which surprised his partners initially but fascinated them once they had got used to it.

After a year of experimentation, Lye found a sponsor – John Grierson, head of the GPO Film Unit, who said to his second-in-command Alberto Cavalcanti, 'This man is terribly important, we must get him going.'[53] Besides Grierson's support for innovation in film (which was informed by his knowledge of modern art), he saw the possibility of using Lye's lively, coloured films to brighten up the Unit's programmes of black and white documentaries. He commissioned a direct film, requiring only that it ended with a Post Office advertising message. The result was the four-minute *A Colour Box*, with a soundtrack of 'La Belle Creole', a beguine or native dance of Martinique that had been a hit in Paris, performed by Don Baretto and his Cuban Orchestra.

As a vehicle to 'carry the motion', *A Colour Box* was very different from *Tusalava*. It was speedy, highly rhythmic and completely abstract, and its images were fluid and painterly rather than sharp-edged. The film danced with extraordinary energy. This was an aesthetic of 'sensation', and the film was a mix of many different visual elements.[54] Also new was the range of brilliant colours, one of the main reasons for the film's impact on the public. Overall, it displayed a new approach to abstraction, distinguished from earlier experimental films by its speed, vibration and painterly texture.

A Colour Box generated so much interest that it ended up being screened all over Britain and seen by millions of viewers. This amazed Lye whose previous work had reached only a small, specialised audience. Viewers were divided between those excited by the new genre who greeted it with applause, and those who saw the film as 'crazy modern art' and shouted 'Take it off!'[55] The film aroused so much debate that newspapers ran stories about it and every reviewer was expected to offer an opinion. Such judgements ranged from Anthony Vesselo's enthusiastic comment in *Sight and Sound* that 'The reinforcements of sound and colour have stirred the abstract film to a new vitality',[56] to the perplexed reviewer of the *Daily Herald* who wrote, 'After watching the waves, stripes, blobs of violent tints, suggesting tartan, bandana, boarding-house wallpaper, fruit salad, chromatic spaghetti and an explosion in a cocktail bar, I half expected to find myself coming to in a dentist's chair.'[57] The film gained cult status among the avant-garde in other parts of Europe,[58] but at the 1936 Venice Festival it was 'met with such loud condemnatory stomping that the screening had to be stopped before the film was over'. The Nazi press gloated over the incident and William Moritz has suggested it was stage-managed by Nazi sympathisers who categorised the film as degenerate art.[59]

A Colour Box was certainly something new, but was it the first 'direct film'? A new category had to be invented for it when it won a Medal of Honour at the 1935 International Cinema Festival in Brussels. The film's publicity constantly stressed originality, and that was a claim nobody disputed at the time. Today, however, we are aware of Ginna and Corra's 1912 essay about their experiments, and Man Ray's use of Dadaist chance techniques. And there were others independently experimenting with painting or scratching on film in some form, such as Hans Stoltenberg, Henri Storck and Norman McLaren.[60] Indeed, in the early days of the medium, many films had paint applied in one way or another, although in most cases the aim was simply to add an overall tint or to enhance the details of black and white photographic footage. When sound arrived at the end of the 1920s, several film-makers – including Jack Ellitt – discovered that the visual pattern of a soundtrack on the side of a film could be painted by hand, producing artificial sounds that anticipated electronic music. We should acknowledge the work of all these experimental film artists, but still see *A Colour Box* as worthy of a special place in the history books. It was a breakthrough because it demonstrated the potential of direct film-making in such a thorough and sophisticated way that the method had to be accepted once and for all as a viable alternative to the camera. Lye had effectively opened up film-making to everybody, since a direct film could take so many forms – from a strip of celluloid that a group of small children covered with felt-tip designs, to a complex art film based on years of experiment. Among the animators deeply influenced by *A Colour Box* was Norman McLaren, who said of his first viewing in 1935, 'I was electrified and ecstatic . . . . Here was the pioneer of the handpainted film . . . . It was for me like a dream come true . . . . Len Lye had shown the way, and shown it in a masterly and brilliant fashion.'[61]

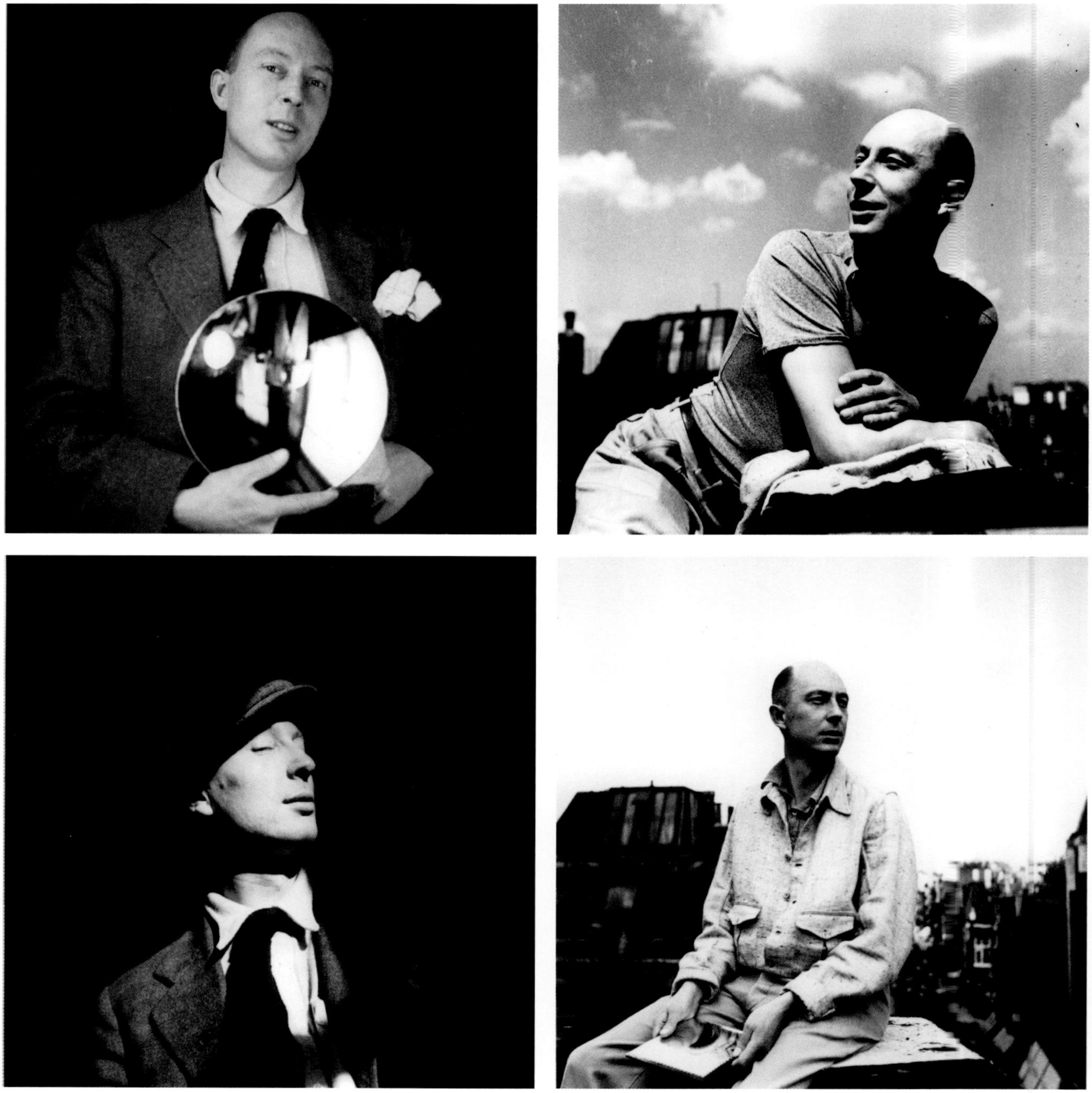

Four photographs of Lye in London, taken around 1936 by Barbara Ker-Seymer, a friend who was a well-known photographer. Courtesy Barbara Ker-Seymer.

Lye described the film to Laura Riding as 'happy go lucky alive stuff for the mind'. It was also 'the only thing I've ever had the result that it faintly pleases me'.[62] He had arrived at a much clearer conception of the art of movement, and for the first time felt ready to write a manifesto. Previously he had concentrated on practice and steered clear of theory, and he was known as a listener rather than a talker in contrast to his voluble, Oxbridge-educated artist friends such as Humphrey Jennings.[63] But Riding and her partner Robert Graves, who had published *No Trouble*, strongly encouraged Lye to articulate his original point of view. Riding got him started in 1935 by collaborating on the essay 'Film-making', published three years later in the first issue of *Epilogue*, a magazine she and Graves edited.[64] Lye found the task of theorising his art gruelling but exhilarating.[65] He supplied the main ideas while Riding expanded the philosophical context and helped him with his expository style. The two parts of the essay – 'Movement as Language' and 'Movement as a Medium' – provided a powerful rationale for *A Colour Box*, and a devastating reply to anyone who supposed that the film was a lucky accident or the work of a naïve artist.

This was the first of Lye's three most important essays on movement, each one written at a different stage of his career.[66] His theoretical concerns were always closely linked with current practice and recent experience. 'Film-making' was an implied revision of the ideas of Henri Bergson, accepting the philosopher's basic conception of time and movement as a constant flow, but arguing that this need not imply an impressionistic blur, since movement could be observed with 'physical accuracy'. The essay also refuted Bergson's argument that the 'cinematograph' was unable to do justice to movement.

Lye and Riding acknowledged 'the lack of a tradition . . . which would enable us to talk about movement' adequately and saw their essay as 'an effort to establish an appropriate terminology'. What was needed was the development of a new kind of 'movement-consciousness' that focused directly on 'physical immediacies' before the intellect got to process them and impose its 'civilised' assumptions. 'Up to a certain point we must leave physical things alone and let them speak for themselves, in movement. We must understand the physical physically.' This meant cultivating the links between mind and body, because an art of movement would represent 'our own physical existence projected outside the mind'. And: 'this gift of physical immediacy, which is the gift of a consciousness of movement, is discoverable through the brain in blood, organs, tissues, nerves'. Although this essay did not refer to the empathy tradition, it was arguing along similar lines.

Lye and Riding criticised the film tradition for being obsessed with realism and with certain kinds of 'meaning'. The true 'language of the cinema is movement', but most film-makers encumbered their work with narrative, 'literary drama' and 'sentimentalities'. *Tusalava* had demonstrated one way of escaping from these clichés, but the essay did not refer to that film; instead, it championed a more fluid type of abstract animation that could work directly with the 'vibration-pattern' of movement. Phrases such as 'dots and lines in the relative perspective of movement' clearly suggested a film like *A Colour Box* in which we focus on 'the rendering of movement in visually immediate experience'. Where the poet Archibald MacLeish wrote, 'A poem should not mean / But be',[67] Lye might have said, 'A film should not mean but move'. If the movement of the film was rapid, the speed would help to keep it a few steps ahead of the meddling intellect. 'Immediacy' was a key word in this essay, along with 'accuracy'. The sense of movement had to be not only precise but also sophisticated, for (as the essay dryly observed) 'it is understood that in speaking of movement we do not speak of the flight of sea-gulls any more than in speaking of painting we speak of sunsets'.

The assertion that 'Film is technically the best method for the isolation of visual movement' implied the existence of other methods, but the essay did not offer any examples. Lye was presumably not yet aware of recent experiments in France – in particular, those of Alexander Calder, an American sculptor three years older than him.[68] These experiments were important enough to justify a brief digression. In 1930, during a visit to the studio of Piet Mondrian, Calder had come up with the idea of introducing movement to Mondrian's abstract paintings. The painter 'did not approve of this idea at all', but Calder went on to develop his own version.[69] He wrote in 1933, 'Fernand Léger's [film] *Ballet Mécanique* is the result of the desire for a picture in motion. Therefore, why not plastic forms in motion? Not a simple translatory or rotary motion but several motions of different types, speeds and amplitudes composing to make a resultant whole. Just as one can compose colors, or forms, so one can compose motions.'[70] Calder's final phrase anticipated Lye's use of the word 'compose' two years later in his essay with Riding. Motion was the main subject in both cases, but Calder took the term 'composition' from the visual arts whereas Lye took it from music. It was also characteristic of Calder to think of a combination of 'several motions' whereas Lye's tendency would be to focus on one 'exactly rendered movement' at a time.

Calder, who had trained as a mechanical engineer, used hand-cranks and pulleys for his first kinetic sculptures, but then changed to motors. After a few years he switched again, to what he called 'mobiles', which derived their gentle, unpredictable motion from the wind, from air currents indoors or from the viewer's hand. Each mobile was a cluster of coloured abstract shapes, usually cut from sheet metal, hanging from wires and delicately balanced. Calder wrote, 'To combine one or two simple movements with different periods . . . really gives the finest effect, because while simple, they are capable of infinite combinations.'[71] Although Lye would admire this work when he later encountered it, his interest focused on different kinds of movement. The cut-out shapes, which were an important component, were too static to satisfy the requirements of his 1935 essay.[72] And 'infinite combinations' left too much room for chance – though that was precisely the aspect that would impress later artists such as the composer Earle Brown, who would see the sculptor's work as a precedent for the kind of open form he sought to create in music.[73] Calder would go on to develop his concept of the mobile with much ingenuity and persistence, and for many years it would be the only form of kinetic art to achieve at least a degree of public recognition.

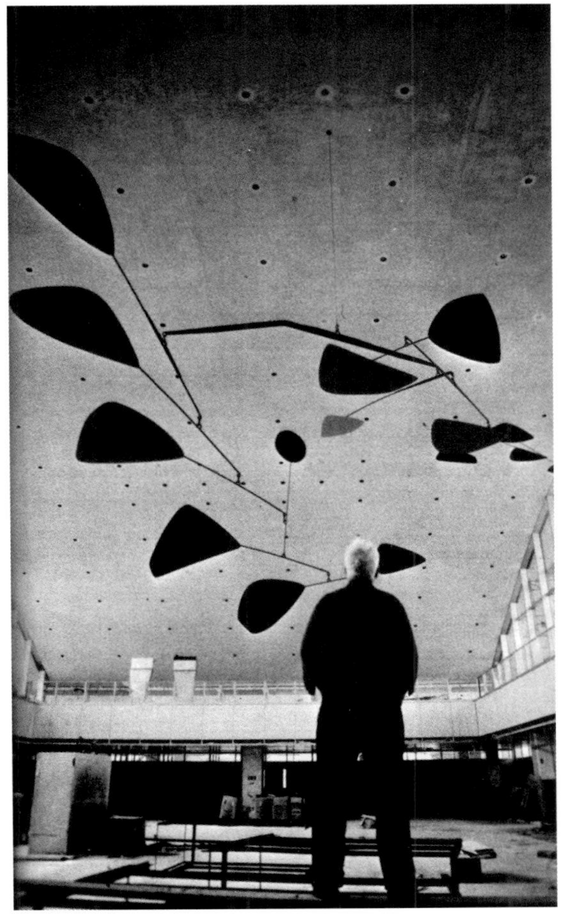

Alexander Calder installs his mobile .125 at Idlewild Airport (later renamed John F. Kennedy International Airport) in New York in 1957. Calder Foundation A00332. Licensed by Viscopy, Australia.

OTHER FILM EXPERIMENTS

After the success of *A Colour Box*, Grierson offered to sponsor a Lye film each year. This was not enough for Lye to live on, but now there were companies interested in sponsoring one of his films for public relations purposes. In Germany, Oskar Fischinger was similarly using the genres of 'music film' and 'prestige advertising' as ways to fund his experiments. Thus, modernist art was entering (or infiltrating) the mainstream. Lye's next project was another direct film, *Kaleidoscope* (1935), sponsored by Imperial Tobacco, makers of Churchman's Cigarettes. He tried with each project to avoid repeating himself, and on this occasion used a number of stencils. The emphasis on rotating forms seemed to hark back to his first kinetic sculpture, but now the film medium allowed him to organise his spinning and rolling shapes with 'accuracy', as choreographed figures of motion.

His next four films returned to the use of the camera but each project did so in a different way. *The Birth of a Robot* (1936) was his first experiment with colour film, a process still new and erratic in its results. Sponsored by Shell Oil, the film was a seven-minute puppet animation which enabled Lye to draw on the experience of *Peanut Vendor*. He put his puppets through their paces as playful versions of animated sculpture, like the circus characters Alexander Calder was creating in addition to his mobiles.[74] To accompany Ellitt's abbreviated version of Gustav Holst's *The Planets Suite*, Lye fashioned a model solar system, like a strange orrery, in the form of a merry-go-round turned by an old-fashioned mangle.[75] The film was seen by more than three million people in Britain, and created much interest by its unusual animation and its bright colours, particularly its multi-coloured storm sequence.

Lye's next GPO films, *Rainbow Dance* (1936) and *Trade Tattoo* (1937), were among his most original experiments in colour and movement. The films grew out of his interest in the new 'colour separation' process which made it possible to control the colours in every image. He realised that this complex technology could be adapted to avant-garde purposes, re-colouring the world of a film and combining painted images with live action. He was not interested in technical experiment for its own sake but he saw it as a way of achieving something he had dreamed of – telling stories without being bound by naturalism. He used a dancer as his solo actor in *Rainbow Dance*, and drew upon his years of thinking about possible ballet films. He was confident that viewers would understand his abbreviated narrative in which symbols functioned as a shorthand, as 'moving hieroglyphics'.[76]

Lye's experiments with colour involved a great deal of complex work and thought, as we can see from his theoretical essays of the period. It could be argued that this diverted him from movement; but his interest in colour was understandable since this was a new frontier for film-making and his work was on the cutting edge. And always underpinning it was his concern for 'rhythm' and 'moving hieroglyphics'. Lye wrote, 'If film is visual movement and progression of scene, then colour . . . must be considered in terms of progression and movement too.[7]

Lye's next project, *Trade Tattoo*, used the separation process in an even more extreme, rapid and intricate way, re-colouring and re-editing documentary footage from the GPO Film Unit and tightly synchronising it to Cuban dance music. This project was a showcase for his new interest in jump-cuts (syncopated or abbreviated editing). It also explored new ways to present words on screen as part of the rhythm of the film. All the elements of *Trade Tattoo* work together as a unified sense experience – the film is a dance of image, colour, movement, words and music.

Excited about the new possibilities he had opened up for the filming and editing of live action, and determined not to repeat himself, Lye was pleased to receive another GPO commission in 1937. This was *N or NW*, a seven-minute black and white film on the theme of using postal codes correctly. Lye transformed this mundane project into a full-scale attack on orthodox film language (camera and editing conventions), which he referred to as 'the Griffith technique', after the film-maker D. W. Griffith who had been the first to make systematic use of it. Lye had always felt an outsider to the conventions of cinema just as he had to the conventions of painting. He had already discovered several ways of getting round the cinematic code – by avoiding editing, by painting on film, by manipulating layers of colour and by the use of pure symbols – but he also wanted to challenge Griffith on his home ground, drama with live actors. Anyone entering the cinema halfway through *N or NW* would have thought they had encountered a Surrealist film rather than a piece of Post Office publicity. Not surprisingly, some viewers also assumed that *N or NW* was the work of a novice director. But the film was enthusiastically received by vanguard audiences around Europe.

In 1937, there was a downturn in the British film industry and Lye received no more work from the GPO. At the same time, John Grierson shifted to Canada to help establish its National Film Board. Although the commissions Lye had received from the GPO had not been enough to live on – four short films in four years – they had allowed him to experiment, and sometimes he had even been encouraged to do so. The infrastructure for experimental work in film was extremely fragile, with no funding of an Arts Council type, and few sponsors. For the rest of his career he would search in vain for another regular funder like the GPO.

Jane Lye gave birth to a son, Bix, in 1937, and three years later to a daughter, Yancy. Lye picked up occasional directing jobs for newsreel companies, but work was scarce. He was able to do special effects for a space travel sequence in the otherwise undistinguished feature film *Mad about Money.* Unemployed for long periods, he turned increasingly to the activity of writing, sometimes to assist his search for sponsors, but more often as an outlet for his never-ending stream of new ideas. Television in Britain was now at a formative stage, and Lye campaigned for an anti-Griffith approach because 'Television must do a job which no existing medium can accomplish – or else there is no point in having television at all.'[78] His essays advanced a range of options – a greater emphasis on movement, a new set of visual conventions, animation gadgets for music programmes and so on.[79] He used the fact that television images at the time were less detailed than film as a reason for the medium to experiment with bolder, more stylised approaches, such as reducing movement 'to its dramatic essentials'.[80] Musical interludes could be accompanied by 'three-dimensional shapes and patterns set in movement' by 'unseen animators'. This idea seemed closely related to kinetic sculpture (as well as to his direct films): 'For solo instruments there would be spirals, crescents, twanging bands, etc., animated by such mechanisms as revolves . . . .' He urged the new medium to see itself as a laboratory, and naturally hoped it could sponsor some of his own experiments.

Alongside media campaigns of this kind, Lye also began writing about politics. Alarmed by the rise of Nazism, he sought to clarify the importance of individuality, which he had always seen as central to art.[81] With the coming of war, he felt urgently compelled to develop and publicise his theory of 'Individual Happiness Now' (or IHN), a personal and political philosophy based on those values. For Lye, it was perfectly natural to use the arts as the basis of a programme that opposed Fascism and championed freedom.

Occasionally he was sponsored to make another direct film – *Colour Flight* in 1938, *Swinging the Lambeth Walk* in 1939 and *Musical Poster #1* in 1940. *Colour Flight* was commissioned by Imperial Airways (the airline that would shortly become BOAC) through a sympathetic publicity manager, C. F. Snowden-Gamble, who had to struggle to reassure his superiors that an abstract film would not damage public relations. In fact, Lye's four-minute animation was very well received, with the American magazine *Time* running a long, enthusiastic story about it: 'Last week in London an original artist named Len Lye, working on a shoe string budget, crashed through with an animated movie called *Colour Flight* which previewers hailed as art, as entertainment, and as the freshest stuff of its kind since Disney arrived.' *Time* went on to develop a vivid David and Goliath comparison between

Lye and the mainstream industry: 'The Disney *Silly Symphonies* are the product of a big corporation employing 75 animators, 150 copyists and a gang of gagmen, musicians and technicians . . . . Lye, however, paints or stencils his designs by hand.'[82] The *Time* story was widely read but did not produce any job offers. Also, *Colour Flight* was classified in the United States as 'imported advertising' and there were regulations that prevented such a film from being distributed.

In 1939, the Lye family had so little money that they often did not know where the next day's meal would come from. Old Grierson associates concerned about their desperate financial situation managed to organise another commission through TIDA (the Travel and Industrial Development Association), with top-up funding from the newly established British Council. This was *Swinging the Lambeth Walk*, a celebration of a current dance craze, the Lambeth Walk. Since this was three decades before the city began publicising itself as Swinging London, the project baffled bureaucrats who could not see popular culture as having any connection with travel – in fact, they were appalled that a government agency should sponsor such a frivolous project. Nevertheless, Lye was able to make the film, and it was one of his best. *Swinging the Lambeth Walk* was, however, unlucky in having its release delayed until 1940, when politically-minded reviewers criticised this joyous film as inappropriate in a time of war.[83]

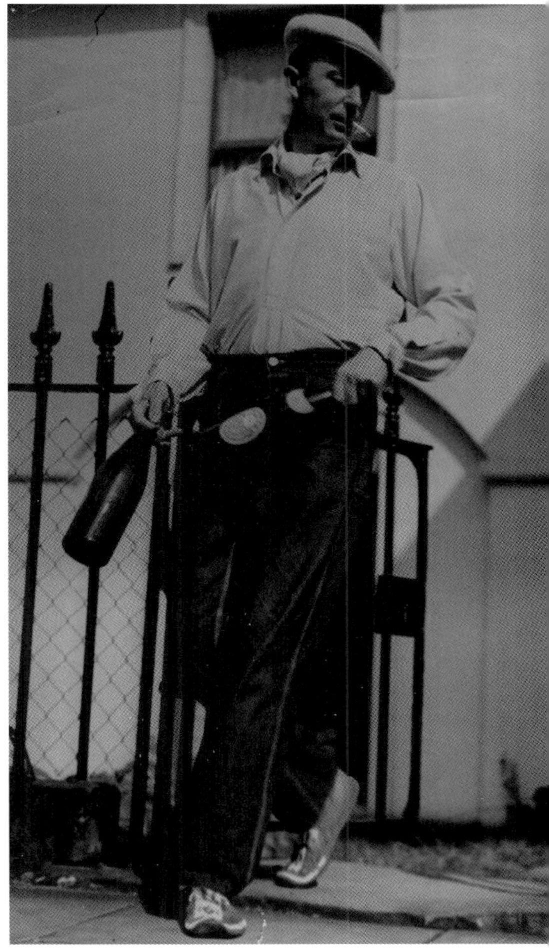

Lye in 1938 heading for the Black Lion Pub to get some beer. Photo John Phillips. Courtesy Len Lye Foundation.

Lye was not called up because the priority was for younger men and because a recent operation for acute appendicitis had involved complications that left him unable to stand for long. In 1941, he obtained a job with the Realist Film Unit which was doing regular work for the Ministry of Information. He was pleased to be involved in the war effort. Realist was a congenial environment for him as it was in many respects an offshoot of the GPO Film Unit, and it was a huge relief to have a steady job, even though the pay was modest. (According to the Realist philosophy, everyone working for the company was paid the same amount.) The six films Lye directed had low budgets and their themes were often prosaic – for example, *When The Pie Was Opened* showed how to overcome the meat shortage by cooking vegetable pies – but he was never capable of making a film without sneaking in some visual or sound experiments. John Taylor, the head of Realist, defended Lye even when people were puzzled by his work because he felt it was essential to maintain the spirit of innovation at a time when film-making was heavily censored and narrowly utilitarian.[84] Also, Lye's ingenuity and preference for stylised story-telling came in handy when making the most of limited budgets or finding a way round wartime regulations.

His most important wartime film was *Kill or be Killed*, a grim dramatisation that explained to soldiers what to do if they came under sniper fire. Brilliantly presented as a kind of old brain struggle for survival, *Kill or be Killed* illustrates the fact that works of kinetic art can turn up in the most unlikely guise.

NEW YORK

Lye moved to New York in 1944 primarily for political reasons. During the war, he had devoted a great deal of energy to his theory of individual freedom. The allied forces might be scoring military victories against the Nazis, but he believed they were losing the propaganda war because leaders seemed unable to talk about democratic ideals except in a stuffy, establishment style. He believed it was crucial to have better ideas ready to guide post-war reconstruction, and he saw his philosophy of IHN as ideal for this purpose. He had had a lukewarm reaction when he approached prominent people in England, but in December 1943 he received an enthusiastic response to his ideas from the American politician Wendell Willkie. Willkie was the author of a 1943 international bestseller, *One World*, which saw the creation of a new global vision or 'sense of common purpose' as the necessary foundation for post-war peace.[85] Potentially he was a powerful ally as he was the Chairman of the Board of Twentieth Century Fox, and a possible future President of the United States. (He had been an unsuccessful candidate once but was expected to try again.) Having received a personal invitation from this politician, Lye was determined to get to New York.

Travel was difficult in wartime, but friends helped him to obtain some directing work with the *March of Time* (the American series of mini-documentaries that was the cinema equivalent of *Time Magazine*), and this enabled him to travel to New York in 1944. Unfortunately, his first meeting with Willkie (in his Wall Street office) was a mixed success – the American politician and the offbeat artist found

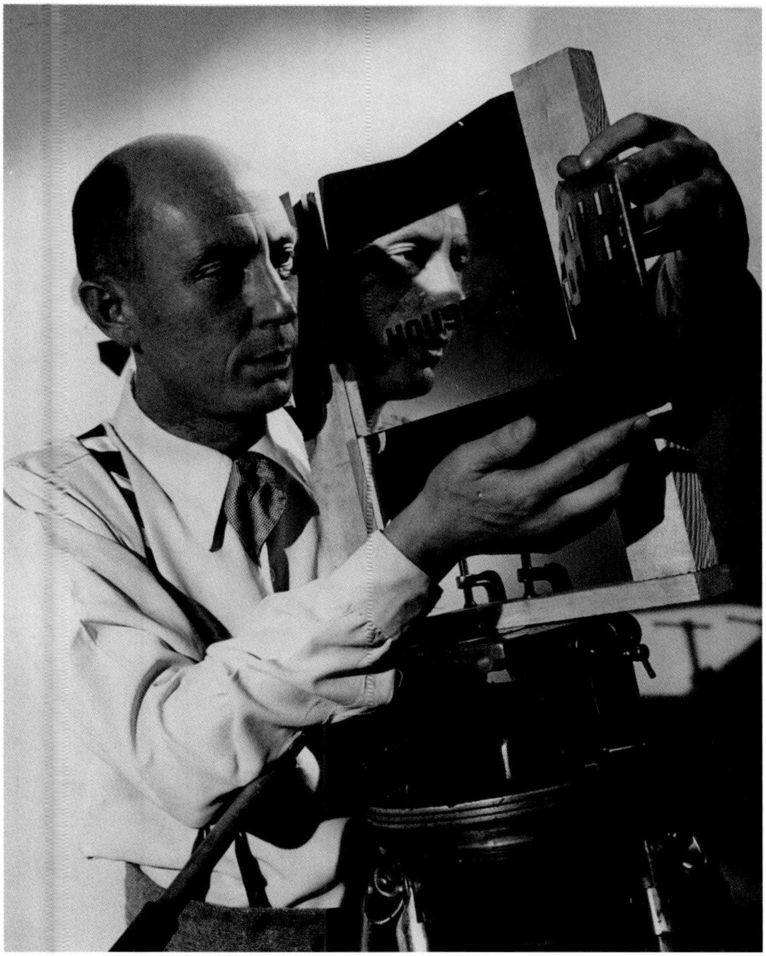

Lye in New York in 1944, making an experiment in preparation for the film *Basic English*. Courtesy Len Lye Foundation.

they had less in common in person than in print. But Willkie did invite Lye to write the script for a film about IHN which he promised to take to Twentieth Century Fox. A month later the 52-year-old politician suffered a severe heart attack and died soon after. The many hopes Lye had built up around Willkie's interest in his ideas came crashing down.

Nevertheless, Lye was immediately impressed by the energies of New York, and he made it his home for the rest of his life. His arrival was well timed since the city was about to supplant Paris as the centre of avant-garde activity. Europe was shattered by the war and some of its leading artists had moved to the United States. New York at this moment in history had the right mix of ingredients to ignite the next creative explosion in art. The artists of what became known as 'the New York School' had interests that matched Lye's, such as a respect for 'painterly' types of Surrealism as found in the work of Matta Echaurren, André Masson and Joan Miró. They studied various traditions of ancient and primitive art. They rejected geometrical abstraction and turned to biomorphic forms or irregular brushwork, because (as Barnett Newman put it) 'only an art of no-geometry can be a new beginning'.[86]

Soon Jackson Pollock took a further step and began to work with large canvases on the floor, pouring paint directly from tubes and cans. Harold Rosenberg stressed the physical aspects in a famous 1952 essay that introduced the term 'action painting'.[87] He wrote: 'At a certain moment the canvas began to appear to one American painter after another as an arena in which to act – rather than as a space in which to reproduce, re-design, analyze or "express" an object . . . . What was to go on the canvas was not a picture but an event . . . . Since the painter has become an actor, the spectator has to think in a vocabulary of action . . . .' While Rosenberg discussed action, process, event and gesture – and referred in passing to motion, muscles, tension and energy – he did not tap any of the traditions of art writing that would have provided him with a more detailed physical vocabulary (such as the empathy tradition, or the manifestoes of movement in art). Rather, he used French Existentialism as his main framework, together with some references to American culture such as Whitman's idea of the 'Open Road'. If this emphasis on physical process had been developed more broadly, it would have helped to set the stage for kinetic art. Unfortunately, Rosenberg's approach was fiercely opposed by critics such as Clement Greenberg, who succeeded in returning discussion to formal qualities such as the flatness of the picture plane, the development of all-over composition and other pictorial aspects that distinguished the new art from predecessors such as Cubism. As interesting and sophisticated as such criticism was, it had the effect of marginalising kinetic aspects. The term 'action painting' was replaced by 'Abstract Expressionism'.

Lye made himself at home in the New York art scene. He was introduced to the younger artists by his old friend Stanley William Hayter, who ran an important print-making workshop. The community of vanguard artists (still small in those days) met at 'The Club' at 39 East 8th Street. Lye enjoyed taking part in 'the cackle and crack of the brain functions' at this venue, and, as he later recalled, 'I met all the abstract expressionist boys before they expressionised. I . . . showed my films there. We'd meet and talk art, then dance and dance, good old day's stuff . . . . I liked all their stuff and I think they liked mine.'[88] During the 1950s, Lye also spent time at the Cedar Tavern (at 8th Street and University Place)

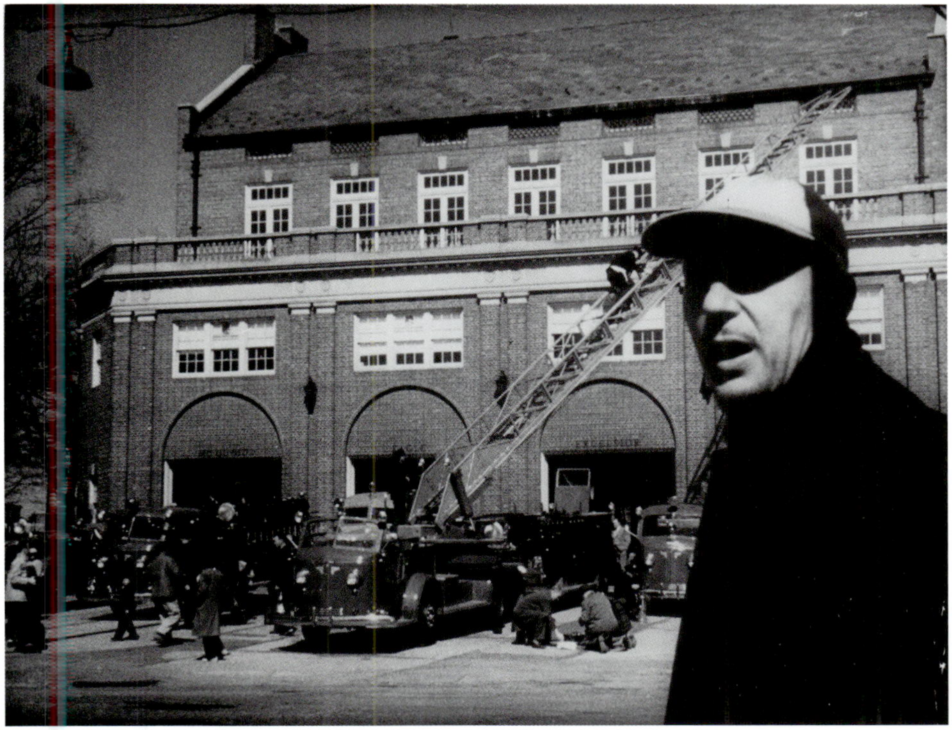

Lye directing an episode of the *March of Time*. Courtesy Len Lye Foundation.

which functioned as a neighbourhood bar for the downtown art community, and he made other contacts through the Museum of Modern Art which held screenings of his films.[89]

By not linking his work with 'the New York School' when it began to attract publicity, Lye passed up one of the best opportunities of his life to gain the attention of critics, museums and buyers. Some of his paintings and the imagery of his direct films had anticipated aspects of Abstract Expressionism, yet he preferred to stay on the margins. This was very characteristic of him – he had also been linked with Surrealism, but was reluctant to become a card-carrying member of any art movement. More generally, he had no interest in the sort of self-promotion and networking that many New York artists accepted as part of the job. Clement Greenberg liked what he saw of Lye's paintings and considered his films 'ahead of their time', but was surprised by the artist's 'lack of drive' which he associated with British artists of that generation in 'their bohemianism

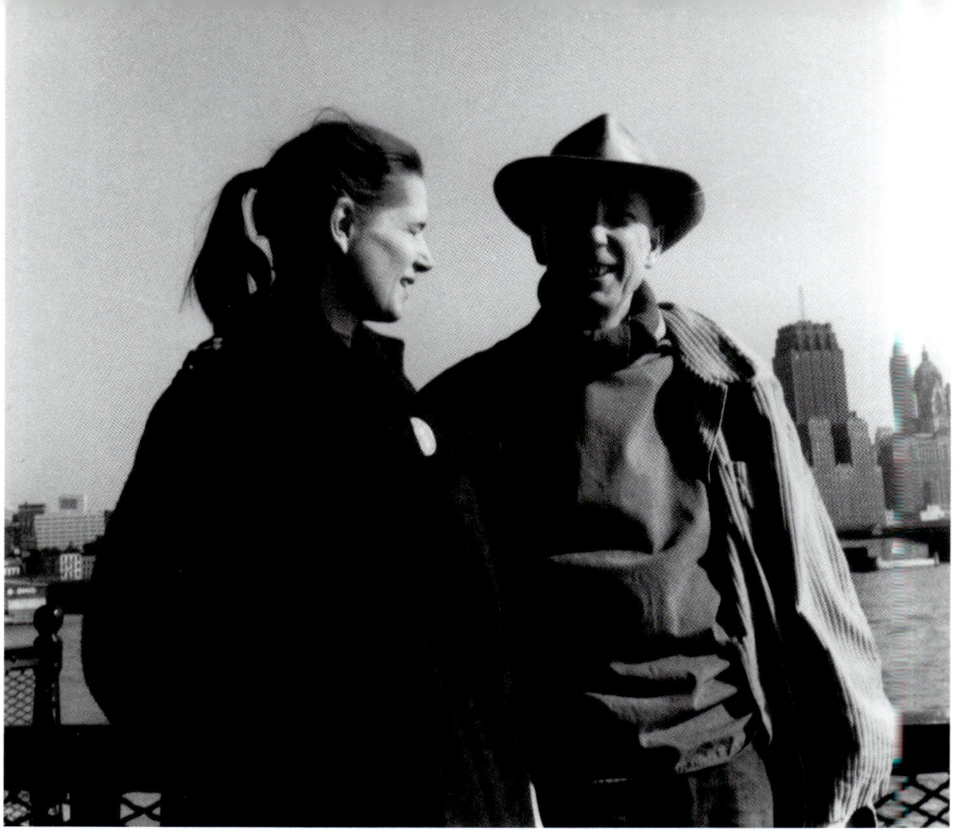

Lye with his new partner Ann on the Staten Island Ferry in New York, circa 1948. Courtesy Len Lye Foundation.

[and] unstudied free-and-easiness'.[90] New York had a competitive, business-minded culture, and Lye would soon discover how hard this was to crack.

The shift to New York brought some important personal changes. Ann Hindle, an American woman he met at the end of 1945, was a lively bohemian with an independent spirit. Their love affair led to marriage in 1948, and this became a lifelong relationship that never lost its intensity.[91] In later years, Ann took over the role of breadwinner, by becoming a real estate broker who specialised in finding apartments and studios for artists. She was also involved in many Greenwich Village campaigns to save old buildings from demolition. Her work yielded a modest but steady income and occasionally she could afford to finance one of her husband's experiments.

For the first seven years, Lye had a steady job as a director for the *March of Time*. This meant working to a formulaic house style, but he found some of the subjects very interesting – for example, one episode included Einstein and discussed the dangers of the atomic age. Such reporting stimulated Lye's interest in science, which he saw as a potential ally in his work on proprioception and the old brain. A particularly influential contact was Nina Bull, a psychologist with a strong interest in neurobiology, who introduced him to scientific ways of thinking about the connections between brain and body.

After the *March of Time* series ended in 1951, Lye was desperate to find a new base for his work. He offered his services as an ideas man and special effects expert to advertising agencies, but found they were on a very different wavelength. He was puzzled why agencies in a city as up-to-the-minute as New York should have so little appetite for taking risks or sponsoring experiments.[92] When colour television arrived in the early 1950s, he was dismayed by the banal ways in which colour was used, but he could not find anyone in television to sponsor an alternative. An impressive range of people involved in broadcasting or music were happy to write letters of support for Lye's campaigns, but no one was willing to commit money. He also tried the dealer galleries, for the Abstract Expressionists were now getting good prices for their canvases. He proposed a series of 'art films' to be sold through galleries where it would be possible to have screenings in one room and to display strips of the films on the wall in another. This idea of a market for limited-edition films failed to catch on.

He continued to work as an artist during this period, but his experiments were spread very broadly and he turned away from literal movement to make paintings, poems and photograms (which were media he could afford). In his photograms, as in his 1930s live action films, he sought to develop an approach to photography that retained a physical trace of the subject but streamlined the image as a 'hieroglyphic'. The process rendered each head as a silhouette (as in *Rainbow Dance*), over which he added symbolic elements. In 1951–52, an idea to which he devoted a great deal of time was 'the dancing atom', an animation invention that made linear shapes with dancing electronic dots of light. Another area of experiment was painting and scratching words on film in search of a more dramatic way of bringing poetry to the screen. This led to brainstorming sessions with his old friend, the Welsh poet Dylan Thomas.[93] They talked of collaborating on a poetry film, but before the project could get very far, Thomas died after a whiskey binge during his 1953 visit to New York.

Some of Lye's most striking prose writing took the form of a stream of consciousness in which physical sensations were foregrounded. Works such as 'Shoe', 'Walking' and 'Mosquitoes in Maine' included some highly kinetic descriptions of the body in motion. He said that he wrote 'Chair' to celebrate 'the wandering sitting resting unlimbering body's body'. His approach was a kind of phenomenology, and his phrase 'body's body' is reminiscent of the explanation of phenomenology as 'the experience of experience'.[94] Though Lye's starting-point was often a commonplace event, he would animate it verbally by exploring all the physical and mental processes involved. For example, 'Brown Paper Bag' described walking along a busy New York street and crossing to the other side:

> I paddle along back to my shaded cove of a room while the objective imagery of me and the street is being transmitted to me by senses of weight and muscle and nerve action helped out by senses of light and sound . . . [with] kerb and street and sidewalk and traffic lights and people as interesting craft with laws of tides and navigation all sychronised in my spatial relationship with them . . . . I am now completely myself, a canoe on the sidewalk, a swimmer in a sea of crocodiles to traverse the road of a river . . . . And this organism that possesses my name got me out into the sunshine to experience being alive . . . a body with a name on its prow.[95]

NEW YORK FILMS

Though experimental film-making in the United States started to grow after the war, it began on a very small scale with few screening venues.[96] One of the catalysts for film-making, as for painting, was the arrival of experienced artists from Europe – including Oskar Fischinger, Hans Richter and Lye. Lye's contacts in New York included film-makers such as Maya Deren, Arnold Eagle and Francis Lee. Meeting Lye in 1945 was a turning point for Lee because 'At that time I was completely alone – I didn't know a soul who was making my sort of independent or avant-garde film.'[97] Another artist who valued Lye's technical advice was 'Ian Hugo' (Hugh Guiler) who turned to film after working as an engraver with Hayter. In 1952, Lye contributed 'abstract colour effects' to Hugo's *Bells of Atlantis*, a dream-like colour film based on the opening pages of his wife Anaïs Nin's book *The House of Incest*. Lye also accepted an invitation from Richter to do some teaching in his film programme at the City College of New York, and later ran part-time film classes at Columbia University and New York University. Over the years, he helped and advised many young film-makers who approached him on an individual basis.

In 1952, he wrote to an old friend Marcus Brumwell who worked for a London advertising agency: 'I have been trying to find an easier way to make direct films. I got very excited when I found that muslin dot fabrics made great patterns and

I dashed round looking for more and more fabrics.' These experiments led to *Color Cry*, completed in 1953. Self-funded, the four-minute photogram film was described as a production by the Direct Film Company (which consisted of himself and Ann). The shapes of *Color Cry* are more blocky than those of earlier direct films but the movement is powerful, especially as it is synchronised with an extraordinary piece of music – 'Fox Hunt' – in which the great blues singer Sonny Terry alternates harmonica playing with animal howls. The film appears to have had only a limited distribution, shown mainly to groups of friends.

During the next few years, Lye continued his frustrating search for commercial work. One of his few paid jobs was *Rhythm*, a commercial for the Chrysler car company. Condensing the assembly of a car to a one-minute montage sequence, *Rhythm* demonstrated Lye's mastery of the jump-cut. It was selected as the year's best television commercial at the 1957 New York Art Directors Festival, but the award had to be cancelled because Chrysler disliked the film so much it never gave it a television screening.

In 1957, Ann Lye agreed to be sole breadwinner for eight months while her husband made a film in reply to an invitation from an International Experimental Film Competition in Belgium to be held in association with the 1958 World's Fair. Lye used this as an opportunity to bring to fruition his experiments with a new form of direct imagery – scratches on strips of leader (black film without images), which suggested the volatility of atomic particles. These scratched lines and streaks had great impact when they flashed and vibrated against a black background. As he used this new approach to create the film *Free Radicals*, Lye relished the rough textures of the scratches, which reminded him at times of cave art. Returning to his old interest in tribal dance rituals, he synchronised the images to traditional African drum music. His increasing perfectionism showed in the fact that it often took him a day to produce a second of film that satisfied him.

Lye despatched his completed, five-minute film to Brussels, which had received 400 entries, including almost

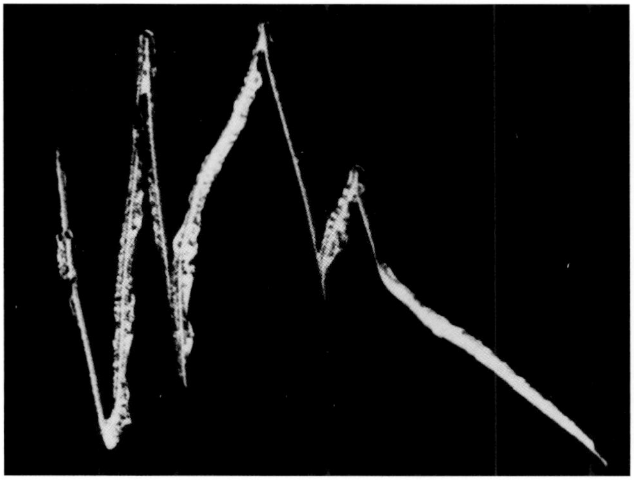

One of the 'new scratchy figures of motion' which were the basis of his black and white film *Free Radicals*. Lye's zigzags of energy moved like lightning. Courtesy Len Lye Foundation.

all the leading experimental film-makers in the world. The competition had an impressive panel of judges – Man Ray, John Grierson, Norman McLaren, the famous animator Alexander Alexeiff and the composer Edgard Varèse. They awarded the Grand Prix to *Dom*, a Polish film of animated objects and extraordinary optical effects, but gave the Second Prize to *Free Radicals*. The Lyes were woken at 3 a.m. in New York by a phone call: 'You've just won $5000.'[98]

Lye greatly valued this encouragement from Europe, and hoped that the award would at last open doors for his work. He was therefore shocked to find that no one was interested in distributing *Free Radicals* in the USA, or in sponsoring his next film. In 1959, after a series of unsuccessful applications to foundations and attempts to obtain screenings, he wrote the essay 'Is Film Art?' in which he announced he was going on strike as a film-maker. Addressed to American readers, the essay challenged the country's miserable record of support for innovation: 'our film and television industries fail to sponsor the experimental film'. In comparison with other media, 'Film is the Cinderella of the fine arts', and this Cinderella was still 'waiting for her glass slipper in order to enthral with her unique kinetic beauty'.[99] Lye noted the irony of the fact that 'the state sponsored Russian popular feature film *The Cranes Are Flying* won top award in Cannes 1958 against all comers [and] the State Cinema of Poland subsidized *Dom*, the ... Grand Prix winner of the Experimental Film Competition at Brussels ... against all comers'.[100] He could also have mentioned the fact that his old friend Norman McLaren received long-term support from Canada's National Film Board.

Lye's strike announcement was partly a rhetorical gesture since he never completely stopped making films. During the 1960s, he prepared and screened various versions of *Particles in Space*, an ambitious sequel to *Free Radicals*. But his statement had a core of truth – he was tired of struggling to raise funding for films and had decided to transfer most of his energies to another medium, kinetic sculpture. In addition to its power as a polemic, the essay was important as Lye's second detailed discussion of the art of movement. In the 24 years since 'Film-making', the context of the art world had changed and his conception of 'kinetic' or 'kinaesthetic' work had expanded. Indeed, neither of those terms had appeared in his earlier essay. Now Lye referred to 'dancing', and saw examples of the kinetic in literature by Samuel Beckett, e.e. cummings, James Joyce, Franz Kafka, Arthur Rimbaud, Gertrude Stein and Dylan Thomas. He also acknowledged the sense of implied movement in the work of the Dadaists and Futurists, and especially in 'action painting' which was 'a notable U.S. contribution to art'. In general, ‘the graphic arts have been visibly exploring the direct sensory appeal of both light and motion . . . . With film, these two qualities are an integral part of it.’[101] (*Free Radicals* had provided a particularly pure, concentrated example.) As yet he was curiously silent on the subject of sculpture, but he looked forward to an ‘increasing emphasis on the kinetic’, and his prediction would be borne out over the next decade.

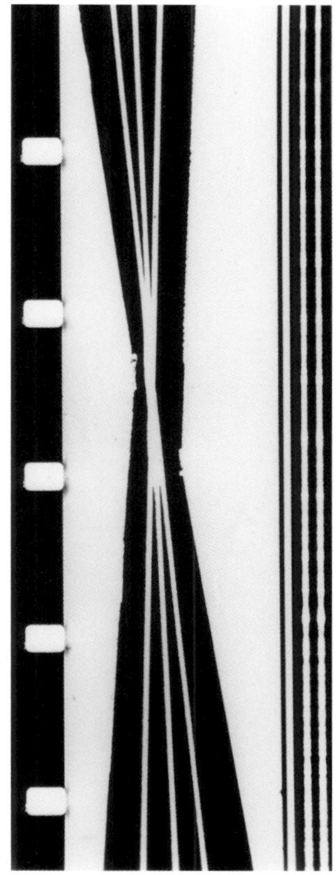

Lye also had a ‘geometrical’ approach to scratching images on film, which is illustrated by this sequence from *Tal Farlow*. He scratched these frames in the 1950s, though the film was not completed until 1980. Courtesy Len Lye Foundation.

KINETIC SCULPTURE

Lye now transferred his skills in composing motion to wood, plastics and above all metal. The way he described his sculpture was reminiscent of his films: ‘I’m interested in something that has a vibratory quality to it and a little shake to it [as a] figure of motion.’[102] Now the energy came not from a projector but from small motors with a reciprocating stroke. As Lye set pieces of metal in motion, the sense of gravity, balance, energy and feedback ensured that ‘bodily kinetic sensation’ was involved. His metal constructions could be thought of as dancers, and the sounds they produced as they swung, twisted and vibrated served as a musical accompaniment. Having identified the key figures of motion for each sculpture, Lye would work out (or choreograph) a programme, a composed sequence of motion and sound, which tended to have a similar length to his films (around five minutes). Even the influence of tribal art was still present in his mechanised sculpture, as he related works like *Storm King* and *Temple of Lightning* to ancient dance rituals and animistic gods. More generally, his way of using metal was clearly linked to his interest in the patterns of nature and the insights of the old brain, an approach that would distinguish his work from kinetic sculpture that was hi-tech and machine-centred. Basically, Lye was applying his old aesthetic to new materials.

The result was an immediate explosion of ideas. In Ann’s words, ‘It was a thrilling time . . . . With sculpture I felt that a lot of things had come together in Len.’[103] He himself was not happy with the term ‘sculpture’ because its history and aesthetics were based on static objects, and he regarded the appearance of a kinetic work at rest as of no importance. He avoided the term ‘mobile’ because it was too closely associated with Calder’s wind-driven constructions. Initially, his preferred term was ‘tangible’ or ‘tangible motion sculpture’ because he was

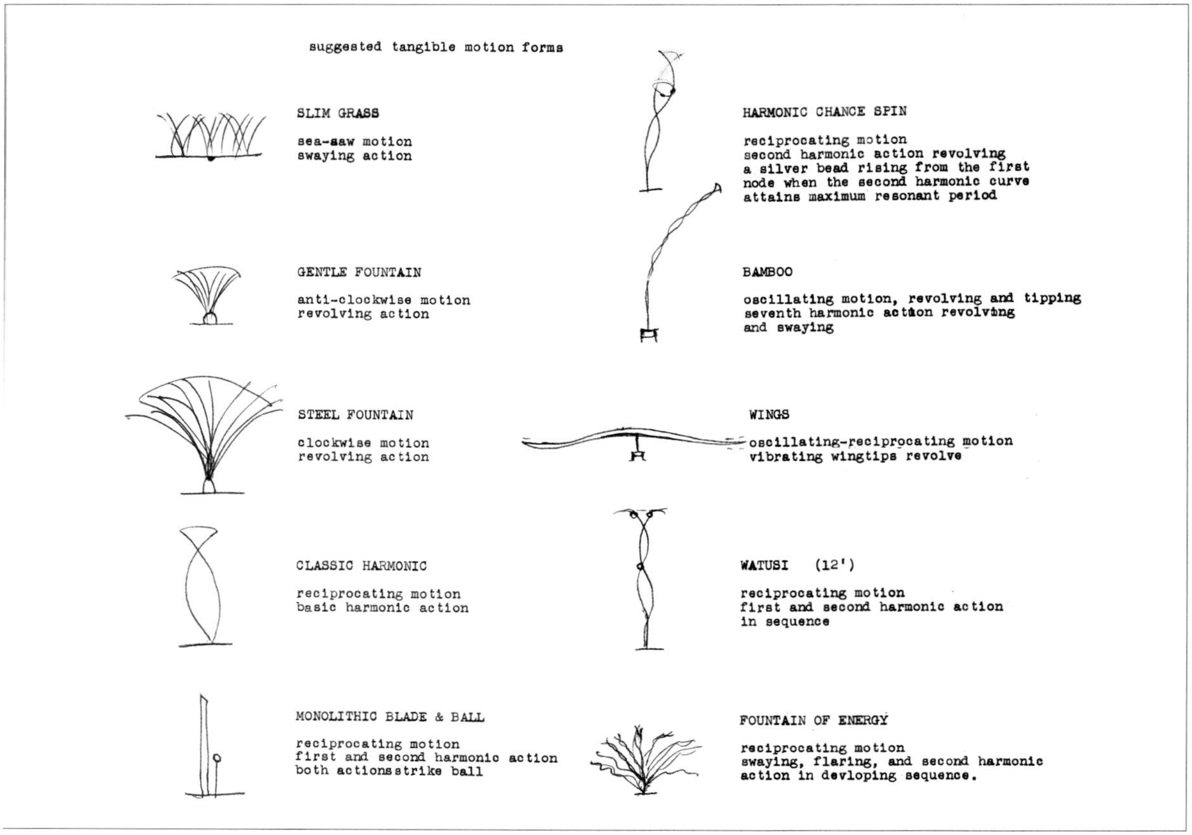

A list by Lye of some 'suggested tangible motion' sculptures. Courtesy Len Lye Foundation.

attempting to make motion (and energy) tangible. 'Tangible' did not imply that the metal should be touched, but it did encourage viewers to respond to the art in a physical or kinesthetic rather than intellectual way. The term did not catch on, however, and he dropped it after a few years.

From his perspective, film and kinetic sculpture were aspects of the same 'art of motion', but he under-estimated the art world's tendency to compartmentalise. Sculpture, painting, film and photography were usually associated with separate audiences, critics, curators and museum departments (who were often fiercely protective of their turf and reluctant to collaborate). Today, most art institutions have come to accept the fact that some artists work in a multi-media spirit, but such acceptance has been slow to develop. When Lye moved from the UK to the USA, he had to rebuild his reputation, and this was again necessary when he shifted at the age of 57 to 'sculpture'. Although he ended up with a significant reputation in sculpture as well as film, few critics or institutions knew his body of work in both areas, and that is often still the case today.

When he embarked on sculpture, it was a lucky accident for him that kinetic art had just begun to develop strongly in Europe.[104] Earlier artists had dreamed of movement but most had found the technology too difficult or too expensive. Although cost continued to be an issue, more technology had now become available, and this was an area of modernism that still held a great deal of unfinished business. The new wave of kinetic art arrived in 1955 in an exhibition called 'Le Mouvement' organised by Pontus Hultén in Paris. By the end of the decade, a number of European artists were involved, in exhibitions such as 'Vision in Motion' in Antwerp in 1959 and 'Kinetic Art' in Zurich in 1960.

Commissioned by the United Nations to make a short film for UN Day in 1959, Lye employed the gentle movement of his kinetic sculpture *Fountain* as a symbol of peace. In March 1961, his work was included in a major survey exhibition at the Stedelijk Museum in Amsterdam. The name of the exhibition, 'Bewogen Beweging', was translated into English as 'The Movement Movement'. The show went on tour to the Louisiana Museum in Copenhagen and the Moderna Museet in Stockholm. On 5 April 1961, the Museum of Modern Art in New York hosted an evening performance of Lye's sculptures. By now he had been signed up by an enthusiastic dealer, Howard Wise, whose gallery was a launching pad for art that involved technology, including video and computer art. Lye hoped that Wise would provide him with the kind of support base he had once had for his film work from the GPO. The dealer put Lye's art into group shows and gave him a solo exhibition in 1965; but though he pursued sales energetically, collectors tended to regard mechanised sculpture as a risky investment. Work of this kind frequently broke down in the course of exhibitions, and Lye found to his dismay that kinetic sculpture was just as dependent on money and technical assistance as film-making had been. Like Tingueley who scoured junk-yards, he developed clever ways of cutting costs, but this sometimes compromised the durability of his work.

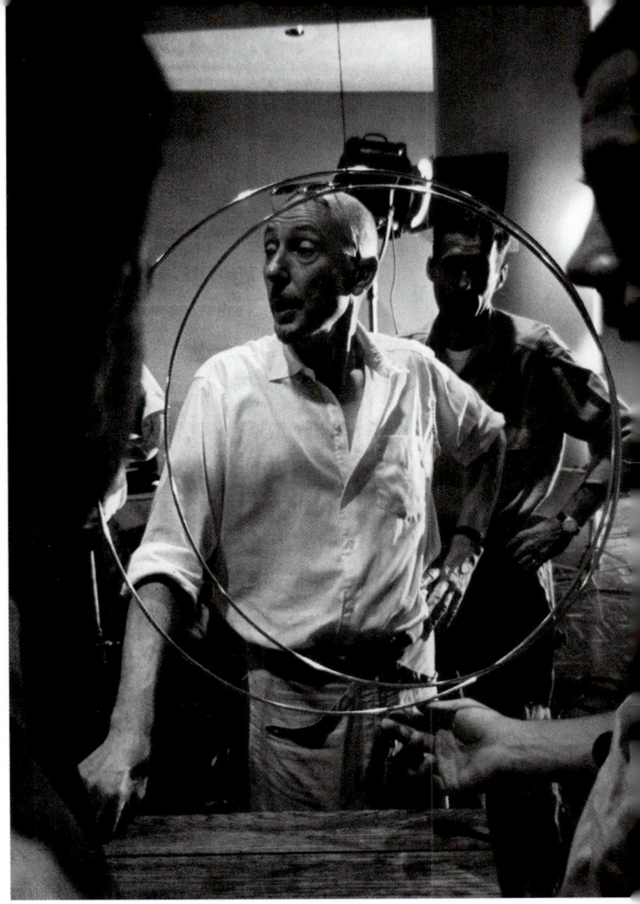

Lye at work on a film for United Nations Day, 1959. The film, known as *Peace*, incorporated *Fountain* and other sculptures. Courtesy Len Lye Foundation.

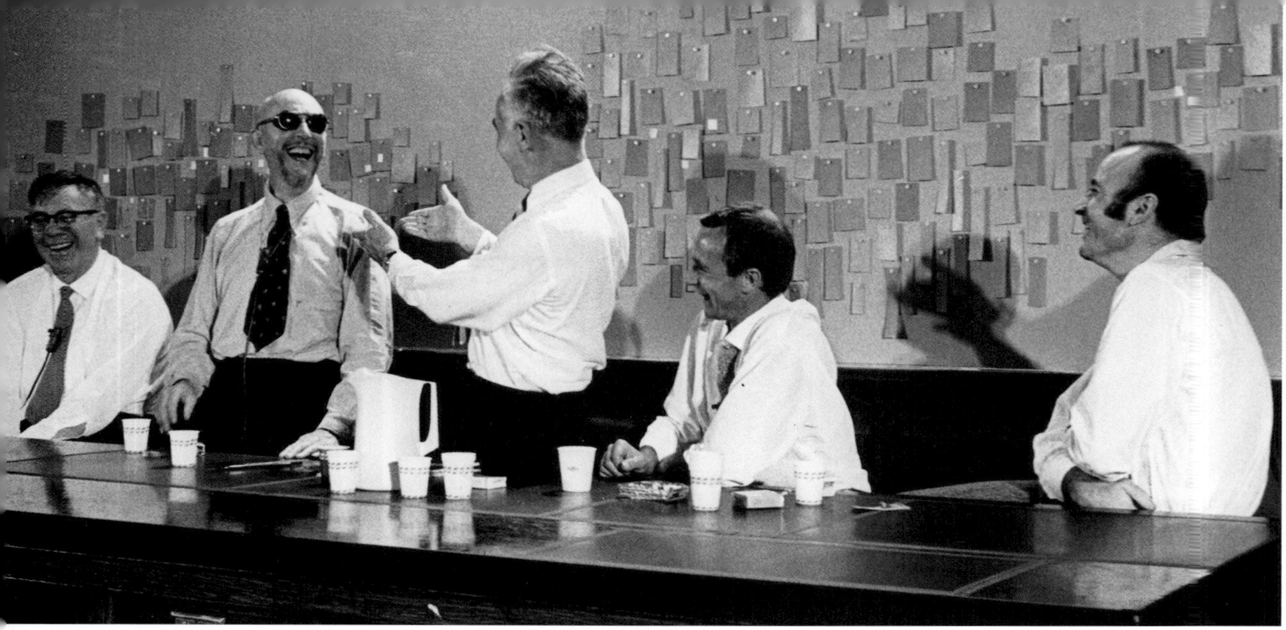

ABOVE Lye on a panel of sculptors, 18 March 1966, during the 'Directions in Kinetic Sculpture' exhibition at the Berkeley campus of the University of California. L to R: George Rickey, Lye, Peter Selz (curator of the exhibition), Harry Kramer and Takis. Photo Ron Chamberlain. Courtesy Len Lye Foundation.
BELOW The last performance of the 'Contemporary Voices in the Arts' series, held at the 92nd Street YH-YWHA in New York. At the table from L to R are Lye (with his back to the camera), Stan VanDerBeek (film-maker), David Vaughan (manager of the tour), Jack Tworkov (painter), Robert Creeley (poet), Billy Kluver (an engineer who collaborated with artists), John Cage (composer) and Merce Cunningham (dancer). The meal was a performance by the artists, with their knives and forks, as well as their voices, amplified electronically. Photo Adelaide De Menil. Courtesy Len Lye Foundation.

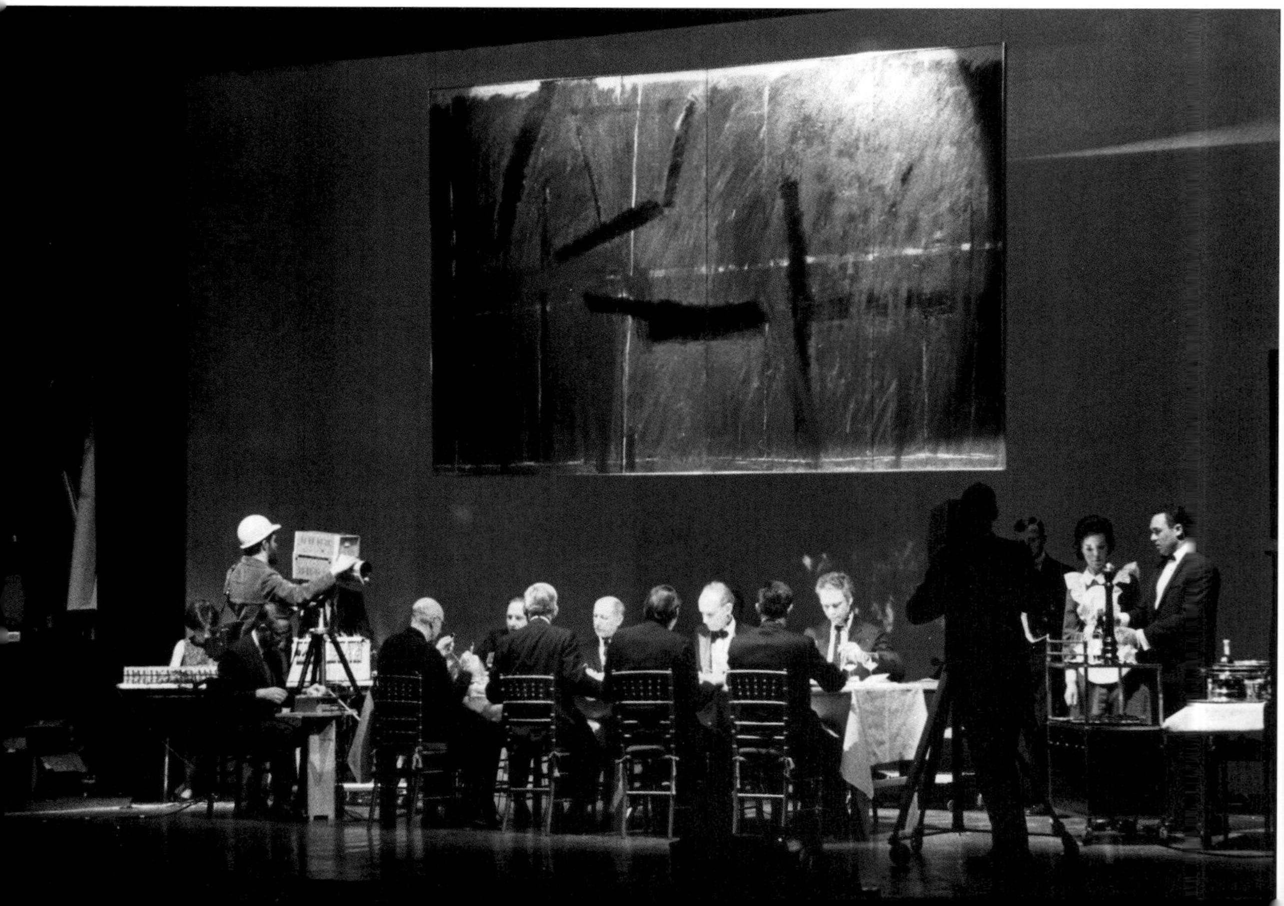

Museums were ambivalent about kinetic art because they were accustomed to objects that maintained a polite silence and did not require repairs. Still, the public responded enthusiastically – exhibitions in the mid-1960s attracted huge crowds and extensive press coverage. Lye was strongly represented in 'Kinetic and Optic Art Today' at the 1965 Buffalo Festival of the Arts, and the following year in 'Directions in Kinetic Sculpture' at the University Art Museum in Berkeley, a show curated by Peter Selz, who – like Hultén – was a leading advocate of kineticism. Such exhibitions also gave Lye opportunities to meet European sculptors with whom he felt a strong affinity such as Jean Tinguely, Vassilakis Takis and Nicolas Schöffer.[105]

The public interest in kinetic art was fuelled by the rise of the counter-culture with its liking for exotic visual experiences. Despite hitting 60, Lye was a suitable role model for the era. Interviewers for hippie magazines were fascinated not only by his art but also by his lifestyle, colourful clothes and free-wheeling speech. The *East Village Other* profiled him as 'The Freest Radical'.[106] But there were less public aspects of his character that did not fit this image. He was a workaholic, not interested in drugs (which seemed to have little effect on him because his senses were already operating overtime), and his thinking about art had been shaped by the most serious and ambitious forms of modernism.[107]

Lye went on creating new sculptures through the 1960s, and museums continued to hold well-attended exhibitions of kinetic art. But by 1970, when the survey 'Kinetics' was held at the Hayward Gallery in London, such art had lost its novelty value. The minimalist work of sculptors such as Donald Judd, Carl Andre and Richard Serra had come to occupy the spotlight, championed by American critics who had always been suspicious of kineticism because they tended to see it as a gimmick, more relevant to Europe than to their own sense of art history. This was a misunderstanding since the work of an artist such as Lye could usefully be seen as an extension of 'action painting', not to mention the kinetic art of Calder, Ray and Rickey, or the American work of Duchamp, Gabo and Moholy-Nagy. Kineticism in the United States never had a critic or theorist of Greenberg's status to argue its case or to distinguish its best examples from the miscellany of 'op art', multi-media psychedelica, 'space-age' novelties and other 1960s interests that tended to dominate kinetic exhibitions. Meanwhile, buyers and curators were happy to focus on minimalism, pop art, and traditional forms of painting and sculpture that did not require mechanical maintenance. More than a few museums that had purchased motorised sculptures could not be bothered keeping them in working

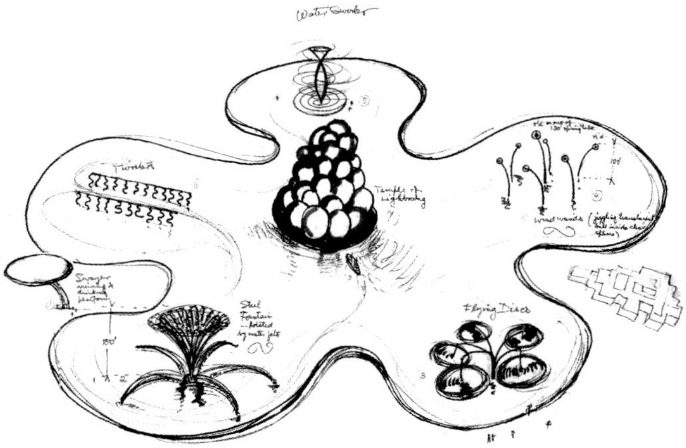

One of Lye's many designs for a 'temple'. Here the Temple of Lightning is located at the centre of a cinquefoil lake, ringed by giant sculptures. Clockwise from the top they include a *Water Swirler*, *Wind Wands*, *Flying Discs*, a *Steel Fountain* rotated by water jets, and *Twisters*. On the left is a *Swayer* viewing platform. Courtesy Len Lye Foundation.

order and relegated them to the basement. The reputation of an artist like Lye, whose lifetime interest in movement had nothing to do with fashion, suffered as a result of the art world's politics and distrust of technology.

In 1970, when Lye contributed to the Howard Wise exhibition 'Propositions for Unrealised Projects', he was already convinced that his plans for large-scale versions of his sculptures could not be realised in his lifetime. Wise had done his best for Lye, even subsidising his work at times, but while the artist had received glowing reviews, his art had never become a magnet for investors. In later years, he also became difficult to negotiate with, as though he was effectively 'going on strike' as a sculptor. He would give a film or sculpture to a friend for nothing, yet when an institution approached him for work he would demand an impossible price. In the 1970s, he devoted more of his energies to writing, theorising and 'utopian thinking'. He thought of his sculptures as prototypes – one day the art world would come to understand their full potential, in the same way they had eventually learned to appreciate other forms of vanguard art. His wife and friends were disappointed that he was turning away from the physical production of art, but they understood his frustrations.

Having done kinetic work in two different media, Lye had now fully developed his aesthetics of motion. In 1964, he wrote 'The Art that Moves', the third of his important essays on the subject. In the course of its ten pages, he explained the history of kinetic art, his own beginnings (such as his Wellington epiphany), the idea behind a 'figure of motion', his fascination with 'choreography', art as an 'homage to energy', the mechanism of feedback, and his concepts of 'the old brain' and the 'neuro-motor or nerve muscle sense'. He also discussed his working method for both sculpture and film, and the idea of film images as a 'vicarious' form of dance to music. Whereas 'Is Film Art?' had referred only briefly to 'empathy', the later essay made it a central theme and explored its processes in detail.

Lye would go on to write a number of other essays – some of which focused on motion, such as 'A Kinetic Biography' and 'Somewhat Autobiographically' – but they tended to revolve round the same concepts. Much of his later writing paid attention to philosophy, values, genetics and the old brain, and it was in those areas rather than motion that he developed new ideas.

NEW ZEALAND

Lye had kept up personal links with New Zealand by exchanging letters with his brother Philip. (His other favourite correspondent, his mother, had died in 1940.) Around 1960, he explored his memories of childhood (such as 'the great flash') in the vivid prose sequence *Happy Moments* (which was published posthumously).[108] During the 1960s, stories about his kinetic sculpture in international art magazines encouraged New Zealanders to contact him in New York. This was a period when New Zealand was 'going modern in its culture', as Lye put it.[109] As artists and curators engaged with contemporary, international trends, they were fascinated to hear about a New Zealander who had already been doing so for more than 40 years.

Lye made his first return visit to the country in 1968 for personal reasons, but while he was in Wellington he campaigned for greater public support to be given

Lye in New Zealand in 1968. He was photographed by Hamish Keith while visiting painter Don Binney at Anawhata. Courtesy Hamish Keith.

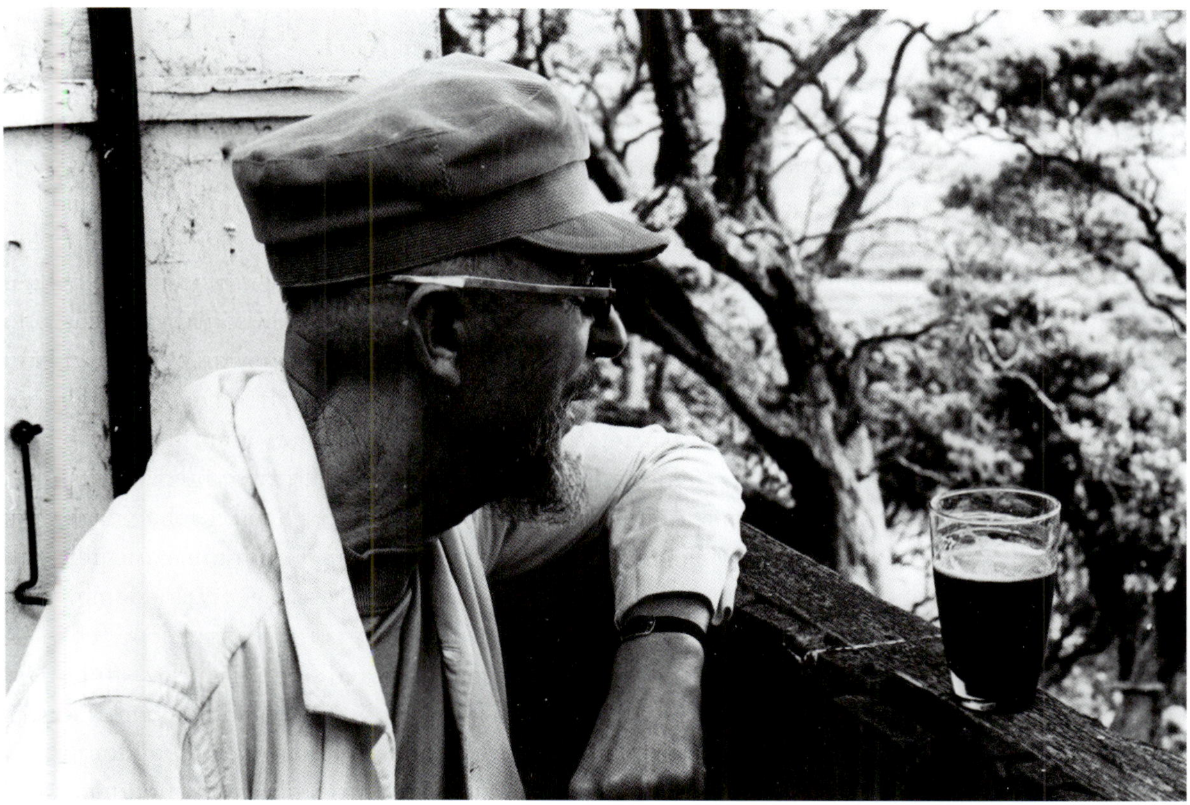

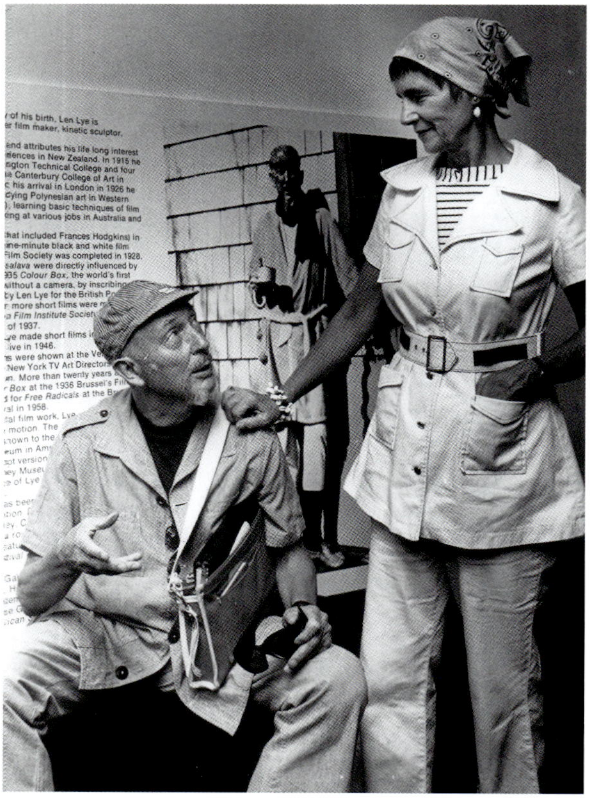

Len and Ann Lye at the Govett-Brewster Art Gallery in New Plymouth in 1977 for the opening of his exhibition. Courtesy Len Lye Foundation.

to independent film-makers.[110] His advocacy was well-timed since an important new generation of film-makers was just emerging. His links with New Zealand deepened over the next few years, and he accepted an offer from the Govett-Brewster Art Gallery in New Plymouth to build some large-scale versions of his sculptures. John Matthews accepted the huge engineering challenge. (The vicissitudes of this project are described in Chapter 6.) In 1977 Lye returned to New Zealand to pass judgement on the results, and was so impressed that he agreed to leave his work to the people of New Zealand after his death, to be administered by a non-profit trust, the Len Lye Foundation, which would house his collection at the Govett-Brewster Art Gallery. The Foundation would have the responsibility of keeping his sculpture in working order, and, as funds permitted, realising his plans for large-scale versions. Lye saw this as the ultimate solution to his lack of a support base. The notion that others would build his work after his death was not easy to reconcile with his perfectionism, but he came to accept it as the best available option. Kinetic sculpture has an inevitable need for ongoing repairs and replacements – an issue to be explored more fully in a later chapter.

Knowing that his health was declining, he concentrated on rounding off his life's work. In Puerto Rico, he returned to his painting preoccupations of the 1930s and completed a series of canvases. Back in New York, he re-edited *Free Radicals*, reducing it to an even tighter four minutes. And he made a final version of *Particles in Space*, a film that had grown out of *Free Radicals* but gone on to develop a new range of scratched images and textures. Funding had finally become available to him – from the New Zealand Film Commission in the case of the first film, and the American National Endowment for the Arts and the Queen Elizabeth II (QEII) Arts Council of New Zealand in the case of the second. The Arts Council and the Len Lye Foundation sponsored work on another short film, *Tal Fallow*, which was completed posthumously.

THE LEGACY

Lye died in Warwick, New York, in 1980. The New Zealand government helped with the cost of transferring his collection to New Plymouth. His sculpture, paintings and documents are held at the Govett-Brewster Art Gallery, which, with the Lye Foundation, continues to function as a support system for the artist's work. Today the Govett-Brewster has a dedicated Lye curator, Tyler Cann. Funding has also come from the New Plymouth District Council, which, in recent years, has discussed the possibility of building a Lye Centre, a museum next to the Govett-Brewster, to be devoted to the artist's work. His films are held at the New Zealand Film Archive in Wellington which is carrying out restoration work. Funding has been a constant struggle for the Lye Foundation as it continues to undertake expensive repairs, research and development. Its activities have been sustained by the sale of a few sculptures and by occasional grants (from the Stout Trust, Creative New Zealand and the New Plymouth District Council), but mostly by personal donations and a great deal of volunteer work.

New Zealand has had a strong tradition of kinetic sculpture thanks to such artists as Andrew Drummond, Sam Morrison, Tony Nicholls, Phil Price, Peter Roche and Evan Webb. The presence of Lye's work should help to ensure that this interest continues to develop. In New Plymouth, his large sculptures *Wind Wand*, *Flip and Two Twisters* and *Blade* have become local icons, and home-made wands have blossomed in many backyards. His *Water Whirler* is a feature of the Wellington waterfront, and there is another *Wind Wand* at Alan Gibbs's Kaipara sculpture park.

Lye has had a broad influence in New Zealand not only on sculptors but also on video artists and makers of experimental films and music videos, as well as on painters and poets. At first, there was some resistance to him because he had spent most of his career overseas, but the country has recently developed a greater interest in its expatriates. The latest history of local art, Hamish Keith's book and television series *The Big Picture: The History of New Zealand Art from 1642*, gives him detailed coverage.[III] The presence of a large collection of his work has attracted many artists to the Govett-Brewster; but Lye's influence is also based on the role model he presents as a creative, independent thinker with a lifetime commitment to experiment. (He was still making innovative films at the age of 78.) Such a personal example is important in a small country where conservative attitudes and limited funding often encourage compromise. The wide-ranging interest of young artists was demonstrated by the conference 'Particles + Pixels: Moving Image Culture after Len Lye' held in Auckland in 2005, which attracted practitioners from a range of media.[112]

Having a base for the work of a kinetic artist is important because of all the upkeep involved, but New Zealand's remoteness has some disadvantages because it is difficult to keep Lye's work under the eyes of the international art world. There have been a few major shows such as the exhibition in Paris in 2000 at the Centre Pompidou, which also published a book on Lye; and during the last few years there has been a flurry of interest by Australian public galleries. The remarkable 2009 exhibition in Melbourne at the Australian Centre for the Moving Image is the first overseas show to offer a broad survey of Lye's sculptures as well as his films. If an exhibition of that kind could travel round the world, it would hugely expand the artist's reputation, especially if his large-scale sculptures were included.

Lye could have left a great deal more work if practical and financial problems had not held him back. Such problems had a big impact on his career and also on the history of kinetic art generally. The media that he used for his art of motion were heavily dependent upon money and technology, and kinetic artists have had to find a base or infrastructure that can support their work during their lifetime and posthumously as well. In Lye's case, his lack of interest in self-promotion and his maverick style exacerbated the problems, though his uncompromising approach also helped at times to strengthen his work. It is fortunate that he found innovative ways to operate cheaply in both film and sculpture; and when we combine his achievements in these media with his paintings, photograms and writings, it adds up to a substantial overall body of work, particularly for an experimental artist who tried never to repeat himself.

Internationally, interest in kinetic art is today at a low ebb. 'Kineticism' tends no longer to be included in surveys of 20th-century art movements. The sceptical mood of post-modernism has discouraged the revival of a movement thought to have been naively enthusiastic about technology. (Lye was enthusiastic about many things but there was nothing romantic in his view of technology.) There have been some attempts to reassess the tradition – such as the ambitious exhibition 'Fields of Force' in Barcelona and London in 2000 – but such surveys have tended to reproduce the whole range of tendencies associated with 'kinetic art' during the 1950s and 1960s.[113] Since art history is always a process of attrition, these reassessments are valuable because they allow us to take another look at neglected areas; but the specific theme of movement tends to get diluted in the process. The costs involved in restoring and transporting kinetic sculptures have also presented an obstacle.

There are hopeful signs that digital technology may create a new wave of interest in 'the art that moves', although robot constructions (of the type associated with the MIT Media Lab, for example) tend to pursue a different set of priorities from Lye's. Some digital machines seem to hark back to the old tradition of mechanised toys. Granted, Lye would have loved to get his hands on this technology.

This condensed biography has focused on Lye's specific interests and influences as a kinetic artist. His work is distinguished by its intense concentration on movement and on the need for the body as well as the mind to be involved in 'the art that moves'. Movement was not his only area of innovation, but it was a lifetime interest, and it provoked his most important work. That is not to suggest that his excursions into other media lack interest. There are continuities that link all his creative work – in painting, photography, poetry and print-making as well as film and sculpture – such as his consistent interest in the old brain. And he brought some original thinking to each of those fields. Other critics have chosen to focus on his experiments with colour, the photogram method, Surrealist imagery, and other themes. (For some thoughtful examples, see *Len Lye*, edited by Tyler Cann and Wystan Curnow, the valuable collection just published by the Govett-Brewster Art Gallery.) The present book has chosen, however, to look most closely at his films and kinetic sculptures and to focus on movement, in order to make the case that this was Lye's most significant contribution to art.

In New Zealand Lye tends to be thought of as a sculptor whereas overseas he is seen primarily as a film-maker. It is still rare for the two aspects to receive equal treatment; yet only by knowing both is it possible fully to understand the art of motion that they share – a whole that is more than the sum of the parts. Similarly, even though aspects of Lye's aesthetic of motion have received close attention from critics and curators, his aesthetic has rarely been discussed in its complete form (as the next chapter will attempt to do). When the missing links are added, we can better understand Lye's argument that a 'new category of art' has emerged, along with a new way of looking at motion.

three the art of motion

OVER THE COURSE OF HIS CAREER, LYE DEVELOPED AN AMBITIOUS and detailed aesthetic of motion. His ideas are brought together here for the first time from a variety of sources – from his unpublished manuscripts, interviews and letters as well as his published essays. His philosophical interests ranged widely, but his aesthetic theories were always closely linked to his practice; hence, as he moved back and forth between different media, his ideas kept changing and expanding, and there is no single essay that provides a complete and final statement of his aesthetic (though 'The Art that Moves' comes closest to it). Despite all the rethinking that went on, however, there is a powerful continuity to his main ideas and interests. Of course, this is only one artist's perspective on 'the art of motion', and in a field so diverse it is not going to suit everyone. But precisely because kinetic art is such a sprawling genre it is valuable to have his definite, fully developed aesthetic as a point of reference. It is also hard to imagine any practitioner or viewer not finding at least some of his ideas useful.

Lye's theory concentrates on the shaping of literal movement. This precise focus distinguishes it from other theories associated with movement that have more to do with time, speed, technology, implied motion, unpredictability, nomadism or other themes. To take one example, Gilles Deleuze's concept of 'the movement-image' was very different from what Lye meant by 'figure of motion' or the 'image' created by movement. Building on some of Bergson's ideas, Deleuze was interested in the potential of movement to reveal something new and unregulated. He also sought to understand 'the thought or the philosophy' implied by particular styles of movement or types of film.[1] Lye always found philosophical writing of that kind stimulating, and he also valued the theoretical work of kinetic artists such as Nicolas Schöffer (*Perturbation et Chronocratie*) and George Rickey (*Constructivism: Origins and Evolution*).[2] Some of Lye's ideas overlap with those of other artists, but his aesthetic combines those ingredients in a new way and has a distinctive thrust

I have grouped his ideas in ten key areas of concern. The first introduces his basic conception of kinetic art, and the second focuses on his concept of 'figure of motion'. The following two ('Training the Senses' and 'Seeing with the Body') describe ways to sharpen our response to movement in art. This emphasis on preparation, for both artist and viewer, reflects Lye's belief that our culture fails to help us develop the relevant skills. The next theme is the important role played by 'empathy', which is followed by an explanation of the relevance of 'the old brain'. Next I discuss his characteristic ways of handling the materials of art, the place for stillness within the spectrum of movement, and finally the concepts of dance and choreography as ways of providing further insights into the art of motion. The subsequent chapters of the book look at how Lye put this aesthetic into practice, his specific methods of making films and kinetic sculptures, and the implications for our viewing of them.

LYE'S AESTHETIC

An Art of 'motion per se'

> Motion sculpture is a distinct form of modern art . . . . My tangible motion sculpture, extending the infinite variety of fundamental patterns of movement, emphasizes the beauty of motion *per se.*[3]

Why did Lye stress the 'per se'? He wanted to explore 'tangible' or literal motion for its own sake, as the primary focus of interest, in contrast to the many types of art in which motion was exploited as a vehicle for other interests. Of cinema he wrote, 'we've all been conditioned to viewing films [not in terms of motion *per se* but] as an adjunct to drama and literature, that is, as a medium for story-telling or as the kinetic illustration of information – all the way from a Hamlet tragedy, a James Bond thriller, to the state of society and the weather'.[4] Of course, some directors and camera operators do have a sophisticated sense of movement but they know that viewers are more interested in the story, actors, dialogue, emotions, music, special effects and so on – so movement is exploited as the vehicle for those aspects instead of being developed in its own right. Ballet is another art of movement, but – at least in its conventional forms – it dilutes the kinetic aspects by highlighting its stars, costumes, music and story-telling. (Dance is discussed more fully later in this chapter.)

Lye used the term 'kinetic art' in a more selective and specific way than did most of the art establishment in the 1960s and even in the ensuing decades.[5] When the theme was fashionable and much talked about, its scope was constantly expanding. Excited curators added to the genre any form of art involving machines, new technologies, optical illusions, light patterns or implied movement. The boisterous public and media interest in kinetic art out-ran any attempt at serious theory or analysis (despite the work of thoughtful curators such as Peter Selz and Pontus Hultén). Not surprisingly, critics questioned the claims of such a diverse body of art to be considered a 'movement' or a radical new aesthetic.

From the beginning, Lye was an exception because he insisted that literal movement was central to his work and that this called for new ways of making and viewing art. His 1935 essay 'Film-making' had spoken of 'movement-consciousness', 'physical explicitness' and 'physical accuracy', which involved developing skills that had been neglected because priority had been given to other forms of sensory experience. The first art critic to understand Lye's emphasis on movement was Roger Fry who wrote to him in 1929 after the premiere of his first film *Tusalava*, 'I thought that you had seen the essential thing as noone had hitherto – I mean you really thought not of forms in themselves but of them as movements in time. I suspect it will need a new kind of imagination to seize this idea fully but you are the first as far as I know to make a start.'[6]

When the hard-to-please sculptor Donald Judd reviewed an exhibition of kinetic sculpture in *Art International* in 1965, he wrote: 'So far, mechanical motion hasn't been used much more clearly . . . . It will be an important aspect of art but it isn't yet . . . . [But] there is less wrong with Len Lye's use of movement than with anyone else in the United States . . . . Subsidiary movement is all right but motion can be *the whole work*. It is, pretty much, in Lye's pieces.'[7]

Judd's comment reflected a tradition of modernism which valued art that was uncompromising and singular, such as the pure forms of abstract art or, in this case, the idea of a pure emphasis on movement. Most of Lye's kinetic sculptures involve an intense concentration on movement, yet to speak of this element as '*the whole work*' takes a step too far. As a sculptor, Lye was still interested in light, colour, sound and (at least to some extent) symbolism. Colour and music played an important role in some of his films, and the two Lye films that come closest to a pure emphasis on movement – *Free Radicals* and *Particles in Space* – dispense with colour but still have musical accompaniment. What Lye demanded was that movement should be the *principal* aspect. The 'subsidiary' aspects needed to be integrated with it, and to help as far as possible to reinforce it.

Figures of Motion

> This kind of kinetic imagery can now be transposed into formal figures of motion by the kinetic artist. He does it in a similar vein to the composer transposing sound into musical figures.[8]

Lye said the idea of 'figures of motion' first came to him as a teenager standing at the top of a Wellington hill watching fast-moving clouds. It became one of his key phrases, and while it is only one of the concepts used to explain his kinetic art, it provides the best starting point. The phrase has two aspects – first, it suggests a way of looking at movement in aesthetic (compositional) terms. And second, it distinguishes Lye's approach from the types of kinetic art that are less focused or less selective.

By 'figure', Lye meant 'form or shape', but what interested him was form as something performed, something that involved a process.[9] One of his reasons for using the analogy with music was because this was an art that took shape over time – musicians had to develop an acute sense of tempo, phrasing and 'melodic line'. There already existed a tradition of modern artists attempting to read form as an unfolding, such as Paul Klee who began his *Pedagogical Sketchbook* (a textbook for the Bauhaus) with this description of a simple curving line: 'An active line on a walk, moving freely, without goal. A walk for a walk's sake. The mobility agent is a point, shifting its position forward.'[10] And Wassily Kandinsky, another Bauhaus instructor, began his section on 'Line' in *Point and Line to Plane* by describing it as 'the track made by the moving point; that is, its product. It is created by movement

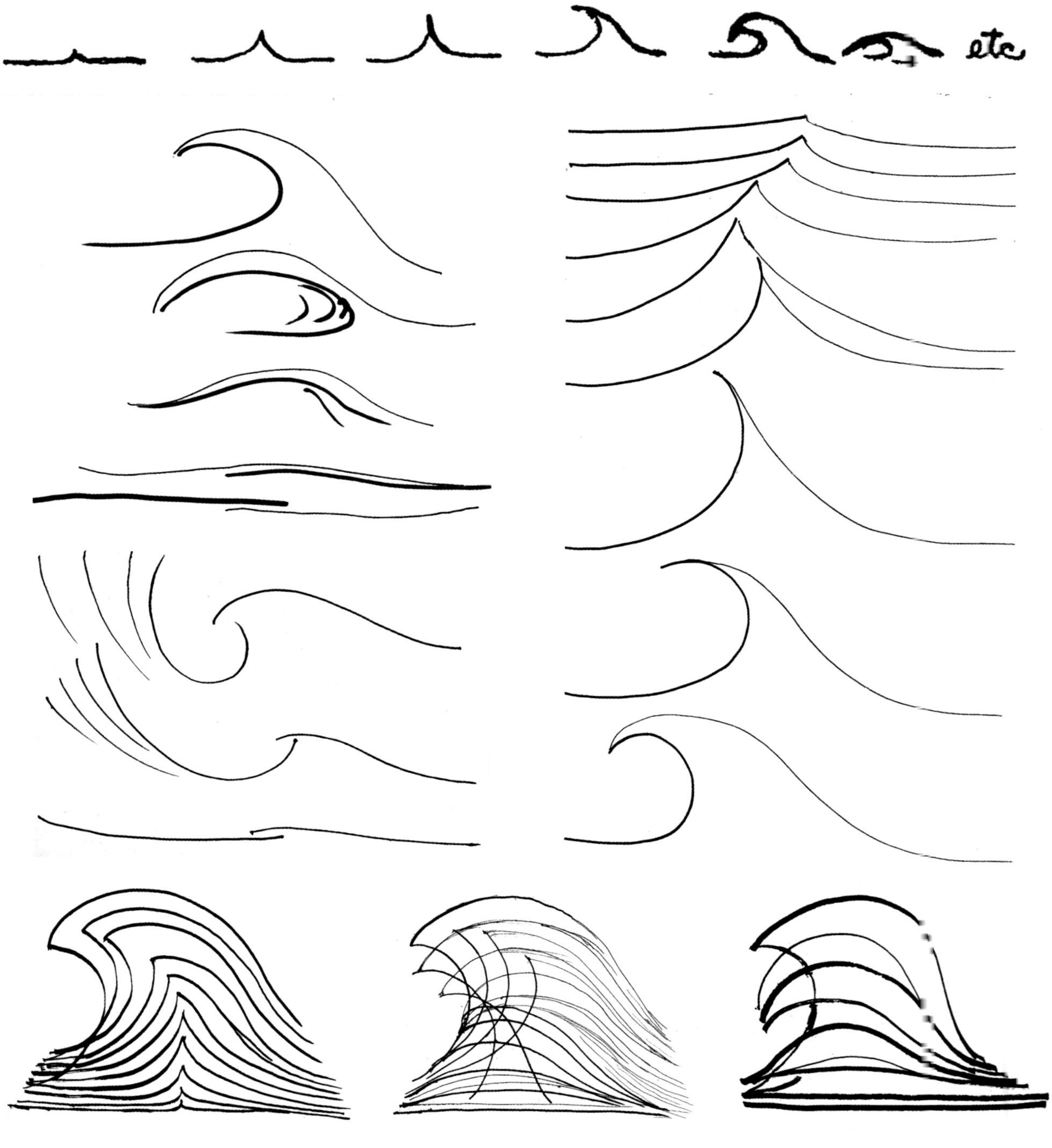

A few of the drawings Lye made when he was designing a sculpture inspired by wave patterns. Courtesy Len Lye Foundation.

– specifically through the destruction of the intense self-contained repose of the point. Here, the leap out of the static into the dynamic occurs.'[11] Whereas Klee and Kandinsky were concerned with implied movement, Lye worked with literal movement. Compare Roger Fry's comment that *Tusalava* expressed 'a new kind of imagination' which 'really thought not of forms in themselves but of them as movements in time'.

The term 'figure of motion' had the advantage of being applicable to films, kinetic sculptures or any movement in nature. Familiar examples included a wave rolling in and breaking, or a graceful 'figure skater' making patterns on the ice. One of Lye's favourite examples was a child waving fireworks on Guy Fawkes Night: 'When a . . . sparkler describes a figure eight, the persistence of after-image isolates its motion as design.'[12] Lye was, however, less interested in the 'after-image' than in the pattern-making implied by the word 'describes'. As he explained, 'of all forms of art, the imagery of motion best describes itself. It's why we say the sparkler "describes" the figure eight; we mean to say the object defines its own action.'[13] It is a struggle to convey this sense of form in words – a shape in motion, a pattern that unfolds. Our mind is busy trying to recognise an emerging form or rhythm ('its motion as design'), but at the same time we are responding to the motion *in the moment*, appreciating its physical energy. This complex experience is something we can also have as we listen to music or watch dancers. The challenge for a critic is how to describe the form of such work without sacrificing some of the richness of the experience (as a purely formalist description does by focusing narrowly on the end-product, on the 'design'). For a kinetic artist, the challenge is how to create art that makes the most of the performance as well as the form.

A vigorous film example is the unstable asterisk in *Free Radicals* that struggles to hang on to the various lines that compose it as they strive to break away – a fascinating process of push-and-pull. A more gentle example is the sculpture *Grass*, in which two rows of slender, flexible, metal rods are planted along a board. A motor and a spring create a see-saw movement. As each end of the board dips in turn, the rods lean forwards and then bounce back in a slow-motion dance. Their figure is a more organised version of what happens when grass stalks bend in the wind. In both these examples, the artist has set in motion a particularly shapely and dynamic figure with a wealth of subtle nuances, creating a rich viewing experience.

In the world of music, 'figure' is one of a group of related terms such as phrase, theme, subject and motif (which is derived from the Latin word for 'movement').

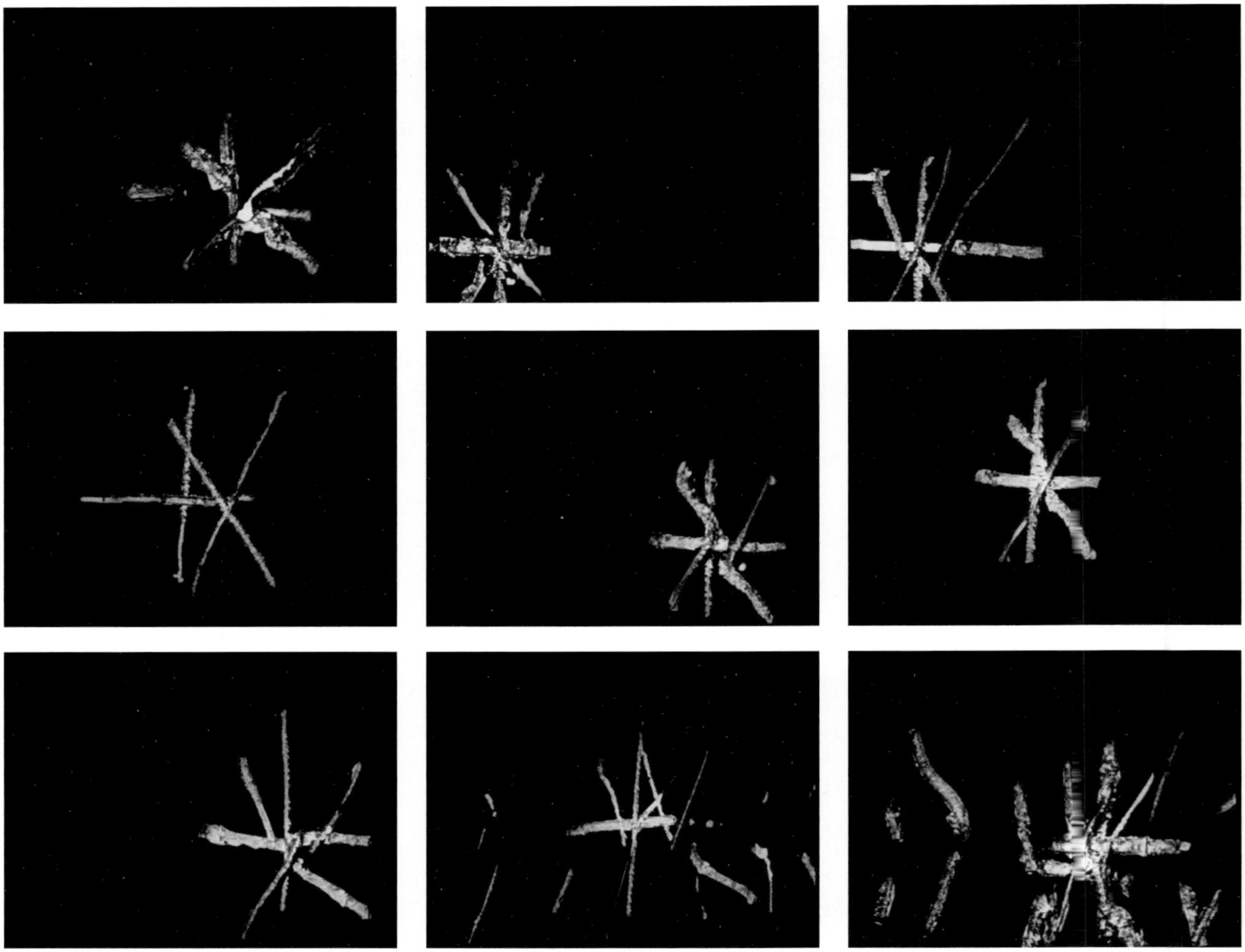

ABOVE Frames from the 'asterisk' sequence of *Free Radicals*. BELOW *Grass* in action. Courtesy Len Lye Foundation.

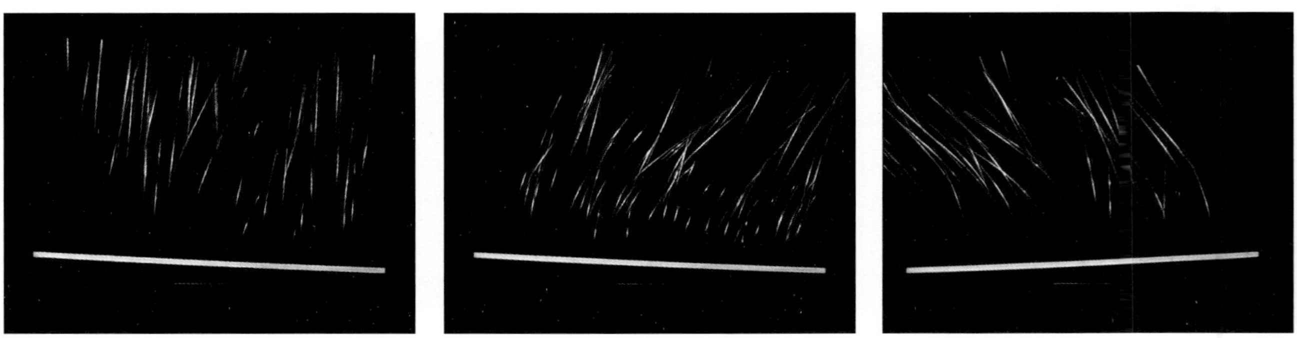

The best-known term of this kind is 'melody' or 'tune', which is similar to Lye's 'figure' in the way a particular sequence of notes can lodge in the memory. A melody can inspire a series of variations, which was the way Lye developed many of his films and kinetic sculptures. He was familiar with this theme-and-variation form in jazz, explaining in 'Voice and Colour' that a 'tune is the foundation on which a musician . . . improvises; or a point of departure for [a] singer with a strong sense of rhythm and melody, who disdains to render the tune exactly, and sings around the melody, investing it with new life and vitality'.[14] This kind of performance could be said to create a number of new tunes, but those tunes have a family resemblance, a shared origin.

The starting point for Lye's art is the kinetic equivalent of a curious, catchy melody – 'a particular form [or figure] of motion which fascinates me because I can't make out why. And I go on with the work . . . while it seductively preoccupies me above all else.'[15] He saw his task as how to 'really get the utmost, to get the god-damn utmost . . . out of the fundamental [figure]'.[16] For the kinetic artist, as for the composer, a good 'figure' is not only catchy in its own right but also rich in its potential to inspire variations.

The other side of Lye's term was its emphasis on selectivity. An interesting figure might produce many variations but it was important to select and isolate the best of them. In his instructions for the sculpture *Dancing Atoms*, he also stressed the need to keep figures separate. Once the work had speeded up to the point where it had assumed a particular figure, 'you must always turn it off and let it coast before you can let it have a different figure'.[17] All of Lye's work reflects the intensity with which he focused on individual figures of motion. Endlessly experimenting and revising, he would paint or scratch hundreds of strips of film as variations on a single idea before selecting the best.

This approach distinguishes his work from a great deal of kinetic art that seeks to immerse the viewer in a field of movement. Early work such as László Moholy-Nagy's 1930 film *Lightplay: Black-White-Grey* used complex, superimposed images. Alexander Calder's mobiles consisted of a number of shapes that maintained an ongoing flux of movement, including chance effects produced by the wind. Some 1960s sculptures created whole environments, and the psychedelic aesthetic encouraged sensory overload. Some computer-based art today similarly builds up multiple layers to create a buzz of hectic activity. Lye was open to many forms of kinetic art but he was not interested in an untidy flurry – he was looking for specific figures of motion. As he said of one of Oskar Fischinger's films, 'Mighty

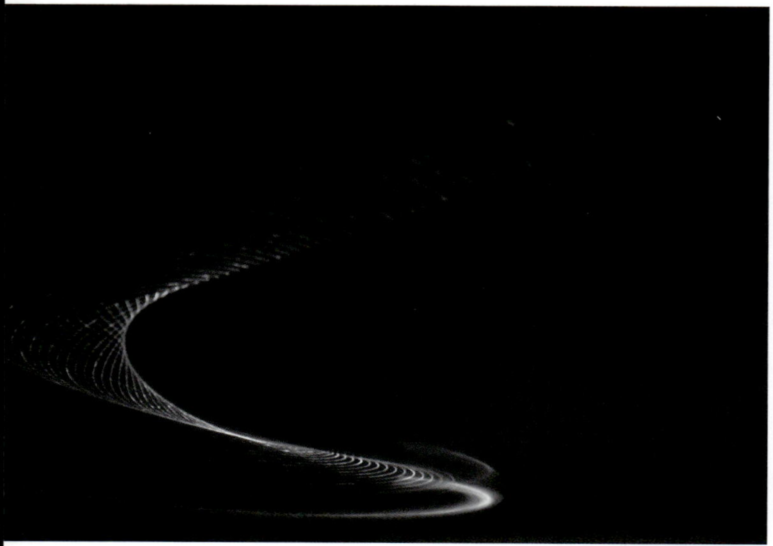

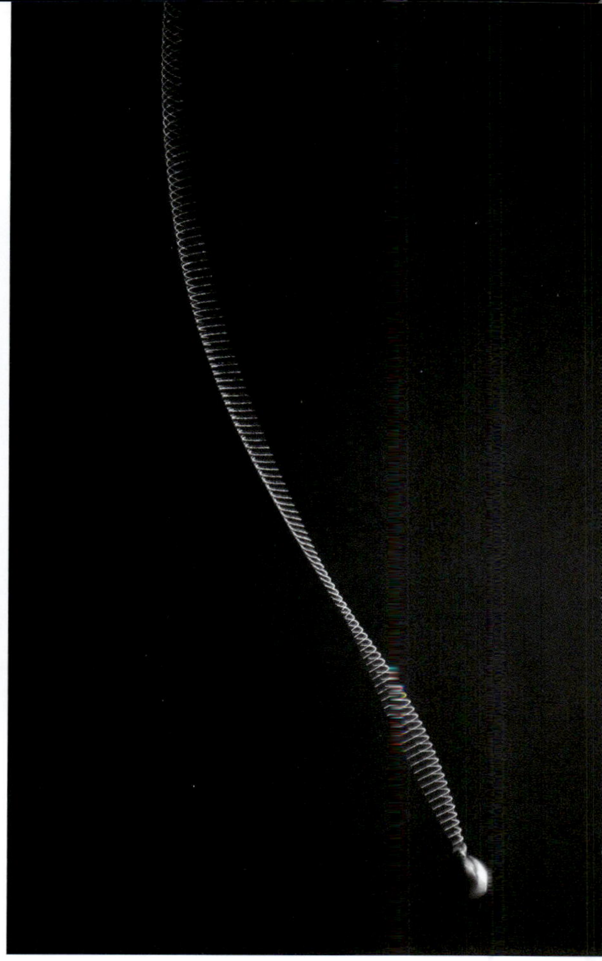

Two photographs of the sculpture *Sky Snake* in motion. Courtesy Len Lye Foundation.

good for some few seconds of it. It's all I aim for, myself, just a few moments of real kinesthesia – there's no other kick of its kind.'[18]

Lye's emphasis on selectivity may seem at odds with the fact that his 1930s films appear very busy. But what creates that impression is the fact that they move so rapidly – each few seconds of film represents a separate visual idea. In a film such as *Swinging the Lambeth Walk*, vertical lines (for the violin) contrast with horizontal lines (for the guitar). His variations include doubling up the lines and using a thicker vertical line for the double-bass. There is also a third figure – circles for percussion – with big, bouncing circles for the drums and clusters of smaller circles for keyboard instruments. These distinct figures are edited to match the phrasing of the music, though never in a mechanical way. To focus on the specific figures of motion in his films calls for alert viewing because the images dance past so rapidly. The blacked-out conditions of a cinema allow us to concentrate without distraction, though many treat this venue simply as a place to relax. Lye's own viewing had an uncanny sharpness.

He built up the programme for each sculpture in a similarly painstaking way. In music, composers are often inspired by a particular motif that 'motivates' (literally, 'sets in motion') the composition, after which the composer 'arranges, orchestrates and improvises' (as Lye described it) to build up a larger form.[19] Lye's basic motif would always be more complex and nuanced than our first impression of it; and in some cases – such as *Fountain*, *Grass* or *Witch Dance* – he would have a number of rods performing the same movement, inevitably with slight differences. He also liked the idea of exhibiting multiple copies of the same sculpture – such as a cluster of *Wind Wands*. In such situations, there is a coherence similar to that of a piece of music in which an interesting melody is passing through a series of subtle variations. Lye carefully choreographed the way his mechanised sculptures unfolded, selecting a sequence of speeds and ordering the variations so that the performance had a satisfying beginning, middle and end. It is also a common practice in music to add a contrasting second theme, and we can see him adopting that approach in a sculpture such as *Trilogy* where the *Flip* and the *Twisters* represent contrasting (and alternating) figures. All of these procedures helped Lye 'to get the god-damn utmost . . . out of the fundamental [figure]'.

Just as it is possible to learn to identify the style of a particular composer, we can come to recognise the favourite figures of a film-maker or kinetic sculptor. Clouds, which first gave Lye the idea of kinetic art, appear in several films (*Rainbow Dance* and *Trade Tattoo*). Waves were always a favourite, with fast-moving, animated waves turning up in several of his 1930s films, and breaking waves provided the starting point for a later sculpture.[20] He was intrigued by the fact that so many types of energy took the form of waves, including the sound waves of music. Lye liked cyclic patterns. Though he was interested in rotation, he was drawn above all to vibration and oscillation. Here is a typical exercise he gave to art students: 'Begin to look at things in terms of their oscillation, say, the branch swaying to extremes of its tensile periods of timing, and note the bounce in the extremities of all the other branches with their disparate timings, along with incidentally the flap and twist of the leaves.'[21] Sculptures such as *Grass*, *Fountain* and *Wind Wand* grew out of his observation of nature. The lines of direct films also have a natural tremor which Lye associated with human muscles under strain or the vibration of guitar and violin strings. A similar tension is seen in sculptures such as *Blade* when its steel strip starts to quiver. As the energy increases, the

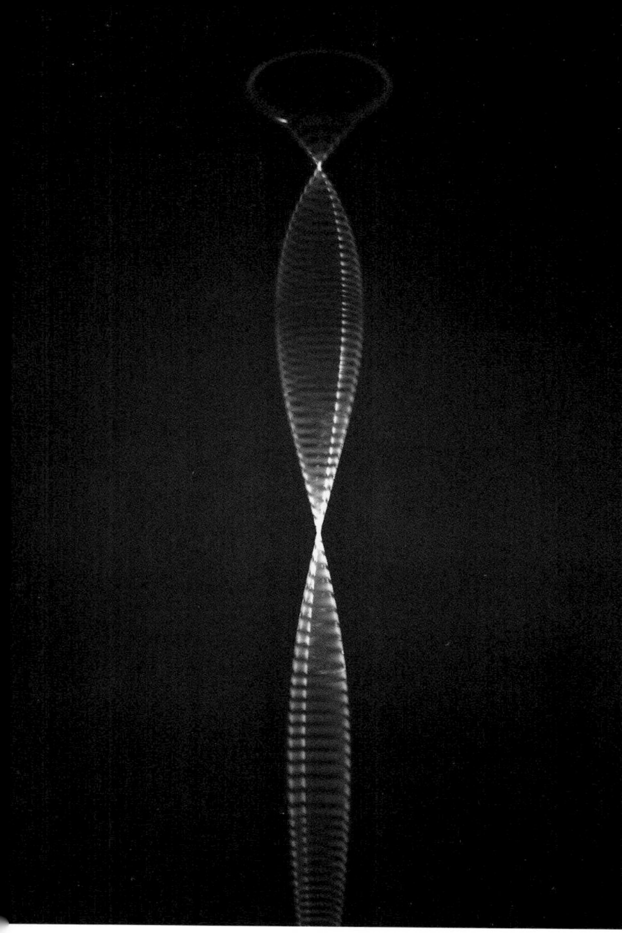

The 'virtual volume' effect created by the sculpture *Zebra*. Courtesy Len Lye Foundation.

strip develops harmonic curves, and those oval shapes – reminiscent of an 'S' or an '8' or (in Lye's words) 'a fish standing on its nose with its tail waggling out above' – were another important element in his visual vocabulary.[22] Also a linear figure spinning rapidly can seem to develop a third dimension, an effect known as 'virtual volume', and he used this figure as the basis of sculptures such as *Zebra*.

In his scratch films, the figures of motion included 'zigzags' of lightning, which he described as a 'particularly vibrant, ziggy little image' with 'terrific zizz'.[23] Steve Jones remembers that when Lye was explaining what he was trying to achieve, he had a distinctive way of gesturing: 'you could almost see the raw movement in his arms . . . . He had a way of detaching himself and just doing a motion for you – you didn't see him, you saw the figure of motion. And then you'd look on a piece of film he'd scratched and there was the same sort of figure.'[24]

One historical question difficult to resolve is when exactly Lye came up with the term 'figure of motion'. In later life, when he described his epiphany on a Wellington hilltop, he always suggested that the term had arrived at the same time; yet he appears not to have written it down until the 1960s. Granted, he seems to have always looked at motion in this manner, and his close friendship during the 1920s and 1930s with the composer Jack Ellitt must have strengthened his awareness of the parallels between music and movement. He spoke of 'composing' motion in his 1935 essay 'Film-making'. Nevertheless, for many years he used a variety of other words and analogies – such as his description of *A Colour Box* in 1935 as 'seven different flowers translated into music and pattern time',[25] and he wrote about his 1936 films as 'a type of sensory ballet' and as 'moving hieroglyphics'.[26] (He had read Ezra Pound's book *Gaudier-Brzeska* which offered a kinetic, 'Vorticist' perspective on 'hieroglyphics'.) Another favourite word was 'image' as a shorthand term for a striking pattern of movement. (This had affinities with Pound's sense of 'image' as a 'vortex'.) But in general, the most expressive term Lye came up with was 'figure of motion', and from the 1960s he used it constantly.[27] Figures of motion, like musical figures, came in many different shapes and sizes, but the term was useful as a shorthand way of describing a precise, unfolding form of movement.

Training the Senses

Lye set out as a boy to develop all his senses systematically, through exercises or games he invented. Through these games he organised his own education, developing a range of artistic skills. Along the way he discovered that he had a particularly strong response to movement. We still have the details of his youthful sense games, which he later adapted for his teaching at New York University. He expected anyone who was serious about becoming a kinetic artist to pay their dues by a lifetime observation and analysis of motion, as he had done. He regarded such long-term practice as more important than stylistic or intellectual virtuosity.

He had developed his first memory game when forced to go to bed early. Having trouble getting to sleep, he passed the time by attempting to remember and relive the sensations of the day,

> . . . starting from which side I woke up; whether I first looked out the window at the weather or guessed it with closed eyes from the feel of the light and the feel of the air in the plain room; how I had laid the fire that morning and how it had caught; the soap in the kitchen when I washed after fixing the fire; how the porridge tasted – thick, thin, lumpy or burnt, it always tasted different; whether I had spread sugar all over it or had dumped it in the middle to make a gradually smaller and sweeter island.[28]

If he was not asleep by the time he arrived at the end of his review, he would return to the incidents that pleased him most, such as 'any good shots with stones' or 'watching seagulls flying'.

This exercise not only passed the time but also had the added benefit of sharpening his senses. Initially, he gave all five senses a workout, but then he began to focus on a different one each night. There were sound days, smell days, taste days and touch days. Sometimes he would select a sense as soon as he woke up: 'The very first image your senses pick up, such as hearing something, or seeing the colour of something, or feeling your bare feet on the linoleum floor – whichever sense it may be, then that is the day it is. If you've just heard someone clanking a nice bit of metal outside your windows, then it's a sound day.' In the case of sight, he began to focus on specialised aspects such as colour: 'On a colour day, I'd remember the first thing that had struck me when I woke up – a gilt picture frame, the floor, the shaded wall, the light at the window, the sky, the tones of the clouds – or the steely colour of the street, horses, clothes, the texture and colour of any peeling paint I had seen, and so on – and which colours I liked best and why.' Gradually, movement emerged as his favourite area of observation, though he continued to explore other areas. These games helped Lye to sharpen his senses and his memory – and later they would make him an extraordinary film-maker and editor, with the ability to remember long sequences of movements.

As a lecturer, Lye encouraged his students to play sense games as seriously as he had done. He did not insist on movement – he wanted each young artist to discover his or her special strengths. ('I would like you to shape your own shoe as you, and only you, know where it fits best.') He encouraged students to have confidence in their own ability and intuitions, but he also emphasised the need to work hard. Using a metaphor from Hemingway's *The Old Man and the Sea*, he would say, 'Right now you should be building your boat to go way out there and catch some really big ones.'[29]

Another memory exercise was the 'moments' game. Around 1960, he delighted his friends by writing a series of *Happy Moments* which recorded his most intense memories of childhood. Many of them were associated with movement. These were not what an adult would regard as major events but moments of special intensity from a child's point of view. He had had many of these experiences when alone, like the youthful epiphanies recorded by poets such as Wordsworth. Lye wrote in punchy, rhythmic sentences full of colours, smells, tastes and kinesthetic feelings. He urged his students to try to capture their early memories in similar fashion.

'Flash' was the name he gave to his earliest memory (described in the biography chapter), when he kicked a metal can and was astonished to produce a great flash of light and a sound like thunder. 'Rainpool', a typical quiet moment, involved watching a pool after rain with 'a puffy wind skidding over it' making 'riddlings in silver scurrying patterns' on the water. Another moment that helped to educate his sense of movement was the sudden appearance of a butterfly as he lay sunbathing on a yacht. 'It felt like the deck of the world from which to watch the great spanking sail belly out firm in the breeze and feel the pull it gave the

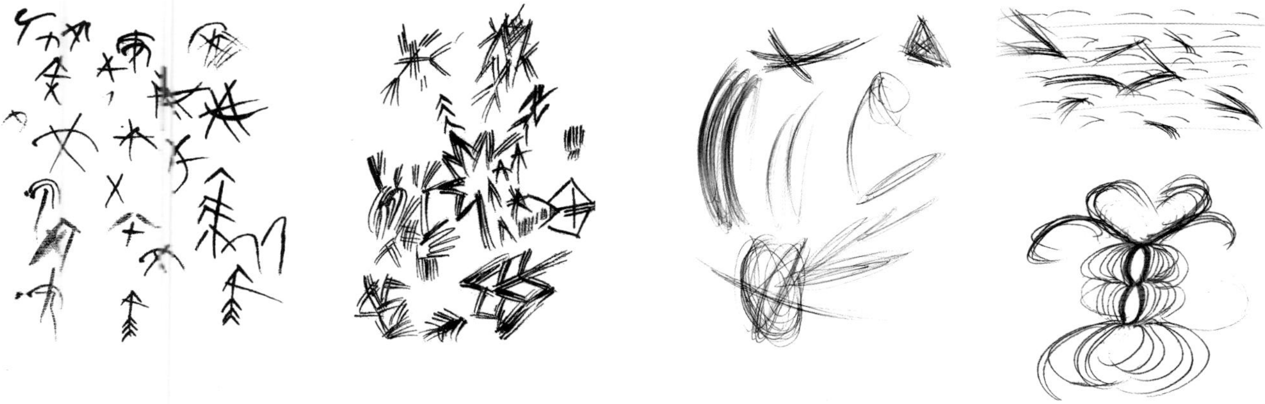

Examples of Lye's 'doodling'. Courtesy Len Lye Foundation.

boat down its mast to the keel and along the deck to my flat back. Then a yellow butterfly stepped out into the blue from behind the creamy sail, and fluttered out against the BLUE.' This was such a precise figure of motion that the memory of it years later could still 'cleave me down the middle like a meat-chopper'. Was it 'the light fluttery motion of [the butterfly's] petal wings? their fragility and strength of purpose? its lightness in contrast to the solid world of the boat and the heavy bouncy sea? or is it that its tremulous flutter was as much part of the breeze as was the sail and my senses?'[30]

He explained to students that whereas most university courses concentrated on strengthening the intellect, he wanted to pay at least as much attention to the body and the senses. He had many other exercises such as observing the movement of an object in great detail (such as a door opening and closing). Everyone was also encouraged to 'doodle' with words, film strips and pieces of metal as a way to generate kinetic or other artistic ideas. Above all, he urged students to practise their favourite exercises constantly, like pianists and athletes who work out every day to 'ensure that the body gets together with the brain at crucial moments'. Lye followed this principle himself in his lifelong study of movement.

Seeing with the Body

> Motion is the province of sensory, neuro-motor aspects of the body, [but] the brain, with its intellect and penchant for literary logic has tried to invest itself with the protagonist [i.e. leading] role in the field of motion, and to make enactment its – the brain's – business, rather than seeking [to portray] the bodily sense of kinetic being which permeates our life . . .[31]

Lye believed that 'in the subject of kinetic art, the body is the primary source of creative inspiration'.[32] Much European kinetic art exploited the intellectual appeal of technology, mathematics and geometrical forms. Many experimental films seemed to him to place too much emphasis on cerebral aspects, and this tendency was encouraged by academic forms of art criticism.

His view of art was reminiscent of the famous jazz slogan, 'It don't mean a thing (if it ain't got that swing).'[33] *Free Radicals* makes many viewers feel like dancing – not only because the music has a strong, rhythmical beat but also because the images have so much kinetic energy. For him, the word 'kinetic' was interchangeable with 'kinesthetic', a term that refers to 'the sensation of position, movement, tension . . . of parts of the body, perceived through nerve end organs in muscles, tendons and joints'.[34]

He was always grateful for having grown up in a country with a strongly physical, outdoors culture. He swam, played rugby and became his school's unofficial boxing champion. He was slight in build but did well on the sports field as a 'runner and zig-zagger'. After leaving school, he spent some years working in manual labouring jobs. But as a voracious reader who loved public libraries, he was certainly not anti-intellectual – rather, he wanted to develop both brain and body, to ensure that in his art-making 'the body gets together with the brain at crucial moments'. Lye used to joke about students being required to leave their bodies at the door of the art school.

Viewing art can vicariously involve the sense of touch when we respond to a work such as a thickly-painted Abstract Expressionist canvas, running our eyes over the textures and imagining the actions of the brush. It is also a physical experience to observe the actions of athletes and intuitively share their sense of strain. A professional tennis player watching an opponent serve has an immediate 'feel' for the likely speed and direction of the ball. An everyday action such as driving a car on the motorway involves not only intellectual calculations of speed and direction but also subtle sensations of touch as our hands adjust the steering-wheel and our foot works the accelerator or brake pedal. If the driver ahead comes to an abrupt stop and we brake just in time, we have a gut-level sense of the solidity of the other car as it comes rushing towards us. Or if we manoeuvre our vehicle through a narrow gap, our eyes function like antennae with a heightened sense of the objects on either side. Kinesthetic feelings of this kind were part of Lye's vocabulary as an artist of motion, and he spoke of them as 'body english'. Originally this colloquial phrase referred to physical signs of encouragement,

Lye paused in the midst of writing an essay to make this drawing. It illustrates his highly physical sense of the writing process. Courtesy Len Lye Foundation.

plain yellow note-paper, & the pen-nib ink flowing on it as the nib makes a pleasant rubbing sound on the sounding board of the bread-board & I can feel its vibrations transmitted to my thigh bone

& I'm dealing with sensation

&

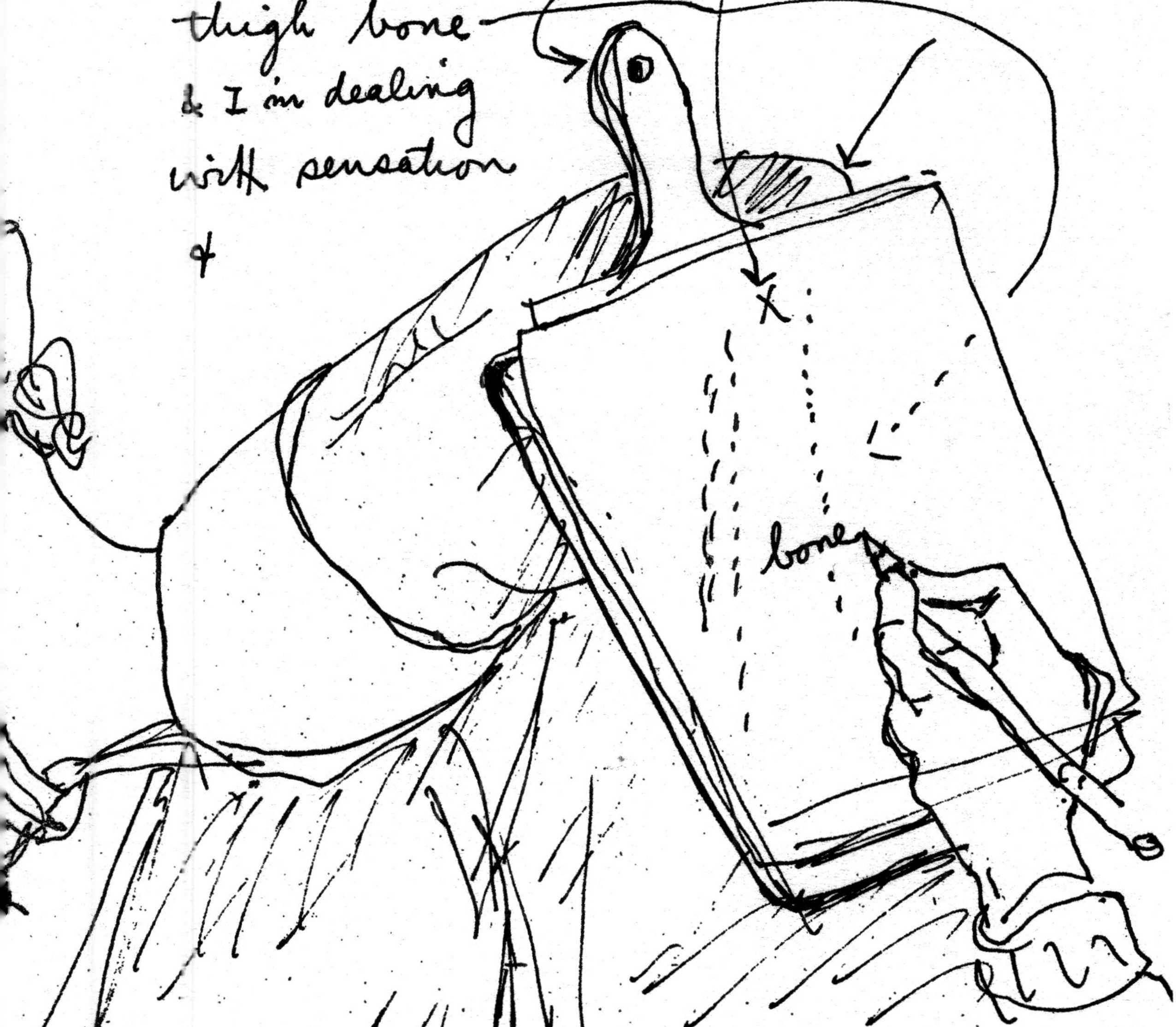

usually unconscious. For example, 'Who hasn't seen the purposeful body english of the putter who attempts to squirm his ball into the hole by remote control as [the ball] rolls towards it?'[35]

It is through the experience of his or her own body that a child learns about balance, energy, speed, tension, resistance, weight and the constant tug-of-war with gravity. This kind of information is constantly passing from the body to the brain through fibres in the spinal cord. As such knowledge develops, it is used not only to control one's own movements but also to interpret those of others. 'Proprioception' refers to the process of gaining information through one's own body in contrast to gaining it through the senses ('exteroception').[36] Sometimes described as the 'sixth sense', proprioception can be as much a source of aesthetic experience as sight and sound. Barbara Montero comments that 'a trained dancer often trusts proprioception *more* than vision when it comes to evaluating aesthetic qualities of his or her movements and positions', and expert musicians may immediately sense they have made the right or wrong move on their instrument, independent of the sound produced.[37] The famous percussion player Evelyn Glennie is deaf but she can play complex music by means of touch and proprioception. While 'much of the proprioceptive information we receive about the movements of others, and even of ourselves, is below the level of conscious awareness' (as Montero observes), a young artist can set out deliberately, as Lye did, to develop this kind of sensitivity through 'sense games'.[38] He wrote:

> When not observing motion I felt it in my actions. For example, [as a young man] I worked outdoors for a living, and I didn't move an inch without consciously trying to feel my various muscles working in rhythm while I enjoyed the motions my body made, shovelling, riding, sewing up wheat bags. My entire world was in motion with never a dull moment. Indeed, I got my feeling for motion down to the most subtle of empathies, such as the way both ends of a pen waggled in relation to one another as I wrote, or how my eyeballs moved in their sockets as I scanned lines of print.[39]

It is important to consider how different the cultural context was when Lye was starting out. Although New Zealand was a strongly sports-minded country, there was still a puritanical, Victorian suspicion of the sexual body. As he summed up this attitude, 'The brain, up there in the head, is thought to be miles better than the body, down . . . below. This up-down lingo is irreparably tied into our definitions of good and bad.'[40] Serious art was meant to cater to the higher instincts,

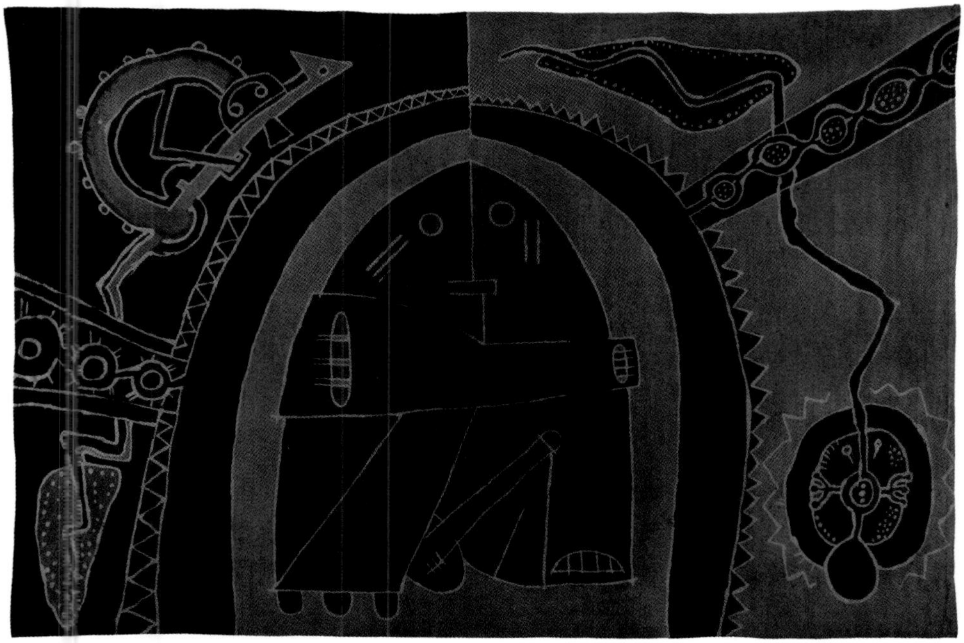

This 1979 acrylic painting *Polynesian Connection* was based on the batik Lye exhibited with the Seven and Five Society in London in 1928. Courtesy Len Lye Foundation.

and the censors were quick to punish exceptions. Encountering a similar prudishness in London, Lye challenged it with images such as *Polynesian Connection*, a batik exhibited in 1928.[41] In the following year, an exhibition of D. H. Lawrence's paintings was closed by the London police who sought to burn the canvases. That Lye's batik escaped the same fate was presumably because the image was so stylised that censors failed to notice the female genitals and erect penis.

Polynesian Connection was inspired by a sexually explicit Maori carving.[42] One of Lye's reasons for valuing Maori and other tribal traditions was because artists from those cultures seemed more at ease with their bodies than their European counterparts. He developed his own interpretation of tribal art that regarded its supposed 'distortions' as logically based on proprioceptive feelings. For example:

> I thought the reason why African sculpture looked so bodily right was because the . . . artist didn't carve eyes, noses, mouths in the way they looked in everyday life . . . but emphasized their dimensional *feeling* . . . . If you close your eyes and think of your nose and concentrate on the feeling of its shape, you can soon come to feel that it is much larger than your mirror version . . . . you can make it keep

> going until it makes a high ridge over your head. Or, try to feel the shape of your face . . . and you'll find that it can seem either to be smooth and round and flat, or have undulating contours in smooth hills and dales. Still with your eyes closed now concentrate on your cheekbones. You'll find they can be felt to protrude even beyond your nose. And the same treatment can be given to get the bodily feeling – rather than the brain's recollection – of your arms, legs and torso.[43]

Whether or not such an interpretation was valid, it provided Lye with a way to engage with proprioceptive feelings. It heightened his response to tribal art, and also to modernist sculpture by artists such as Constantin Brancusi.[44]

Other aspects of Lye's art that reflected his emphasis on the body were a preference for organic rather than geometrical forms in his paintings and batiks, and his use of dance music in films in contrast to the classical music favoured by European experimental film-makers such as Fischinger. In the 1940s and 1950s, he was strongly interested in emerging forms of psychology that focused on links between body and brain, and his comments about 'sensory, neuro-motor aspects of the body' (quoted above) reflected this influence. While Lye's sculptures of the 1950s and 1960s did not directly represent the human body, they certainly evoked many forms of 'bodily feeling'. For example, the critic Dore Ashton spoke of their 'erotic undulation' like 'a belly dance'.[45] Emily Genauer of the *Herald-Tribune* regarded *Blade* as so erotic that she felt its value as art was compromised.[46] And Ann Lye judged *Flip* to be 'the sexiest sculpture Len has ever made'.[47]

Lye's criticisms of the 'false brain/body value dichotomy' linked him to an alternative 20th-century tradition of artists and theorists who called for more attention to be given to proprioception, kinesthesia and 'neuro-motor aspects'.[48] Mabel Todd, author of *The Thinking Body* (1937), was one of several theorists of this kind whose work had an impact on modern dance. Others included Frederick Alexander and Rudolf Laban. In *The Phenomenology of Perception* (1945), Maurice Merleau-Ponty called for a greater awareness of the body in philosophy. Poet Charles Olson's essays 'Projective Verse' (1950) and 'Proprioception' (1960) explored the implications of the fact 'that one's life is informed from and by one's own body', including the act of writing. Olson's interest in 'kinesthesia', 'movement' and 'energy' was shaped by his powerful sense of 'the DEPTH implicit in physical being'.[49] These writers developed their ideas independently, in separate subject areas.[50] Some, such as Olson, were strongly resisted by the arts establishment.

Lye appears not to have known of writers such as Olson or Merleau-Ponty; but he did know and feel strong affinities with the work of the dramatist Samuel Beckett, as he explained during a 1966 panel discussion:

> He [Beckett] seems to say, 'Well, there's something being overlooked around here, and that's our feeling of bodily being, the bodily sense of our physical, daily routines' . . . . And so he is an example of an artist taking one of the many facets of our 'bodyness' out of ourselves to examine it and respond to its reality in this strange, new way . . . . Well, anyhow, to me kinetic art is plucking this kind of kinetic, sensory twanging of experience which we take for granted in our bodily sense of presence. For instance, you're sitting around there, and you would not feel the actuality of your existence unless you felt, sitting there on your fanny, that you had all your bodily weight to anchor you to your reality.[51]

When Lye watched narrative films, he devoted much of his attention to body language. He would vividly characterise actors in physical or gestural terms such as 'the nifty Balinese hand motions of a James Cagney'; or 'the mollasses of a James Dean spreading his bodily attitudes all over the armchair'; or 'the celery stick walk of that stick of celery, *High Noon* star Gary Cooper'; or 'the knobbly cast of the star Elliott Gould, bemused, his mouth full of marbles, finally flapping his foot-flippers enroute insouciantly to some horizon or other'.[52] Movie-going companions would be surprised when Lye declared that the highlight of the film was the 'choreography' of a brief action sequence they had scarcely noticed. Underlying all of his responses to films, literature and the visual arts was his commitment to a style of seeing that incorporated 'the bodily sense of kinetic being'.

Links with Science

Over the past 20 years, new scientific methods of scanning and imaging have revolutionised our understanding of the brain and its relationship with the body. Lye would have been fascinated by these developments, and they have given scientific support to ideas he arrived at intuitively. Recent discoveries have confirmed the sophisticated ability of the brain to combine information from many parts of the body and from the senses. Complex processes are involved in assembling our image of the visual world within the cerebral cortex. Although there is an intricate map of interconnections, creating a unified end product, there are regions of the brain that specialise in particular aspects of seeing. Researchers have identified an

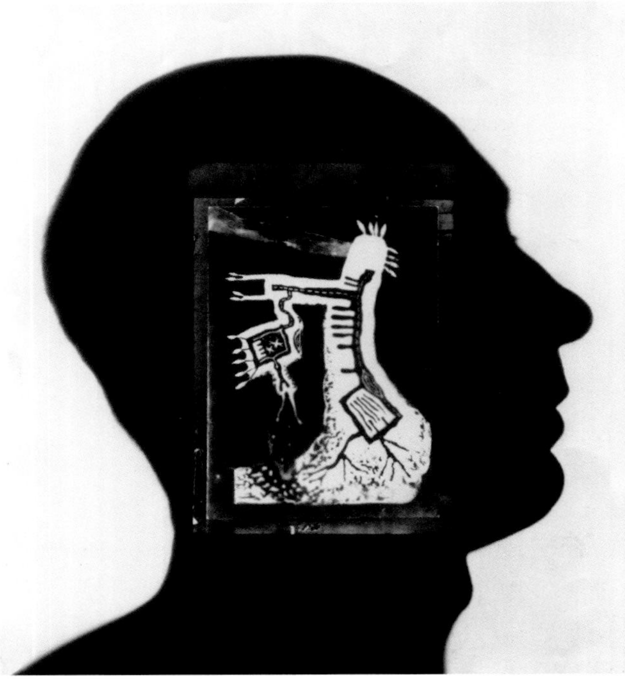

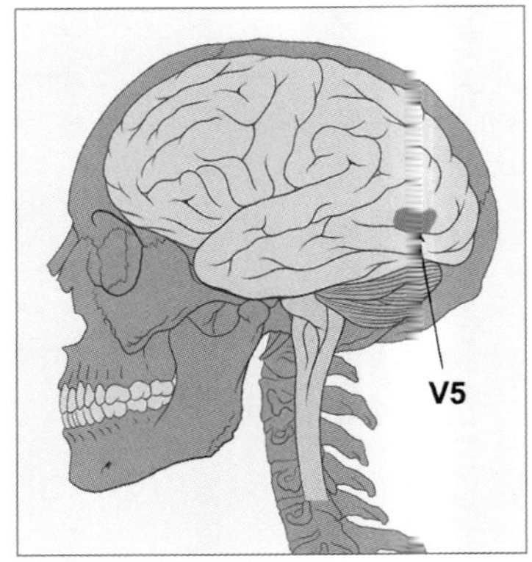

LEFT Lye's 1947 photogram *Self-Portrait*, which incorporates his 1930 photogram *Self-Planting at Night*. Courtesy Len Lye Foundation. RIGHT The 'V5' area of the brain specialises in the processing of motion. Drawing of skull and brain by Patrick J. Lynch, medical illustrator, and C. Carl Jaffe, MD, cardiologist.

area known as 'V5' or 'MT' ('middle temporal area') that specialises in movement. In 'The Neurology of Kinetic Art', a much-discussed 1994 essay in the journal *Brain*, Semir Zeki and Mathew Lamb argue that V5 'is optimally responsive to any visual stimulus in which motion predominates, which is of course what happens in kinetic art'.[53] V5 is a notably old region of the brain, shown by the fact that it is more mature at birth than many other regions. It works closely with another area – V3 – which also analyses forms in motion but focuses on edges and lines, a type of information more relevant to 'the mobiles of Calder' which the authors interpret as an early, partial form of kinetic art.[54] They add, 'Just as physiologists have managed to identify visual areas in the cerebral cortex specialized for visual motion so artists, through their experiments, have unknowingly developed an art form [kinetic sculpture] seemingly tailored for an optimal stimulation of these visual areas.'[55]

The authors 'do not mean to imply that the resulting aesthetic experience is due solely to the activity of V5 but only that V5 is necessary for it'.[56] They note that V5 receives a variety of inputs, which is 'in keeping with the view that each area of the cerebral cortex will use any kind of visual information . . . to undertake its function'.[57] Although this is a paper written for scientists, it reflects an informed interest in kinetic art. More recently, Zeki has remarked, 'I hold the somewhat unusual view that artists are in some sense neurologists, studying the brain with techniques that are unique to them, but studying unknowingly the brain and its organization nevertheless.'[58] Lye would have been delighted with the confirmation that his 'new category of art' corresponded to a specific area of the brain, which was very old in evolutionary terms, but I think he would add, 'What makes you think artists are "unknowing"?'

Recent research has strengthened the link with proprioception through the discovery in 1995 of 'mirror neurons'. So far these have been studied in detail only in monkeys, but there is growing evidence that a similar system exists in human beings. Scientists have discovered that the same neurons fire in the brain whether one is performing a task or merely watching someone engaged in a similar activity. There is, then, a direct link between perceiving and proprioceiving. This suggests that mirror neurons are an important part of education – babies can learn by watching adults because behaviour rehearsal takes place in the brain. Vilayanur S. Ramachandran wrote in a 2006 essay, 'I predict that mirror neurons will do for psychology what DNA did for biology: they will provide a unifying framework and help explain a host of mental abilities that have hitherto remained mysterious and inaccessible to experiments.'[59] This noted neurologist also suggested that when the mirror neuron system in human beings evolved to a higher stage than in apes, it permitted the rapid development of language, culture and art – the 'great leap forward' in human evolution that researchers have known about for a long time but have not previously been able to explain.

Neuroesthetics – the application of neuroscience to the arts – remains controversial, but kinetic sculpture is one area in which it clearly succeeds in raising useful questions.[60] Such research also lends support to the tradition of incorporating the physical dimension within discussions of art – the kind of holistic approach Lye always championed.

Empathy

> In spite of the shock that terms like neuromuscular, motor-sensory, empathy and so on may give to the sensitive, philosophically-minded, introspective artist and critic, they will have to get around to such terms if they want eventually to bring the arts into relation with the age we live in. It is an age of scientific reference to the natural world . . . and to the life we enact and experience. Art manifestos and explanations of work in many catalogues these days look medievally inadequate.[61]

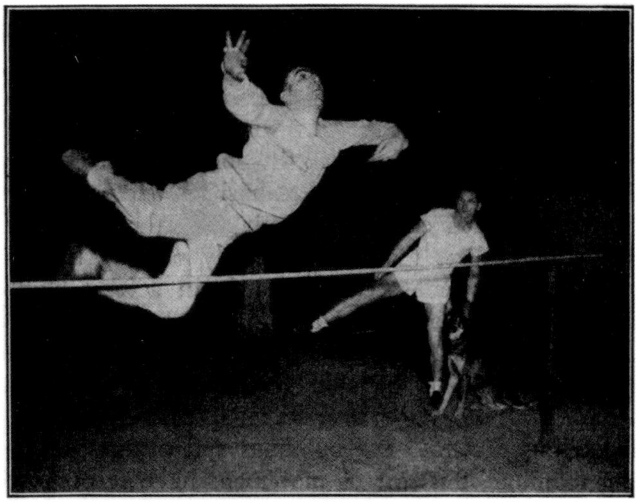

This photograph illustrated the section of a psychology textbook that introduced Lye to the concept of 'empathy'. The caption reads: 'Blind Bill Kelley clearing the pole, with his trainer Peter Bennett watching. Notice the empathic response of the trainer.' The author, Herbert S. Langfeld, also described spectators intently swaying as they watched an acrobat.

In an earlier chapter, I discussed the rich tradition of art criticism in the late 19th century based on the concept of empathy. This was inspired by the psychology of its time. Today, science has given that concept a new lease of life by discovering a basis for it in the brain – the system of mirror neurons – as a 'mechanism' that enables direct experiential understanding of objects and the inner world of others'.[62] During the intervening years, however, the concept of empathy passed generally out of favour. Worringer's influential book *Abstraction and Empathy* dealt a blow to the tradition by linking it with naturalism and suggesting that abstraction was more relevant to modern art. The term continued to have a specialised use in other fields such as psychoanalysis, but seldom cropped up in art criticism.[63] Lye appears to have had no direct knowledge of the 19th-century 'empathy' tradition, and this was hardly surprising as it was primarily German and most of the texts were untranslated; but he was excited to discover the concept in 1946 through a two-page summary in an American psychology textbook. The author was Herbert S. Langfeld whose 1920 study, *The Aesthetic Attitude*, was mentioned in my earlier discussion of the empathy tradition. Lye remarked, 'I've wondered what to call the biggest part of all experience, and now I know.'[64] Two sentences in the textbook perfectly articulated his own approach: 'It is as if we had projected our own experience into the object of our perception. This sort of perception has been termed *empathy*, or a feeling of ourselves into the object of regard.'[65] Langfeld emphasised the physical dimension and included a photograph that was a classic illustration of 'body english' (an athletics trainer leaning forwards anxiously as his blind student leapt over a hurdle).

Lye may also have heard the term empathy being used by the painter Hans Hofmann, who rescued it from Worringer's talk of naturalism by applying the concept to abstract art. For Hofmann, empathy was an 'intuitive faculty' that made an artist sensitive to 'formal and spatial relations or tensions',[66] but he did not stress the body aspects that were Lye's key concern. The term also began to be championed by psychotherapists like Carl Rogers.[67] It is clear, however, that the version of 'empathy' that most excited Lye came from scientists such as Langfeld who sought to combine psychology with physiology. In the 1940s, Lye turned away from 'literary' forms of psychology and psychoanalysis, and instead immersed himself in body-oriented, scientific studies. He was fascinated by W. H. Sheldon's book *The Varieties of Temperament: A Psychology of Constitutional Differences* (1942) which explored links between personality and body type.[68] Lye asked Sheldon if he could make a film about him and his ideas, but the psychologist declined the invitation because of ill health. Lye also discussed film possibilities with Nina Bull whose 'Attitude Theory of Emotion' linked emotions to 'neuromuscular events' such as facial expressions, changes of posture and breathing patterns. Bull challenged common sense by insisting that physical response preceded emotion, and she used the provocative title *The Body and its Mind*.[69] Lye did not like the more extreme behavourist aspects of Bull's work, but he was fascinated by her attempt to bring mind and body together.

'Empathy' was seldom mentioned in scientific literature, but psychologists turned to the concept when they needed to discuss how people interpreted and responded to one another, and biologists used it to debate the role of social feelings in evolution (another area of science that interested Lye). There were attempts to establish methods of detecting and measuring feelings of empathy objectively. Lye took the term and developed it in his own way. In some respects, he was rediscovering the ideas of the 19th-century tradition. He started with the assumption that the activity of seeing involved the body as much as the mind. Expanding on Langfeld, he wrote, 'Some degree of empathy occurs with all "image" formation' because there is always 'a bit of projection of . . . your bodily sense to it.' And: 'Empathy prances blatantly into the picture when that world is given space and dimension, for dimension and space are but ideas dragged out of the organism's own sense of its neuromuscular and spatially motor functioning body.'[70] He also argued that one reason why each person's vision of the world is unique is because no two bodies are identical.

Such ideas were not original, but he had new twists to add, such as his heightened emphasis on movement. For him, 'movement' and 'identity' were so intimately linked that he could have reworked Descartes' famous *cogito* formula as 'I move therefore I am'. Earlier writers in the empathy tradition had paid a great deal of attention to implied movement but they had not talked about literal movement in art. Also, many of these writers had been purely critics or theorists whereas Lye's approach was that of a practising artist. His discussions of empathy were a form of preparation for making art or for viewing it in a more active and physical way. By connecting empathy with the idea of figures of motion, he also helped to shift the focus from naturalism to abstract patterns.

Lye's first exercises in empathy had been his attempts with eyes closed to think his way in to the form of ancient African sculpture. Then in the 1940s he adopted 'shoes' as a favourite metaphor. He wrote both a poem and a long prose work entitled 'Shoe of my Mind'. The colloquial phrase 'learning to walk in someone else's shoes' is usually applied to sharing the emotions of another person, but Lye extended it to the sharing of bodily feelings and kinetic sensations. For example, 'Empathy is the sweat in the soles of your palms when you walk in the shoes of the tight-roper as you sniff his height from down here in your seat. What a mess should he fall with you in his shoes . . . feeling your weight as he balances a facsimile weight on his rope.'[71] Watching a tight-rope walker had been used as an example by earlier empathy theorists such as Theodor Lipps and Herbert Langfeld, but Lye with his 'sniff' and 'sweat' heightened the physicality.[72]

Another of his favourite themes was the act of walking. He was fascinated by the experience of instant physical empathy with a fellow pedestrian – such as watching someone slip and almost fall on an icy pavement. To catch that person's eye just as they recovered their balance was an experience close to telepathy. In 'Chairmanship', a lengthy exploration of 'our bodily feelings towards chairs', Lye spoke of his empathy for the kinesthetic poetry of Arthur Rimbaud, such as this satirical vision of conservative old men glued to their chairs:

> They've grafted in long, epileptic love-embrace
> Their weird bone-structures to the big, black skeleton
> Of every chair; their feet endlessly interlace
> With the rachitic bars, while days go on and on.[73]

Lye enlarged the scope of his 'shoes' metaphor to include every form of movement in nature:

> I got so that I could feel myself into the shoes of anything that moved, from a grasshopper to a hawk, a fish to a yacht, from a cloud to the shimmering rustle of ivy leaves on a brick wall. Such shoes were around in profusion . . . . I could levitate with the curling smoke, scud with the wind-blown leaf, sashay with the reflection of masts on water, shimmy with the flapping flag, glide with the snake.

He turned empathy into another sense exercise:

> . . . when you look at the linear direction and timing of the interstices described by the lines of flight made by a flock of gulls soaring around in some updraught, you try to feel their flight by imagining it seeping into your bones by some kinetic kind of osmosis. Soon there you are, high above with outstretched arms and flight-held body banking and following the gull's lines of flight, while at the same time aware of the patterns and figures of motion you'd *all* be making.[74]

His most original contribution to the tradition of empathy was the idea of explicitly internalising movements in nature by matching each one with a similar movement in the observer's body – in other words, turning exteroception into proprioception. 'The Art that Moves' described this process of 'inner echo' in detail:

> I can be noting how the shining black back of the speeding porpoise humps over on its line of dive down into the emerald sea, while at the same time searching around inside myself to find a spot to which to attach the feeling of the porpoise's motion. In this instance, I come to feel the spot is my right shoulder. I feel as if I am putting my shoulder to a wheel of waves breaking in the same direction as its motion . . . . so that now . . . I have only to feel my . . . shoulder [to remember the porpoise] . . . . I relate the floppy up-and-down motion made by the wings of a flying heron to my lungs (perhaps because the heron's wing-work unconsciously reminds me of the way a wind-bellows works) . . . . When a cat stretches, it's not my back which empathizes with its action; instead, it's the way my instep feels when I stretch back my toes.[75]

He extended this exercise to the body's own movements, such as the assignment about breathing he gave to his New York University students: 'Close your eyes. Breathe in and make the air coming in at the tip of your nostrils feel like the peak of a huge comber. (Hiroshige's wave as an image.) Then, as you breathe out, make your belly the back wash of the wave from the beach into the sea for the next breath which is, of course, another huge comber.'[76] This was empathy in reverse, comparing one's own experience to a movement in nature.

He saw his constant absorption of figures of motion through empathy as a way of feeding the mysterious process of imagination. The reverse process was 'projection' – making and exhibiting a film or kinetic sculpture that others could empathise with. His aim was never merely to reproduce what he had already seen in nature or art but to bring something new into the world, a 'form of motion which fascinates me because I can't make out why . . . . Later I may see some association with the motion of a diving fish, but if I'd seen this sort of thing at the start, I'd more than likely drop the project.'[77] (For Lye, the art of empathy was not limited to naturalism as earlier critics had assumed it was.)

Figures of motion could be projected on any scale. Lye was accustomed to seeing his tiny hand-drawn images blown up by the projector onto large cinema screens. There were, however, two opposing tendencies in his art. On the one hand, he was interested in movements of any size, and the images in his paintings suggested discoveries made with either the microscope or the telescope. His ability to paint or scratch on film proved that he could work superbly on a tiny scale. On the other hand, he wrote:

> It's mostly the bigger the better [because] our Muse [of motion] . . . increases empathic tension through an increase of scale . . . . For example, the falling motion of a small shrub in contrast to that of a giant redwood tree, or the tiny wavelet on the beach and the big comber, have distinctly different effects on the degree of our empathic response. There are identical principles of gravity and arced lines of motion in each of these instances. But our lack of response to the smaller objects is in marked contrast to the feeling we get from the larger.[78]

He found that if kinetic works were small, people tended not to take them seriously but to associate them with toys or games. He was fascinated by the tradition of the 'sublime' in art. For all these reasons, he was greatly drawn to size and deeply frustrated that he never had an opportunity to make monumental sculptures. He did not agree that large-scale 'projection' meant losing a sense of human relevance, for it was possible to empathise with any movement if we related it back to our bodies. Still, he conceded that at least some of his sculptures worked better on an intimate scale with a concentrated figure of motion. (Of *Singing Blade* he said, 'it's impressive that such a small object can kick up such a racket . . .')[79]

The Old Brain

When Lye argued for a greater awareness of the body in art, he also championed what he called the 'old brain'. There was much overlap between these two themes, but the old brain represented the body's *deepest* level of intuitive awareness. For him, this was the way of thinking about the 'unconscious' that was most relevant and useful to a kinetic artist. Artists, including Lye himself, had been hugely influenced by the ideas of Sigmund Freud and Carl Gustav Jung, but Lye felt it was time for a new model that gave primary emphasis to the body. Each of us has a surface level of knowledge about the body's movements, but we can also seek to explore deeper levels. Lye came to think of this exploration as re-establishing links between human experience and the ancient, intensely kinesthetic world of animals and reptiles, in which instincts were sharpened by the struggle for survival.

In the mid-1930s, he was happy to exhibit with the Surrealist movement as the most lively avant-garde group in London, but their notion of the unconscious seemed to him too 'literary'. Though he made an exception for Surrealists with a free, abstract style such as Joan Miró, he was not impressed by the much talked-about imagery of Salvador Dalí. In his 1936 essay 'Notes on a Short Colour Film' (1936), he wrote: 'In contemporary art, intelligent people have been influenced by psycho-analysis to exploit the literary content of the dream element in our mentality . . . . Many of these painters still use realistic imagery, because, perhaps, they cannot yet use the pure visual impulses of their minds . . . . But we should understand that dreams . . . represent a kind of mental process that, as a guide for visual imagery, is lazy, chaotic and unreliable.'[80] He resumed the argument two years later in his poetic prose sequence 'Song Time Stuff', suggesting that the Surrealist aesthetics 'ruffles only the top of the lake' instead of floating down 'to lake bottom'.[81]

He greatly valued the Surrealist method of doodling (or 'automatic drawing and writing') as a starting point for his art, but in his own experience this resulted not in dream-like images but in abstract lines with kinetic energy. When he was painting or scratching a film, he felt he produced his very best results when he entered a kind of rhythmic trance. For him this was a matter of tapping the bodily unconscious, in the same way dancers can create a greater flow and excitement in their movements by letting their bodies take control.[82] He understood, however, that this was the fruit of years of practice.

The alert, physical directness of an animal remains part of our human potential. Ted Hughes (a poet frequently drawn to this theme) wrote in 'Thrushes':

> Terrifying are the attent sleek thrushes on the lawn, . . .
> Triggered to stirrings beyond sense . . . .

Is it their single-minded-sized skulls, or a trained
Body, or genius, or a nestful of brats
Gives their days this bullet and automatic
Purpose? Mozart's brain had it, and the shark's mouth . . .[83]

Lye was fascinated by the earliest stages of evolution, when movement was the key to survival and life was directly interwoven with the processes of nature. *Tusalava* and most of his paintings, batiks and book covers were visions of this pre-human state. He was interested not in dreams but in what Aboriginal culture calls the Dreamtime. His 1948 story 'A Tree has its Heart in its Roots' illustrated his ability to imagine this environment, describing the experience of a blind, prehistoric creature at the precise moment when evolution invented eyesight: 'He knows all things by feeling them with his feet. Where this is a big black log he finds it. He thinks of what he finds so hard a waterfall of seeing comes out of his head and it falls on the end of the log. So he sees with his head what he feels with his feet and it is the world in the shape of a black log.' A red snake and a green snake emerge from the log, and 'the first great Seer' (as he has now become) is able to recognise their colours and watch them go about their activities. And he is able to intervene to help others evolve. The story ends many thousands of years later in the age of human beings: 'Today when people stand up straight and still on hills and feel the earth with their feet they are most like a tree because a tree has its heart in its roots. And people still know most about the earth from planting things in it and standing like trees.'[84]

A decade later, Lye was delighted to learn that neuroscience had confirmed the existence of an ancient area of the brain which contained the functions that had developed first in the course of evolution. This was a relatively large region, separate from the small 'movement' centre discussed earlier in this chapter. The implications were spelled out by Paul D. MacLean:

> Man, it appears, has inherited essentially three brains. Frugal Nature in developing her paragon threw nothing away. The oldest of his brains is basically reptilian; the second has been inherited from lower mammals; and the third and newest brain is a late mammalian development which reaches a pinnacle in man and gives him his unique power of symbolic language. This can be said with some assurance, because the big brain which sits on top has been more thoroughly investigated than the other two.[85]

MacLean's terms 'old brain', 'mid-brain' and 'new brain' were picked up by the media and became firmly established in the field of popular science. Lye saw 'the old brain' as coinciding exactly with what he had been describing for years as the deepest level of the unconscious.

MacLean characterised the old brain as 'reptilian' because it specialised in the kinds of instinctive behaviour found, for example, in snakes. In humans, it consisted of the brain stem (which regulated the heart, digestion and breathing) and the cerebellum (which coordinated muscles, posture and balance). In other words, the old brain was concerned with the body, with physical survival and with movement. The mid-brain was the 'limbic system' or 'mammalian brain', which added emotions and provided better memory storage. This was also an ancient part in evolutionary terms, and Lye sometimes incorporated it in his 'old brain'. MacLean also did so at times because the brains of the earliest mammals consisted of only these two parts, a combination he described as 'the old mammalian brain'. The large 'new brain', also known as the 'neo-cortex' or 'neo-mammalian brain', added the powers of language, logical thinking and conscious control. MacLean stressed that while each of the three centres had a distinct character and specialised functions, they were profoundly inter-connected.[86] Less thoughtful versions of the theory tended to assume a hierarchical relationship, with the 'new brain' necessarily in control and the 'old brain' described in negative terms as primitive and inflexible. As MacLean noted, this reptilian brain had been less 'thoroughly investigated' than 'the big brain which sits [literally] on top'. It was basic to Lye's approach that there should be no hierarchy – artists needed to cultivate their old as strongly as their new brain.

As the Surrealist notion of the unconscious had inspired a great upsurge in art, Lye saw the cultivation of the old brain as having the potential to make a similar impact, particularly in kinetic art, which had been too much dominated by the intellect. In his writings on the subject, he saw one of the functions of the new brain as helping him to advocate for the old; but both centres had a part to play in sculpture, which combined the logic of engineering with the intuitions of the old brain. He had great respect for science and was delighted to use new technologies when he had access to them, but he saw kinetic art as needing to remain firmly grounded in nature and the body. It needed to have 'its heart in its roots' so it could continue to tap the most subtle kinesthetic instincts. The old brain represented the deepest layer of knowledge. This notion of a mother lode which enriched the best and most intuitive works of art was Lye's equivalent of

Jung's 'collective unconscious', a region of the mind so deep that artists were only rarely able to penetrate or draw from it.

Around 1966, when there was much talk about genetics – by artists as well as scientists – Lye added a further dimension to his theory. If scientists were correct in suggesting that the history of evolution was still encoded in our genes then an artist attuned to the old brain could access images from that ancient database. Therefore art had the potential to anticipate scientific discoveries about evolution or about the fundamental workings of nature. Lye offered some of his own paintings and films as evidence.[87] Because he based most of his case on static images, however, this aspect of the old brain lies outside the scope of the present book.

Since Lye's death, new developments in neuroscience have shifted attention away from MacLean's ideas. His basic conception of 'the triune brain' has never been disproved, but brain scanning has provided so much new detail that researchers have focused on the micro rather than the macro scale.[88] When all the intricate networks of neural circuitry have been mapped and it becomes possible to return to the big picture, it is hard to predict how closely the new model will still resemble MacLean's. Nevertheless, Lye would have been pleased with several of the research findings to date. In addition to the discovery of V5, researchers have confirmed that there is a constant, two-way flow of information between the cortex and the 'sub-cortical' areas (where muscles, joints and tendons are at work). The cerebellum functions as a kind of way-station, both receiving data and passing it on. (Interestingly, the word used for this transmitting of data is 'projection'.) The thalamus, which helps to link the cerebellum to the cortex, is thought to function as a translator, processing body information into a form readable by the new brain. There is so much dialogue occurring within these intricate networks that a simple hierarchical model no longer makes sense.

Research develops so rapidly that Lye's notion of the 'old brain' may become dated from a scientific point of view, but it should still be useful to artists as a guide to their becoming better attuned to signals from that source. This is a matter of accessing not only body knowledge (proprioceptive and kinesthetic information) but also the old brain's flashes of insight into the workings of nature. Such an artist will be 'Triggered to stirrings beyond sense', like the brain of a reptile – or a new Mozart.

Working by Hand

In a field such as kinetic sculpture, the making of things has increasingly become the domain of the computer and automation. Lye understood the value of technology but his art serves as a reminder that there is much to be gained by retaining some 'hand-made' aspects, particularly in the initial stages. This went with his habit of developing art by a long process of trial and error, and his very direct and physical response to materials. Because he thought of his sculptures as performers rather than objects, he wanted an intimate knowledge of how a particular kind of steel or aluminium was likely to behave. This involved a long dialogue with his material, which gave time for 'old brain' ideas to surface. He was like a choreographer watching his dancers doing exercises, looking for signs of grace or tension, figuring out what they could do best and what their limits were. Metal for him was as much a part of nature as the body since it had to obey the laws of energy, gravity and natural harmonics, and it responded to context and changing ambience (such as wind and temperature). Lye also liked to experiment with the sounds he could make with each piece of metal. He described the initial process as doodling:

> If it's to get going on a solid figure of motion, then it's a . . . messing-around doodling sort of attitude that nabs me. I go around my studio looking at this or that, picking up bits of wood or steel or, say, a piece of rope. I might lift up the end of the rope and slip it down to make it waggle like an undulating snake along the floor . . . . From the rope I progress to a long band of steel I'd picked up in the street. It undulates up and down, more like a sea serpent than a snake.[89]

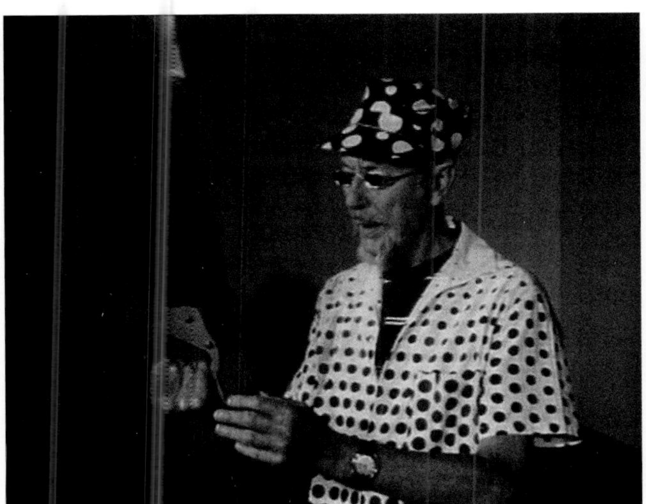

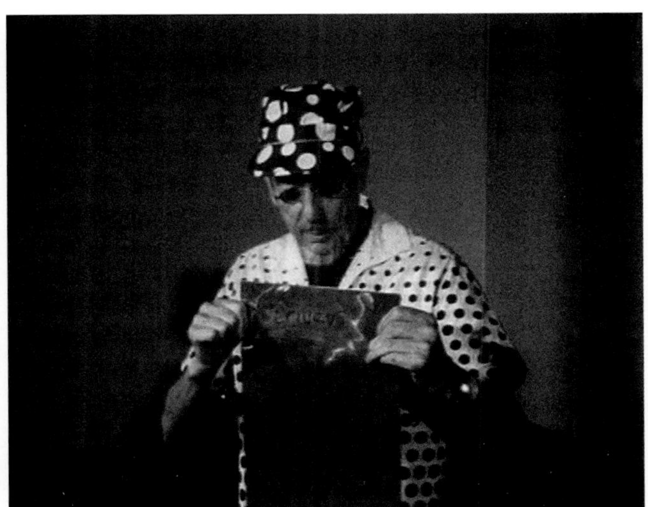

Lye liked to begin work on any kinetic sculpture by hand. Here we see him waggling a saw and shaking a piece of steel, to demonstrate how he 'doodled with metal'. Courtesy Len Lye Foundation.

This creative approach distinguished Lye from kinetic sculptors whose initial concept was mathematical or geometrical. Their high-tech approach tended to involve the imposition of form onto material, whereas he was interested in the unique forms that the material had the potential to deliver. While the shapes that his sculptures create are purely abstract, it is always easy to empathise with and respond to them physically. Lye was acutely sensitive to the physical properties of each piece of material – its weight, thickness, surface texture, lustre, flexibility, springiness, sound and so on. To quote some of his typical comments about materials, he said of *Universe*: 'Above the [steel] band hangs a compressed cork ball. Now that compressed cork is very important because we tried all sorts of material – plastic, glass, metal, wood, leather, baseballs . . . . And we found that this compressed cork, which we went all over the place to find, made the best tone of all . . . this sonorous sound.'[90] On the board for *Grass*: 'This was an absolutely fantastically weathered seasoned piece of mahogany that made this beautiful Stradivarius-type perfect resonant sound.'[91] On *Moonbead*: 'It was a very tricky thing to find the right bead that would spring up from the shoulder it was resting on where the two rods join. That bead had to be a certain thinness and to have a certain width in its relationship to the diameter of the rod it was on. If I had it too heavy, it wouldn't swing up, or if I had it too light it would go too far . . . . It didn't work until it had the exact proportions it has now.'[92]

Unlike kinetic sculptors such as Gabo and Calder, Lye never trained as an engineer. But engineers acknowledged that he had developed a remarkable intuitive sense of how metals behaved. This enabled him to come up with ideas that seemed to defy orthodox practice. It also earned him a place in the tradition of self-taught innovators that New Zealanders describe as masters of 'no. 8 fence wire'. Once he had developed the parameters of a sculpture, Lye was happy to pass on his requirements to a production team – but they needed to share his aesthetics. For example, the above description of *Moonbead* was to help John Matthews understand the aesthetics involved. Lye added, 'If a larger version of *Moonbead* was made, there would have to be a lot of trial and error, and not to get dispirited by the fact that it didn't work [at first] . . . .' Today, in realising his plans for 'larger versions', the New Plymouth team must to some extent employ his trial-and-error method in order to arrive at the required figures of motion. This makes such attempts difficult to budget for.

Lye's film-making was as much a process of working by hand as his sculpture. The film-maker Hilary Harris watched him scratching *Free Radicals*:

> I admired the way he really got into it, he gave himself over to the process completely. When I saw the results I was amazed at what could be done with scratch film. Len had developed a kinetic use of his hands. It reminded me of when I was editing film, I'd get into a similar rhythm of work. But his hands had developed such a keen rhythm there was a real coherence in the way things progressed from frame to frame. His films are outstanding in terms of kinetic integrity and what I call aliveness.[93]

'Aliveness' is a vivid way to describe the distinctive energy of Lye's hand-made images.

In an essay on three film-makers – Lye, Norman McLaren and Pierre Hébert – Marina Estela Graça has spelled out the far-reaching implications of making animated films by hand: 'According to each one of these [film-makers], movement should never be understood as a formal, external aspect, of a mechanical character, but as an expression of the physical existence itself, projected externally and seen as a manifestation of life.'[94] Graça quotes a 1948 statement by McLaren about working by hand which shows how close his thinking was to Lye's:

> [The] conception and execution of most of my work for the National Film Board [of Canada] has probably depended on four things:
> (1) Attempting to keep at a minimum the technical mechanism standing between my conception and the finished work.
> (2) Handling personally the mechanisms that do remain, in as intimate a way as a painter his painting, or a violinist his violin.
> (3) Making the very limitations of these mechanisms, when brought in touch with the theme, the growing point for visual ideas.
> (4) Making sure of a chance for improvising at the moment of shooting or drawing.[95]

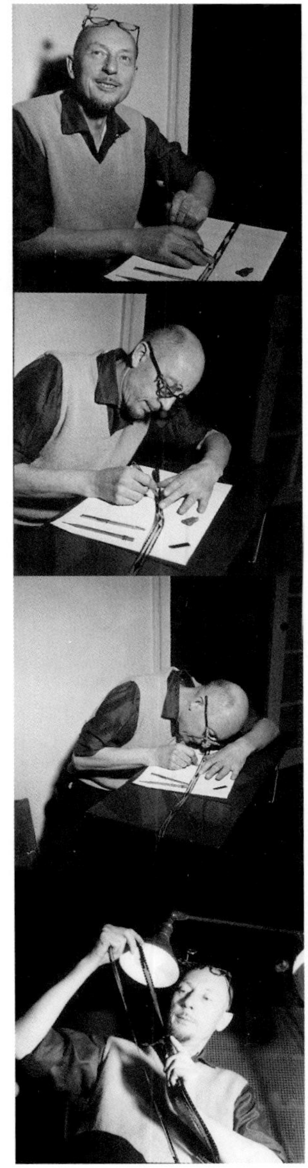

Lye made many of his films by hand. Here, circa 1966, he is scratching strips of 16mm black and white film. Photos by gin briggs. Courtesy Len Lye Foundation.

Energy

Energy was important to Lye as a material he worked with, as a way of looking at the world, as a theme for his art and as the basis for a new critical approach. An abundance of energy is one of the strongest impressions created by his art – painted lines vibrate like guitar strings, single-celled creatures struggle to evolve, 'free radicals' and 'particles' of energy zip through space, strips of steel quiver and dance. Those who knew the artist were struck by the extent to which his work reflected his personal energy, sense of humour and *joie de vivre*.

From Lye's perspective, 'movement . . . is absolutely nothing or everything, ask any electron, atom or molecule, light, sound or any vibration mental or otherwise . . . . So movement needs all the insight possible . . . .'[96] In this 1930 passage, Lye could easily have written 'energy' instead of 'movement'. Energy was essential to movement, so for him the two words were often interchangeable – and interchangeable with the word 'life'. The apparent solidity of objects concealed the scientific fact that at the level of 'electron, atom or molecule', the whole world was in movement. In the middle of the 19th century, scientists had also come to understand that all forms of energy were interrelated.[97] That encompassed the energies of nature, of machines, of human bodies and of human minds. The translation of one type of energy into another was happening all the time. In 1905, Albert Einstein made the discovery that energy and mass could also be exchanged. Sometimes Lye's sculptures seem a perfect illustration of that process, as an object speeds up and becomes a pure pattern of energy (or figure of motion), before slowing down and returning to its original metal form.

He took a deep interest in all aspects of energy, and assumed that any kinetic artist would do the same. This theme was one of his main ways of linking film and kinetic sculpture. He liked to reflect on the process of direct film-making – how the energy of his mind and hand movements could produce images on a small strip of celluloid, which were then animated as a screen-size visual dance by the electrical motor and lamp of the projector, while an optical soundtrack pattern was converted into the energy of music. Evan Webb has drawn attention to Lye's grasp of energy on different scales:

Lye's *Rotating Harmonic* is a shiny metal rod that begins by forming a lateral harmonic curve, and then, in its struggle to absorb additional energy, goes on to produce increasingly complex patterns. Courtesy Len Lye Foundation.

> *Roundhead* and *Universe* are two of my favourite [sculptures] because they encapsulate Len's remarkable ability to work (and think) both small [*Roundhead*] and large [*Universe*]. In these works I can see his understanding of both the atom and the cosmos. I think he intuitively understood the relationship between particle-sized and sun-sized energy. I guess this understanding came about from years of working with the tiny scale of film frames knowing that while scratching and painting with the aid of an eye-glass, the final image might be magnified as much as 500 times [as] a dazzling energy burst from scratch to screen . . .[98]

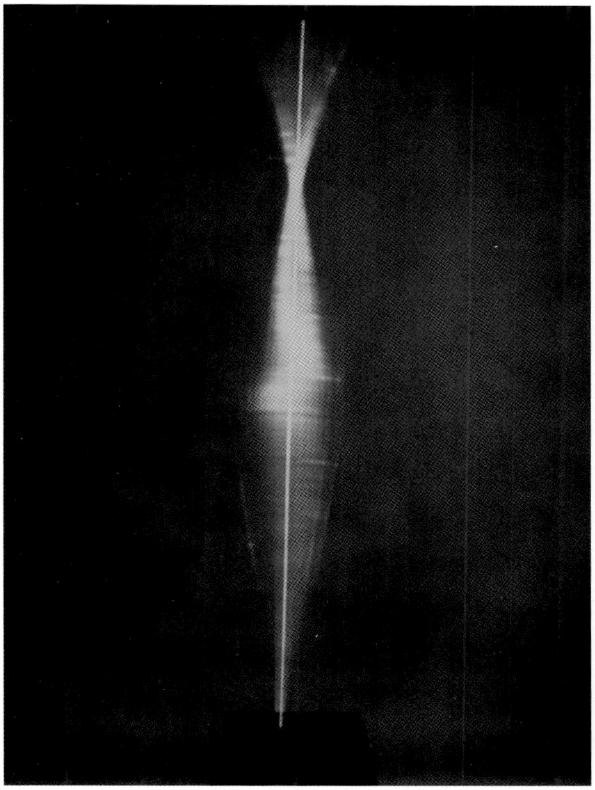
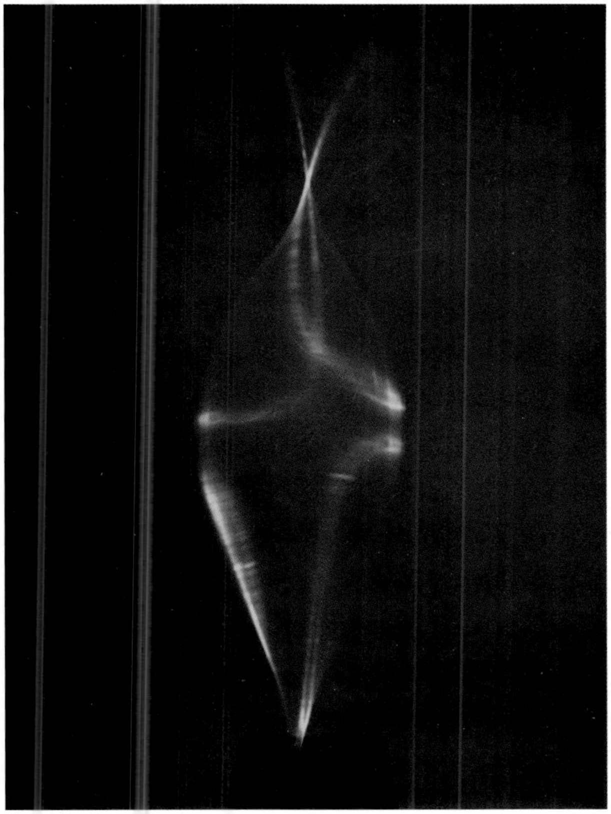
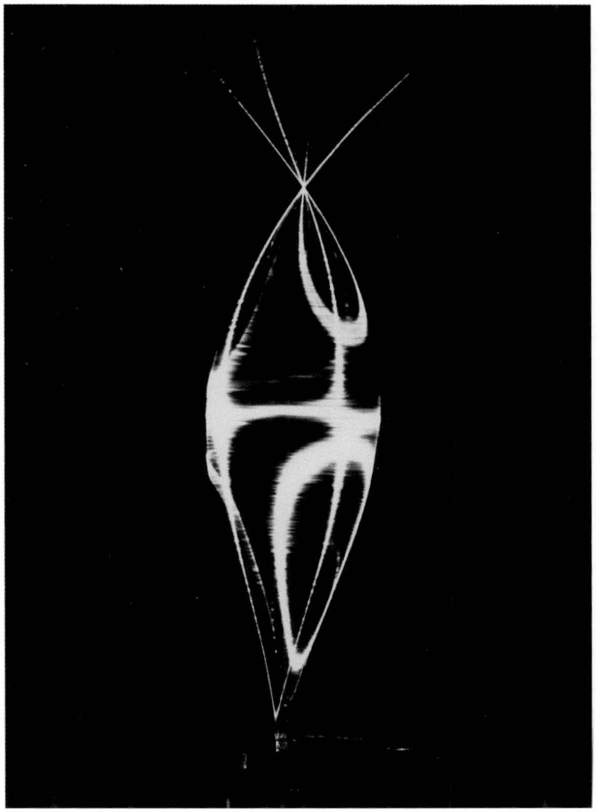

Each of his sculptures was a drama set in motion by charging a certain kind of material with energy. Excess energy created feedback effects, as Lye said of *Rotating Harmonic*: 'The shiny metal rod can be made to form a lateral harmonic curve, and then to struggle dramatically to absorb extra energy by achieving a rotating motion. The range of motion allows for many effects of composition, and perhaps this four-foot rod will remain the most classical example of composed energy of any of my kinetic sculptures.'[99] Sometimes he compared a sculpture with the way the human body handled energy:

> We are physically organized to individuate energy and direct it to creating end-effects of value. And so is motorized motion sculpture. Many parallels exist between the way our organism handles energy and the way a motorized kinetic work 'programmes' energy. In some of our conditioned reflexes we feed back energy to help control our actions . . . . When the artist was making *Rotating Harmonic* he was also expending energy under the control of his own anatomical feedback system . . . . [for example] when he reached for a wrench . . .[100]

Energy takes many forms but there are similarities between the different types of tension or vibration seen in hand-drawn film images, string instruments, strips of metal and human muscles. Not surprisingly, Lye treated energy not only as a material but also as a theme. In fact, he thought of all his art as ultimately a tribute to energy. Religion had once worshipped the energies of nature in the form of gods. He saw his films *Free Radicals* and *Particles in Space* as a dance of energy particles, and was delighted to learn that a piece of drum music he had already selected for the soundtrack of *Particles* was linked to the cult of Shango, the African god of thunder and lightning.[101] Lye had earlier paid homage to this figure when he gave the title *Storm King* to one of his sculptures. He had read how the Yoruba (a Nigerian tribe) 'tie their sense of self to the natural energy of thunder and lightning. They personify it through their god [Shango] . . . and emphasize their affinity with him in drum and dance.' He treated this kind of worship with respect because it spoke the language of the old brain and was attuned to the deep structure of nature. He made it clear, however, that his own thinking was more secular: 'I do it [celebrate energy] with *Storm King* not as a god, but as art.'[102] On another occasion, he said that 'the marked vibration and oscillation, rhythm and spinning, undulation and orbiting' in his work served ultimately 'to isolate an image which portrays the fundamental force of nature – energy'.[103] He saw this as the meaning of his art at its deepest level – its old brain meaning – deeper than the images conjured up by titles such as *Fountain* or *Grass*, and deeper than any Freudian or sexual associations.

Lye liked to link the artistic impulse to the process of evolution: 'Scientists seem to refer to the individuation of energy when they speak of the "directional force" of evolution. I believe that this force, whatever it is, is the same energy which drives the creative imagination.'[104] Webb comments: 'This is an important quote because Lye makes a conceptual leap that takes the energy equation out of the realm of physics . . . . and humanises it. I think this is where Lye is more comfortable – when he talks about energy not as an abstract concept as Einstein did, but as a real lived experience – as something rooted in our humanity. To move (to be kinesthetically aware) is to be alive.'[105] This 'real lived experience' gave Lye a clear understanding of artistic form in terms of the shaping of energy – an action perspective very different from the more formal approach that dominated mainstream art theory at least up to the 1960s. Critics tended to focus on structural qualities, and on product rather than process. We have already mentioned one alternative theorist, Harold Rosenberg, who clashed with Greenberg in 1952 over his conception of 'action painting'. Another process theorist was Charles Olson, the controversial poet who wrote the manifesto 'Projective Verse' in 1950. (His essay 'Proprioception' was mentioned earlier in the chapter.) Olson and Lye appear not to have known each other but the poet's conception of art was remarkably close to the artist's, as shown by the beginning of Olson's description of 'projective verse':

> The kinetics of the thing. A poem is energy transferred from where the poet got it (he will have some several causations), by way of the poem itself to, all the way over to, the reader . . . . Then the poem itself must, at all points, be a high energy-construct and, at all points, an energy-discharge. So . . . what is the process by which a poet gets in, at all points energy at least the equivalent of the energy which propelled him in the first place, yet an energy which is peculiar to verse alone and which will be, obviously, also different from the energy which the reader, because he is a third term, will take away.[106]

Olson's conception of art as 'energy-construct' is relevant in an extremely literal sense to Lye's work, if we focus on the energies of sculpture or film rather than 'the energy . . . peculiar to verse'. Lye spoke of the impact of kinetic art as a kind of 'kick' – the viewer was energised by it. His desire to scale up his sculptures was an attempt to increase their 'energy-discharge'. Both he and Olson focused on the conversion of one kind of energy into another as the process moved from artist to artwork to audience, attempting to maximise the flow of energy at each step along the way. Both artists described this process in physical, kinesthetic terms, incorporating the artist's body as well as mind, and they celebrated the individual ways this occurred.[107] The projective approach also assigned an active role to the viewer who must be prepared to invest as well as to 'take away' energy. (Lye's sense exercises are a useful investment for viewers as well as for artists.) Combining the ideas of both theorists would yield a powerful aesthetic relevant to any medium. Lye's contributions would include his idea of empathy, his sense exercises and his kinetic sense of form ('figures of motion'). Linking them to Olson's aesthetic would be simply a matter of substituting the word 'energy' for the word 'movement' or 'motion'.

The Experience of Stillness

> [T]hough we may know that at bottom everything in space is in motion, we also know that when we talk of a static image we mean something that appears to be still in contrast to something that appears to move. We simply 'feel' that a mountain is there, and will stay right there, or that this or that sculpture or painting will remain exactly as it is while we look at it; that a humming bird may also be right 'there', but not for long for it will soon dart off; or that a kinetic work will soon move or appear to move.[108]

Every kinetic artist turns occasionally to drawing or painting. Calder not only created mobiles but also static sculptures that he called 'stabiles'. Lye made paintings, batiks and photograms, and, as an artist with a philosophical turn of mind, he thought a great deal about the relationship of static to kinetic images. He saw stillness as occupying a place within the spectrum of movement. Although 'at bottom everything . . . is in motion', the subjective 'feeling' of stillness had a definite role to play in his aesthetics. His essays explored the relationships that these contrasts made possible. For example, in 'Is Film Art?' he wrote, 'immobility, stillness, quietude have a contrapuntal effect on our sense of motion as silence emphasizes sound'.[109] And in 'Tangible Motion Sculpture': 'these give us examples of complementary elements in our empathy to both stillness and motion. In like manner, an unexpectedly vibrating metal sculpture, through its movement, will enhance the serenity of an architectural environment.'[110]

When he looked at a painting, Lye tended to have a heightened response to its very stillness, as the following passage suggests: 'in static painting and sculpture, the artist freezes the passing cloud, the facial expression, the cast of body, the abstraction. He captures and holds the changing mood, the transient flesh, the seasons, the falling wave, the formal structure, the calligraphic statement. He arrests them and holds them frozen in their tracks forever'.[111] He talked about how – with the help of empathy – it is possible to read static images in kinetic terms:

> A Hiroshige woodcut makes us aware of the power and weight of a curled mighty wave about to break; we feel an emphatic response to the decorative grace of a bird elegantly poised on a branch; we respond to the taut spatial relationships of a Cézanne painting; we may almost quiver to the ecstatic stillness of a Zurbaran still life; as equally as we do to the glowing candesences of the Impressionists.[112]

Here he was perhaps describing the wave tingling with energy in Utagawa Hiroshige's woodblock print *View of Mount Fuji from Satta Point in the Suruga Bay*. As a young artist, Lye was fascinated by Paul Cézanne's paintings because of their 'static sculptural quality', which struck him as 'the opposite of motion but part of it, like the opposites silence and sound'.[113] The still-life paintings of Francisco Zurbaran displayed cups and jars with an intense sense of presence in their stillness. And in his early years, Lye had been strongly drawn to the Impressionists because of their attempt to record transient effects of light and atmosphere; but now that he was involved with literal movement, what struck him was the 'frozen' aspect of their paintings. He associated static images with a desire for 'durability' because 'deep in our hearts we would all like to be impervious to change'.[114]

His own work seldom pursued this kind of 'ecstatic stillness', but he did create a few memorable examples. For example, 'Wave', a piece of prose writing from his *Happy Moments* series, froze a memory from his first visit to Australia:

> On Coogee beach there was this glass-clear twenty-five-foot-high walking wave of green sea. Twenty-five-foot! Alive and swimming straight along its curling middle was this huge shark . . . . What's the frantic magic? Simply feeling, hey, there's a mighty rising mass of energy forever gathering, never stopping, preserving a fish in amber, gone greeny forever. That big slow curling wave never comes down.[115]

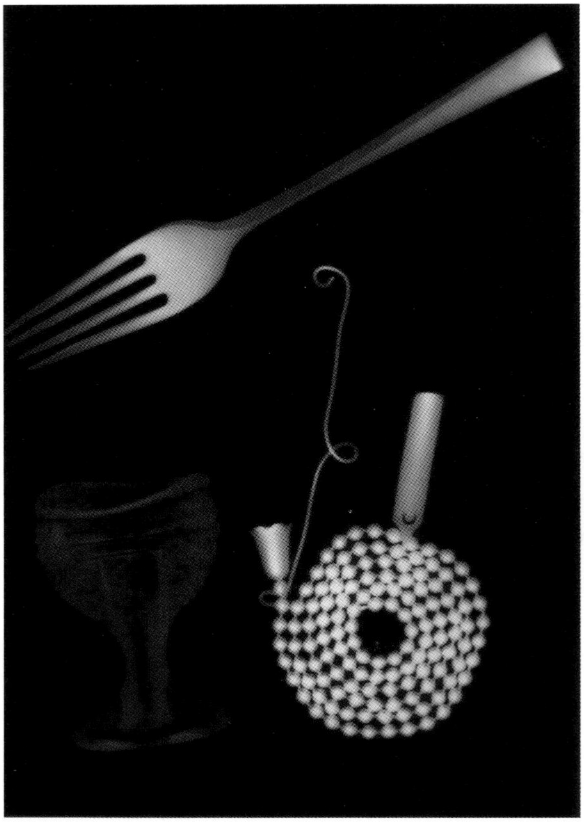

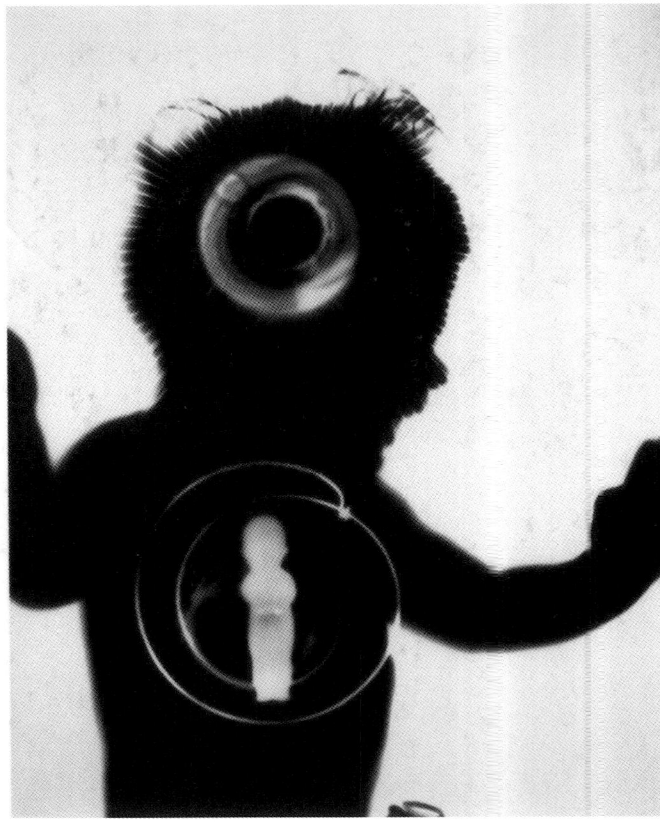

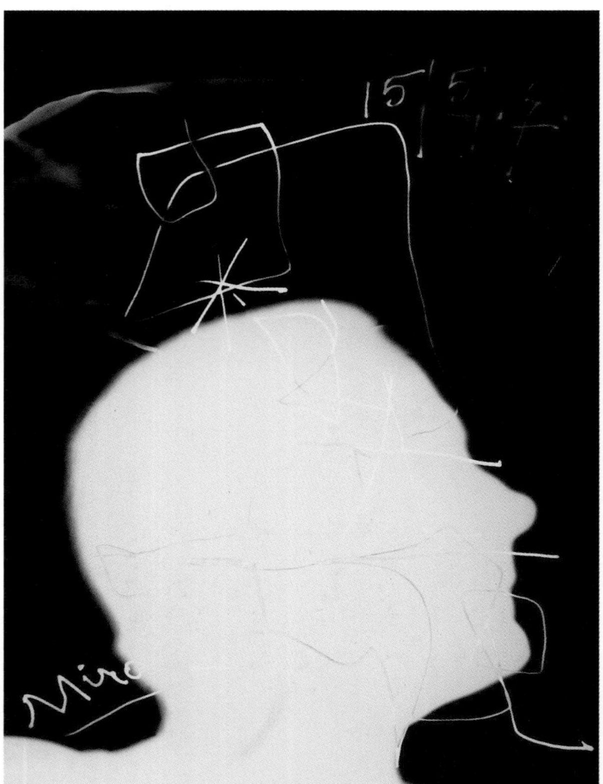

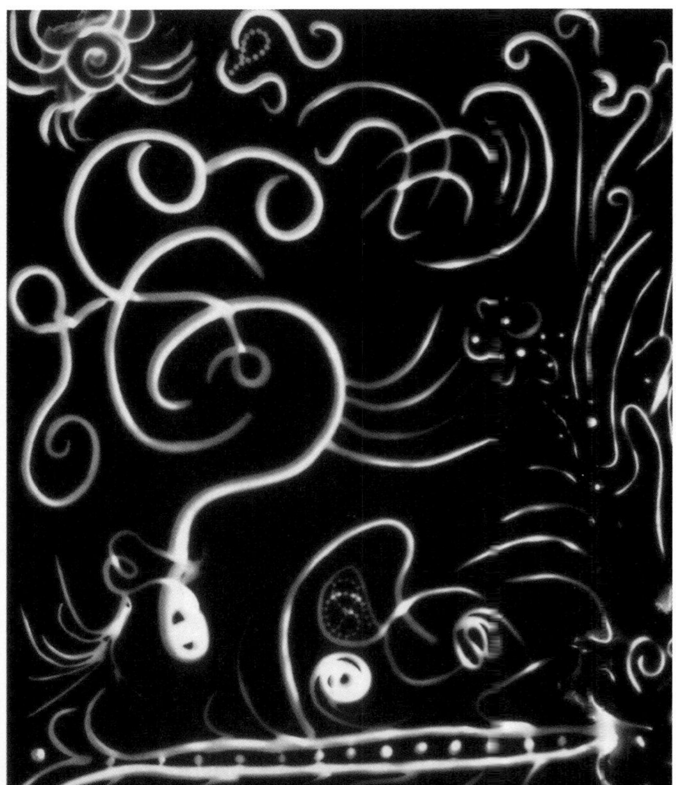

Lye's other forms of art explore the contrast between static and kinetic in subtle ways. Around 1947, he made an evocative series of photogram portraits of friends and neighbours, superimposing relevant words, objects and doodles so they floated around or across the static silhouetted heads. Because these were dynamic personalities (such as W. H. Auden, Joan Miró and Ann Lye) and their outlines were blurred, the silhouette heads conveyed a vivid sense of mental energy, as though Lye was anticipating today's brain scanning. At the same time, the heads retain a strong physical dimension as they are the trace of the person making direct contact with photographic paper. (To create a photogram, the subject had to lie on the floor in the dark, on a piece of photographic paper, until an overhead light was switched on.) Among the most kinetic examples were *Child Collage* the image of a new-born baby, and Lye's *Self Portrait* in which a strangely mobile tree-like figure (a photogram he had made circa 1930) filled his silhouetted head as though to reveal all the activity in his old brain. In Lye's terms, these static images 'allow us to identify the feeling of [an] essential self with some . . . quality of individuality', and each 'captures and holds . . . the transient flesh'.[116]

Lye started out as a painter and returned to this medium at various stages of his life. In the 1930s, he made several paintings such as *Helium* and *Snow Birds Making Snow* in which the lines and brushstrokes were exceptionally dynamic. These works alligned him with the 'painterly' side of the Surrealist tradition (particularly with Miró), and they looked forward to the 'action painting' that emerged in the late 1940s. They also linked up with his lifelong practice of doodling, his interest in graffiti, and his study of cracking, flaking, staining and other signs of natural energies at work.[117]

Most of Lye's other paintings seem more static. When he made them he was primarily concerned with tapping the old brain. The paintings illustrated 'organic life in a primary stage'.[118] The images look curiously timeless, like the sacred images or totems of some long-lost culture. It must be added, however, that Lye himself saw plenty of movement and drama in them. Most paintings have a protagonist figure or figures at their centres, and from the artist's point of view each of these powerful protagonists had its own unique style of movement. There is an amusing sequence of photographs showing Lye adopting various poses in front of the paintings as he responded to their implied movements. He considered turning *God of Light* into kinetic sculpture as 'a big figure with three legs and prongy feet. It was very spastic and it compressed its three legs and sharp elbows all together, then suddenly they sprang out. This springing sideways

Four of Lye's photograms. Top left is his earliest known photogram – from the late 1920s – which juxtaposed an eye bath, a fork and a coiled light chain. The other three were made in 1947. Top right, *Child Collage (black on white)* combines a doll with a new-born baby. Bottom left is *Miró (white on black)*, which incorporates some of that artist's doodles. And bottom right is *Photogram of a Doodle*, whose patterns Lye appears to have created by the kind of modelling clay known as plasticine. Courtesy Len Lye Foundation.

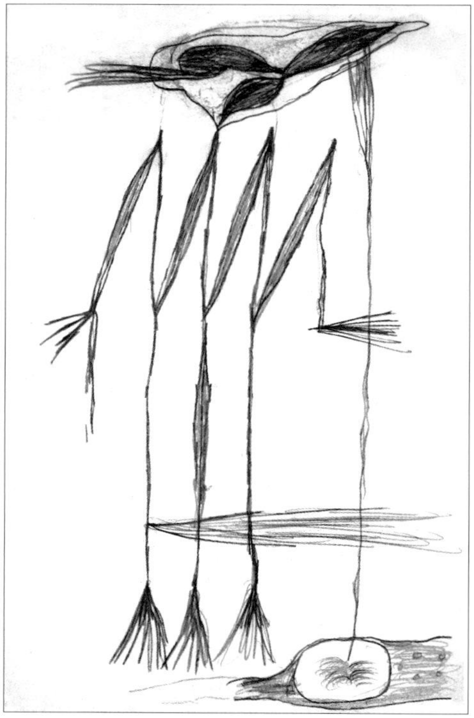

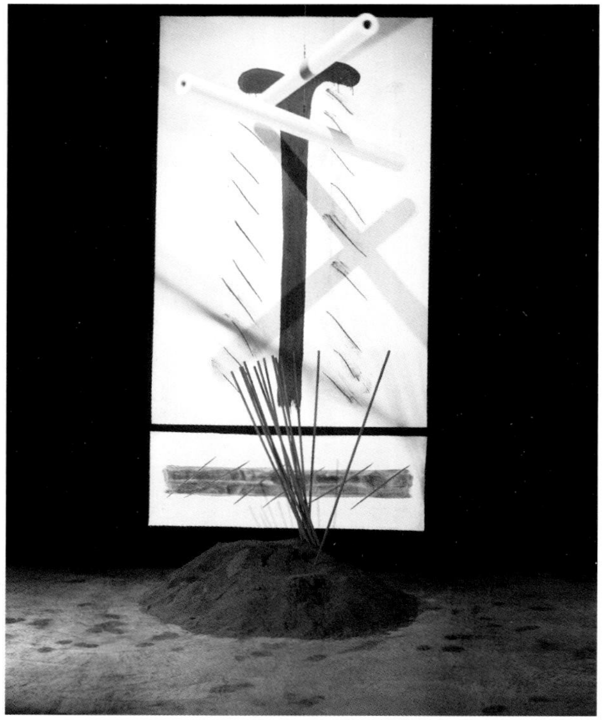

LEFT Lye associated this 1933 pencil doodle with *Cagn*, 'an African Bushman god'. He used it as the starting point for a painting in 1933 and again in 1977 (*God of Light*). He liked to imagine what Cagn would look like when he walked, with 'no knees' and legs that 'moved sideways one at a time, crab-fashion'.
RIGHT Some of the props for a performance Lye planned to accompany his painting *Rain Tree and Earth*. They included mounds of black earth and red and black stylised arrows. Courtesy Len Lye Foundation.

action would cause it to sidle sideways like a crab. A very spectacular figure with its three eyes gradually turning round and blinking.' (Lye got as far as experimenting with a folding gate!) He also liked the idea of stylised performances in front of the paintings, to highlight their implied movements and their symbolic or mythic elements.[119] Such performances were to resemble tribal rituals, Japanese Noh dramas or Javanese marionette plays. In the case of *Rain Tree*, he planned a happening that involved mounds of black earth, red and black stylised arrows, rotating white tubes (symbolising bones) and the reading of an Aztec poem.

Lye's paintings were set in the same prehistoric (or Dreamtime) world as *Tusalava*, and indeed some of them began as story-board images for the two films he had planned as sequels. They were full of implied 'nature-processes' – growth, impregnation, birth and metamorphosis (evolutionary change), in the context of sun and moon, rivers, lava flows, fires and storms. The implied movement is not always clear, but Lye wrote prose poems (in capital letters) to accompany many of the pictures. Like an Aboriginal interpreting an ancient rock painting, he would translate each image into a kind of narrative with old brain or evolutionary implications. For *Watershed*, for example, he wrote:

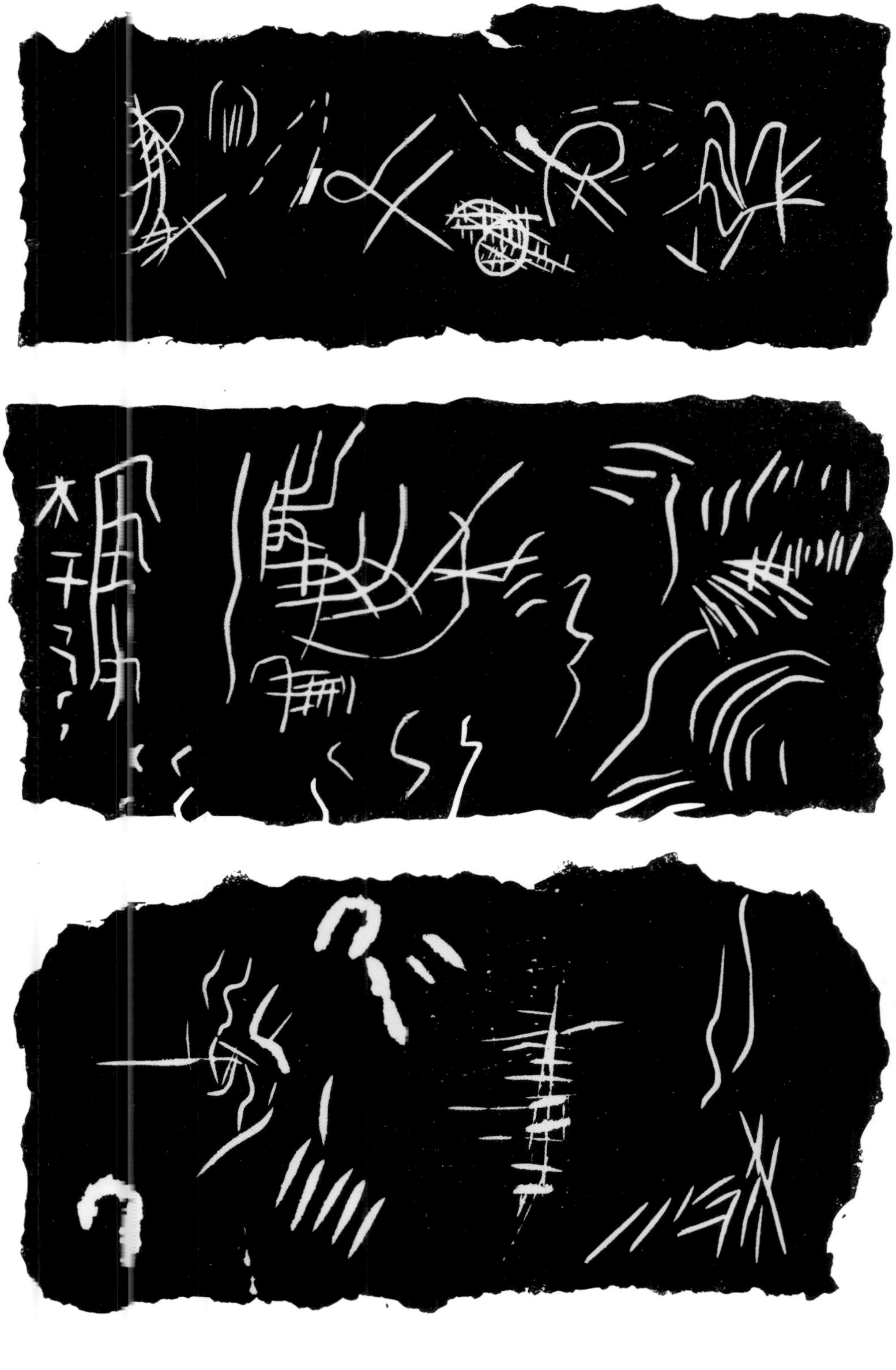

Lye's 1940 woodcuts for the Surrealist magazine *London Bulletin* are rich in implied motion. They also anticipated his scratched black and white images many years later for the film *Free Radicals.* Courtesy Len Lye Foundation.

WATER HAS CLEANED THE SKY AND WIND IS BLOWING THINGS THROUGH IT. SPANGLES OF POLLEN ARE BLOWN FROM A HILLTOP. OUT OF THAT BANK OF STRAIGHT UP STRATA COMES POLLEN WHICH IS WASHED DOWN TO A LAKE UNDER THE GROUND AND BECOMES SMALL WATER THINGS . . . . THE GREAT SPRING WATER PUMPS ARE DRAINING A WATERSHED FOR ALL OF THIS.[120]

And for *Land and Sea*:

THE SEA MAKES A FORCE THAT BECOMES A THUNDERBOLT OF THE SEA. THIS THUNDERBOLT RISES OUT OF THE SEA TO STRIKE AT THE LAND. THE SEA IS ALWAYS AGAINST THE LAND AND THAT IS THE IDEA OF IT. NOW THE SEA THUNDERBOLT IS STRIKING LIGHTNING AT A CAVE IN A MOUNTAIN OF ROCK THAT IS LAND STRATA.[121]

Lye's paintings tend to be more interesting for their old brain strangeness than for their implied sense of movement; and it must be acknowledged that some aspects of the old brain appear to have no connection with the art of motion. Nevertheless, the prose poems help us to understand the strong sense of 'nature-process' that is always present in Lye's art, as in the activities of the old brain. That sense of process is clearly linked with movement, so that *Land and Sea* was one of the starting points for his potentially largest and most dramatic sculpture – the proposed *Sun, Land and Sea* in which the 'God of the Sea' shoots lightning at a 'Cave Goddess'.[122]

In the case of his films, Lye sometimes exhibited a static arrangement of painted strips, but their projection as moving images remained his first priority. His films tended to be characterised by rapid, constant motion, but now and then he would exploit stillness as 'a contrapuntal effect'. Twice in *Rainbow Dance*, a leaping figure leaves behind a train of brightly coloured silhouettes, the stages of his movement frozen as in a Futurist painting. In his black and white direct films, the occasional black frames function like moments of silence in a piece of music.

But it is in his kinetic sculptures that stillness becomes most clearly part of the continuum of movement. It is always a dramatic moment when a sculpture, having rested, suddenly springs to life in a quiet gallery; and the routines of many of the sculptures incorporate moments of stasis as well as variations of speed from slow and gentle to fast and furious.

Dance

It may seem odd for Lye to talk about the 'art of motion' as something new when there had been such a long tradition of dance. He was very aware of dance but there were two reasons why he wanted to take a fresh approach and to go beyond what appeared to be widespread understandings of dance as an art form. First, this art as it existed in his vicinity seemed to him to have solidified into a stodgy ritual – the Victorian tradition of ballet. It lacked the rhythmic energy and sexiness that he felt in jazz or the experimental energy that he found in new forms of art. Second, the modern age had introduced the medium of film and other new technologies that could drive and control the motion of objects. In Lye's words, 'until recently the only art form which expressed [an] all-embracing sense of individual being was dance. Kinetic art has freed us from the restricted anatomical range of dance movements'.[123] As Lye's wording suggests, the new 'kinetic art' would still be based on 'individual being' – including the experience of the human body – but now artists could express their sense of movement as images on a screen or as moving pieces of wood or metal. He himself was inspired by the movement of clouds, waves, tree branches in the wind and other patterns in nature directly, rather than by the imitation of those movements in ballet.

While he was always most fascinated by movement in the natural world, dance remained a key interest for him and a useful concept for understanding his art. Dance joins 'movement' and 'energy' as interchangeable words – energy is the source of movement and dance is the shape it makes. Lye's habit of comparing kinetic art with choreography follows naturally from his idea of musical 'figures'. It is, however, important to know that he associated dance not with classical ballet but with styles that were either very modern or very ancient.

As a young adult, he read anthropology books voraciously looking for information on tribal dance rituals linked to ancient times. He saw this as a way of uniting his interest in 'primitive art' with his interest in movement. He was aware that ancient cultures did not restrict the concept of dance to the movements of the human body but applied it to the whole of the natural world. For example, the notion of a dancing world was developed by the ancient Greeks, then reworked in Christian terms during medieval times.[124] The assumption that God – or the gods – had created a well-ordered universe gave rise to the idea of 'the music of the spheres' and the related notion that the heavenly bodies moved in a sort of dance. The main Hindu gods are also associated with dance, and from the

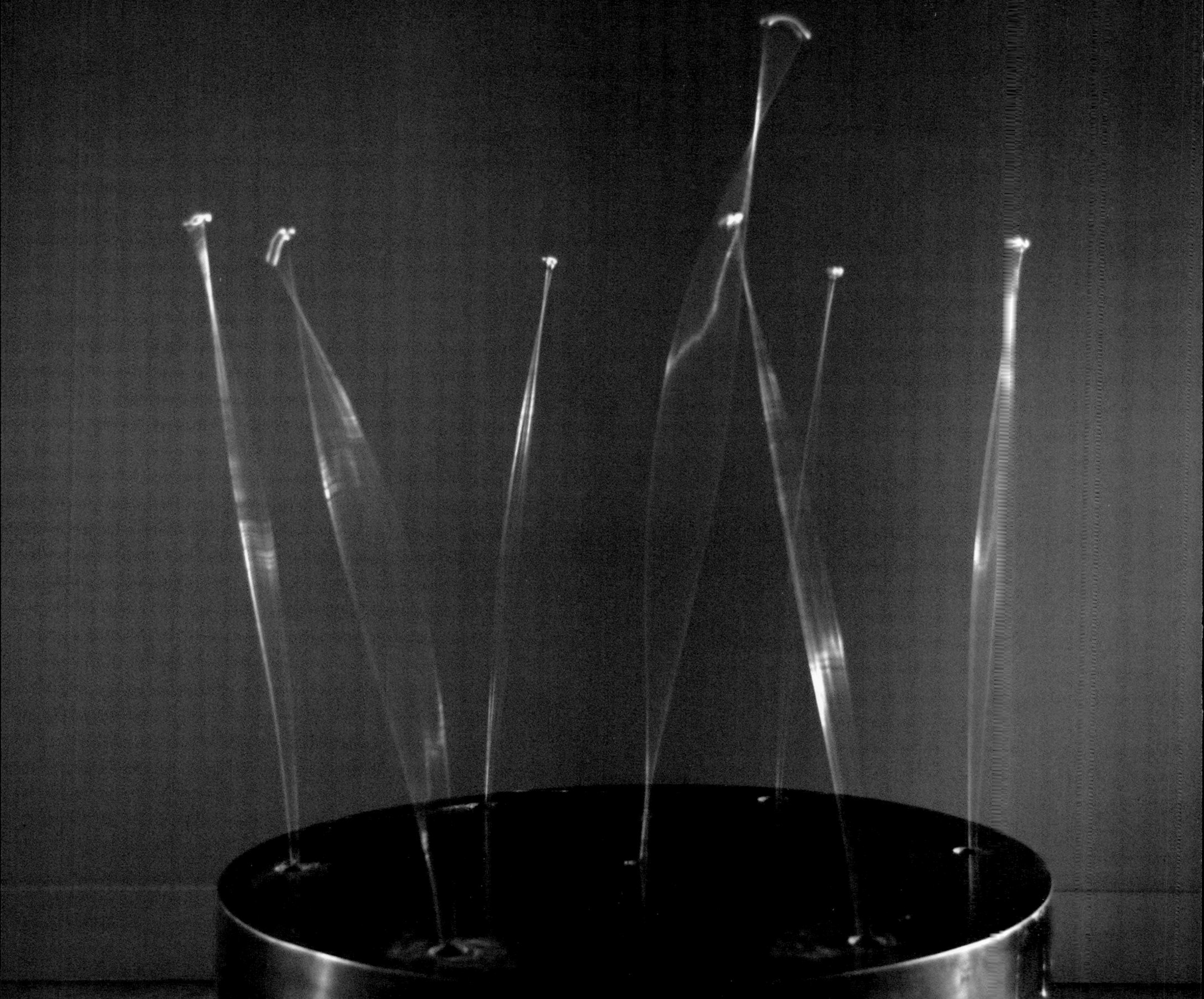

Lye's sculpture *Witch Dance*. Courtesy Len Lye Foundation.

13th century the Darwish (members of the Mevlevi order of Islam) adopted the 'whirling dervish' dance as a route to religious ecstasy.[125] In these and many other ancient cultures, the widespread emphasis on dance in religion (as well as in other areas of life such as 'love, art, work') encouraged a heightened awareness of the rhythms and patterns of nature.[126]

Lye was particularly interested in the dance forms of Africa, Australia and the Pacific. By combining scenes of tribal dancing with the modernity of motion pictures, *Pearls and Savages* convinced Lye that film could be the key medium for his desired new art of motion.[127] And the inspiration for his first film, *Tusalava*, came from pictures of an Aboriginal tribe preparing for a ritual dance to celebrate the witchetty grub. *Tusalava* was created as a silent film but Lye asked Jack Ellitt to write music to perform with it. Later he proposed Eugene Goossens' *Rhythmic Dance* as an alternative accompaniment. Arguably, the film has something of the feel of a dance since it has groups of 'dots' or 'microbes' moving in formation, while solo characters interact in a rhythmical way. Lye did some detailed planning for the sequel which he described as a 'ballet of natural objects with marionette models'.[128]

He became involved with many forms of modern dance in London during the so-called 'Jazz Age' of the 1920s. In his words, 'To be in one's twenties during The Twenties was to hear a continuous roar made by some sort of ozone fallout which affected everyone into feeling loose planks in their shanks.'[129] He attended a wide range of dance events with his first wife, Jane, who was a professional dance instructor. His films of the 1930s were based on popular dance music, mostly with a Latin jazz flavour. The previous chapter has mentioned his dance projects *Quicksilver*, *Peanut Vendor* and *Rainbow Dance.*

In the 1936 essay 'Notes on a Short Colour Film', Lye championed 'good swing dance music' as a basis for kinetic forms of film-making. He implied that jazz had an energy and physical dimension that other forms of music had lost. It retained 'a strong pulsation or sensation element', whereas music 'based on classical traditions' had 'succumbed to literary influences' and had 'wallowed in mood colouring for so long . . . that it is dead beyond recovery'. He likened jazz to the music and dance rituals of ancient ('primitive') peoples, whom he admired for 'their use not only of sound, but also of colour and imagery'. Lye did, however, end by acknowledging the limitations of jazz and popular dance music, such as their 'restricted' rhythms. He expressed the hope that a new form

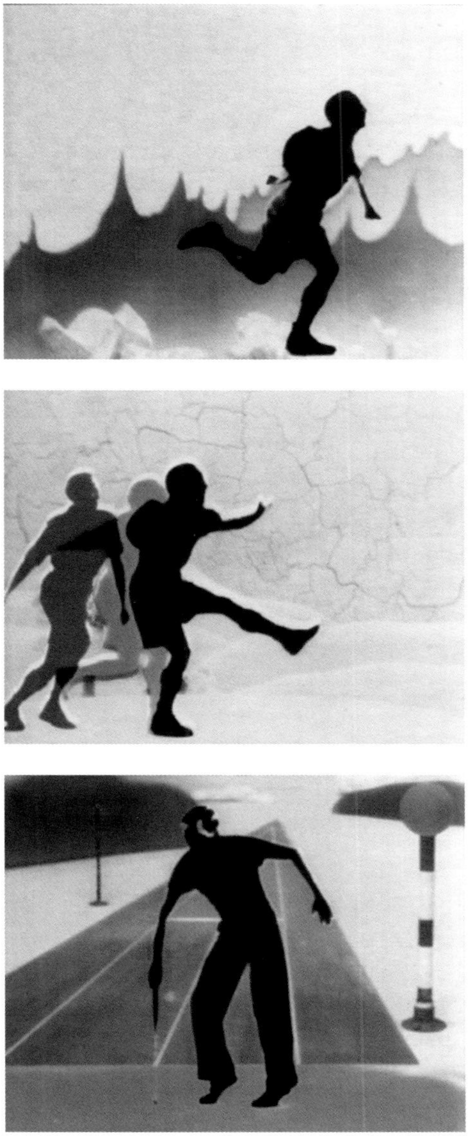

Dancer Rupert Doone in Lye's film *Rainbow Dance.* Courtesy Len Lye Foundation.

of serious music might develop – 'a pure sensation music . . . which would be a pure sound construction, perhaps in ranges of sound not yet made use of'.[130]

Practising his Aesthetic: Images as Vicarious Dance

In *Free Radicals* (1958) and *Particles in Space* (1979), Lye returned to his old interest in African tribal dance music. In the 1967 essay 'A Note on Dance and Film' (which described his work on an early version of *Particles*), he said he had come to the conclusion that the abstract images of such a film functioned as 'a vicarious form of dance to the music'.[131] This is a useful concept for understanding all of his music films, though it is important to realise that Lye understood dance as a dialogue with the music and not as a simple accompaniment. We have mentioned that he was popular as a dance partner at parties and that his style was famously idiosyncratic. Today, when computer programmes translate music automatically into abstract shapes, the results are fundamentally different from his films. His 'vicarious form of dance' was independent, quirky and syncopated, shaped by his sense of physical empathy.

A possible approach to understanding his art is to consider whether Lye's films and sculptures have affinities with modern forms of dance. Selma Jeanne Cohen has attempted to sum up the main differences between classical dance (or ballet) and modern dance in these terms: 'Classical rhythms tend to be regular . . . . Unison movement and symmetry tend to characterize ensembles, though any balanced and ordered arrangement would be consistent with the other elements of the style.'[132] Other common attributes of classical ballet include 'the clean line of the movement', 'verticality' and above all 'lightness', as an illusion that 'natural laws' (such as the law of gravity) have been transcended by the skill of the dancers. In contrast, modern dance tends to prefer 'an emphasis on path rather than goal in space; on weight rather than lightness in the body; on sharpness of accent rather than flow; on asymmetrical rather than balanced design; on exposure rather than concealment of process'.[133] In another essay, Cohen contrasts classical with modern dance in terms of 'rigid torso' becoming 'writhing torso'; 'long, unbroken line' becoming 'angular line'; and 'lightness and ease' being brought down to 'the floor plane'.[134] She puts forward these generalisations cautiously since there are so many 'species of modern dance', but they seem strongly relevant to Lye's sculptures and his direct films (particularly his later ones).

Although vertical lines are a favourite motif for him, they are forever wandering or dancing to the side (in the case of his direct films) or vibrating and bending (in the case of his sculptures). Lye liked clear visual ideas but his lines are nervous and nuanced rather than 'clean'. Sharp 'accents' are a favourite aspect not only of his films but also of his sculptures (with their collisions and percussive sounds). A sculpture such as *Universe* or *Roundhead* starts with a symmetrical shape, but once it is set in motion it becomes complex and unpredictable. Apart from his habit of concealing the motors of his sculptures (so as not to divert attention from their figures of motion), Lye's work seems closely related to the aesthetic of modern dance, particularly in its strong emphasis on 'natural laws' (such as gravity and harmonics), and the complex relationship between sound and sight in his films. As Lye says in his 'Note on Dance and Film', 'Merce Cunningham very O.K.'.[135]

His sculptures can be seen, then, as engaged in a modern form of dance. The music they make is a kind of 'pure sound construction', quirky and unpredictable, with their clicking, beating, straining and shuddering sounds.[136] When Lye experimented with recorded music to accompany them, he turned to both ancient and contemporary forms – old African tribal music with a strong beat (the 1963 television footage of *Witch Dance* provides a wonderful example), and avant-garde music with complex rhythms (such as *Le Marteau sans Maître* by Pierre Boulez). The sculptures engage in 'a vicarious form of dance' to this music, with a particularly lively pairing in the case of a work like *Fire Bush*.[137] For most sculptures, however, music is not at all necessary as we can enjoy the singular way they dance to the metallic noises they themselves create, 'in ranges of sound not [previously] made use of'.

'Choreography' was a word Lye often used, and it certainly applies to the way he planned the programmes of his sculptures and the form of his films.[138] When he worked on a film, he selected music and analysed its structure in much the way a choreographer does. Since his sculptures are like dancers with a specific set of abilities, the 'choreography' is designed to make the most of what each can do. As previously noted, some of his sculptures may be described as solo acts (such as *Water Whirler*), while others are duets (*Blade*), trios (*Flip and Two Twisters*) or groups (a cluster of *Fountains*). Both his films and his sculptures are choreographed to run for a brief but busy period of time, with variations on a basic figure of motion (or in some cases several figures), faster and slower episodes, and an eventual climax.

Dance theorist Roger Copeland has described the actions of Jackson Pollock – as recorded in Hans Namuth's famous 1950 film of the painter at work – as a demonstration 'that the fundamental impulse behind abstract expressionism was *the desire to transform painting into dancing*'.[139] Copeland links this with Pollock's interest in 'primitive art' and the 'ecstatic dancing' thought to have been associated with it. Whether or not this is an adequate description of the painter's work, it is certainly applicable to Lye's working methods for his late films where the very process of scratching images became a kind of dance. His assistant Steve Jones has described the way Lye taught him to work: 'It's like learning to dance . . . To scratch film you have to let go of your inhibitions and let your body move . . . . You can tell when [the images] have a real elasticity to them, a movement that's more like muscle.'[140]

These are a few of the many possible ways of relating Lye's art to dance, both ancient and modern. In general, the dance analogy helps to remind us that while 'Kinetic art has freed us from the restricted anatomical range of dance movements', the human body continues to stand at the centre of Lye's aesthetics. It is the starting point for so many aspects of his work – such as sharpening the senses, seeing with the body, shaping by hand, developing empathy, linking the kinetic with the kinesthetic and tapping the intuitive knowledge of the old brain.

Because Lye was uneasy about seeming to tell people what to do, he liked to end any discussion of his aesthetics on a modest note. In 'The Art that Moves', he wrote: 'These personal exercises for getting to the core of motion are not given as sure-fire guides to the practice of kinetic art. Each student will have his own anatomical cast of temperamental affinities with aspects of motion, such as weight, poise, balance, gravity, magnetism, energy. Each artist knows best where the shoe of his creative imagination pinches most.' He could not resist adding, 'But, unlike the other arts, there are very few shoes around to try. The kinetic student has to cobble his own.'[141]

Lye did a remarkable job of cobbling his own aesthetic – the result was a sturdy and thoroughly practical pair of 'shoes'. And he was happy to pass on this 'shoe of my mind' (as he had once called it) to any 'kinetic student' who might be interested.

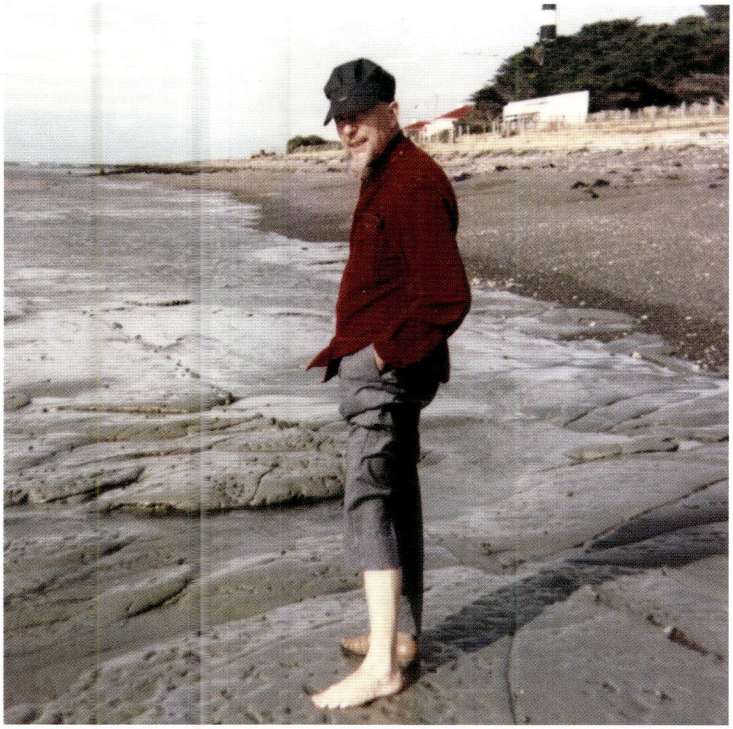
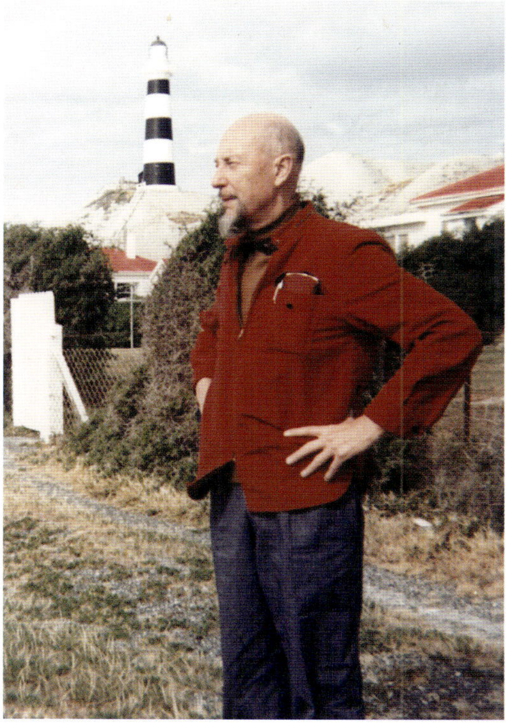

ABOVE In 1968, Lye revisited the lighthouse and the 'rocky beach' at Cape Campbell which had made a deep impression on him during the period he had lived there as a child. Courtesy Len Lye Foundation.

BELOW John Constable, *Study of Cirrus Clouds*, oil on paper, 1822. © Victoria and Albert Museum, London.

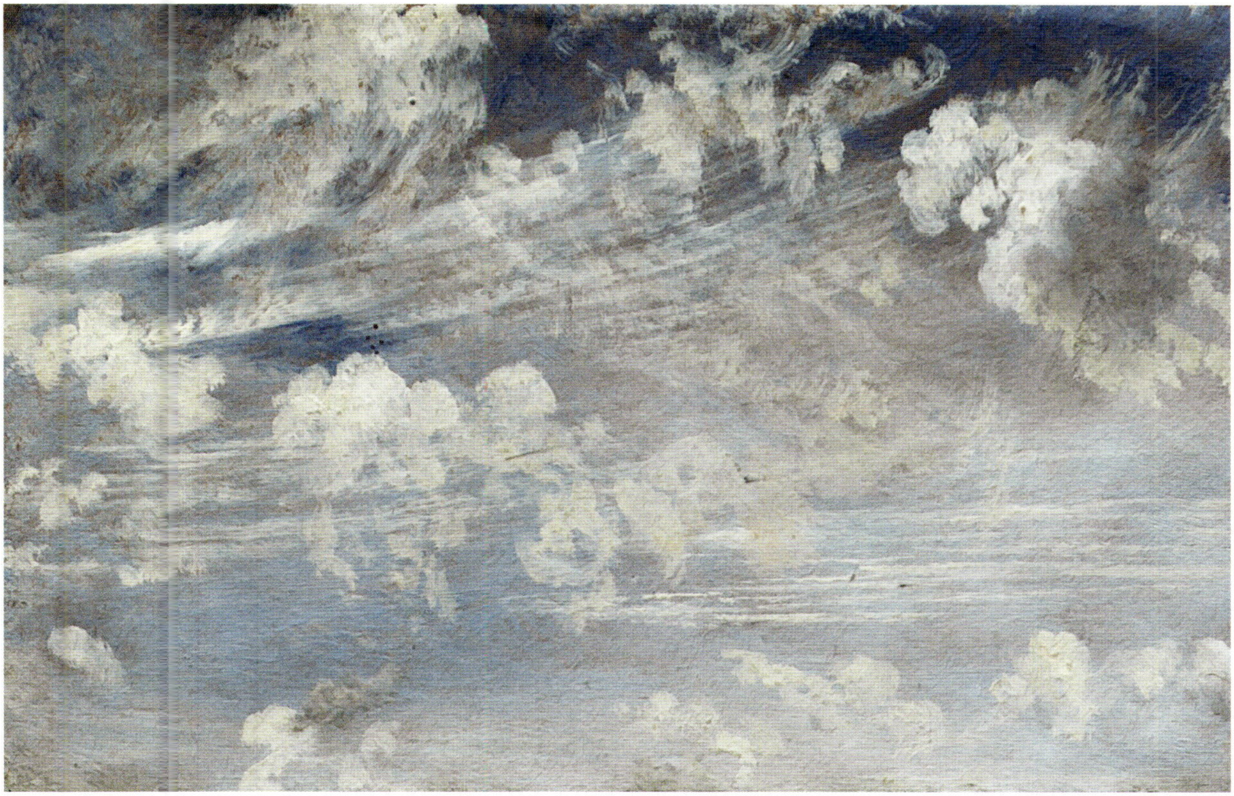

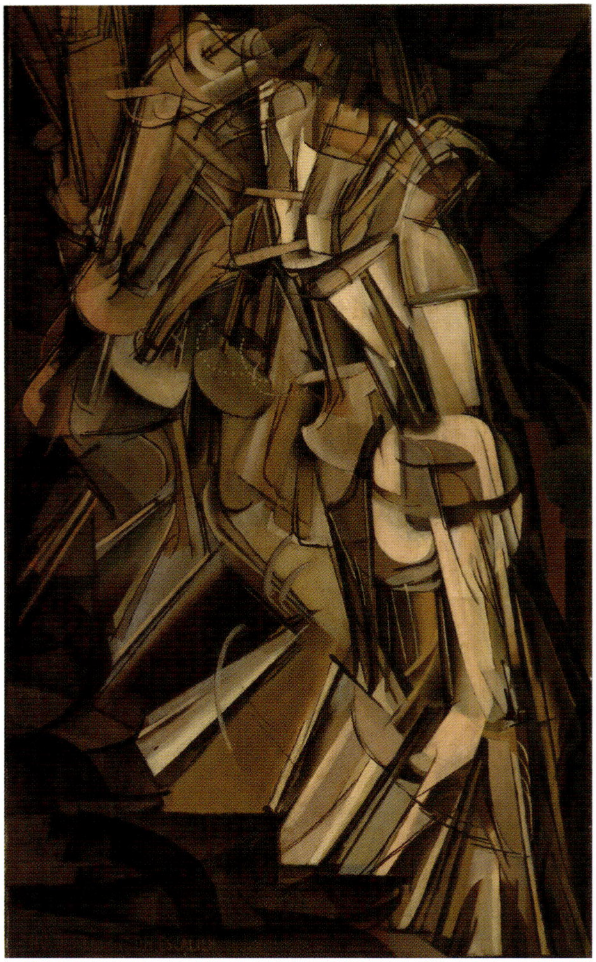

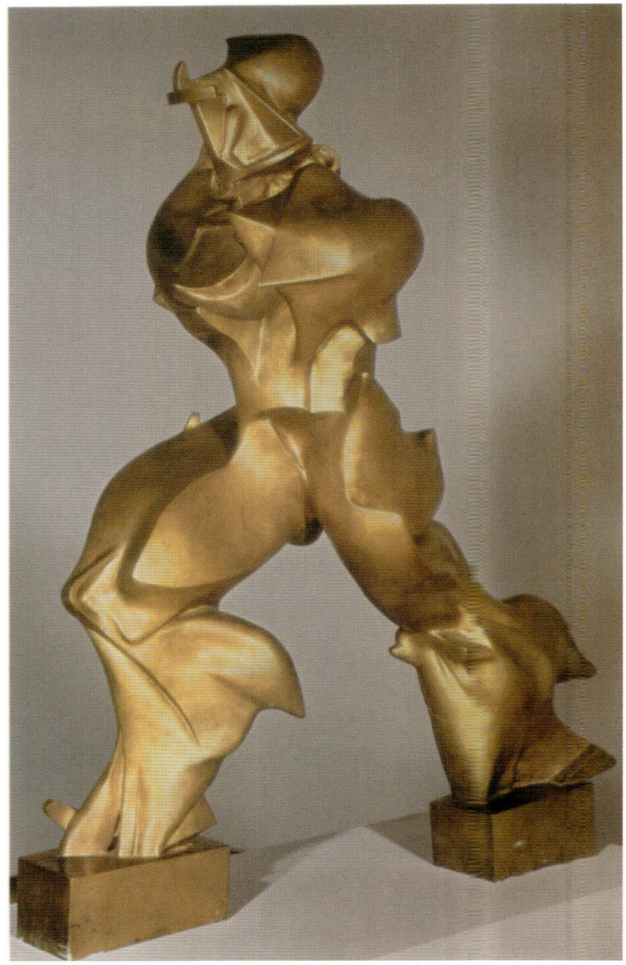

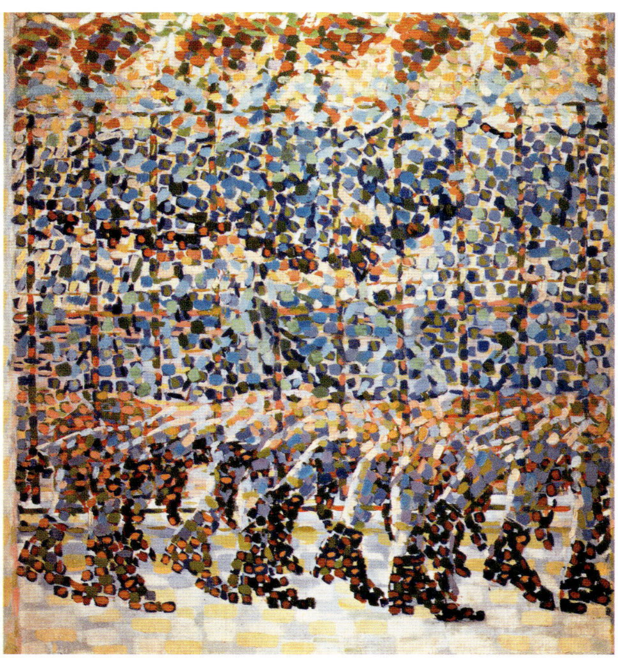

ABOVE LEFT Marcel Duchamp, *Nude Descending a Staircase No. 2*, oil on canvas, 1912. Licensed by Viscopy, Australia.

ABOVE RIGHT Umberto Boccioni, *Unique Forms of Continuity in Space*, bronze sculpture, 1913.

LEFT Giacomo Balla, *Girl Crossing a Balcony*, oil on canvas, 1912–13. Licensed by Viscopy, Australia.

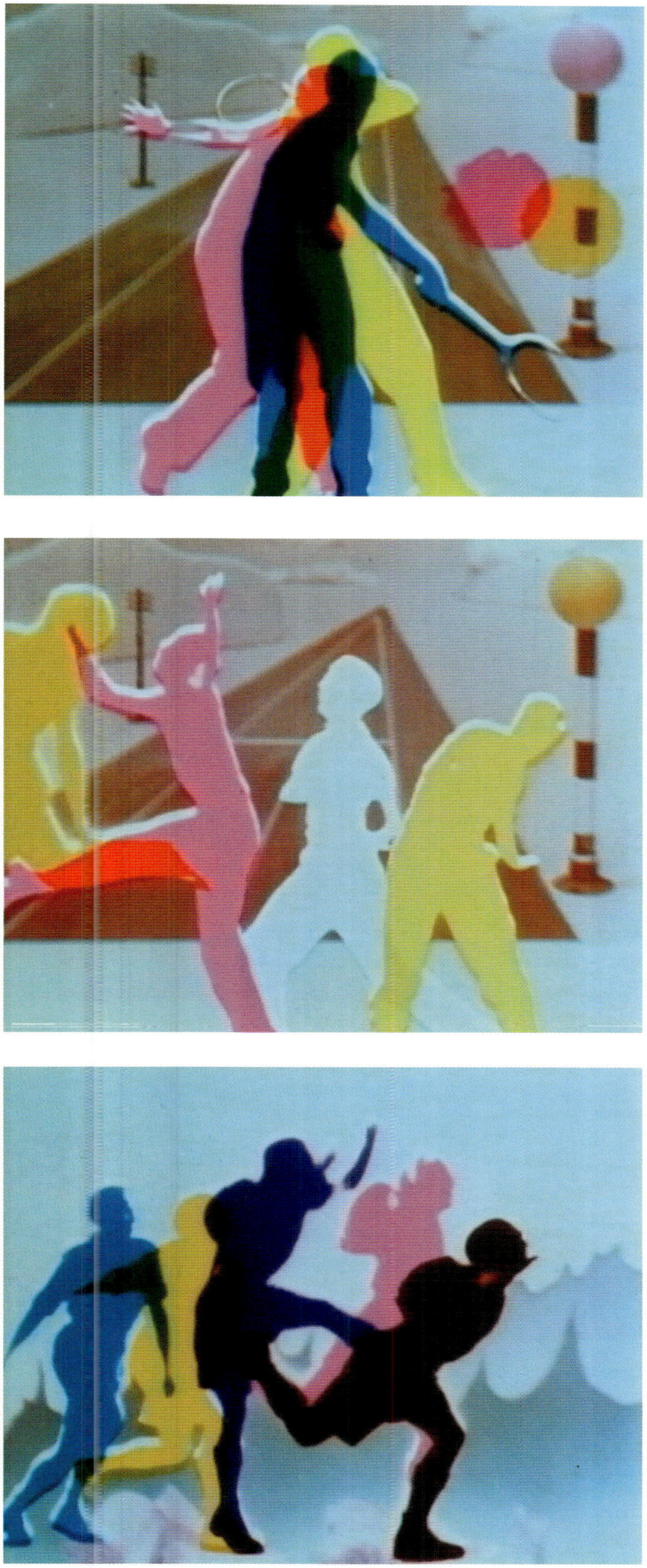

Lye, frames from the film *Rainbow Dance*, 1936. Courtesy Len Lye Foundation.

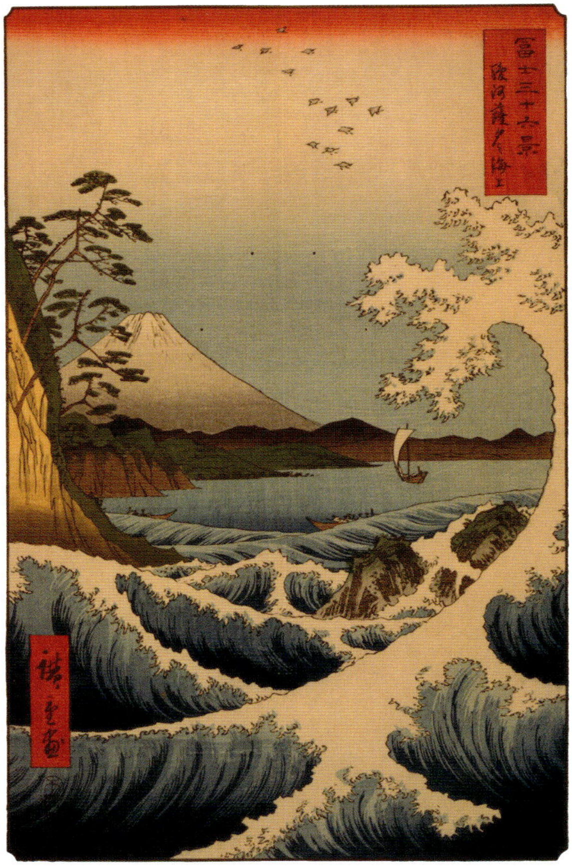

LEFT AND BELOW Lye admired these 19th-century woodblock prints by Japanese artists, *Breaking Wave at Satta Point on Suruga Bay* by Utagawa Hiroshige and *The Great Wave off Kanagawa* by Katsushika Hokusai. Mount Fuji appears in the background of both prints.

OPPOSITE, TOP AND BOTTOM Lye's paintings *Land and Sea* (oil on canvas, 1977, based on a 1920s batik) and *The King of Plants Meets the First Man* (oil on canvas, circa 1936). Courtesy Len Lye Foundation.

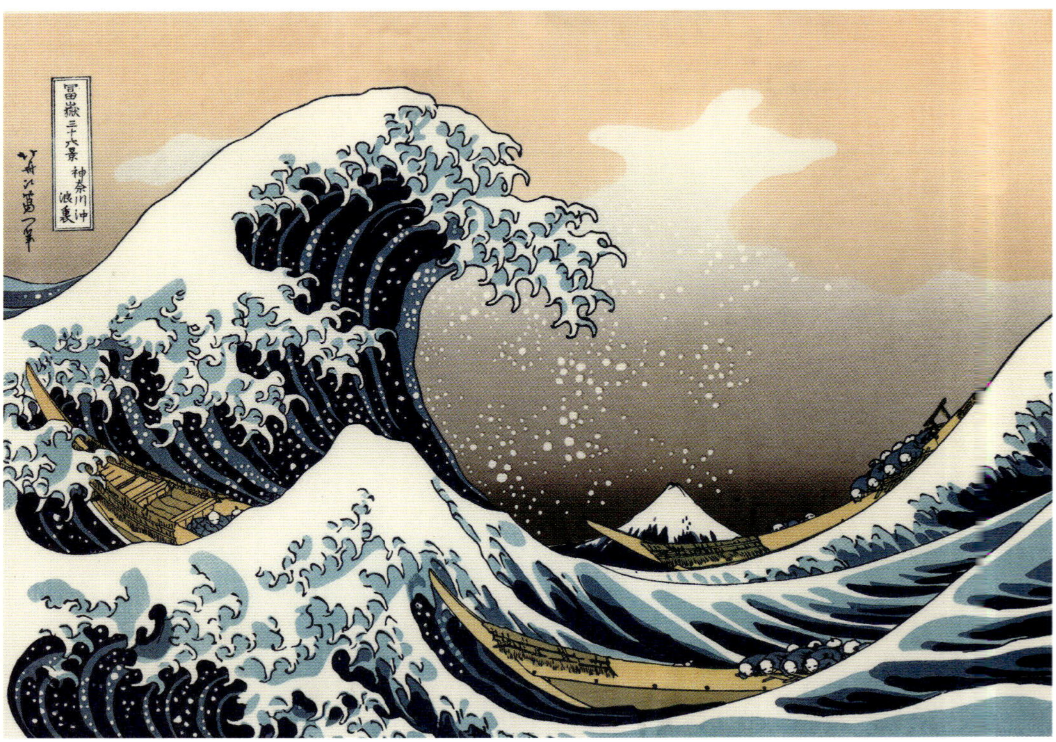

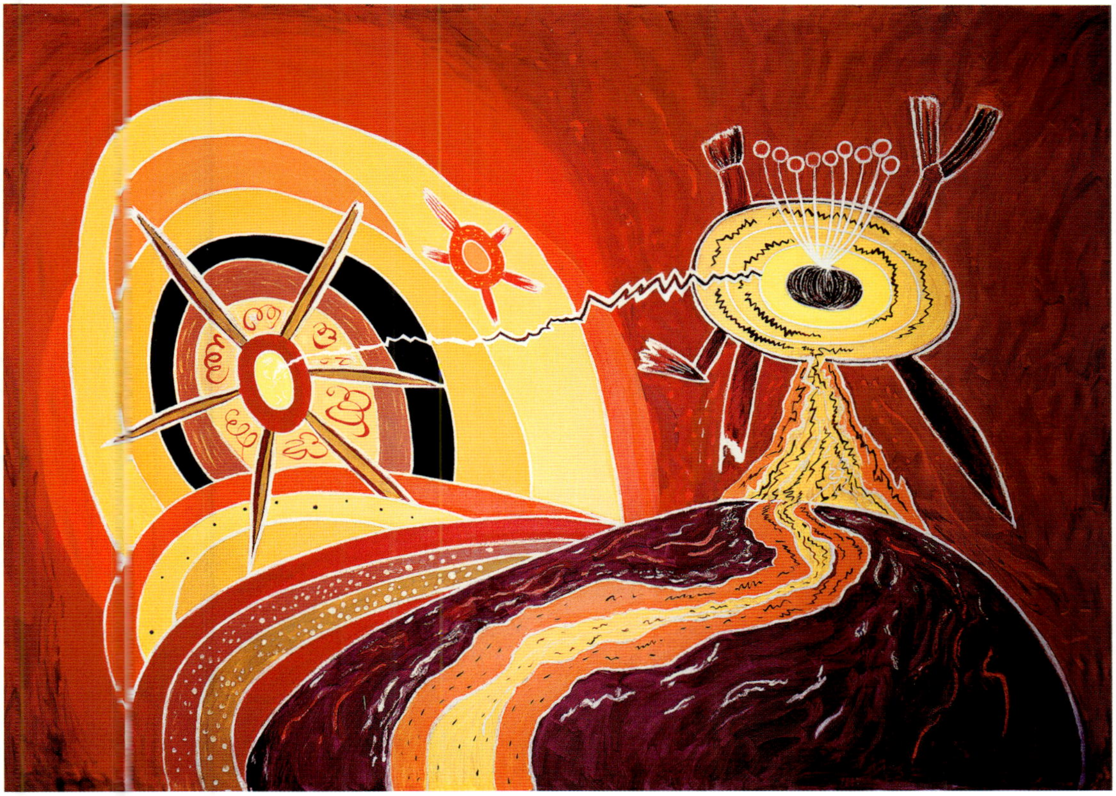

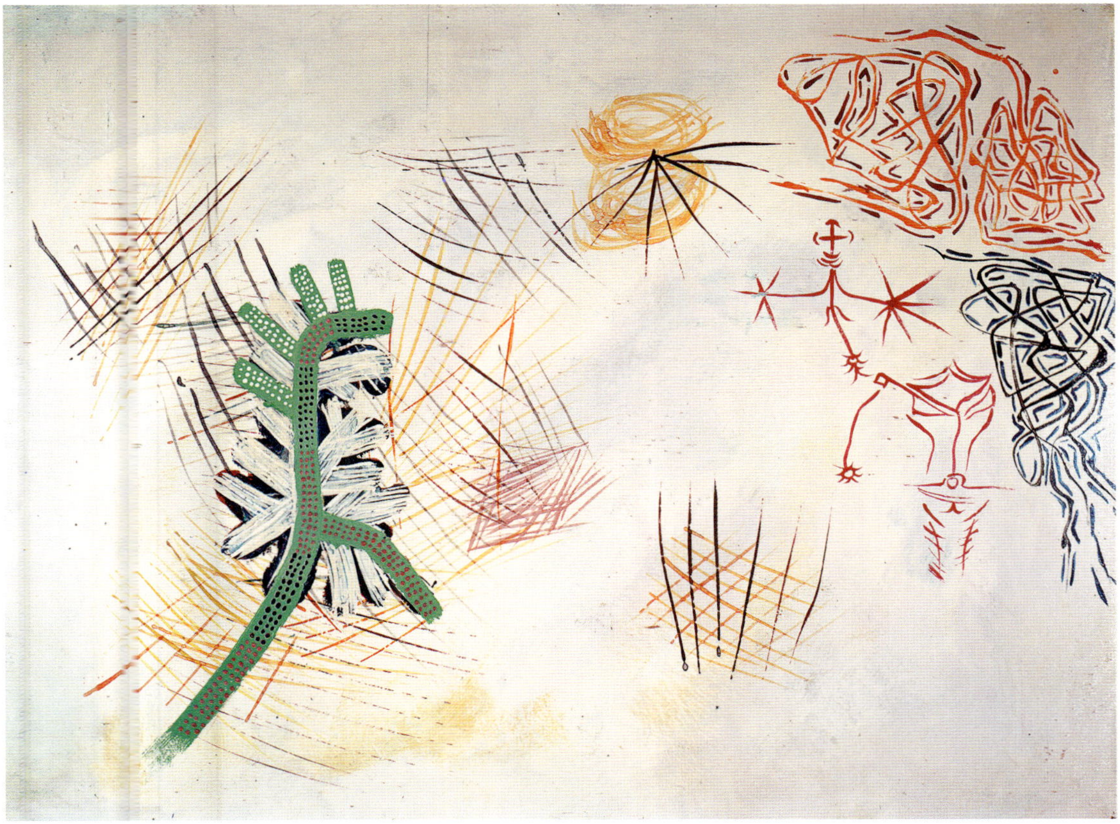

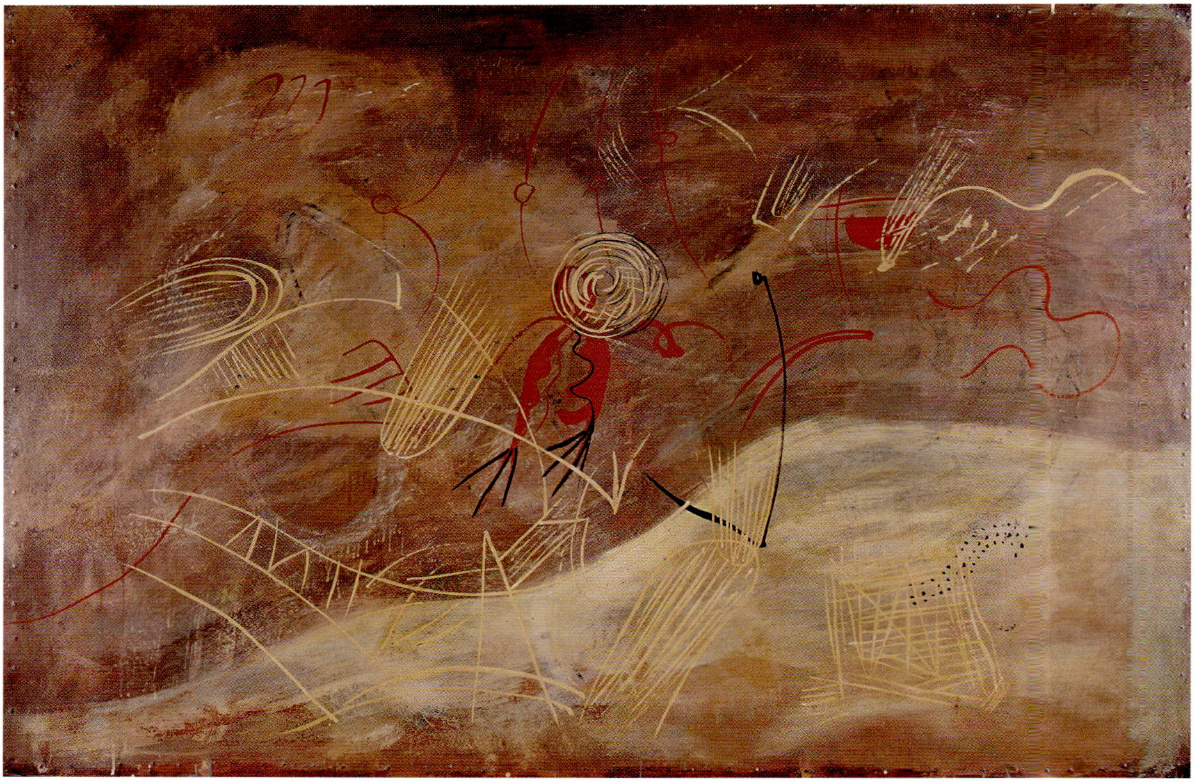

Lye's paintings *Snowbirds Making Snow* (oil on board, 1936), and *Helium* (acrylic on canvas, 1978, based on a 1938 oil painting). Courtesy Len Lye Foundation.

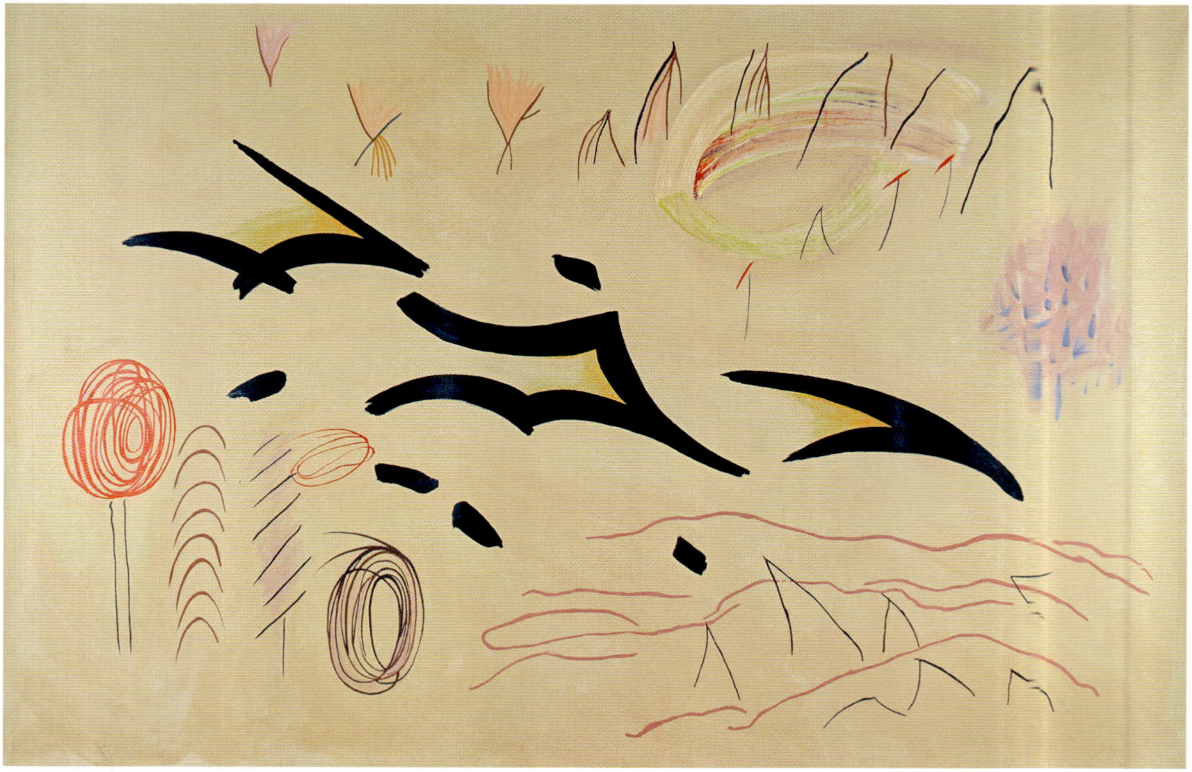

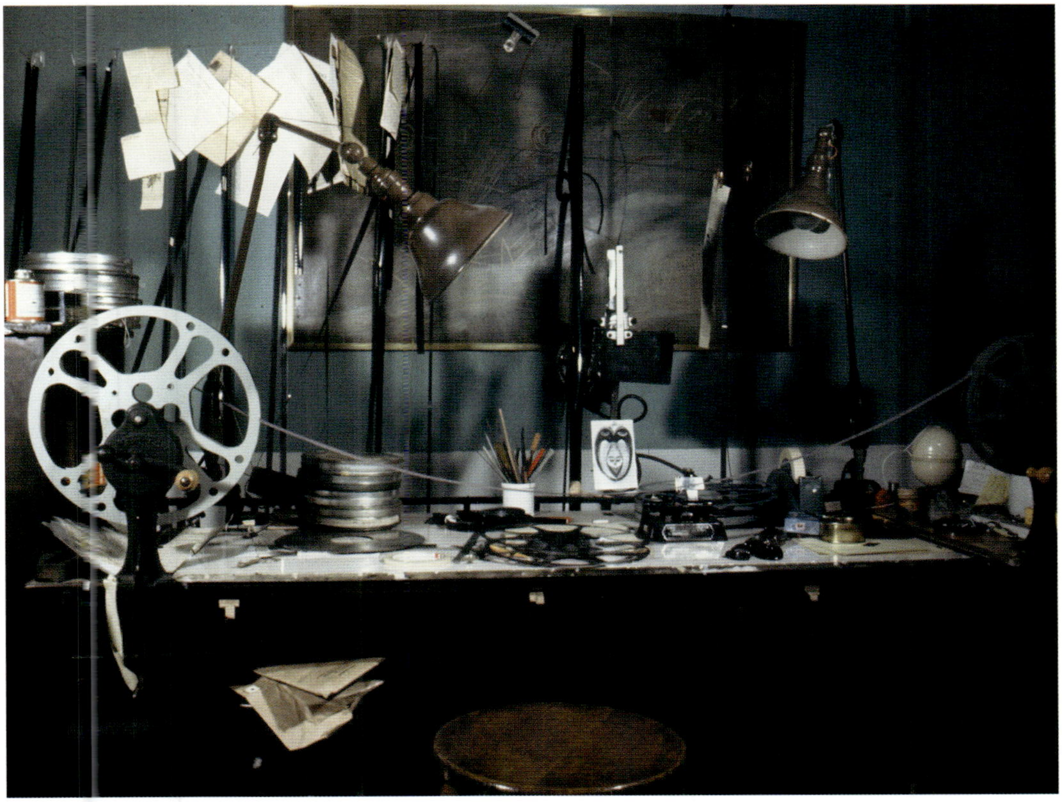

ABOVE Lye's work bench for making films in the 1950s. BELOW Some of the stencils he used to make hand-painted films in the 1930s. Courtesy Len Lye Foundation.

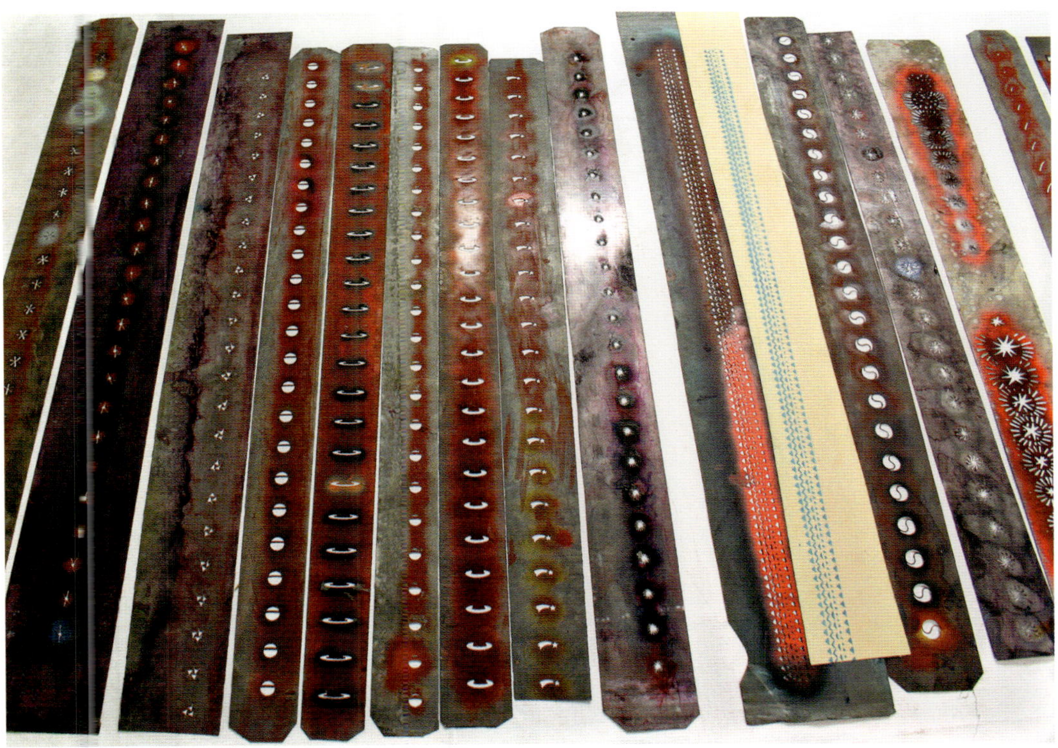

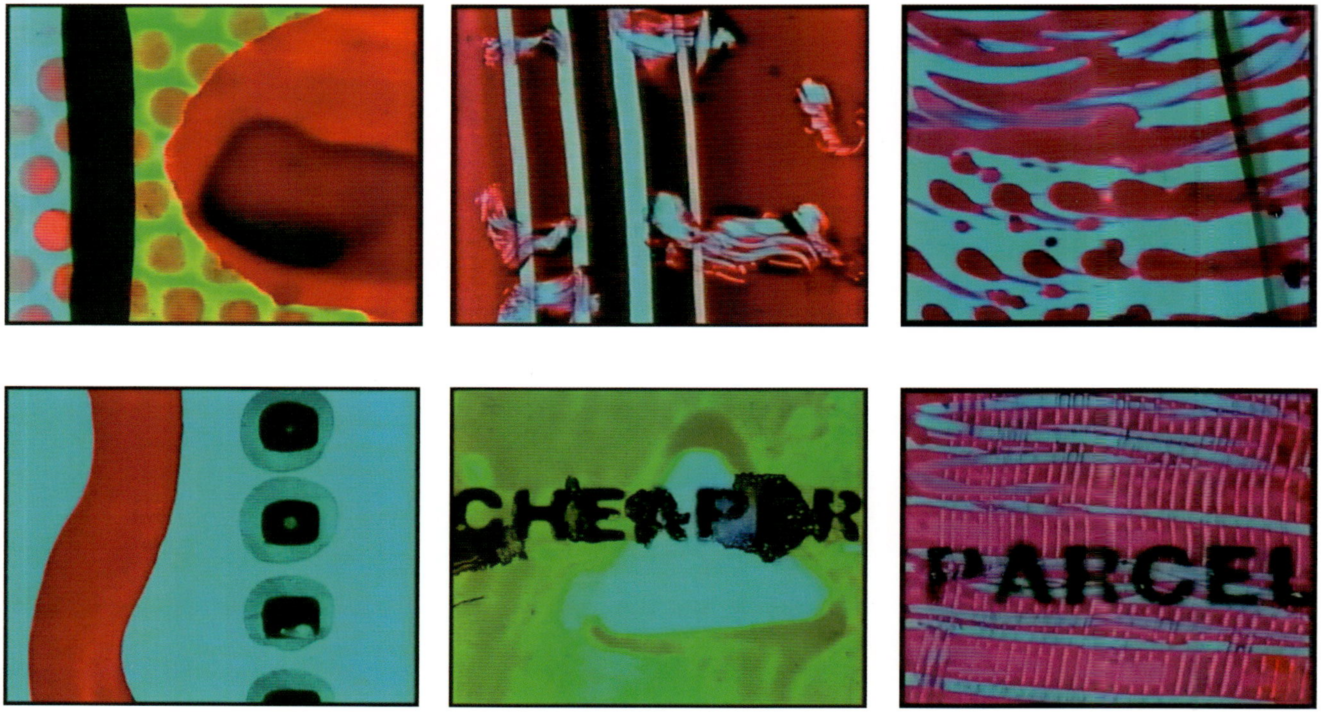

ABOVE Sample frames from Lye's film *A Colour Box* (1935). Courtesy Len Lye Foundation.

BELOW Three frames from *Musical Poster No. 1* (1940). Such images in Lye's films anticipated the shapes created eighteen years later by his kinetic sculptures. Courtesy Len Lye Foundation.

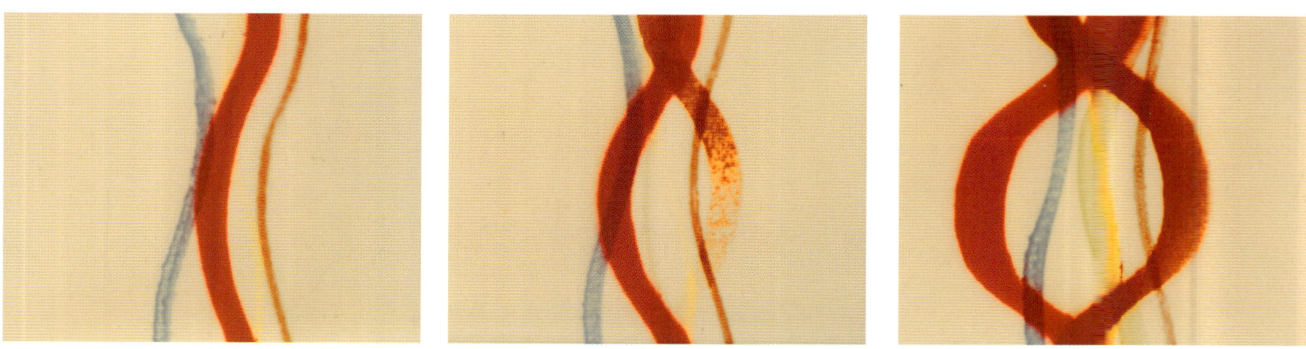

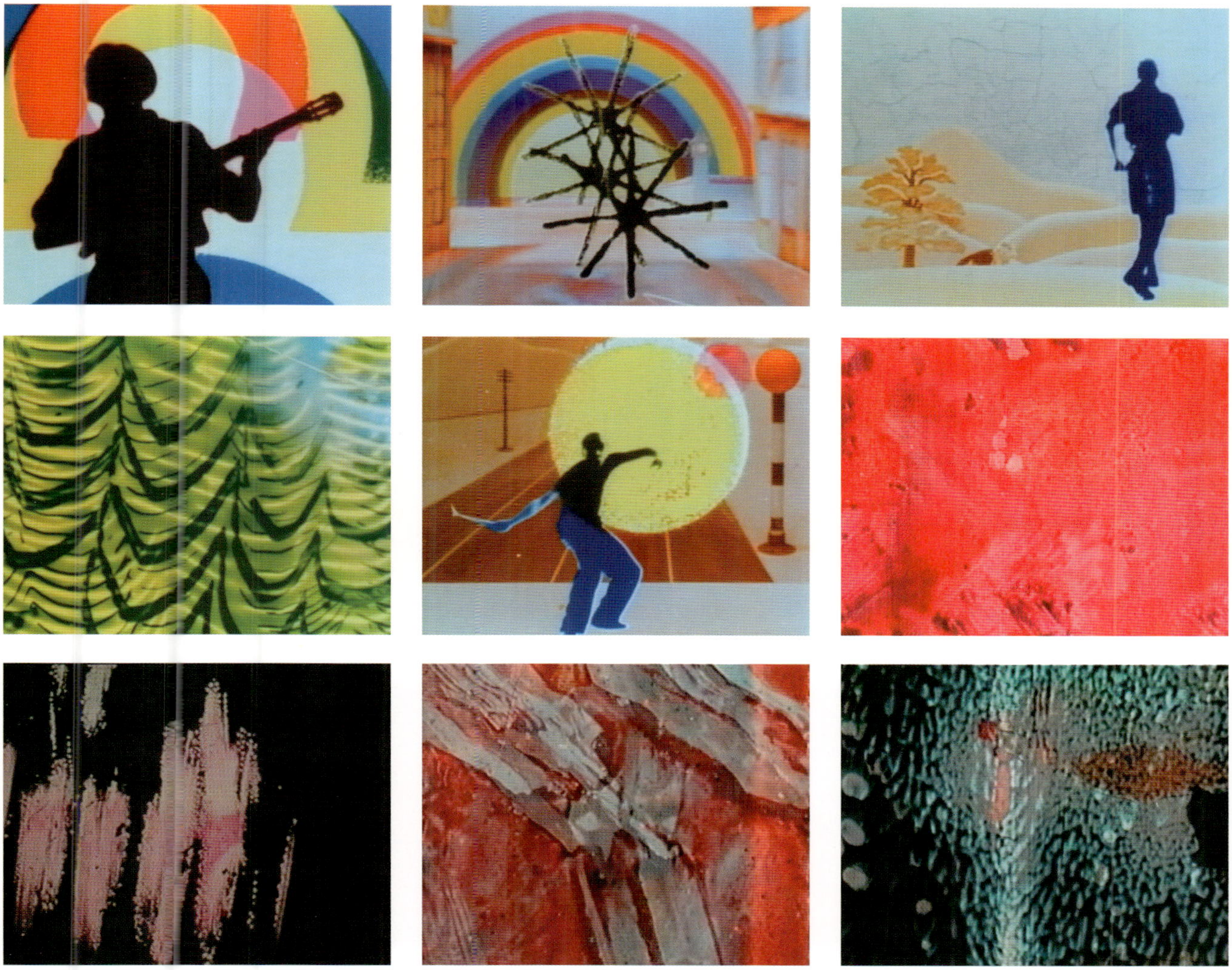

The first five frames are from *Rainbow Dance*, 1936, illustrating Lye's creative approach to colour processing and his symbolic method of story-telling (through the use of 'moving hieroglyphics'). The fourth image represents the sea, the fifth a tennis match. The last four frames are from *All Souls Carnival*, 1957, a showcase for a new style of 'rhapsodic' abstract imagery. Courtesy Len Lye Foundation.

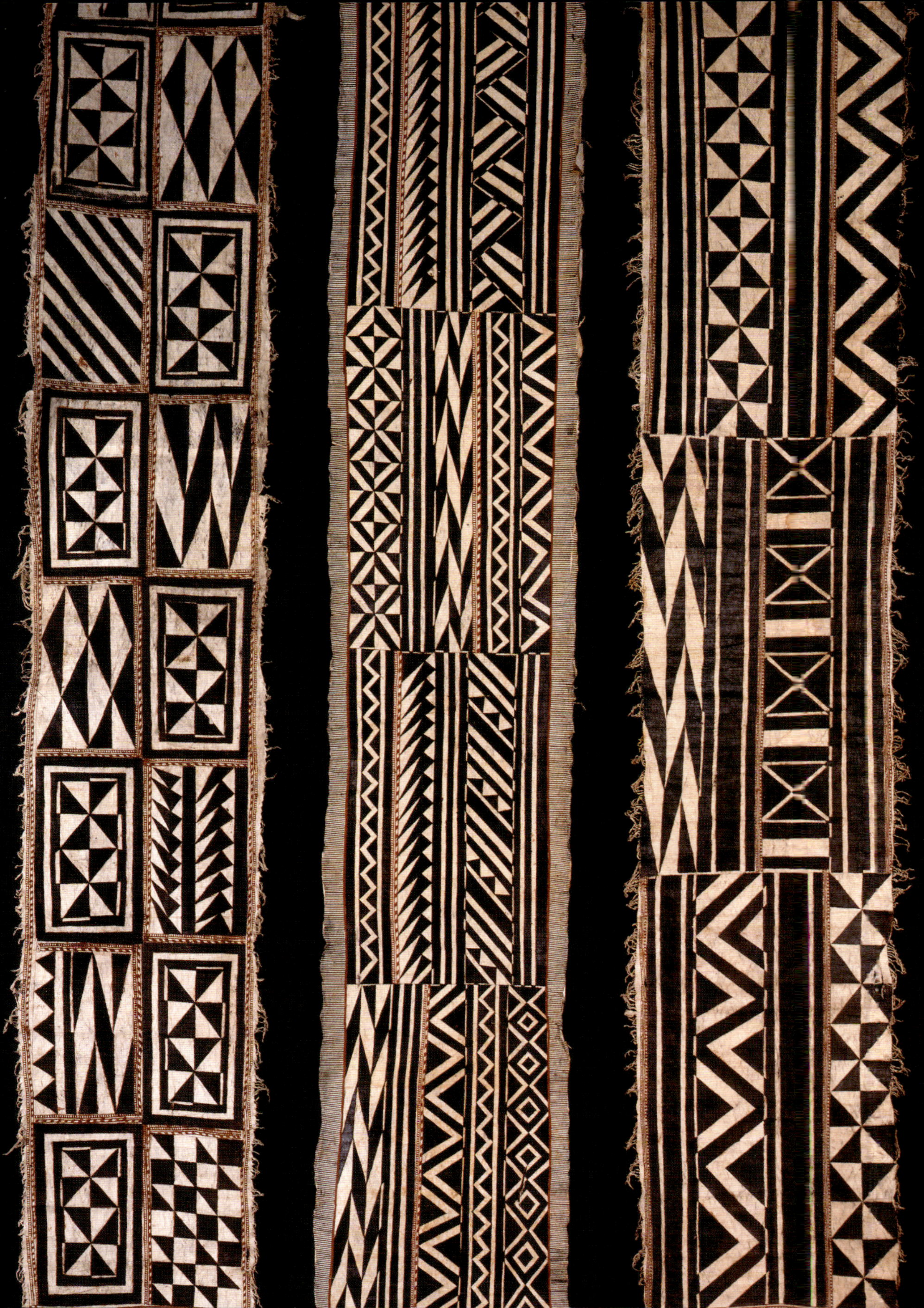

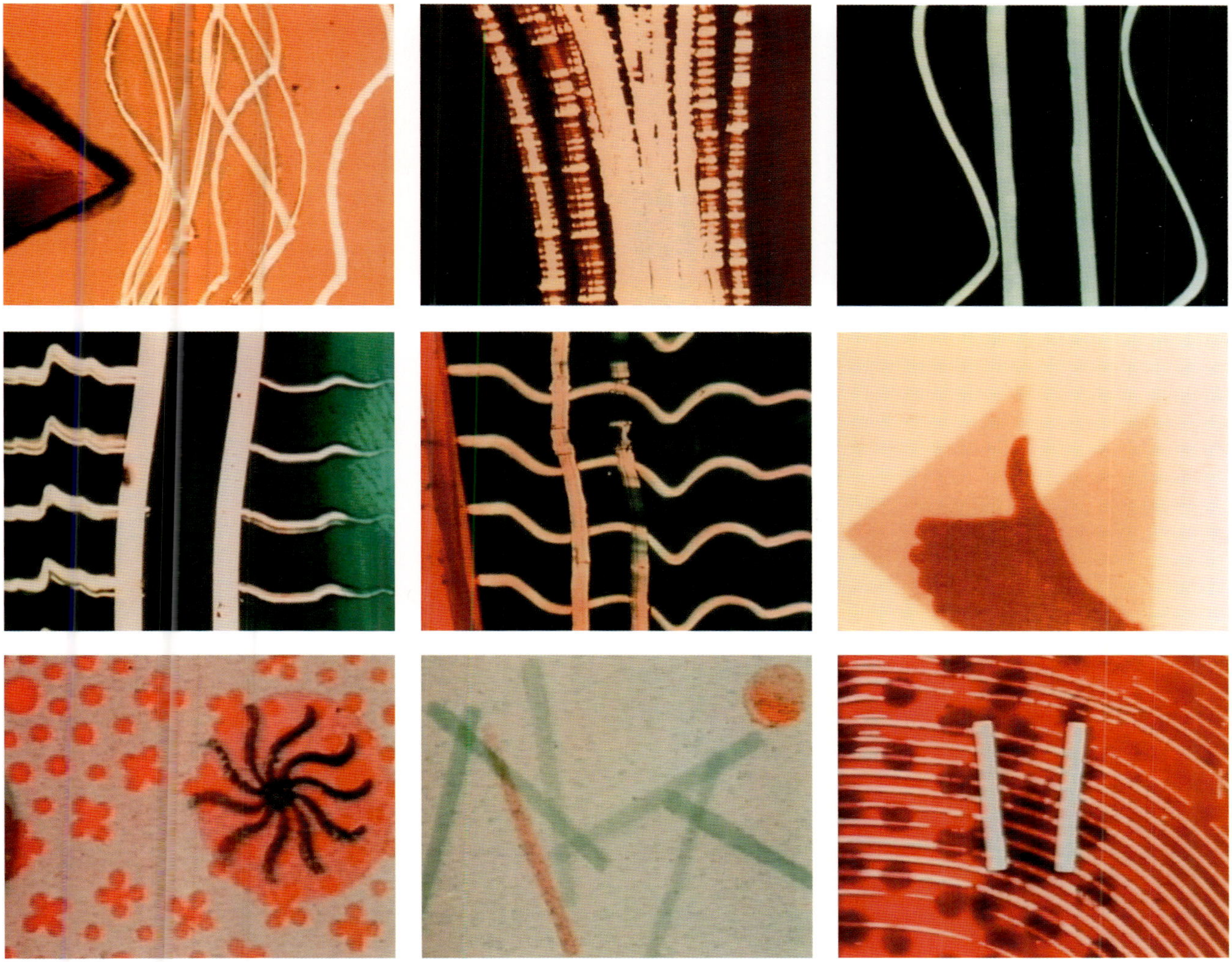

ABOVE The first six frames, which combine hand-painting and scratching, are from the film *Swinging the Lambeth Walk* (1939). Some of these images look forward to the shapes made by sculptures such as *Water Whirler*. The sixth frame, which employs stencils, is the thumbs-up 'Oi!' gesture associated with the Lambeth Walk dance. The last three frames are from *Kaleidoscope* (1935), a film that uses a variety of stencilled shapes to create rolling and spinning movements. The two cigarette shapes dance together. Courtesy Len Lye Foundation.

OPPOSITE Examples of Fijian *masi* (tapa) design. These striking, hand-painted patterns, made before 1930, are from the Cakaudrove district. Courtesy Auckland Museum, Tamaki Paenga Hira (collection numbers, left to right, AM 4138.1, AM 8487, AM 13760.1).

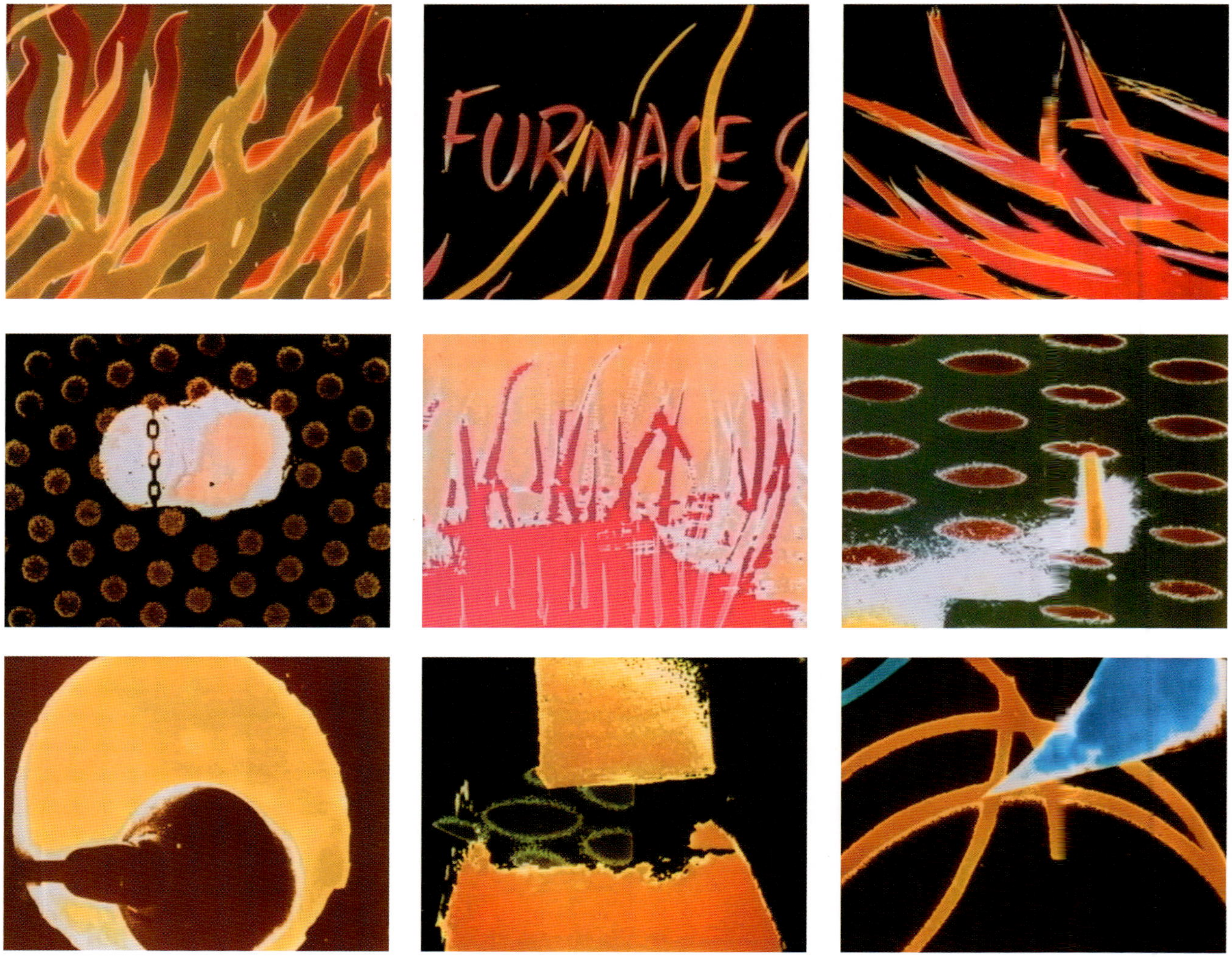

Frames from the 'furnace' sequence of *Trade Tattoo* (1937). Courtesy Len Lye Foundation.

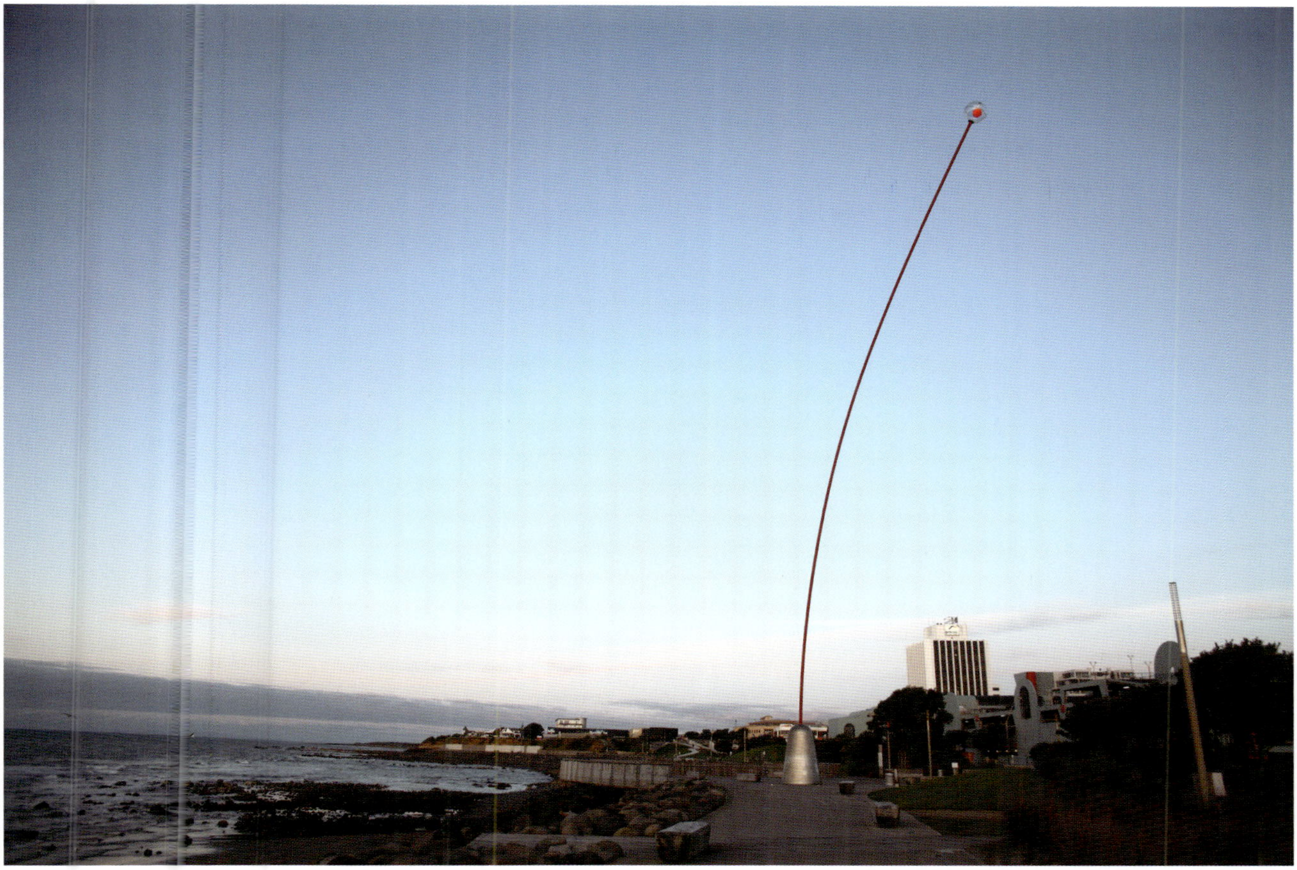

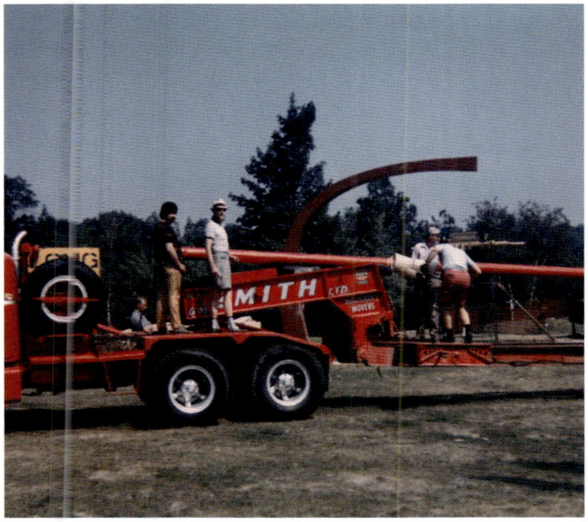

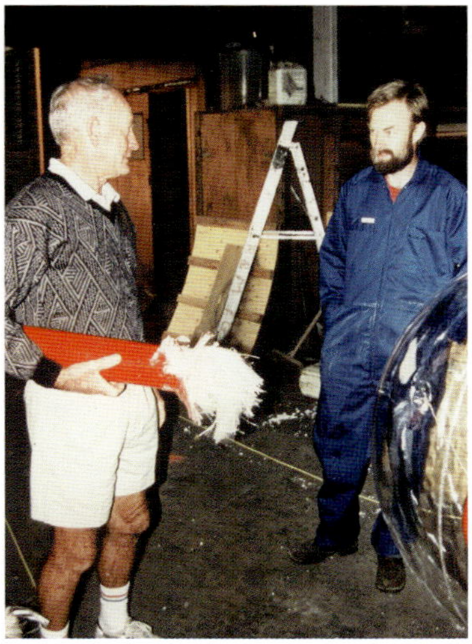

The 45-metre *Wind Wand* on the New Plymouth waterfront (above), and Dave Marks and Evan Webb who played key roles in building this sculpture. FAR LEFT Lye in Toronto in 1967 for the erection of a 25-metre *Wind Wand*. The artist was dismayed to see that his instructions had not been followed correctly. Courtesy Len Lye Foundation.

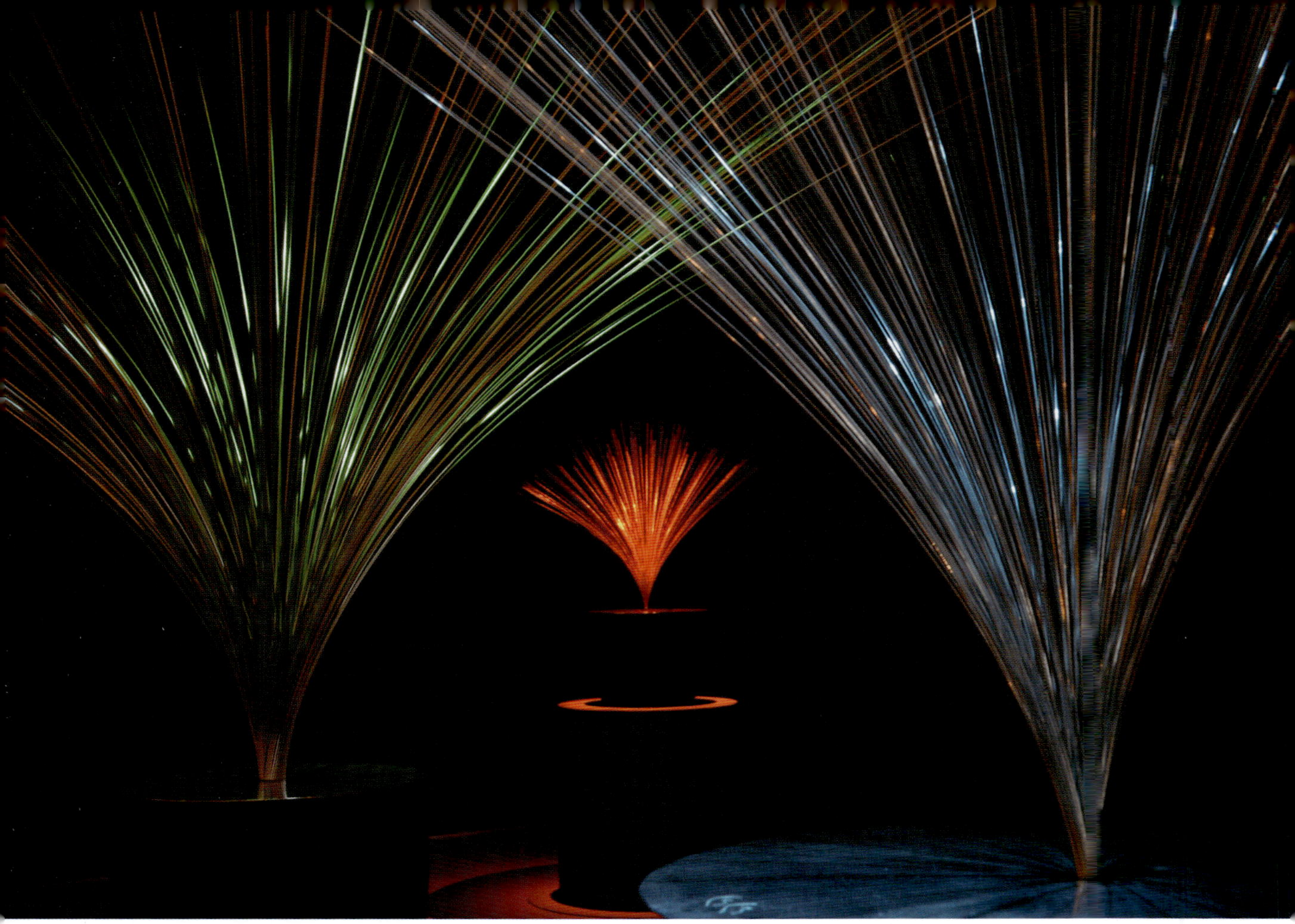

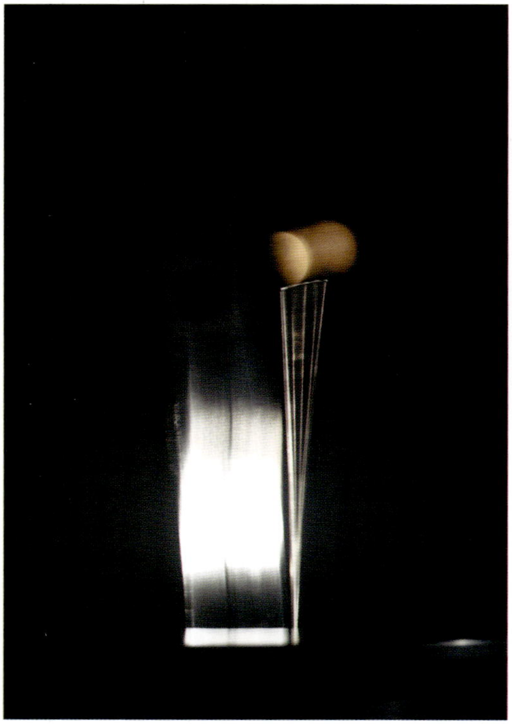

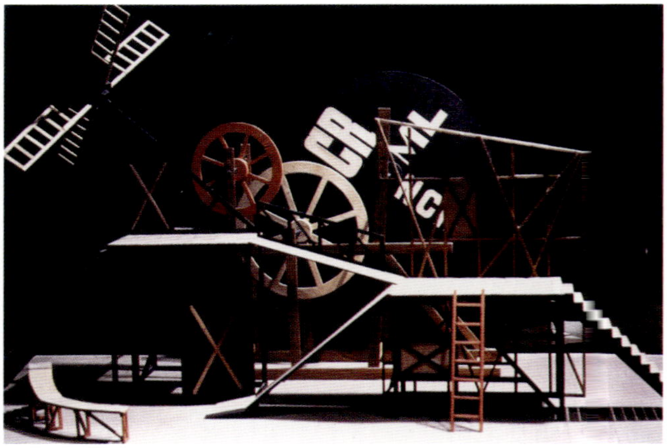

TOP *Firebush*, with two versions of *Fountain* in the foreground. From Tyler Cann's 2007 Lye exhibition *Five Fountains and a Firebush*. Courtesy Govett-Brewster Art Gallery. LEFT Lye's sculpture *Blade* in motion. Courtesy Len Lye Foundation. ABOVE Lyubov Popov's stage set for the Meyerhold Theatre's 192[illegible] production of *The Magnanimous Cuckold* in Moscow. The set resembled a large kinetic sculpture, and when Lye saw a picture of it he was so impressed that he made plans to travel to Moscow.

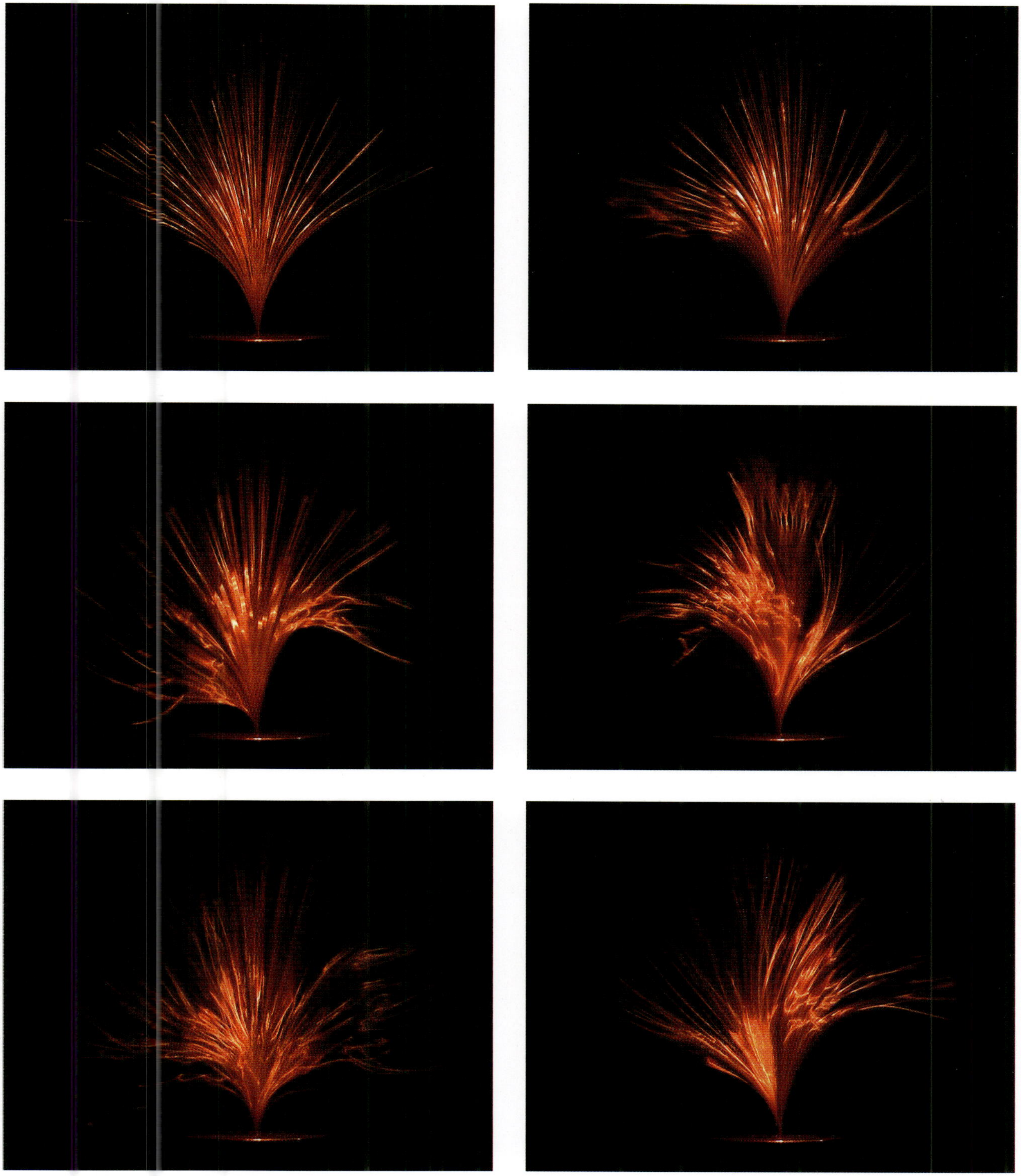

ABOVE Six images of *Fire Bush* in motion. Courtesy Point of View Productions.
OVERLEAF *Water Whirler* in one of its most active phases. Courtesy Govett-Brewster Art Gallery.

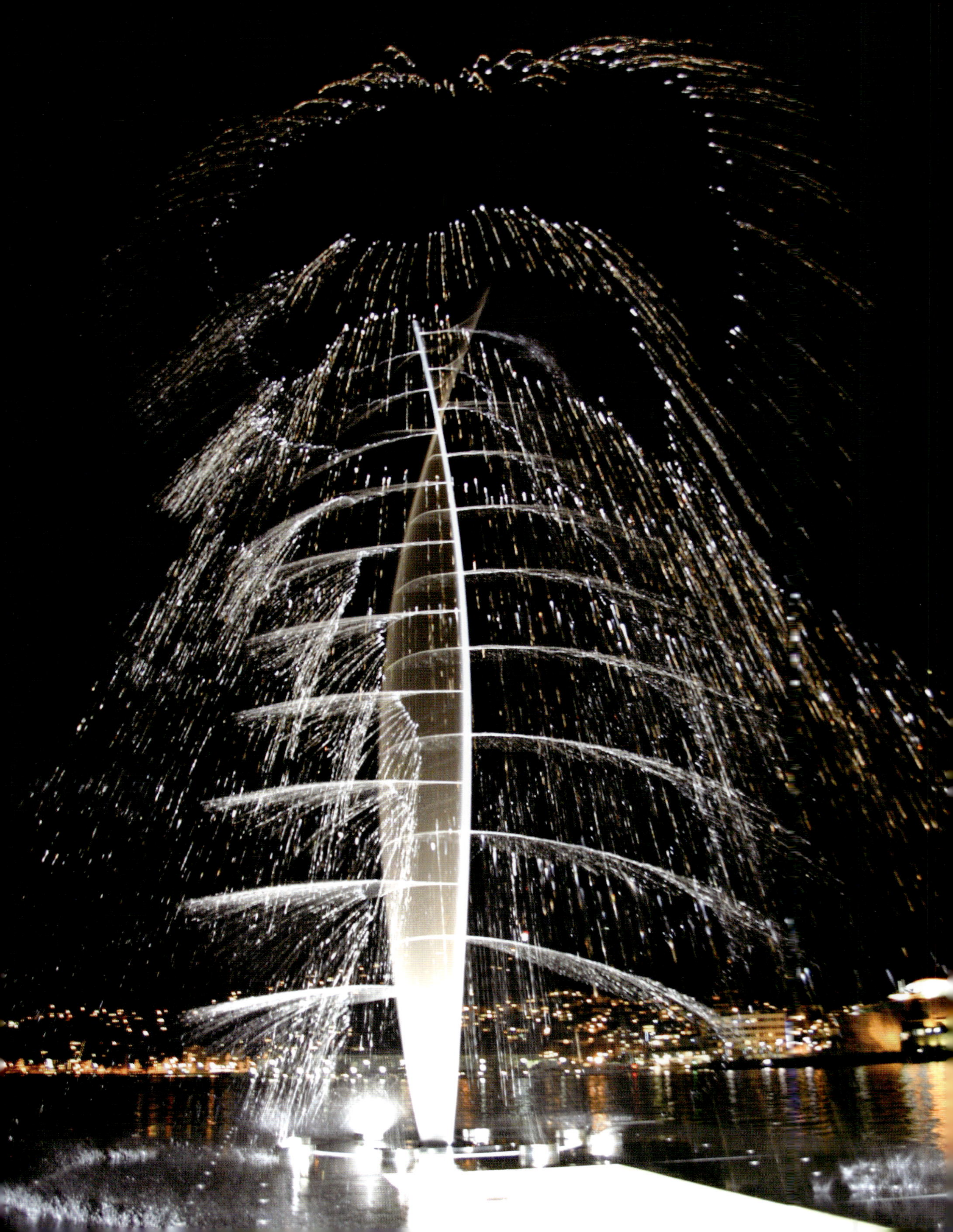

four the films

JOHN TAYLOR, AN IMPORTANT FIGURE IN BRITISH DOCUMENTARY-making who was Lye's boss at the Realist Film Unit, said of him, 'I've been in the film industry for 50 years now, and I think he is probably the one truly original thinker I've met in that time. He had completely his own approach to everything.'[1] Alberto Cavalcanti, a leading figure in the GPO Film Unit, summed up Lye's approach similarly: 'Len Lye could be described in the history of British cinema by one word – *experiment*.'[2] And Lye himself commented, 'Every film [commission] I got . . . , I tried to interest myself in it by doing . . . something not previously done in film technique.'[3]

For his first film *Tusalava*, Lye used orthodox animation with a camera, but created a unique visual style through his choice of imagery and unusual sense of composition. In his direct films, he pioneered a new method of animation, dispensing with the camera and painting images directly on celluloid. Determined not to repeat himself, he continued to expand his camera-less techniques – scratching images with a variety of sharp-pointed tools, using stencils and an airbrush, learning to animate words and letters, and employing the photogram method to print fabric patterns onto film. He kept discovering new possibilities within each of these methods, so there are striking differences between (say) the abstract paint patterns of *All Souls Carnival* and those of *A Colour Box*, or the scratched shapes of *Free Radicals* and those of *Tal Farlow*.

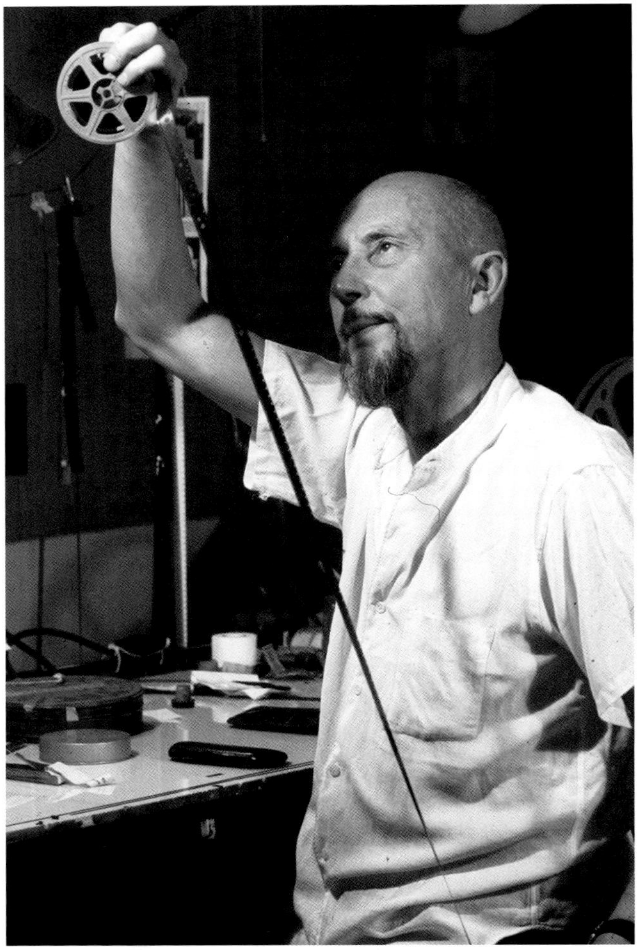

Lye in New York working on a film, circa 1958. Courtesy Len Lye Foundation.

With the introduction of new film stocks in the 1930s, colour became a major area of experiment for Lye. During this period, he was generally better known for colour than for movement. As one reviewer wrote, 'You've not seen a colour film till you've seen a Len Lye effort.'[4] His colour experiments brought him back to the use of the camera (in *Rainbow Dance*), but he transformed this technology by an innovative approach to the processing of film, which created a new style of representation. Impatient with conventional forms of realism, he pushed the possibilities he had opened up in *Rainbow Dance* to a further stage in *Trade Tattoo.* In *N or NW*, when he engaged more directly with the activity of story-telling by means of actors and the camera, he took a simple GPO cautionary tale about addressing letters correctly and turned it into a radical attack on the narrative language of film. Lye championed a less linear, more kinetic approach to continuity editing. This summary does not exhaust the scope of his experiments. He also developed puppet (or 'stop motion') animation in *The Birth of the Robot* and *Peanut Vendor*, and he experimented with sound in *When the Pie was Opened* and with cinéma vérité (or 'fly on the wall' documentary filming) in *Work Party.* These last two films were among those Lye made during the Second World War for the British Ministry of Information, and although he was required to work to a tight brief, he always managed to add a few surprises.

All of Lye's films were informed by his appetite for experiment and by his eye for movement. Movement was not his only concern but it strongly informed his thinking about animation, editing and story-telling. Unfortunately, he sometimes included more experiments than the audience could handle. Hence there were two conflicting tendencies in Lye's work. On the one hand, his films were never solemn or pretentious, as avant-garde art sometimes is; their exuberance and their use of dance music gave them the potential for broad appeal, and David Curtis has pointed out that *A Colour Box* was seen 'by a larger public than any experimental film before it and most since'.[5] On the other hand, some viewers were puzzled by his innovations and dismissed the films as quirky and eccentric. *Newspaper Train* was unlucky enough to be selected as one of four wartime films followed through the nation's cinemas by a Ministry of Information audience study, which reported that viewers found it confusing and 'over-intellectualised'. The researchers concluded that MOI films needed to be more straightforward and less 'cinematographic'.[6] Nevertheless, it is precisely their 'cinematographic' qualities that enable Lye's films still to seem fresh 60 or 70 years later.

Lye found that even camera-less film-making was expensive – in terms of materials, music rights and the making of prints – and so he needed commissions. He was fortunate in England to find sponsors such as John Grierson who understood the importance of his work even though it polarised audiences. As Cavalcanti explained, 'When you see these publicity films you'll realize that it would have been futile to expect people to post more parcels after *Colour Box*, smoke more cigarettes after *Kaleidoscope* or save more money after *Rainbow Dance*. [But] a Len Lye film brought a great amount of prestige to its sponsors.'[7] It was also an opportunity for the sponsor to sneak an advertisement into the cinemas, albeit an odd sort of advertisement. Many cinemas actually paid to rent *A Colour Box* because it was creating so much public debate.[8]

The challenge was how to incorporate the advertising message in an interesting way. In *Colour Flight*, Lye made vivid use of the Imperial Airways 'speedbird' symbol, creating a flock of many-coloured birds. He attempted to integrate the Post Office slogans in *A Colour Box* by stencilling the words in a style reminiscent of Cubist painting, constantly changing their colours and flying them onto the screen from different angles. This ingenuity helped audiences to accept the slogans with good humour. A *Daily Express* reporter wrote, 'We guarantee a good laugh when a blob totters on and says, "3 lbs for sixpence".'[9] And Ernest Betts observed, 'I doubt if Ginger Rogers could make a more startling appearance.'[10] While Lye knew that slogans were the only way to finance his work, he remained deeply troubled by them. In his later years, he would sometimes make disparaging comments about his films of the 1930s, partly because they were not relevant to his current theories about genetic imagery in art, and partly because his time in New York had left him fed up with commercial sponsors. He remarked in 1963, 'You can't go and put a pack of Chesterfields on the brow of Michelangelo's *Moses* and call it fine art.'[11] Nevertheless, Lye's failure to find sponsors in the USA meant that his production of films slowed down considerably. The forms of public funding available today were not established until late in his career, and he never had the advantage of personal wealth or rich patrons. In the light of that situation, no one interested in the art of film – or the art of motion – can afford to be squeamish about the occasional advertising slogans that intrude on these remarkable films.

INDIVIDUAL FILMS AND LYE'S FILM TECHNIQUES

Tusalava and the Principles of Animation

Lye taught himself the basic principles of animation by creating *Tusalava* between 1927 and 1929. He employed the conventional process – making drawings and then photographing them, one frame at a time – but approached the medium from a fresh perspective. He was the first film-maker to model his imagery on Australian Aboriginal art. There had been a strong influence of tribal (or 'primitive') art on modern forms of painting and sculpture, but it had not yet reached animation. In terms of film technique, he took an unusual approach to the screen by dividing it into panels and by moving his creatures around the edges. He refused to follow the emphasis on montage (sequences of rapid editing) that had become fashionable thanks to the work of Sergei Eisenstein (whose London workshop Lye attended in 1929). Instead, *Tusalava* avoided any suggestion of editing or camera movement – the action was continuous and the framing remained constant throughout the film. This was clearly not the result of inexperience as Lye drew attention to this aspect in programme notes for the première: '*Tusalava* is a drawn film relying on the intrinsic form to convey the meaning without the use of "mounting" [montage] or camera technique to heighten the sequence. Rather, the form is developed continually from the original motif . . . without the motif leaving the screen.'[12] In one sense, this was a return to the early days of film-making, but for Lye it was a conscious aesthetic. Today, we may relate this approach to his later sculptures which operate continuously from a fixed base.

The imagery of *Tusalava* suggested forms of life in the dawn of history – growing, splitting by binary fission, attacking or absorbing one another, and in the course of this activity evolving. The main motif of the film was the Australian witchetty grub, which he imagined as a 'lumpy worm' that would 'wiggle quietly' while he taught himself animation.[13] It gradually developed into a more complex creature with some of the characteristics of a 'monstrous python' or 'octopus'. At first, Lye found it hard to build up speed: 'it was a goddamned drugged grub . . . I tried to push [it] around with my drawings.'[14] But though the animation was somewhat jerky, even mechanical at times, it seemed to suit these strange creatures. The grub, as he described it in *No Trouble*, had 'cog-chain movements'.[15]

The action became more fluid in the second half of the film when the 'monstrous python' attacked an almost human form that had developed within a womb shape – a 'cocoon or core' – on the right-hand side of the film. Incidentally, in the last few years there has been a controversy about the correct orientation of the film, as some prints place the embryo on the left. But in his detailed account in *No Trouble*, Lye clearly imagined the figure on the right.[16] Whichever way round the film is presented, it is a dramatic moment each time the 'python' succeeds in penetrating the barrier that separates the two sides of the screen. The embryo seems passive and helpless. This is the most kinetic section of the film, anticipating the vigorous action of Lye's later sculptures. The monster (whose arms have grown more muscular) pushes the embryo back and forth, then leaves it to rock from side to side. This complex dance continues with the monster rotating while concentric circles in the embryo pulse. Then, like an octopus, the monster squirts ink into the embryo, turning it into a kind of black egg, which it sends spinning. When the ink clears and we can see the embryo again, it moves with a wobble, having become 'grey and soft and ready for mastication'. The monster toys with it like a yo-yo, but then, when it sticks its tongue into its prey, it triggers off a great explosion. Concentric circles ripple forth and fill the screen.

Tusalava was originally conceived at silent speed, but Lye later came to feel that the film moved too slowly.[17] Nevertheless, the effort of single-handedly producing ten minutes of film at the rate of one second per day – 'it takes two whole months to do one minute's worth of drawings'[18] – trained his hands and eyes in the subtleties of animation. He thought of the film as the first part of a trilogy and did an enormous amount of planning for the sequels, but he was not able to raise the necessary funding.[19]

Tusalava remains unique in film history, with its Samoan title and its mixture of modern and Aboriginal art. From the Aboriginal tradition, Lye borrowed dots, concentric circles and egg shapes – all associated with witchetty grub mythology – and the python motif.[20] Another reason the film was surprising was the way it employed whimsical cartoon animation for avant-garde purposes, giving it a complex tone that recalled the paintings of Miró and Klee. Many viewers of *Tusalava* lacked a context in which to place the film, but Oswell Blakeston in *Close Up* applauded the radical way in which Lye had rejected editing: 'There is no cutting, beloved of the Russians, or jugglery with the camera; the screen is considered instead of the camera.'[21] At that time, Blakeston was collaborating with Francis Bruguière to make *Light Rhythms*, another film without conventional editing and with musical accompaniment by Jack Ellitt.[22]

A Colour Box and its Sequels: Direct Film-making

Around 1934, Lye moved on from the *Tusalava* method of animation to the process of painting directly on film. One of the practical problems was to find types of paint that would not crack or peel off the surface of the film, while being transparent enough to produce the right colours when projected. This involved a slow process of trial and error until he settled on a particular range of lacquer paints. As tools, he used a camel-hair brush and various homely objects such as a fine-tooth comb which he wiggled through wet paint to make 'striated wavy lines'.[23] He is said to have started by making a trial film (since lost) called *Full Fathom Five*, based on a famous song lyric from Shakespeare's *The Tempest*. This film was not entirely abstract but included 'flashes' of found footage.[24]

The five direct, animated films that Lye made between 1935 and 1940 can usefully be taken as a group: *A Colour Box*, *Kaleidoscope*, *Colour Flight*, *Swinging the Lambeth Walk* and *Musical Poster #1*. What were his working methods? In each case, he had first to find a sponsor who was not going to impose too many conditions. Then, having developed some visual ideas, he looked for a suitable piece of music. This had to be rhythmic, with a strong sense of 'swing' or body resonance. The music needed to have popular appeal yet not cost too much for the rights. London was just then in the process of discovering Cuban and Caribbean dance music, styles that had already gained a following in Paris. For *A Colour Box* and *Kaleidoscope*, Lye obtained the right to use tracks by Don Baretto and his Cuban Orchestra, and in later 1930s films he used Cuban music by Rico's Creole Band and the Lecuona Cuban Boys. *Colour Flight* included jazz by Red Nichols and his Five Pennies, and Lye's cut-and-paste soundtrack for *Swinging the Lambeth Walk* sampled at least five recordings of the Lambeth Walk, a current dance craze. (His favourite version was by Le Quintette du Hot Club de France, with Django Reinhardt on guitar and Stephane Grapelli on violin.)[25] Lye hoped that such soundtracks would help make his films more accessible, but, in any case, it was music he enjoyed for its sensuous swing. The Baretto tracks were based on the beguine, a dance originally from Martinique that encouraged a slow, sexy rolling of the hips.[26]

Next, he had to 'chart' (analyse) the music he had chosen. Lye was assisted in this by two brilliant composers, Ellitt (up to 1937) and Ernst Meyer (from 1938 to 1943). The dance music usually had a clear structure and this provided the framework for Lye's animation. For example, a song would follow an AABA pattern or some other regular form, and a jazz-style solo was generally structured in four- or eight-bar units. Lye was not interested in simply illustrating the music but he would observe the main changes and junctions – the entry of a new solo instrument, say, or the repeat of the main theme at the end. *Lambeth Walk*, for example, began and ended with a very similar visual sequence, though he changed the colours. He also liked to add 'accents' (stabby black triangles that appeared momentarily on the left or right of the frame) to mark the pauses in a solo, in the way that a jazz drummer might fill a gap with extra beats. Lye would get the music printed in the form of an optical soundtrack because, translated in that way, the shape of a phrase would occasionally give him a visual idea. Despite these various forms of interplay, the images of the film retained a great deal of independence.

As he painted the film, he worked on strips of celluloid up to a metre long. The film frame was a tiny canvas on which to do detailed work – it was 35mm wide and 24mm high, approximately the size of a postage stamp. After the advent of sound films at the end of the 1920s, 24 (rather than sixteen) separate frames made up one second of film. A metre of film now ran for approximately two seconds. Lye would pass rhythmically along the strip as he drew a series of consecutive frames. To control the movement of images, he needed to paint or scratch each

One of Lye's stencils for film-making. An instruction written along the top says 'Revolve', and along the bottom 'Repeat 1st turn or this turn & reverse turn as sync accent . . .'. Courtesy Len Lye Foundation.

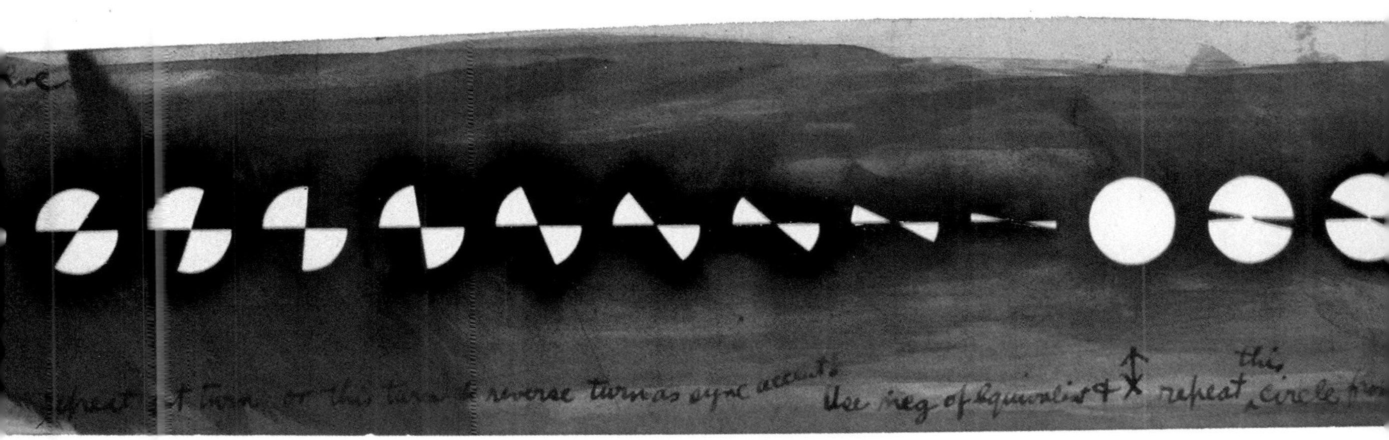

ACCENTS

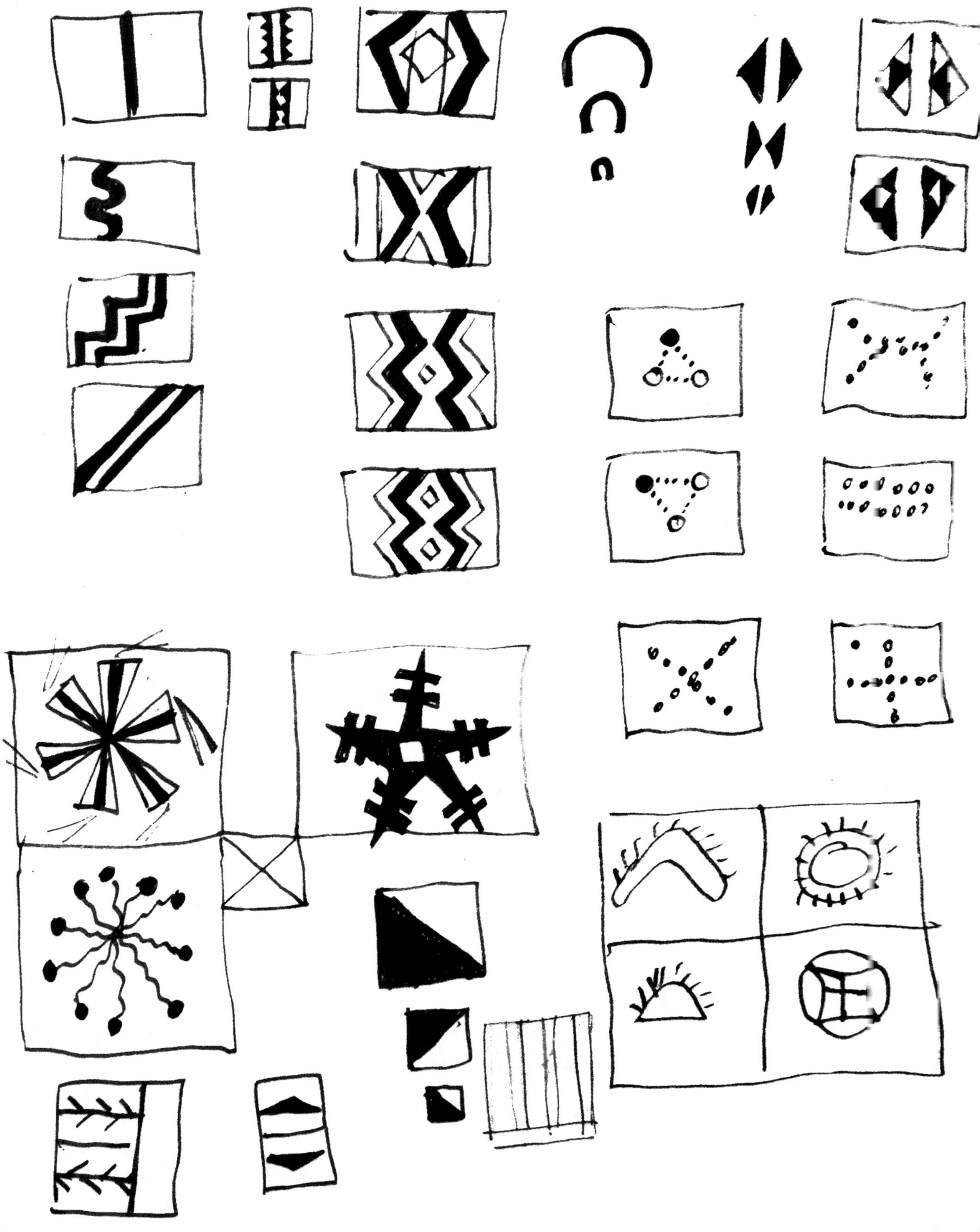

frame separately, although backgrounds could be painted across several frames as a wash, and a vertical line could be drawn down the film. Such a line became a favorite motif and Lye developed a masterful control over it – he could make it sway, wriggle, jump or glide. Most striking, however, was the attention he paid to each individual frame, making his films rich in details and textures, with the image constantly changing.

During the making of *Tusalava*, it had taken him a day to produce a second of film; now, with direct animation, he could produce a couple of seconds in one burst of activity. But drawing on such a small scale was a less controlled process, and he had to keep checking whether he had realised his idea successfully. He would start each strip with a sense of what he wanted, but the small size made it necessary to work by 'feel', and this left room for surprises. He had to allow the film strip to dry (there were strips hanging from clothes-lines all over his apartment), and he would then check the results on an editing bench at the GPO Film Unit. He revised constantly. The one film he made rapidly was *A Colour Box*, presumably because he was able to reap the benefits of a year of experiment. After that, he made films at the rate of two per year.

He developed a basic range of visual motifs (or figures of motion). He tended to match drumming with bold bouncing circles, using this for the title sequences of several films. He associated the piano, another percussion instrument, with a swarm of coloured blobs – dots, small circles and sprocket hole shapes – which suggested a flurry of notes. Other solos – by wind or string instruments – tended to be accompanied by vertical lines – thin or thick, painted or scratched, sometimes dividing into several parallel lines. They swayed from side to side, quivered and twanged. Deep, resonant playing on a tenor sax or double-bass called for a bold line, thick or very textured. A guitar became a horizontal line or mesh of lines, like vibrating strings.

It must be stressed that this was not a fixed vocabulary, only a starting point. It accompanied many of the instrumental solos of *A Colour Box*, *Swinging the Lambeth Walk* and *Colour Flight*. For passages of ensemble playing, Lye would combine a variety of motifs. And each film contained some special figures of motion – such as the dynamic triangle during the first piano solo of *A Colour Box* (1 minute 43 seconds into the film) that twists and turns as it rises and falls, like a kinetic sculpture. And early in *Colour Flight*, there is a lively blob in the middle of the frame that bounces and sways in time with the music while the rest of the pattern keeps changing. (This starts at 1m 16s and ends at 2m.) Other favourite

In one of his 1930s sketchbooks, Lye explored various kinds of visual 'accent'. Courtesy Len Lye Foundation.

motifs not linked with a particular instrument include the rolling wave which appears several times during *Colour Flight*'s title sequence, and also turns up in *Lambeth Walk* and *Musical Poster #1*. Lye also liked kite and fan shapes, and there is a dynamic effect like a curtain opening and closing, seen in *Kaleidoscope* (starting at 1m 10s) and at the beginning and end of *Lambeth Walk*.

These figures of motion pass so rapidly that, unless we watch closely, we will miss some of them. To give them more space, Lye would splice together a series of variations on the same basic figure of motion – say, half-a-dozen strips of film, each of them one or two seconds long – to accompany a brief instrumental solo. But as he worked on so many short pieces of film, he could not resist changing colours and details, so the images were constantly in flux.

This flux helped to produce the fluid sense of space that Lye described as '3½, 3, 2½, 2D'.[27] His painter friends used to tell him they were frustrated they were not able to freeze particular frames.[28] Certainly a freezing of selected images in his 1930s films would show that he had anticipated later forms of abstract painting. (To mention one example, there are frames in *Lambeth Walk* that look very much like Morris Louis canvases with vertical colour stripes and diluted pigment.) But Lye had only a limited interest in single frames – his primary concern was to use the energies of the medium to explore 'sensation-stimuli' and figures of motion.

The visuals provide 'a vicarious form of dance to the music', but viewers can also enjoy this group of Lye's direct films for other reasons such as their exuberance, bright colours, painterly textures and whimsical sense of humour. The lines retain something of the playfulness of cartoon characters, and there are tongue-in-cheek touches such as the four circles turning clockwise in formation in *Lambeth Walk* (2m 39s into the film) that recall the bouncing balls in sing-along films of the period.[29] In other words, the films are not solely concerned with movement, nor do they always have the physical resonance of Lye's sculpture. But every film does include some moments of powerful empathy. In *Lambeth Walk*, for example, the whimsical circle sequence is followed by some serious kinesthesia. A funky Django guitar solo is accompanied by the tense twanging of a horizontal line. This dynamic sequence is followed by a double-bass solo (from a different jazz recording), closely synchronised with a thick, vibrating, vertical line that rocks and stomps. Changing colours and patterns accent the pauses. Ray Thorburn remembers Lye describing these guitar and bass passages (each about twelve seconds long) as 'one of his best interpretations of jazz music'.[30] He had liked the music so much that he had made designs 'very specifically', and

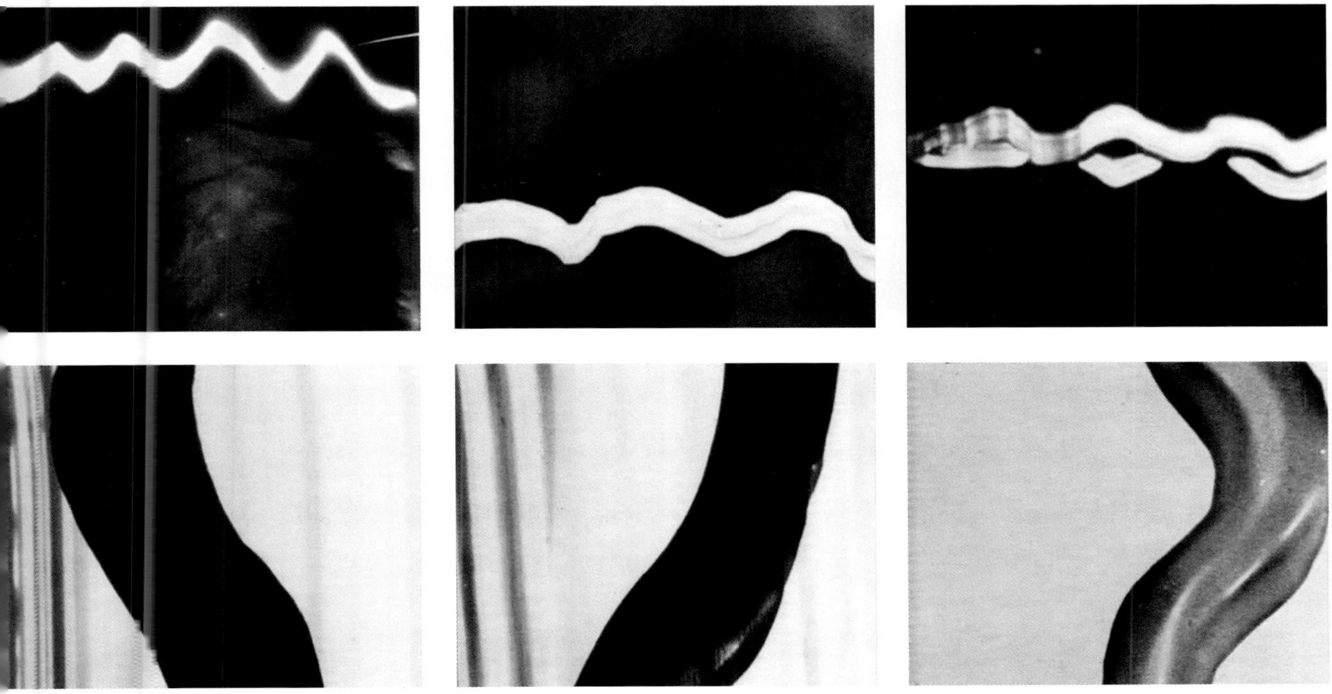

Frames from *Swinging the Lambeth Walk*. The top three accompany the guitar solo and the bottom three accompany the double-bass solo discussed in this chapter. Courtesy Len Lye Foundation.

'the image is almost a copy of a guitar string'.[31] Lye described the bass solo in a letter as 'a spiffing sequence of twangs . . . yes! I mean Hoorroo, Hoooorooo0, Hoooooooo'.[32] This sequence may also have been the music on his mind when he wrote in a Surrealist magazine soon after finishing the film, 'Everything is XXXX cellent and the hum on the double-bass is so extreme that one's cord quivers in sympathetic response or should we say ecstatic response.'[33] This 'cord' image could be seen as referring not only to the strings of the bass but also to the vibrating line on screen and to the way it produces feelings of empathy. Such moments also look forward to Lye's kinetic sculptures – to *Blade*, for example, when its strip of steel is quivering with tension. Few direct animators have been able to give such a strong physical dimension to their images.

Lye was delighted to have found a way to transform the high-tech medium of film into something hand-made. The direct method also allowed him to tap his memories of tribal art, such as the patterns of tapa cloth he had studied in Samoa.[34] The artists of the Pacific used brushes, sticks or fingers to paint tapa, and there were also wooden forks to draw parallel lines and stencils for a range of patterns. Lye liked to drag a comb through wet paint, and he applied stencils with the help of an air-brush. He had stencils made for favourite images such as 'stars,

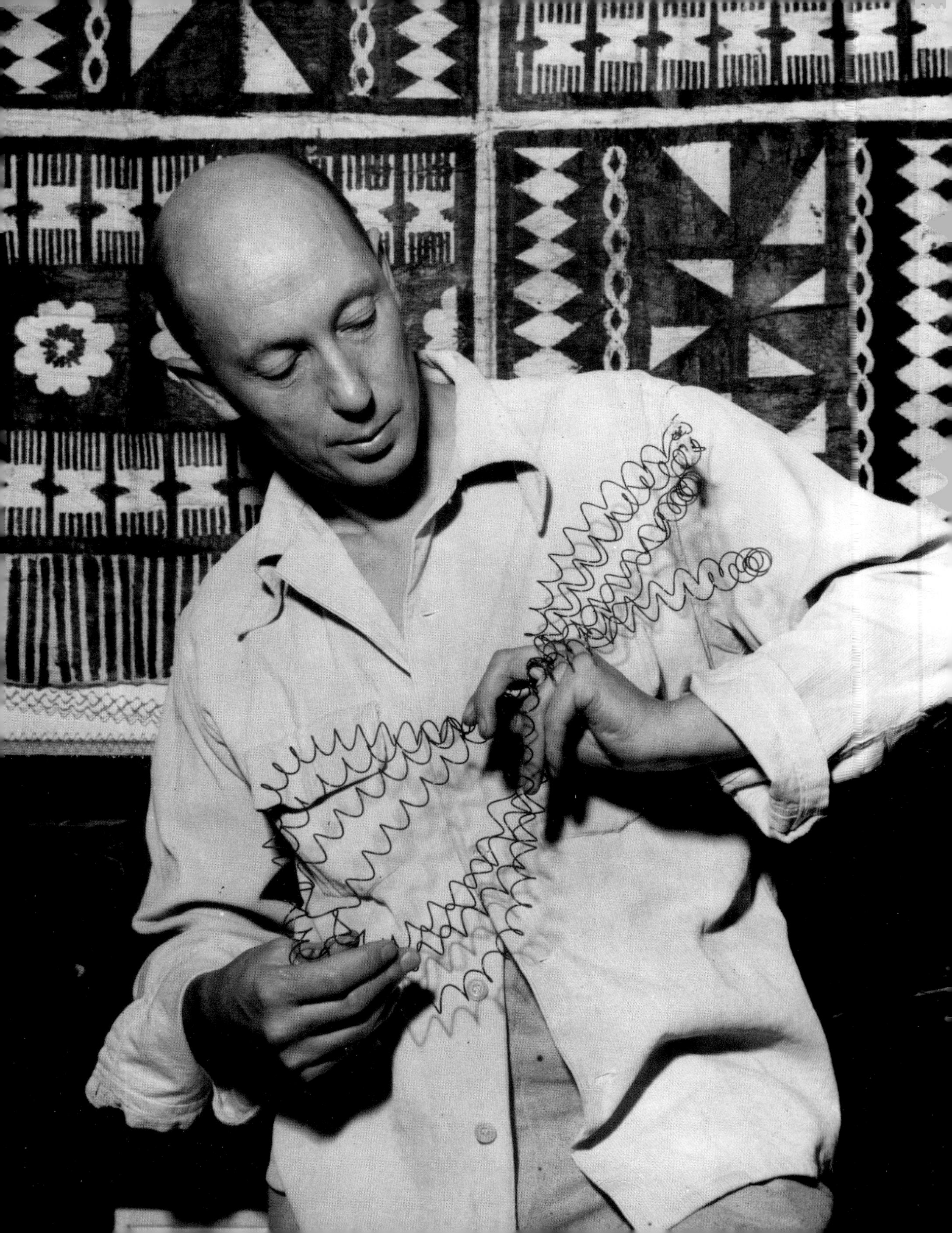

circles, triangles, and yin-yangs', and he improvised others, such as a fish slice which was ideal for rows of dots.[35] Smudged dots could be as interesting as tidy ones. Though he focused more on painting than scratching, he also experimented with various types of scriber, and their sharper or more fibrous line added variety and suited the sound of some solos.

After *A Colour Box*, a very painterly film, Lye shifted his attention to stencilled imagery in *Kaleidoscope*. This film, which deserves to be better known, looks forward to his kinetic sculpture in the way he took a variety of stencil shapes and animated them with an emphasis on circular movement. Besides rotating, most of the shapes moved horizontally across the screen to left or right, like wheels spinning – although some (such as the yin-yangs) rolled first one way and then the other. Since the film was sponsored by Churchman's Cigarettes, its climax involved a dancing cigarette. For the première, Lye cut the cigarette shapes out of the celluloid so that the direct light of the projector made them a very intense white.

Rainbow Dance and *Trade Tattoo*: Colour Separation Methods

Colour film stocks were still new and temperamental in the 1930s, and one of the biggest headaches for Lye was trying to obtain copies that were true to the colours he intended. The lab would make a negative from his painted original and then produce multiple prints. Lye was horrified by the inconsistent colours, and he kept changing from one film stock to another in search of better results. Along the way, he learned a great deal about film processing, which provided the starting point for his next set of experiments (in *Rainbow Dance* and *Trade Tattoo*). Lye took a perfectionist attitude to the physical condition of his films. He would surely be appalled today to witness the decline in standards now that celluloid is passing out of fashion and skilled film technicians and projectionists are becoming a rare breed. Those who know Lye's work only from low-resolution copies on YouTube can have almost no sense of the luxuriant colours and textures of the 1930s direct films in their original form.

Lye in New York in 1946, making spiral shapes out of wire. He is standing in front of a Pacific tapa cloth. Courtesy Len Lye Foundation.

Rainbow Dance and *Trade Tattoo* are among Lye's most important films. They are based on his discovery of a new way to use colour processing, as surprising a leap of lateral thinking as his idea of direct animation. While this development focused on colour – and that was certainly the aspect of the two films that caused the most public comment – Lye was also experimenting with movement. He was coming to terms with the camera and with live action, and the films explored new approaches to editing and story-telling. *Rainbow Dance* embodied a new kind of filmic 'ballet', and *Trade Tattoo* showed how to take existing footage and to charge it with kinetic energy by means of jump-cutting. Both films were synchronised to dance music and had a powerful sense of overall rhythm.

All the radical ideas and hard work that went into *Rainbow Dance* and *Trade Tattoo* were clearly reflected in Lye's theoretical essays of the period, which (among other themes) explored the relationship between colour and movement.[36] As he explained in 'Experiment in Colour', changes of colour could be synchronised with music: 'rainbow shapes [in *Rainbow Dance*] float upwards in movement while the divisions of colour alternate exactly in time to strong rhythmic music'.[37] In the fluid world of these films, the colour of a person or object could be changed at any time, and those changes could be developed as a 'counterpoint to the movement of the object carrying the colour'.[38] He could also create '2D, 2½D, 3D' effects by subverting spatial assumptions. For example, 'Some theorists say that Red is a "near" or "approaching" colour, [and] that Blue is a "distant" or "receding" colour . . . . [But] Blue . . . could be turned into an approaching colour with all the more significance, by making it approach.'[39]

Lye's new methods exploited the various colour film stocks that were emerging at the time. Colour printing in books and magazines was based on different colour layers being printed in succession, one on top of another, but to adapt this method to motion pictures required a special 'beam-splitter' camera that could split the scene being filmed into three negatives, each recording a different colour. This was achieved in the camera with the help of a prism, mirrors and colour filters. The printing process was also complex, with an intermediate step by which the negatives were printed as positives with a particular kind of gelatin surface, before being combined to make the final film print.[40] This separation method continued until the early 1950s when it was replaced by 'tripack' film stocks (such as Eastman Color) that accommodated the three layers of colour on a single strip of film. But cumbersome as the separation method was, it produced pure colours and the results were long-lasting. In contrast, a crisis later occurred with the early tripack stocks when it was discovered that films gradually lost their colours as the three layers leaked into one another.

In 1936, Lye was impressed by the 'clean' colours of the separation process, but what intrigued him most was the fact that two of the stages – the original negatives and the intermediate positives – were black and white. Ultimately, the three strips represented separate colours – cyan (blue / green), magenta (red / blue) and yellow – but this translation did not occur until the final stage. Lye realised that any black and white footage could be fed into this system and converted into colour. The black and white material might be new or old, positive or negative, filmed or hand-painted – there were no limits. When this material was translated, the laboratory had total control over the balance between the three colours and the strength of each colour (from the palest hint to the greatest intensity). Lye realised that such a printing process was like a musical instrument just waiting for a bold performer to create wild cadenzas of colour.

Why had others not employed the technology in such an imaginative way? One reason was the amount of work involved. And, basically, most film-makers and lab technicians still thought in realist terms, so their first priority was to make the colours as true to life as possible. Lye, on the other hand, came to the medium with an interest in modernist art and old brain imagery. He asked, why not 'a strange yellow tree in deep blue sky' with 'vibrant colour spots'?[41] He saw the new colour process as a way to achieve non-naturalistic story-telling that used live actors as freely as cartoon characters. Today, computers have made it very much easier to create elaborate, multi-layered images, compared with the sea of details that Lye had to navigate in creating his colour-separation films, frame by frame and colour by colour. Yet arguably this necessary attention to detail gave his films a precision that has ensured their lasting value.

Lye's takeover of colour methods typified his approach to technology. He had no specialised training but he could intuitively understand a technical process and then come up with a new way to use it that caught the experts by surprise. For *Rainbow Dance*, he persuaded the Gasparcolor laboratory to allow him to redesign their usual procedures, although its manager, Adrian Klein, was skeptical that anyone could juggle the colour elements in the complex manner proposed: 'It is a problem in non-Euclidean geometry to predict the results.'[42]

Funded by a Post Office commission, Lye wrote a simple script for a four-minute 'film ballet' about a traveller who 'sets off on holiday activities and dances in a fantasy of colours'.[43] The music was *Tony's Wife* played by Rico's Creole Band.[44] The dancer was Rupert Doone, a key figure in the Group Theatre, one of London's most adventurous theatre companies.[45] Working entirely in the studio, Lye filmed Doone against a white background. He added a variety of painted images and stylised props, all black and white so that the colours created during the printing process would be as pure as possible.

Lye's aim was to represent everything purely as a sign or symbol. The man was filmed as a silhouette, with changing colours and patterns superimposed. Rain fell as darting dashes of colour accompanied by percussion. A railway train looked blatantly toy-like and a yacht resembled a paper cut-out. Waves were combined with jumping cartoon fish. A tennis game became a dance, with a player leaving coloured silhouettes in his wake. Lye wanted the transitions between scenes to be very fluid, replacing realist conventions with 'moving hieroglyphics'.[46] For example, Doone in a dark raincoat was transformed, as soon as the sun came out, into a rainbow-coloured troubadour. Setting out on his journey, he became an asterisk rolling across the screen, then a hiker silhouetted against a moving map. The most striking transition in the film occurred when the traveller, tired at the end of his tennis game, simply lay down to rest on the court and its surface changed suddenly into his bed at home.

Lye's instructions to the laboratory produced bright rainbow colours. Bold poster effects have since become a familiar feature of music videos, but in 1936 they were still a startling novelty. Animator Norman McLaren was so impressed that he subsequently used Lye's method of translating black and white images into colour for a number of his own projects.[47] *Rainbow Dance*, over 70 years later, still seems fresh and original. What could have been a pretentious experiment was swept along by its energy, rhythm and whimsical sense of humour, qualities which may remind us of classic musicals. When the film turned up much later on television as part of a British film history survey, it still held the 'shock of the new' for photographer Barbara Ker-Seymer:

> The other evening there was a programme of 1930s documentaries, all very worthy and very dull films of miners down the pits and trains puffing through the night, when suddenly the screen lit up with a burst of colour, design, and movement. It made you sit up as though you had suddenly drunk a very strong cocktail, and I recognised *Rainbow Dance*. It was amazing, it was as though there had been a mixup in the projection room and an extract from a contemporary avant-garde film had got in by mistake.[48]

The word 'tattoo' in the title of the film *Trade Tattoo* refers to a mass display involving marching and music, in which drumming plays an important part. Lye took this form of large-scale choreography as a metaphor for the activities of people all over Britain during a typical working day. He had been impressed by the 1927 documentary *Berlin: Symphony of a Great City*, a survey of a day in the life of a city directed by Walther Ruttmann, an experimental film-maker with a keen eye for patterns of movement. When Lye was commissioned by the Post Office to make a film about the need to 'post early', he came up with the idea that the British working day had an underlying rhythm – a kind of overall figure of motion for society as a whole, in much the same way Ruttman had seen a day in Berlin as a 'symphony'. Although Lye was never as involved with working-class politics as some of his left-wing colleagues in the GPO Film Unit, he was sympathetic to their ideas and embarked on *Trade Tattoo* as an attempt to convey 'a romanticism about the work of the everyday, in all walk/sit works of life'.[49]

The most striking aspect of the film was the richness of its colours and textures, for it carried colour separation possibilities even further than *Rainbow Dance*. It also experimented with movement through its visual rhythms, its kinetic presentation of words on screen, and its fast, syncopated editing. It showed the extent to which the pace of Lye's work had speeded up since *Tusalava*.

His soundtrack was more varied than usual. This five-minute film drew upon five dance music recordings by the Lecuona Cuban Band, offering a variety of tempos.[50] Lye would apply the same cut-and-paste approach to the music for some of his later films, such as *Lambeth Walk*.

Trade Tattoo contains more words than most of his films, but it is particularly successful in incorporating them into the flow of movement. Avoiding voice-over commentary, Lye presented the words visually, animating them in a mix of styles from hand-painted to typewritten. The words appeared in rhythmic bursts and moved round the screen. In one sense, he was returning to the convention of 'intertitles' in silent films.[51]

This time he did not undertake any live-action filming but reworked leftover footage from documentaries made by the GPO Film Unit.[52] Malcolm LeGrice has described *Trade Tattoo* and *Rainbow Dance* as historically important because of the way they 'prefigure, in an extraordinary versatile and accomplished way' one of the 'major directions' of later experimental film-making, 'that based on the transformation of film images through printing and developing techniques'. Lye's explicit use of film strips and sprocket holes as visual motifs also reflects his 'awareness of the material aspects of film as a major basis of language and content'.[53] Arguably, the dot stipple patterns of *Trade Tattoo* could also be seen as an allusion to the grain structure of film images.

Lye collected black and white shots of mail-sorting, welding, cargo loading, steel milling and other types of work, and gave them the once-over. He used the colour separation process as a kind of Cubist machine that swallowed naturalistic footage and converted it into brilliant, multi-coloured fragments. Not entirely satisfied with Gasparcolor, he decided this time to try Technicolor, the rival process which had just established a lab in England. Ellitt recalled that 'Len got a colour chart from Humphries Laboratories which showed 32 different colour changes which could be made on the printing camera. He worked out frame by frame what colours he wanted.'[54] He made each of the three strips (or matrices) a composite, so that *Trade Tattoo* became one of the most intricate exercises in multiple-printing ever attempted. Bernard Happé and Leslie Oliver of Technicolor Ltd were amazed by their client's ability to visualise in detail the results of such complex printing procedures, but Lye saw the job as 'simply a matter of knitting – two pearls, one plain, etc'.[55]

He incorporated many different kinds of visual material such as a hand-painted drum sequence, photogram-style film strips, and cartoon drawings of letters, clouds, a comet and the planet Saturn. Much of the live footage was printed in high contrast or as a negative so that figures and objects became silhouettes on which Lye then superimposed bright stencil patterns. These patterns (dashes, dots, asterisks and stars) were always in motion, growing larger or smaller, and changing from one colour to another. This added another dimension of movement to the film, in counterpoint to the movement of people and objects. The result was a complex push-and-pull, with the abstract patterns sometimes upstaging the representational images. Lye seemed to be experimenting to see just how far he could go; but the film managed to avoid overload because each of the ingredients had been so carefully chosen.

Clever visual transitions carried the film from one location to another. The many remarkable images included: a signalling railway guard whose arm was covered with dashes like Morse code; the silhouette of a plane in flight covered with a buzz of polka dots; and jump-cut (abbreviated) waves breaking kinetically off a ship's bow. The loading of cargo (just over two minutes into the film) was a vivid sequence of rapid, jumpy editing that danced closely with the music.

The 'furnaces are fired' sequence (just over a minute into the film) showed how successfully Lye could combine his interest in colour and texture with his sense of movement. The sequence began with a rush of busy music and fiery bursts from the furnace of a steel factory. Freely painted words and flames, flowing and flickering, were intercut with blurred stencil patterns. Then, in contrast to this rapid editing, a container of hot metal swung gracefully through the air in a slow, continuous, left-to-right movement. A pattern of dots pulsated in the background, and the colour of the container underwent a series of subtle shifts – from white and yellow to apricot – until it completed its arc and disappeared behind a pillar. In Lye's terms, 'the colour movement' (changes of colour) and the dancing dots added 'a form of counterpoint to the movement of the object'.[56]

N or NW and *Kill or be Killed*: Experiments with Live Action Films

Among the other films Lye made in England, *N or NW* and *Kill or be Killed* stand out as unique experiments in live action filming.[57] Lye 'always wanted to get out of the D. W. Griffith technique' and to develop a completely new kind of film syntax;[58] and he had already explored several options, ranging from the continuous, un-edited movement of *Tusalava* to the rapid-fire editing of *Trade Tattoo. Kill or be Killed* returned to a more continuous style of movement, while *N or NW* made constant use of jump-cuts. Unfortunately, the section of *N or NW* that Lye saw as his most radical experiment was removed and subsequently lost. He had hoped that this sequence of a young woman getting dressed and going for a walk would have a big impact on the film world – his *Nude Descending a Staircase*, so to speak.

What has survived of *N or NW* is uneven but the film has a definite curiosity value. Its appeal was well summed up by Cavalcanti in 1947: 'The new ideas seem to follow each other in rapid succession. It has a strangely poetic quality ... which is purely filmic.'[59] Subsequently, the film seems to have been largely forgotten until the 1980s when it was rediscovered by a few critics (such as David Curtis) who were very struck by its strangeness. Innocently commissioned by the Post Office as publicity about the need to take care in addressing letters, the film is full of extreme closeups, strange camera angles (from over an actor's shoulder, or from below through a glass-top table), odd shifts in space (shots that 'cross the axis'), unexpected changes of focus, superimpositions, dissolves and jump-cuts (so that, within the course of a single sentence, there may be two or three separate shots of the person speaking).

As Ellitt recalled, 'Off Len went [to make this film], and immediately found himself in difficulties. He kept on changing, kept on shooting and changing. I was absolutely astounded [at] what caused Len so much trouble, because the project was so simple and so direct, with two practically static people talking occasionally.'[60] *N or NW* brought Lye's long collaboration with Ellitt to an end because the music editor had lost patience with the director's obsessive search for a way to escape the standard language of film.

Most of Lye's jump-cuts in this film were not primarily a way of adding kinetic energy or matching the accents of the music, but, rather, a way to evoke the stream of consciousness. We may recall Robert Herring's description of *Full Fathom Five* (Lye's direct film that was lost) in terms of the mind at work: 'It is rather like a speech [in the process of] being made, there is mind-movement in the shapes, mind pictures in the occasional flashes, inserts . . . .'[61] In *N or NW*, Lye's way of escaping from 'Griffith' was by turning to 'mind-movement'. In the period during which he made this film, he was very involved with Surrealism, not with its 'literary' excesses, but with the way art could 'keep [all] my mind's layers accessible to me'.[62] His essay 'Voice and Colour' speculated about how a film could represent the rhythms of 'subjective' experience – from 'continuous' attention to 'staccato and dramatic' feelings.[63] He suggested that 'Degrees of meaning in speech could . . . be emphasized by depicting objects *subjectively*.'[64] It is in this spirit that *N or NW* presents the conflicted interior monologues of his two central characters (a young man and woman writing letters to each other after a quarrel) as a jumpy succession of thoughts, perceptions and memories.

In addition, there are some interesting moments of physical movement such as the posting of a letter, a sequence that begins with a strange, subjective closeup of the envelope in the man's hand as he approaches the postbox. The letter's travels are conveyed symbolically by a dancing postbox superimposed over a map and a tracking shot along a row of trees, followed by a shower of letters through the clouds. Lye makes witty use of three jazz songs with relevant lyrics ('I'm gonna sit right down and write myself a letter' by Fats Waller, 'Gimme a break baby' by Bob Howard and 'T'aint no use' by Benny Goodman); and in depicting the travels of the letter, the film becomes a kind of music video version of the Goodman number.

Frames from the 1937 film *N or NW*, starring Evelyn Corbett and Dwight Goodwin as two lovers trying to communicate by letter. Courtesy Len Lye Foundation.

For actors, Lye chose to use non-professionals, not merely to keep the budget down but also because the acting of professionals seemed to him too theatrical. What mattered most to him was the look of an actor, and, above all, how he or she moved. For *N or NW* he chose a young GPO Unit assistant named Evelyn Corbett with no drama experience. She and her co-star Dwight Goodwin did indeed have an interesting look, and a critic praised Corbett for her 'charming

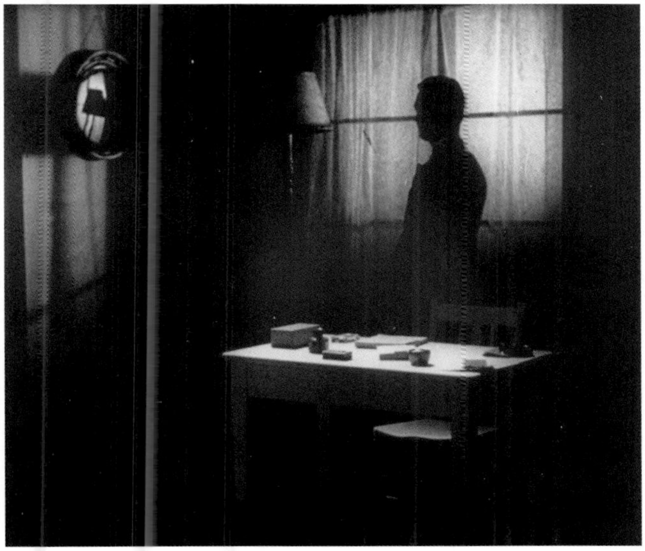

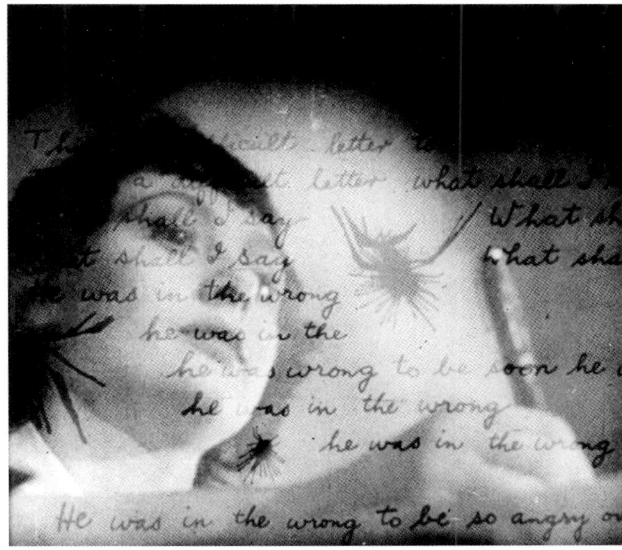

he was in the wrong
he was in the
he was in the wrong

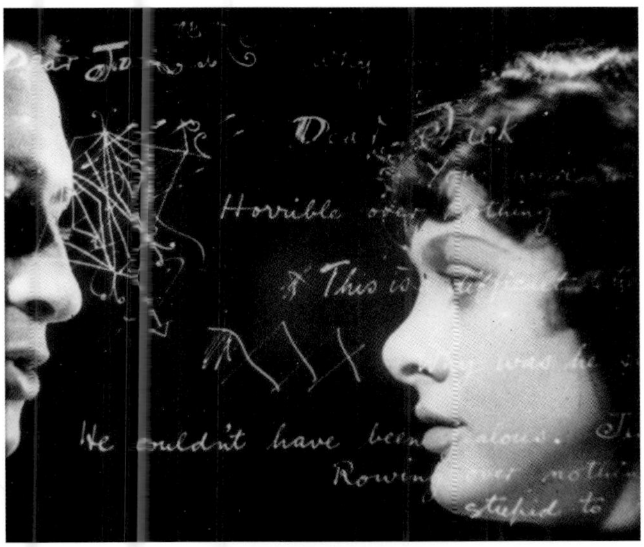

Horrible
This is

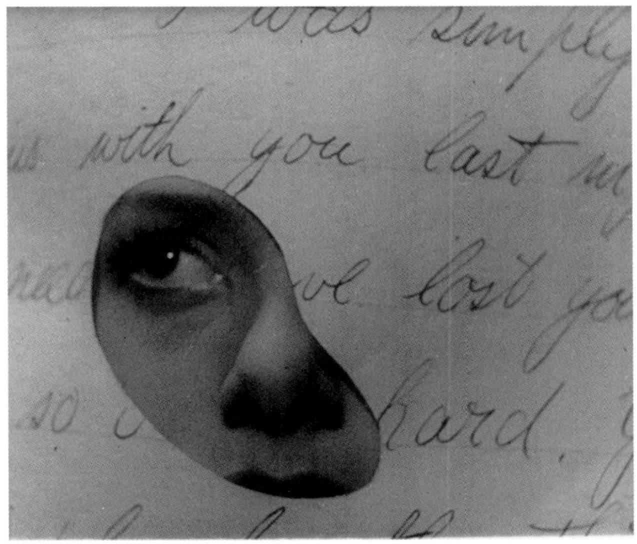

with you last
lost
hard

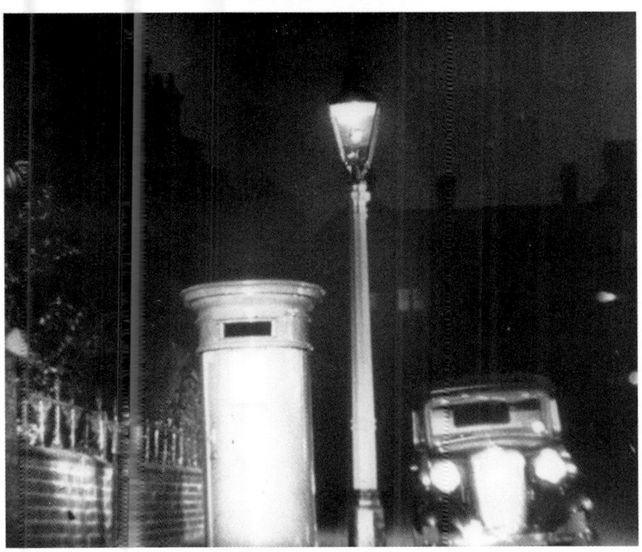

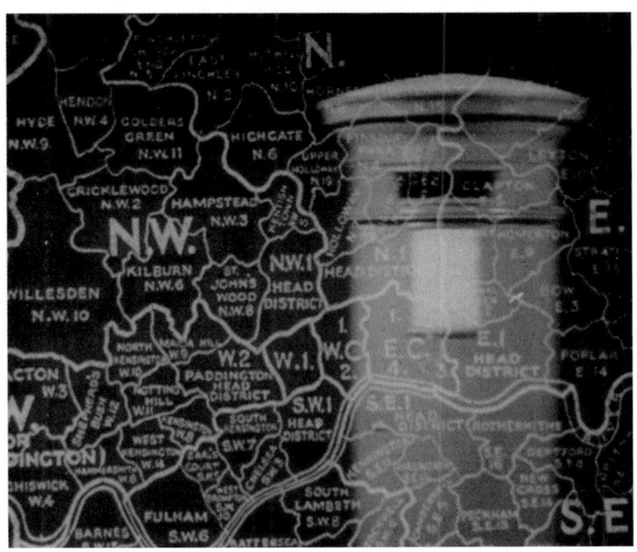

N.
HENDON N.W.4
GOLDERS GREEN N.W.11
HYDE N.W.9
HIGHGATE N.6
CRICKLEWOOD N.W.2
HAMPSTEAD N.W.3
N.W.
KILBURN N.W.6
N.W.1 HEAD DISTRICT
WILLESDEN N.W.10
W.2
PADDINGTON HEAD DISTRICT
W.1.
E.
E.C.
E.1 HEAD DISTRICT
POPLAR E.14
ACTON W.3
S.W.1 HEAD DISTRICT
S.E.1
SOUTH LAMBETH S.W.8
FULHAM S.W.6
CHISWICK W.4
S.E.

natural London voice', but, not surprisingly, some viewers found their acting gauche.[65] The film survived such problems because its real stars were the editing and the camerawork. Lye used amateur actors more successfully in *Kill or be Killed*, a film to which physical movement was absolutely central.

N or NW proved to be the last commission he received from the GPO. The English film industry experienced a severe downturn in 1937, and he was driven to seek free-lance work from newsreel companies, whose house styles left no latitude for experiment.[66] Between 1941 and 1943, he worked for Realist, a company commissioned by the government to make instructional films. Each of Lye's wartime films had some interesting aspects, but the most memorable, particularly from a movement point of view, was *Kill or be Killed*. Indeed, some critics have described it as one of the best of all wartime films.

Kill or be Killed was a fictional enactment of the deadly contest between a British soldier and a German sniper hiding in a tree. Lye wrote to Robert Graves, 'I just made a simple film – The War, as played by a Lovat scout versus a German sniper – and it is 18 minutes of crawling and jumping.'[67] Or as he put it years later, 'It exemplifies a slow unfolding rhythm, a rhythm that creeps into one's buttocks, as does Samuel Beckett's body imagery.'[68] The part of the British soldier was played by Duncan Chisholm, a Scotsman with no experience as an actor but many years of experience as a soldier and as a deer stalker. (Before the war he had been head

The British soldier (played by Duncan Chisholm) and the German sniper (played by Alistair McIntyre) stalk each other in the 1942 film *Kill or be Killed*. Courtesy Len Lye Foundation.

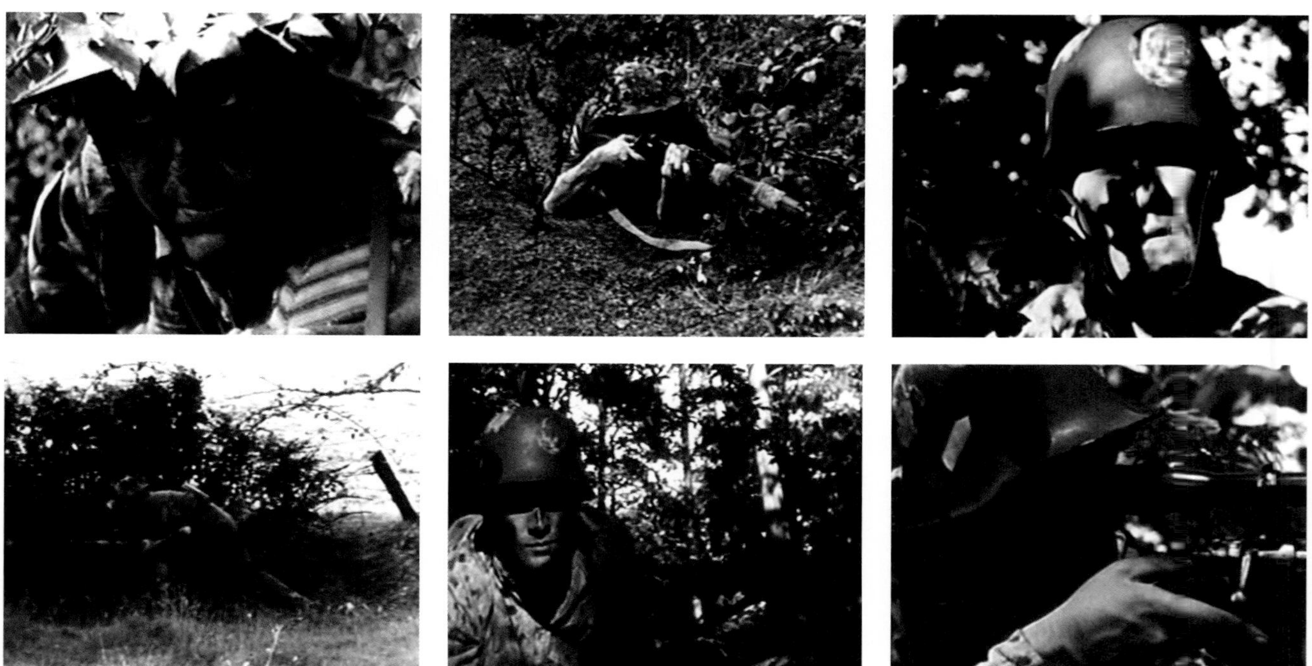

gillie in a large game park.) Lye was excited by his agility – 'his movements are smooth and rhythmic like a cat'. Chisholm had to do so much crawling for the film that his trousers wore thin.[69]

The film's primary aim was to train soldiers, though it was also shown to many groups of civilians who would have needed to take up arms had the Germans invaded Britain. Since most army instructional films were straightforward and didactic, *Kill or be Killed* gained impact from Lye's decision to replace commentary with drama. The film stayed close to the point of view of each protagonist, and (as in *N or NW*) their thoughts were made audible. Richard MacNaughton, an editor who had worked on many films of the period, commented, '*Kill or be Killed* is small-scale and very precise – each scene motivates the next. John Grierson used to say: "When you come to make a film, think in terms of boxing, and the famous film of the cobra and the mongoose. You saw the cobra doing his thing, and then you saw the mongoose attacking. That movement, where one attacks and the other reacts and hits back, was exactly what you'd get in boxing, so the actions were always motivated and always alive".'[70] Lye succeeded in giving his elemental struggle for survival a similar old brain resonance.

While the alternation of viewpoints was a familiar narrative device, the camerawork of Lye's film was extraordinary. He used numerous tracking shots, some very close-up, as the soldiers crawled and stalked each other. There was no Steadicam in those days – and no possibility of using a dolly – so the heavy camera had to be hand-held or hung on leather straps from a rifle being carried through the bushes by Lye and Adrian Jeakins.

Fellow film-makers recognised its exceptional story-telling. Cavalcanti wrote in *Sight and Sound*, 'To praise without reservation is the critic's most difficult task and about this [film] I cannot but say that it has the weight of a classic Greek tragedy. *Kill or be Killed* keeps also, in a slow tempo, the same sense of rhythm that we find in *Colour Box*.'[71] The *Documentary News Letter* review summed it up as 'without doubt one of the most exciting films ever made'. It added,

> Here warfare is reduced to a primitive, man to man contest, in which the colour of a leaf, the sudden movement of a horse, the keenness of one's eyes or ears, may mean life or death . . . . The film has the very magic of cinema in it, every legitimate device has been used with an integrity that is rare in film making . . . . It is well worth your while to hunt it out – that is if you don't mind being shaken up, frightened and fascinated.[72]

Its presentation of warfare was so matter-of-fact and lacking in sentiment that today it shocks viewers who have grown up on conventional war (or for that matter anti-war) movies. Even in 1942 it ran into problems. Tom Matthews remembered attending a preview of *Kill or be Killed* in the company of American army officers who found the film so stark that they resolved to prevent its proposed theatrical distribution in the United States.[73] Some prints of the film in circulation today omit the brutal last few minutes which show the British soldier setting up the body of the German as a decoy to pick off the five members of a scouting party who come to investigate.[74]

Color Cry: Photograms and Direct Film

In 1953, after many unsuccessful attempts to obtain commercial work in New York from television broadcasters and advertising agencies, Lye returned to 'fine art film' by selecting some of his many photogram test strips as the starting point for *Color Cry*, a four-minute direct film. After a long search for suitable music, he hit upon something that 'fitted like mad' – 'Fox Hunt', recorded in 1938 by blues musician Sonny Terry as a solo in which he played the harmonica and gave wild, wordless hollers. As Lye described it, 'The fox chase is simulated by repetitive yelps of hounds, the pounding of horses' hooves and, once in a while, by Terry emitting a blood-curdling, high-pitched cry of pain and fright.'[75] (Foxes have an eerie wail.)

Someone who regarded the music merely as a novelty number might have combined it with playful cartoon animation, but Lye – who had been dismayed by the racism he had seen in the USA – had a far more serious perspective. Knowing that Terry came from the South, he imagined that the music evoked the situation of a black slave fleeing from a lynch mob. This was more a matter of mood than of literal interpretation. *Color Cry* did include some explosions of bright colour, but there were enough dark backgrounds and bars to convey an anxious sense of being blocked or enclosed.[76]

When Lye returned to the film years later, he came up with a new interpretation, focusing on organic-looking images such as the clusters of red circles. The images now suggested to him 'blood cells, nerves, bone and marrow, rib-cage, sinews'.[77] Whether we link the images with the workings of the body, or with a frantic struggle for survival, the film's combination of spine-tingling music and strange, intense visuals seems to channel the elemental power of the old brain.

Lye had worked with the photogram (or 'shadowgraph') method for still photographs in the early 1930s and again in 1947. He had continued to experiment by applying the method to moving images, using the patterns of fabrics (such as muslin) and miscellaneous objects such as string, ribbons, mosquito netting, metal stencils, spoons, pieces of black film, spiral wires and thin saw blades. He 'flash-exposed' them on strips of 16mm colour film, adding changes of colour by means of gels. He did not use expensive processing methods as he had in the 1930s – he no longer had the budget for special effects – and he now employed 16mm rather than 35mm film. This provided the direct animator with an even smaller canvas on which to work, but it was less expensive, and Lye's skills and experience gave him the necessary precision.

Making a photogram film involved months of experiment in the dark. In his words:

> One stretches out a length of film on a bench; lays a perforated strip of metal over the unexposed film (still in the dark); then a coloured sheet of gelatine is spread over both and the film is quickly exposed by the on-off switch. When developed, the strip of film shows up as a length of coloured patterned footage. If one shifts the perforated . . . strip of metal on the exposed film and changes the coloured gel, one will get a three-colour complex formal pattern.[78]

Lye added motion by playing off fabric patterns of dots against the film frames, or by manipulating objects along the film. In his words, 'You twist a ribbon and that produces a turning effect. Working in the dark you get into a very inventive mood. Your fingers arrange shapes across this strip of film which will unreel whatever energy you can put into it.'[79]

He built up *Color Cry* from short strips, mostly between sixteen and 40 frames long. Though he would group together similar strips (such as the same pattern re-coloured) to provide more continuity, the film still moved at a rapid pace. The diversity of his templates created a whole new range of textures for direct film. While there were still familiar patterns such as vertical lines, there were new fabric textures and bold, blocky shapes which made it like a moving version of the new abstract painting of the day. (In 1948, for example, Barnett Newman had begun using vertical lines which he called 'zips'.)[80] The use of double exposure to combine two differently coloured versions of the same lattice pattern – so that it seemed to cast a coloured shadow – was one of several ways the film created a complex sense of space. The illusion of depth kept changing – the image would suddenly open up as though one were looking at a landscape from the air, but then return abruptly to a flat surface.

Terry's powerful music was 5m 30s long, and Lye cut about 1m 4s, omitting the opening section (for harmonica only) and the ending (when the piece slowed down). The remaining music had a continuous intensity. The music's qualities of agitation, urgent movement, strong accents and trembling vibrato were perfectly accompanied by the jitter of direct animation, the fast editing, the textured backgrounds and the twitching lines. The ribbons that twisted and rotated (such as the sequence beginning 2m 36s into the film) were a particularly striking figure of motion, and one that looked forward to kinetic sculpture.

All Souls Carnival: Extending Direct Animation

All Souls Carnival is not as important a film as *Color Cry* but it illustrates another of the many ways in which Lye strove to extend the range of direct animation. In 1957, he was experimenting with a new style of 'languorous, rhapsodic' imagery based on new kinds of lacquer paint and felt-tip marker pens. He was always on the lookout for new direct film tools, commonplace objects such as an old toothbrush which could make intricate whorls in wet dye (like finger-painting), or a rubber pad with bristles, the kind of pad kept next to a cash register for picking up change, which could produce complex patterns of dots. His blobs, bands and washes of colour in *All Souls* were reminiscent of the painterly styles of abstraction being created by contemporary artists such as Sam Francis, Philip Guston and Helen Frankenthaler. The painter Max Gimblett said that the first time he saw *All Souls*, he was startled to realise how deeply appropriate was the term 'film painter' as applied to Lye.

The music was provided by Lye's friend Henry Brant, an innovative but underrated American composer.[81] *All Souls Carnival* was something new for Lye in its use of contemporary classical music and its choice of loose counterpoint rather than close synchronisation. He had occasionally collaborated with jazz musicians (such as Count Basie) by screening films as the background to a performance, but this was the first time he had made a film especially for the occasion.[82] Brant wanted *All Souls Carnival*, his suite of chamber music, to be performed live because 'Len's work was so direct, with the actual paint on the film. So I wanted the organic sound of acoustic music.'[83] The composer and the film-maker decided not to link their work closely but to allow the images and the music to proceed side by side, similar in spirit but independent of each other. Viewers who expected the film to 'illustrate' the music were likely to be disappointed, but those open to a free-spirited dialogue could enjoy the ever-changing parallels and contrasts (which continued to change from one live performance to the next). That kind of independence was starting to be pioneered in dance by choreographers such as Merce Cunningham.

Rhythm: Jump-cut Editing

Perhaps the best demonstration of Lye's sharp eye for editing is the film *Rhythm*. He took one-and-a-half hours of straightforward black and white footage documenting the assembly of a Chrysler car, and edited it down to an extraordinarily kinetic one-minute film, consisting of many split-second shots. He used jump-cutting and synchronised the results to some of his favourite recordings of traditional African tribal drumming and chanting – one of the many times he juxtaposed the ancient with the modern. There were some brilliant examples of synchronisation such as a tyre bouncing down a conveyor belt in time with the music, and a drill-like machine that twitched rhythmically to the beat. The editing process was rendered extremely difficult because he could not afford to make a print and had to work with the one and only copy of the footage.

Despite being rejected by Chrysler, *Rhythm* won a major award and acquired cult status among experimental film-makers who had never seen jump-cutting used in such a dynamic way. In an interview with Peter Kubelka in *Film Culture*, Jonas Mekas asked, 'Have you seen Len Lye's 50-second automobile commercial?

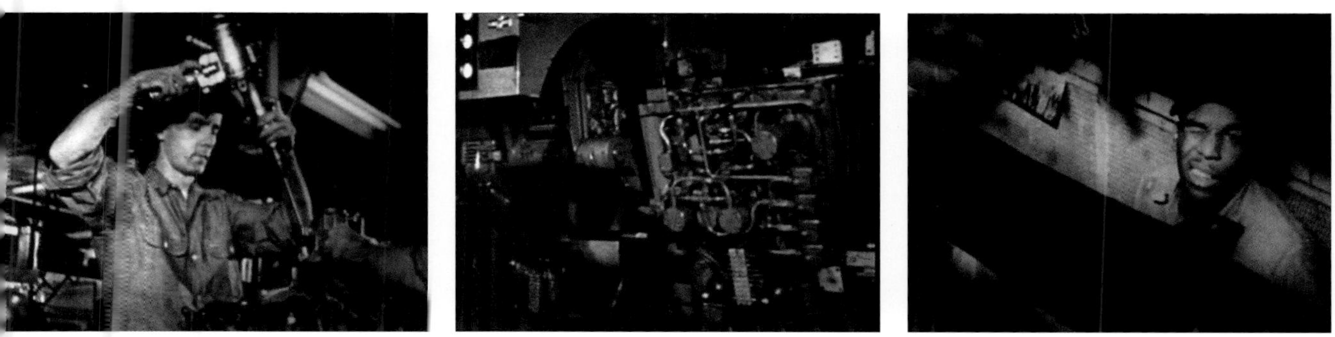

Rhythm (1957) reflects Lye's interest in machine rhythms. One of the reasons the Chrysler corporation rejected this brilliantly edited film was the (split-second) shot of a workman winking at the camera which they assumed to be ironic. Courtesy Len Lye Foundation.

Nothing happens there . . . except that it's filled with some kind of secret action of cinema.'[84] And P. Adams Sitney wrote in his book *Visionary Film*, 'Although his reputation has been sustained by the invention of direct painting on film, Lye deserves equal credit as one of the great masters of montage.'[85]

Free Radicals: Scratching Film, Shaping Energy

There is general agreement that *Free Radicals* is Lye's greatest film and *Particles in Space* is a worthy sequel. Stan Brakhage, the American experimental film-maker summed up *Free Radicals* as 'an almost unbelievably *immense* masterpiece (a brief epic) and . . . *Particles in Space* [is] its contemplative equivalent'.[86] *Film Quarterly* critic John Adams described *Free Radicals* as 'the most stylish, condensed, and formal work' in the field of direct animation, adding, 'If proof had ever been needed that Lye, the pioneer in this field, is the real – and for some the only – master, here it is.'[87] *Free Radicals* also provides the clearest film example of his aesthetic, in terms of its concentration on motion, its physicality, its shaping of energy, its hand-made authorship and its vitality as 'a vicarious form of dance'. I will therefore take a particularly close look at this film.

A burst of experiment in 1953 had given Lye tantalising glimpses of 'a new scratchy figure of motion' which had him 'salivating holy water'.[88] He was inspired to 'mess around' for several months with a film he called 'Ions' or 'Anions'. These terms referred to atoms or molecules with an imbalance between their electrons and protons, a condition that made them highly reactive. Lye felt that his new scratched imagery could evoke the volatility of these atomic particles, but after a while he gave up because 'I could not make a "jump" image that matched up with the ephemeral image-feeling I felt at the back of my skull.'[89] He returned to the project in 1957 and completed the film in eight months of concentrated work.

Scratches are normally the last thing that any film-maker wants to see. Lye's idea went back to his very first film-making in Sydney when he had drawn 'fiddly scratches' on black leader.[90] During the 1930s, he had scratched as well as painted images for colour films such as *Swinging the Lambeth Walk*. But black film created a whole new range of effects, because the darkness gave added impact to the sudden emergence of a white image, like light flashing in the night sky. It also produced after-images. In 1955, the potential of intermittent imagery scratched on black film was vividly realised by Norman McLaren in *Blinkety Blank*. Lye had

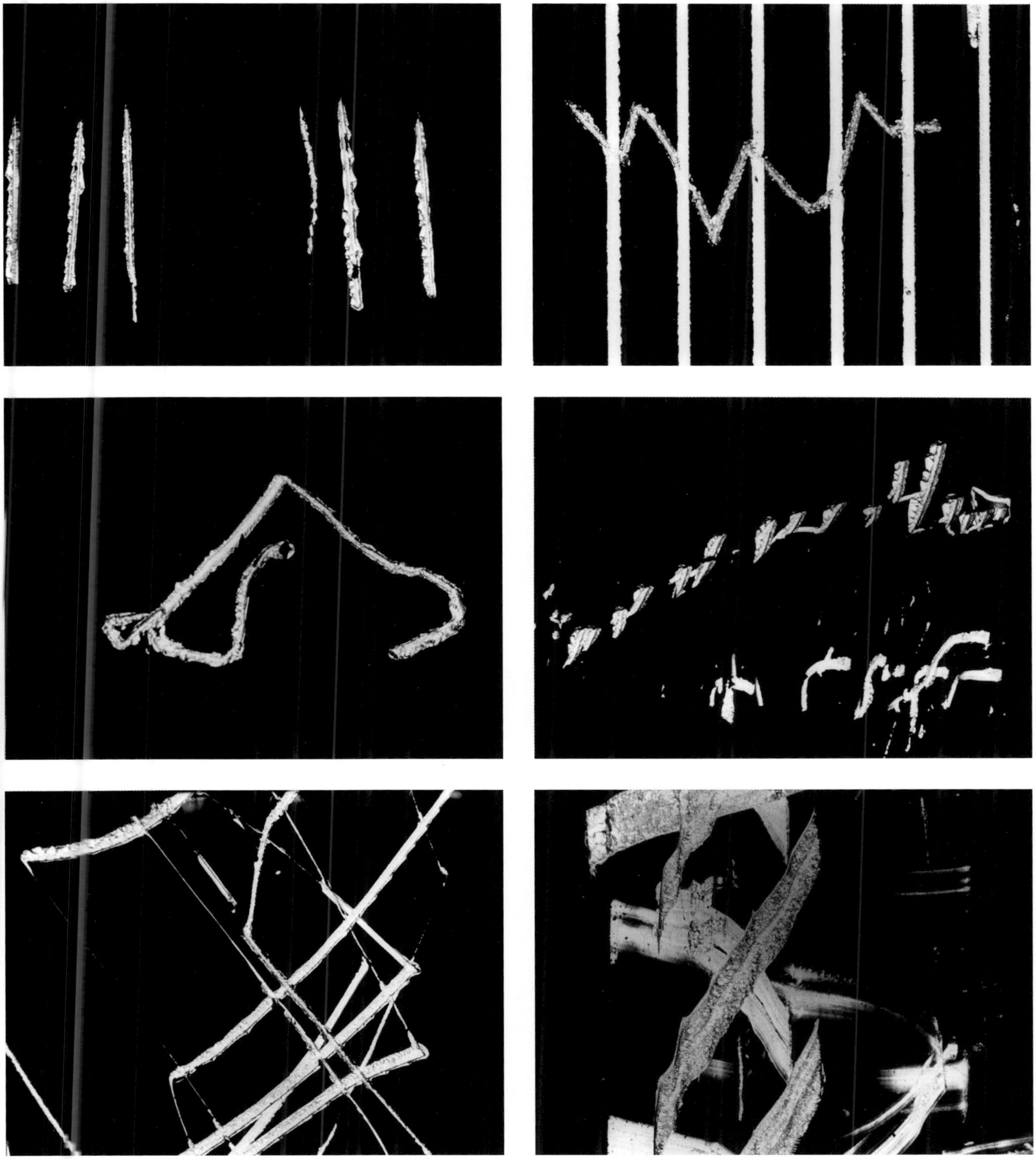

Six frames from *Free Radicals*, illustrating some of the shapes and textures of its scratched imagery. Courtesy Len Lye Foundation.

already arrived at his own version of the method two years earlier, but he and McLaren maintained a lifelong interest in each other's work, so it is possible that Lye saw and was influenced by *Blinkety Blank*. The difference in their approaches lay in McLaren's use of colour rather than black and white, and in his figurative imagery.[91] Also his work tended to be elegant and whimsical, whereas Lye by this time had an uncompromising, avant-garde approach, seeking to maximise the physical energy of his film.

Free Radicals became the name of Lye's film for scientific as well as political reasons. Free radical was a broader category than ion but it implied the same chemical and electrical volatility. Lye liked the description of a free radical in the science section of *The New York Times* as being like a compressed spring ready for release.[92] He thought of his title as a colourful analogy – he was not trying to represent such particles literally, though he felt that his imagery was coming closer than ever before to expressing pure energy. He also enjoyed reducing the film medium to its most basic elements – light in darkness. By scratching the black emulsion side of the film so that the beam of the projector flashed through the clear celluloid base, he could evoke the energies of nature such as lightning. With his admiration for the most ancient (as well as the most contemporary) forms of art, he was delighted to imagine that he was cancelling out the thousands of years that separated modern technology from the scratching of designs on cave walls. He even added some ancient Native American arrowheads to his tools, 'for romanticism', as he put it.[93]

After testing many types of black film, Lye settled on DuPont leader because its emulsion peeled away cleanly. He haunted second-hand shops looking for scribers small enough to suit 16mm film. The most useful were dental tools, nails, needles, wire brushes and sections of fine-toothed saw blades. Much concentration and precision were required to draw on such a small scale, to scrape vigorously enough to make the images bold and energetic, and yet not tear the celluloid.[94] In his words: 'You stick down the sides [of the film] with Scotch Tape. You spit on or dampen the celluloid with a sponge . . . . You've got sprocket holes to guide you. When you hold the needle you dig it in through the black emulsion into the film and then start doing pictographic signatures.'[95] And: 'My wife said one day when passing me working at my bench, "Len, I didn't know you were spastic". She saw me crouched over a piece of film with my etching needle stuck in it. I wriggled my whole body to get a compressed feeling into my shoulders [and] a pent-up feeling of precision into the fingers, and with a sudden jump I pulled the needle through the celluloid and completed my design. So, I called to Ann on her way back, "Hey, I'm not spastic; but wait till you see these things". On film they are very controlled yet very kinetic.'[96]

He would begin each session with a particular figure of motion in mind which he would draw for hours, checking the results with a jeweller's eyepiece or through the projector.[97] As the strips accumulated, music was needed to accompany these 'little zig-zags of electricity'.[98] He had followed his usual practice of developing a new type of imagery before looking for relevant music. Later he wrote, 'I came across an absolutely marvellous field tape of the Bagirmi tribe. It had the same kind of feeling [as the images], the same resonance, the same attack.' Its singing and drumming seemed to 'rattle the marbles in your skull'.[99] Lye was delighted to learn later that this African music was a tribal homage to Shango, the god of thunder – an ideal way to accompany his visual lightning.

The selected music was a traditional dance piece which might be described as a funky four rhythm (emphasising what drummers call 'the and-of-two'), performed by one musician beating a pair of drums and another shaking a rattle.[100] Lye relished the 'quality of zizz' in the drummer's 'short, sharp, rhythmic figures'. The crisp sound perfectly suited the energy and abruptness of the images.[101] The fact that the tempo was steady and the music somewhat repetitive made synchronisation easier. The most marked changes were a burst of singing after the opening titles and occasional passages of more syncopated drumming. Lye constructed distinctive visual sequences around these variations.

In visual terms, *Free Radicals* can be understood as a set of variations on the technique of scratching black film. In the course of its four minutes, there are nine or ten major variations (though this is a subjective estimate as the variations flow one into another, and sometimes overlap, with a sense of continual metamorphosis). Each variation (or figure of motion) can be broken down into smaller sequences, typically one to two seconds long, though a few strips of film last longer and some are as short as one or two frames. This is the scale on which Lye worked, usually scratching around 24 frames (a second of film) during each pass. As always, having discovered an interesting figure, he would continue for days to make variations. He was also open to chance, quick to seize on interesting accidents.

Like the main theme introduced at the beginning of a piece of music, the film kicks off with one of its principal figures of motion – the 'zig-zag of electricity' which darts like lightning, or like the snake-like kinetic sculptures he would build in the 1960s.[102] It is interesting to compare the snake-like forms in *Free Radicals*

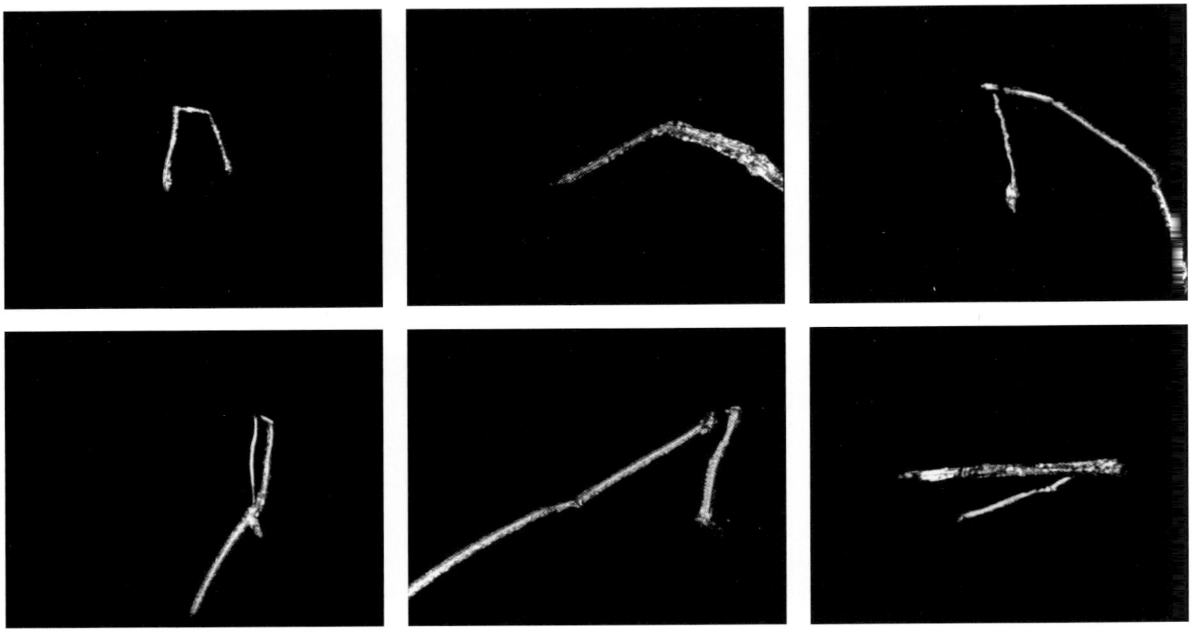

These frames from *Free Radicals* (1958) create the impression of a graceful dancer pirouetting or a skater spinning. The sequence illustrates the film's fluid sense of space. Courtesy Len Lye Foundation.

with those in his first film, *Tusalava* – or the dot patterns in the two films – as proof of the progress he had made in developing a more dynamic style of animation.

After thirteen seconds, a cleanly scratched vertical line moving sideways across the screen functions as a kind of optical wipe to clear the way for the next section (the title sequence). When the hand-scratched titles appear, they have a tense vibration, and the letters are like an energetic group of dancers jumping back and forth to the drum music. Lye had developed this style of scratched words in the early 1950s while preparing to make a poetry film with his friend Dylan Thomas.[103] Other film-makers (such as Brakhage) would imitate this method, but Lye remained the master of it.

Next, the singer's voice is associated with a group of parallel vertical lines that sway gracefully as they keep shifting from side to side and forming new pairs. Such lines are another of this film's figures of motion (and they later formed the basis of *Tal Farlow*). The following sequence consists of a diverse range of scratched images in brief bursts, mostly only a few frames in length. It is clear that the intervening black spaces are an integral part of the visual rhythm. Many of the images resemble numbers or letters, but they change constantly. There are also some more complex tangles of lines.[104] All of these white shapes leap out of the darkness like fireworks, reinforcing the sharp beats of the drum.

The following section, approximately a minute long, is more continuous, and in some respects it represents the heart of the film. It consists of a wonderful series of turning, twisting or spinning movements. Lye had found that shapes like letters could be made to pivot or turn inside out, creating a sudden illusion of depth. This sequence is one of the best examples of the fluid space of his films ('3½, 3, 2½, 2D'). Performing within the frame as though on a stage, some of the shapes create the impression of a dancer pirouetting or a skater spinning. In this rapid, giddy series of variations, it is difficult to tell where each dance (or strip of film) begins and ends.

The next section is a miscellany of zigzags and lines, which includes some short sequences such as momentary flashes of lightning first at the top and then at the bottom of the frame. They are followed by two of the most memorable figures of motion. The first figure (approximately half a minute long) accompanies a passage of syncopated drumming. An asterisk shape comes into existence as a number of lines run together from different directions. Once in place, the asterisk struggles to remain intact. It is tugged around the screen as the individual lines engage in an energetic push and pull. Finally it splits in two, like a dancing couple who separate.

A few seconds later there is a beautiful sequence of broad banner or feather-like scratches which curl or whiplash across the screen, as though rippling in the wind – another striking example of the film's complex space.

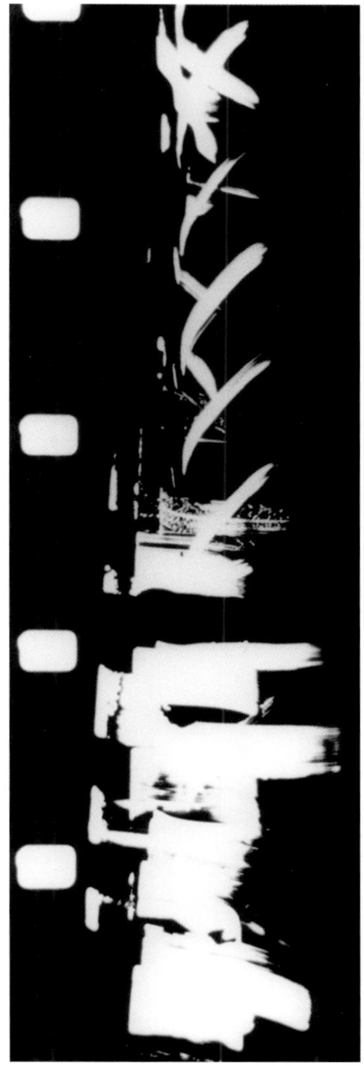

This strip of film is part of the 'banner' sequence near the end of *Free Radicals*. It consists of five frames (as the sprocket-holes indicate). Courtesy Len Lye Foundation.

Paul Barnes, Lye's assistant at the time, recalls that he 'was as fussy with the [making of prints] as he was with everything. You would think a white-on-black image would be relatively easy to achieve, but one of the things [he] liked about etching was the fact that at times there was a certain depth to the lines. There were gradations of grey within the etched-out areas and that gave the lines a bit of substance.'[105] The images were meant to be as 'scratchy' as his earlier films had been 'painterly'. No processing lab had ever seen a film like this before, and Lye had to try a number of labs before he could get what he wanted – a pure black background so the images appeared to be floating in space, along with enough grey texture in the scratches to add a subtle hint of three dimensions.

The original (1958) version of *Free Radicals* was five minutes in length. Despite having won a major award for it, Lye returned to the film in 1979 and re-edited it, removing some short sequences where he (or his wife Ann, whose opinion he greatly valued) 'wasn't happy with the clarity of the line, or the way the images were synched to the music'.[106] His perfectionism required every second of the film to make a clear contribution.[107] The version that he ruthlessly condensed to four minutes is the one in circulation today and the one described above. A section he dropped was the opening title that linked the film to Lye's theory of Individual Happiness Now: 'Brancusi said: "Do not look for obscure formulae or mystery, it is pure joy that I bring you". I say: "Film is advanced art, not science, education, nor box office – but utopia".'[108]

Critics have not always followed Brancusi's advice – for example, Parker Tyler saw Lye's choice of title as 'a morally motivated pun on the Marxist dialectic as formulated in montage by Eisenstein'.[109] Marxism cannot help us to appreciate the 'advanced art' of *Free Radicals*, but there are three contexts that do provide useful starting points. The first is Surrealism. From the 1930s, Lye was interested in the most free-wheeling (or 'painterly') aspects of Surrealism such as its interest in automatism, doodling and graffiti as sources of original images.[110] The style of *Free Radicals* echoes some of Lye's earlier paintings and woodcuts, such as the repertoire of zigzags, asterisks, dots, dashes and other energy signs that he shared with the artist Joan Miró.[111] The obvious difference is that Lye's radicals literally move and morph.

A second context is Abstract Expressionism, with its emphasis on open form, physicality, gesture and the pure energies of the medium. Not only the images of *Free Radicals* but also Lye's film-making process had affinities with 'action painting'.[112]

The fact that the film's title sequence is a form of handwriting suggests a third context, semiotics. In semiotic terms, the scratches are not only indexical (Lye's 'signatures', the traces of his authorship), but also symbolic (suggesting letters) or iconic (taking the form of lightning, say, or a dancer) – but they are not symbolic or iconic consistently. A scratch can have many possible readings – interpreted as an atomic particle, a bird in flight, a snake, an ideogram or purely a vector. The film can be said to explore the extreme limits of language. Yann Beauvais describes it vividly when he says its lines are 'in a continual state of becoming. *They are the signature of movement itself.* They are like the trails of shooting stars, abysses of energy. These are lines of force, and not lines of figuration.'[113] Earlier, I spoke of the figure of motion as a form in process, a form that unfolds, and *Free Radicals* offers some of the most dramatic examples.

Lye's aesthetic also provides other relevant contexts. The imagery of *Free Radicals* creates a powerful sense of physical empathy. Lines stretch, spin, wriggle and sway, subtly reminding us of the human body in movement. And the music is directly related to his old interest in African tribal rituals. At the same time, the images are sufficiently abstract to invite other analogies besides dance – including old brain associations such as the inner workings of the body (like the urgent patterns of an electrocardiograph), flashes of lightning or the collision of atomic particles. Such analogies do not contradict one another, for this artist was always inter-relating different natural energies. *Free Radicals* is the greatest film example of his (and Olson's) conception of art as energy transfer.

Particles in Space: Extending the Scratch Technique

Particles is even more extreme than *Free Radicals* in the apparent roughness of its scratchy textures – a striking contrast to the tidy styles of line drawing that characterise most animation. While using the same black and white methods as *Free Radicals*, it is based on a new motif – the particle, a tiny scratch or very compact 'zizz of energy', with a fluid shape that can vary from dot to flash to streak. Lye described it as 'the smallest bit of anything I could isolate in the vastness of space'.[114] The other key motif in the film is a line so freely scratched that it breaks up at times into separate particles. At a late stage of his work on the film, Lye was fascinated to read in the *New York Times* that the crew of the

These sample images from *Particles in Space* (1980) show 'nests of energy', a line that moves vigorously from side to side, lines that fly from the bottom to the top of the frame, and particles of various kinds which Lye described as 'floating in space'. Courtesy Len Lye Foundation.

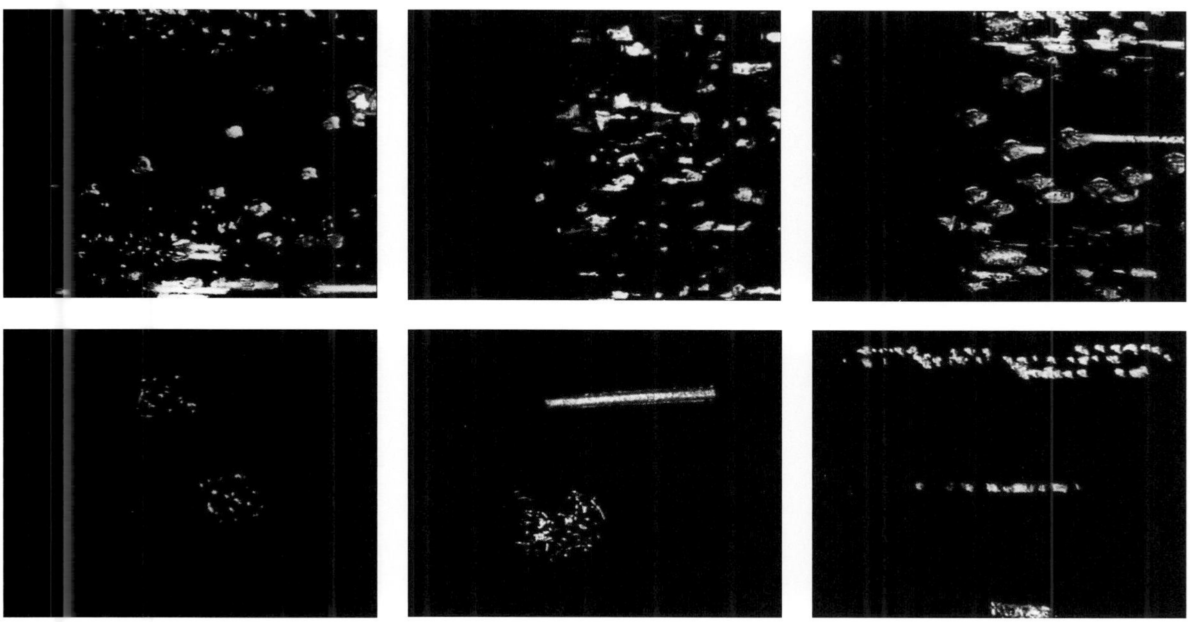

Apollo 14 moon mission had been startled to see energy particles in space. The particles were of 'three types – pinpoint or starlike lights; explosive flashes; and thin streaks of light'.[115] The sense of space as a field full of energies sounded exactly like his film.

After the title sequence, the action begins with a single particle, which is then joined by a glittering swarm of particles. Lye scratched this motif on black leader with a small cluster of stiff wire bristles that he had extracted from larger brushes. The bristles flaked off the emulsion in small speckles, creating showers of particles that filled the screen with movement. At times, they resembled sparks but at other times they were like gleams of light on a dark expanse of moving water. Lye spoke of the smaller, more compact clusters that moved around the screen as 'nests of energy floating in space'.

Particles was a film intermittently in progress for many years.[116] In 1978, knowing that his time was running out, Lye selected the existing footage that he liked best, then made a final version of the film with the help of his assistants Paul Barnes and Steve Jones. Under Lye's supervision, each produced an additional variation on the particle motif.

Unlike the continuous music of *Free Radicals*, *Particles in Space* has a cut-and-paste soundtrack. During the film's 3m 20s, there are at least nine different passages of sound. Each has a different tempo and visually is paired with a different figure of motion.[117] Lye drew his music from two Folkways albums of traditional drum music – *African and Afro-American Drums* (F-4441) and *Drums of the Yoruba of Nigeria* (F-4502). Drums are the principal musical instrument of the Yoruba, and Lye sampled three important types – Igbin or log drums, Dundun or pressure drums (which have variable tuning and can function as 'talking drums'), and Bata, a cone-shaped, two-headed drum with a reputation for complex rhythms. From the other album, Lye took two samples of 'Jumping Dance Drums' from the Bahamas. When he later learned that, like Yoruba drumming, this music reflected the Shango tradition (which had spread through the West Indies), he felt that his old brain must have intuitively sensed the connection.[118]

He also combined two sound recordings of his Shango-related sculpture *Storm King*. This provided a striking accompaniment for his superb title sequence. Lye had become so expert at scratching letters that he could make them rotate like kinetic sculptures.[119] At the end of the film, he added the crashing sounds of his sculpture *Twister*. All of the sound sources for the film were chosen for their dynamism, resonance and physicality – drums beaten by hand and metal sculptures

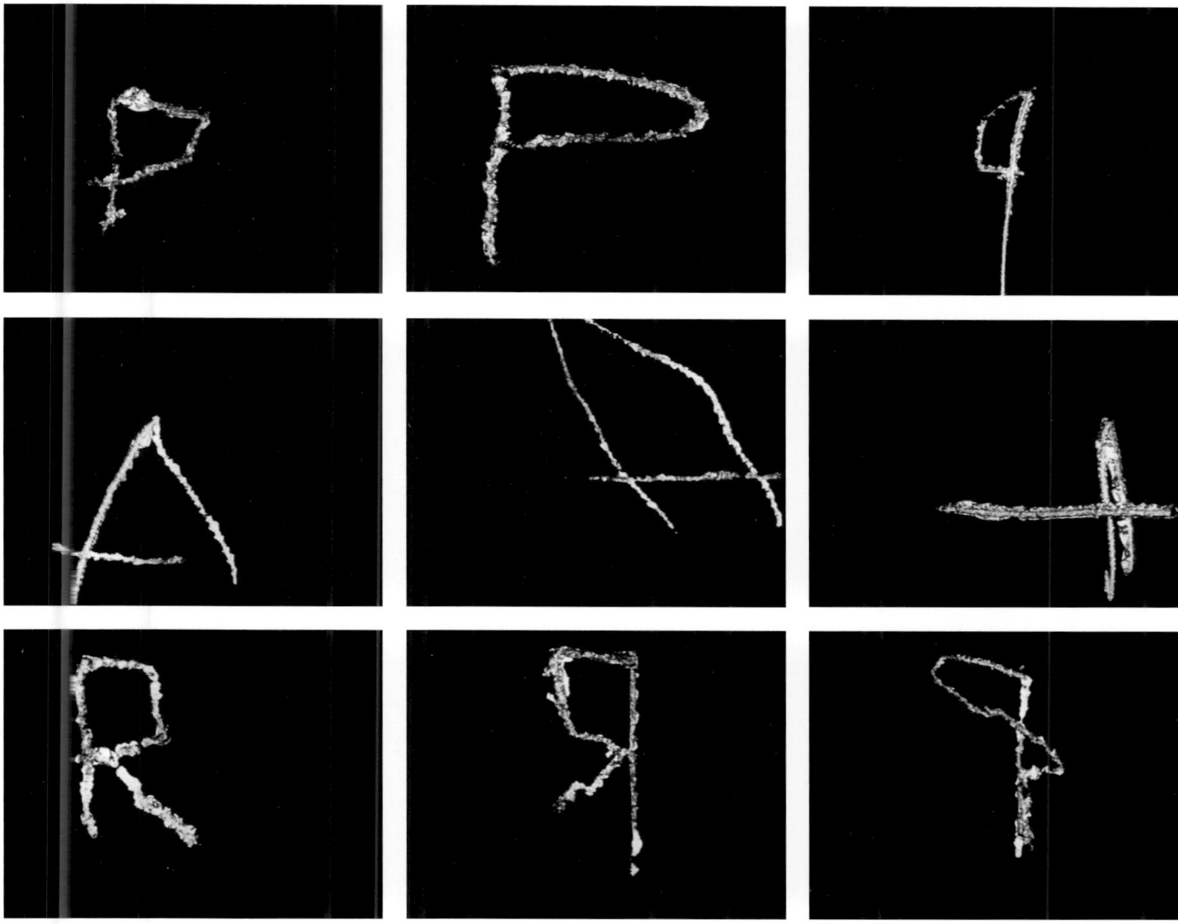

The first three letters of the title, *Particles in Space*, whirl like a dancer. Courtesy Len Lye Foundation.

shaking wildly. The result is a fast, funky soundtrack which combines with the rapid movement of the images to create a sense of urgency.

Barnes recalls that:

> Generally Len never wanted a sequence of images to run longer than a second. The sequence would be 10 frames, 12 frames, 18 frames. In *Free Radicals* there are sections of long straight lines that run for a number of seconds in counterpoint to the shorter, more staccato sequences – they work that way rhythmically in the film. But in *Particles* he wasn't interested in that kind of imagery. What he wanted now were shorter, tighter, more precise sequences.[120]

This gives *Particles* a less continuous flow than *Free Radicals*; but because related ideas have been grouped together, it is still possible to see the film as having nine sections, both visually and musically, with each section exploring a set of variations on a basic figure of motion.

One section, beginning at 2m 43s, is like a direct continuation of *Free Radicals* – a beautiful series of turning and spinning forms. But even here there are new ideas added, such as the parallel zigzag lines (at 2m 50s) that shiver like lightning. More typical are the many variations on the particle motif. There are also three sections based on dynamic horizontal lines. To match a passage of particularly fast drumming, Lye imagined an elbow thrust out repeatedly from the body, like the action of rowing but with a 'snap' to it. He started with a dot (particle) and stretched it sideways to make a line, then let it contract – all in less than half a second. This dramatic stretching movement was also reminiscent of someone exercising with a chest expander, though no person could move so rapidly. Lye at the age of 77 found his own fingers were letting him down, so he got Barnes to scratch these images for him. The end result of several months of experimentation was a sequence (starting at 2m 8s) in which the dot performed its 'concertina' motion over 20 times in the space of eight seconds. Focusing on the way a single particle changes, this is one of the most concentrated kinetic images in the film.

In another memorable sequence (at 1m 38s), also accompanied by rapid drumming, horizontal lines rise from the bottom of the frame and fly to the top (an action Lye described as 'climbing' or 'reaching'). In another related section (at 2m 32s), a short line zaps back and forth between the opposite sides of the screen, above a 'nest' of particles. These variations on lines and particles and the (deliberate) roughness of the scratchy textures, broke new ground for direct film-making.

Even during the final weeks of his life, Lye was working to complete another film based on rhythmic patterns created by clean-cut vertical lines, as a vicarious dance to *Rock 'n' Rye* by the jazz guitarist Tal Farlow. He had scratched these images around 1957 but had not finished synchronising them. Although he regarded this as a minor film, he liked the way it demonstrated yet another range of 'scratch' possibilities. Lye did not live to finish the project, but he arranged for the editing to be completed by Steve Jones under the supervision of Ann Lye. It serves as a short but very stylish display of Lye's more linear or 'geometrical' style of doodling, as distinct from his 'main stuff' which he described as freer and more 'biological'.[121] Like all his animated films, *Tal Farlow* has a very physical sense of swing.

five the sculptures

WHEN LYE WENT 'ON STRIKE' AS A FILM-MAKER AND SHIFTED MOST OF his creative energies to kinetic sculpture, he had to learn new engineering skills, but he could continue to follow his basic aesthetic with its emphasis on movement, kinesthesia, choreography and figures of motion. He was still working by hand, and still seeking to 'project' or 'blow up' his images on a large scale. His new knowledge of metal and motors did, however, give him a fresh perspective on movement; and it seems no accident that his most detailed theoretical writing about kinetic art followed his most intense period of sculpture-building.

We have seen that Lye's major films of the late 1950s became more austere, embracing black and white and using music that focused on rhythm rather than melody or instrumental colour. An interesting perspective on this development is provided by an essay mentioned earlier that related the art of motion to neuroscience. Semir Zeki and Mathew Lamb distinguish three stages in the evolution of kinetic art, represented by the Futurists, Calder and Tinguely. The third stage involves a shift away from colour and from clearly defined form (such as the cut-out shapes of mobiles); instead, the effect of the work is 'to approximate the stimulus . . . as nearly as possible to the physiology of area V5', the area of the brain that specialises in movement.[1] *Free Radicals* seems to qualify for this most advanced stage, but what of the kinetic sculpture that followed it?

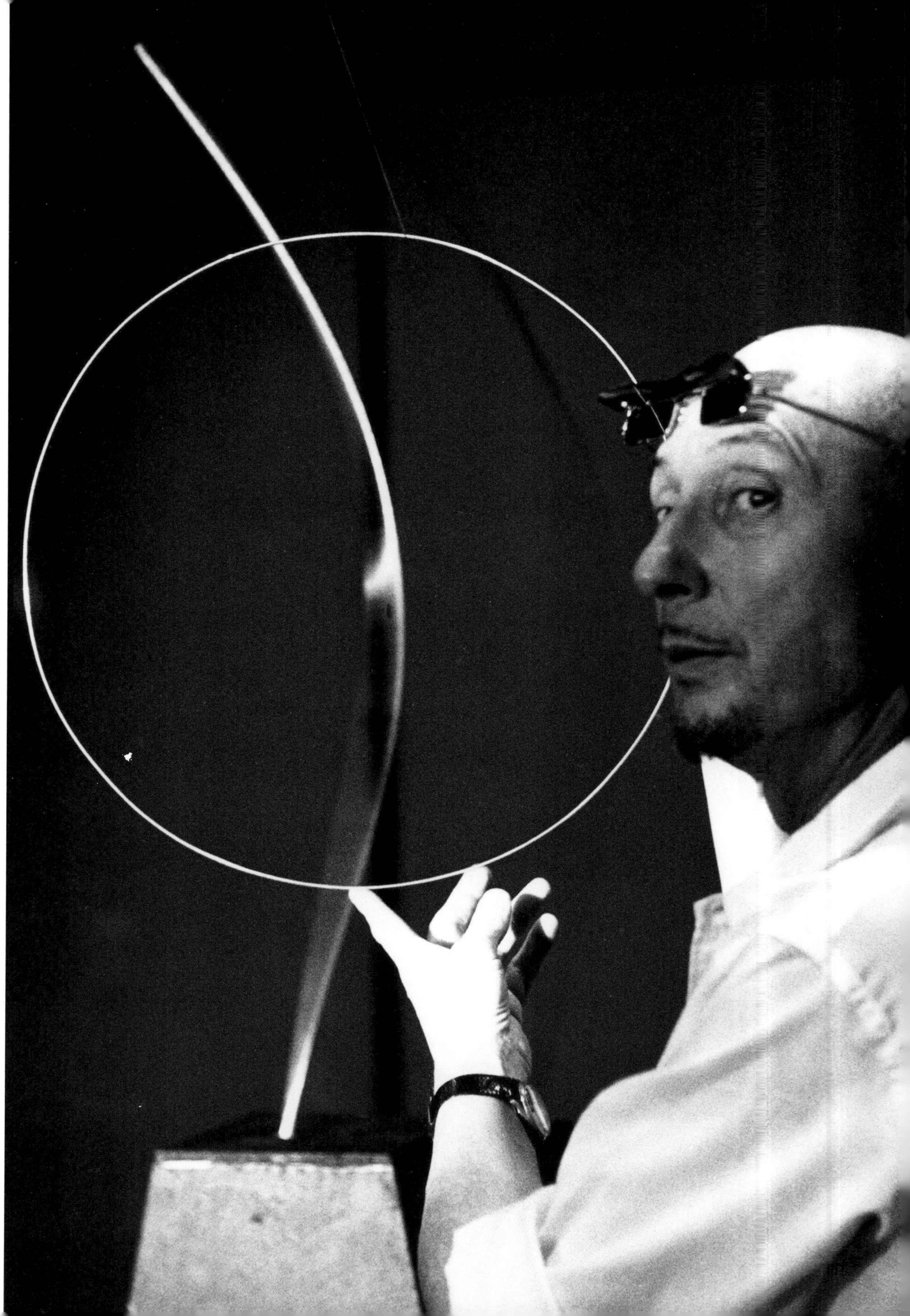

It would have been possible for Lye to combine colour and music with his sculpture, and he did occasionally explore those possibilities, but he always put his primary emphasis on movement.[2] The range of possible movements was more confined than in film, because most of the sculptures needed to be attached to a base – but this had the effect of focusing attention on those movements that were possible. Also, the artist's relationship with the pieces of metal and the way they moved involved empathy in a very direct way. His shift to kinetic sculpture could therefore be seen as a logical follow-on from the concentrated style of *Free Radicals* and as part of the 'evolution' described by Zeki and Lamb. This is not to assume that specialised art is necessarily better than more eclectic forms.[3] Lye's talk of 'movement *per se*' did not imply that it had to be the only ingredient, but he always gave precedence to movement. He succeeded in transferring to his sculpture the same sophistication and subtlety of movement he had achieved in his films.

It is not surprising that some of his favourite filmic figures of motion turn up in his sculptures – for example, spinning, oscillation, bouncing movement like branches in the wind, and tense, muscular vibration. There are moments when the showers of water thrown out by *Water Whirler*, spotlit against the night sky, resemble the energy swarms of *Particles in Space*. And when the two *Twisters* become a blur of motion, they are reminiscent of *Free Radicals* as their polished steel surfaces create darting flashes of light. When Lye spoke of using motors to propel the sculptures, he used the term 'animation'.

Another basis of comparison is the fact that many of the sculptures are programmed to perform for around four minutes, a similar length to many of his films. The artist was genuinely concerned about the risk of boring the spectator. (In his words, 'three to four minutes . . . seems a long time. I mean, a TV spot would last 20 seconds.')[4] A few sculptures such as *Water Whirler* do, however, require a longer period for the 'unfolding' of their figures of motion. Lye saw timing and programming as key aspects of kinetic art:

> So far as the means of the craft in kinetic sculpture [are concerned] – for compositional control and presentation of various kinds of unfolding motion, such as reverse action, rotation, reciprocating action, the flow of acceleration and deceleration – it must be noted that industrial timers and electronic programmers are what brush, paint and canvas are to the painter; chisel, welding torch and casting material are to the sculptor; pencil and paper to the poet; or musical instruments to the composer.[5]

Lye, circa 1959. Courtesy Len Lye Foundation.

LYE'S SCULPTURES

Lye built or designed at least 32 kinetic sculptures: *Atomic Dance*, *Bell Wand*, *Blade* (aka *Plinth*), *Bones*, *Dancing Atoms*, *Fire Bush*, *Flip and Two Twisters* (aka *Trilogy*), *Fountain*, *Grass*, *Harmonic (Rotating or Revolving)*, *Jump Fish*, *Large Fountain*, *Moon Bead*, *Ribbon Snake* (aka *Convolution*), *Roundhead* (aka *Rings* or *Orrery*), *Sea Serpent* (with *Sun Ball*), *Singing Blade* (with *Thunder Sheet*), *Sky Snake*, *Spinning Disc*, *Storm*, *Storm King*, *Swaying Steel Fountain*, *Swirler*, *Swirling Harmonic*, *Thunderbolts*, *Universe* (aka *Loop*), *Wand Dance*, *Water Whirler* (aka *Water Swirler*), *Wind Wand*, *Witch Dance*, *Wave* and *Zebra*.

He occasionally changed names, and when there were two words in a title he would sometimes combine them (for example, *Windwand* or *Moonbead*). He

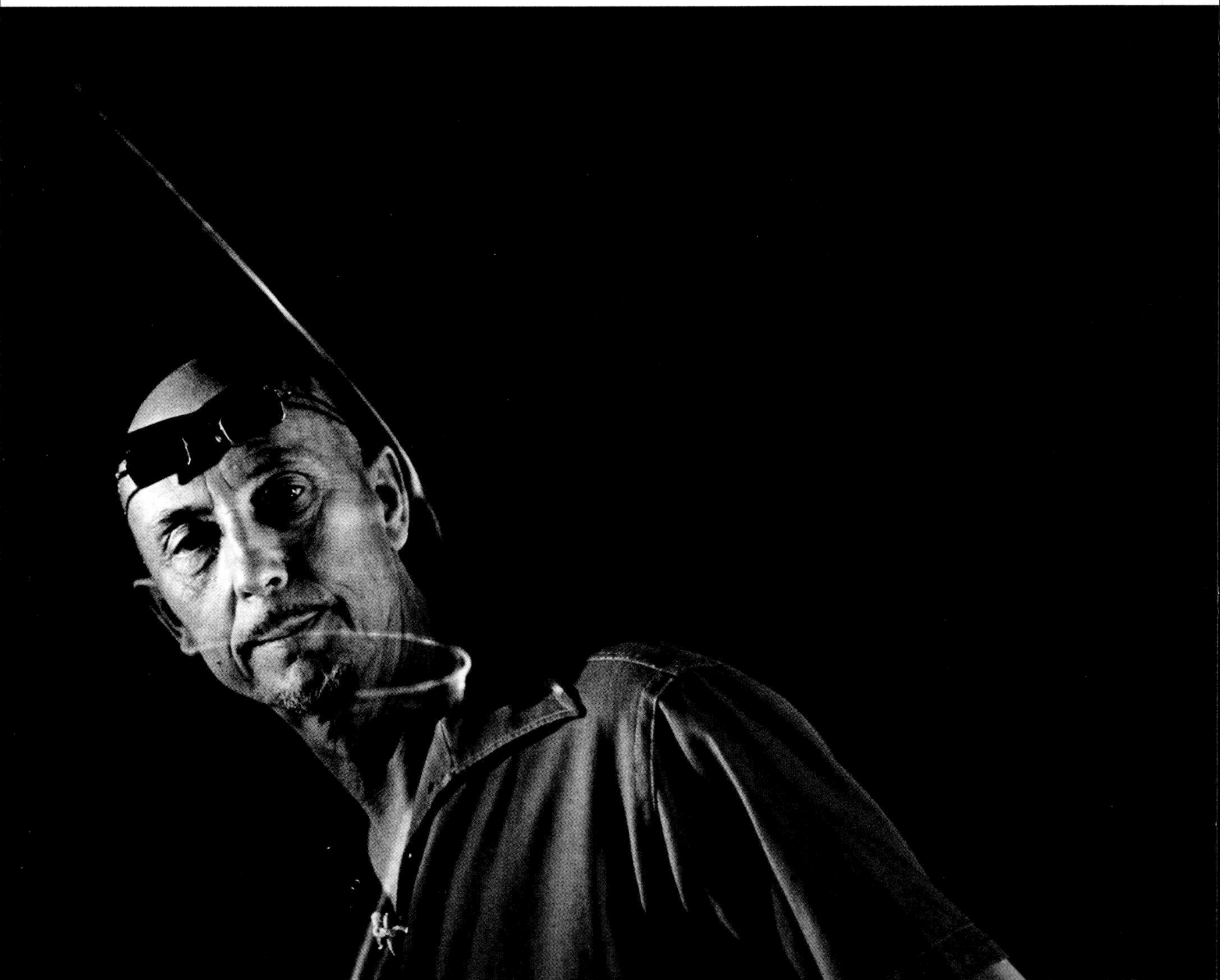

Lye watching a sculpture in motion. Courtesy Len Lye Foundation.

planned to assemble several of the works (or 'protagonists') as a large-scale tableau that he called *The Temple of Lightning.*[6] There are probably a few more ideas for sculptures hidden in the Lye collection which is yet to be fully catalogued. The list is also complicated by the fact that he occasionally proposed variations on a work – the addition of new members to the same family, so to speak. He made several copies of each of his completed sculptures during his lifetime, increasing the scale when he was able to do so; and the Lye Foundation has continued this tradition after his death (as the next chapter will explain). The editions remain small, however, and no edition has reached double figures.

Fountain was the best-known Lye sculpture during his lifetime, exhibited at the World's Fair and used by the United Nations in 1959 as a peace symbol. It was widely exhibited because it was one of the easiest of his sculptures to ship and install. It was also the idea most often pirated, turned into countless desk-top ornaments. Today, his best-known works are probably *Wind Wand*, *Water Whirler*, *Blade* and *Flip and Two Twisters*, which exist in giant versions. The first two are installed outdoors, and *Blade* has performed at outdoor festivals. Four other sculptures – *Grass*, *Roundhead*, *Storm King* and *Universe* – have also become well-known, with *Universe* the only large-scale Lye work based in Auckland. Most of the others in the above list are in the process of being restored. Evan Webb and Stuart Robb have recently completed work on *Fire Bush* and *Ribbon Snake*, and the remarkable nature of those sculptures suggests that there are other big surprises in store for us.

HOW LYE CREATED HIS SCULPTURES

A survey of Lye's working methods needs to start by looking at his 'doodling' process for generating ideas, then at how he selected and developed a particular idea, fine-tuned the details and 'choreographed' the overall performance of a work, before he decided on the best ways to exhibit it.

In the 1950s, one of his favourite haunts was Canal Street in downtown Manhattan, an area where manufacturing co-existed with a crowded marketplace of shops and tables selling cheap goods. He was 'looking for metals and springs and motors and mechanical tools and gadgets galore which are stalled out on the pavement for all the young Einsteins and Edisons to pick and choose and put two and two together and make a wonderful press-button affair out of scraps and rejects'.[7] In those days, there were still a number of engineering workshops in

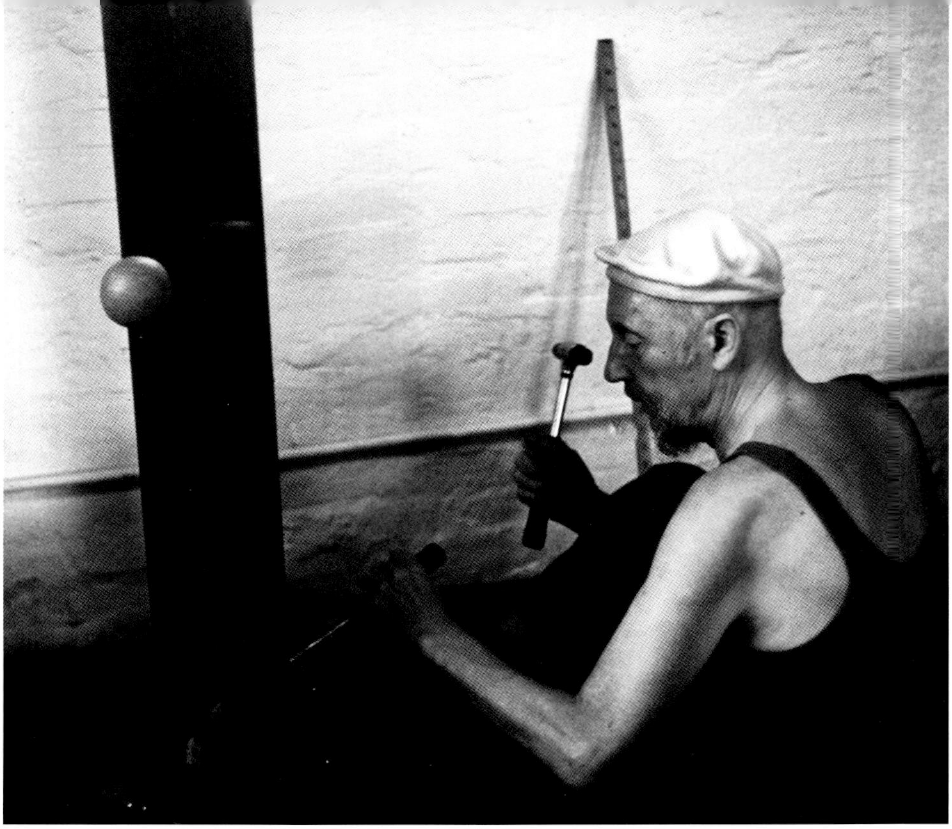

Lye in his studio in 1974 at work on *Blade*. Courtesy Len Lye Foundation.

the West Village and SoHo, and Lye would make the rounds of them in search of leftover pieces of metal. Paul Barnes recalls that the pieces –

> . . . came from all over, which was partly a money-saving device and partly a socia thing on Len's part. He'd run across these individuals, old machinists who could modify motors for his needs. There'd be some sort of crazy interchange and amusing relationships would develop. They looked on Len as an oddball, an alien from outer space, but as much as they thought he was crazy it was the event of their day when he came to see them. And he really loved these people, he had such respect for the work they could do, it was amazing the rapport that could develop.[8]

The off-cuts of metal that Lye would collect – rods, strips, sheets and occasionally a roll – were reminiscent of the trims of film he had collected from film studios when he had started to experiment with direct animation. He familiarised himself with iron, aluminium, brass, steel and many other metals. Steel came in a variety of forms, depending on the amount of added carbon or other alloys such as chromium. Each mixture altered the look and texture, hardness and tensile strength, as did the type of heat treatment. Lye developed a feeling for metals – a sense of 'affinity' or 'empathy' with 'the identity of the material', as he put it. Each type had its own 'plasticity', its way of bending or stretching, so that each was a potential 'performer' with its own kind of dance. At times, Lye worked with other materials such as wood (for the base of *Grass*) or water (for *Water Whirler*).

In his workshop, he would play with the rods and strips, shaking and waggling them. He called this process 'doodling' because he saw it as similar to the free-wheeling, trial-and-error, hands-on process he had used to draw on paper and to paint on celluloid.[9] After years of practice with those processes, he was acutely sensitive to literal or implied figures of motion. What Klee called 'taking a line for a walk' became for Lye the manipulation of a strip of steel. He wanted to explore the possibilities of sound, but his search was primarily for a movement 'that looks kind of magical, that keeps fascinating me'. For example, a roll of steel could produce an 'undulating, snake-like effect'. Not that Lye was interested in the symbolism – he was looking for an intriguing pattern that had a physical 'resonance'. Once he had glimpsed a potential shape, 'What I think of are the limits of the material, and the motions I have available. If I [continue to] like the image that the motion is forming, then I try to create some interplay which seems to me to get the best figure.'[10]

A type of small motor that Lye bought on Canal Street could produce rotation or rapid back-and-forth movement (reciprocation). For example, there was a sanding machine with a flat plate which he adapted so that a metal strip could be attached instead of sandpaper. Small as it was, this eight-dollar motor could shake metal much more rapidly than his hand, creating an astonishing sense of energy and noise, and a range of wave-like patterns. When a Variac motor was added, he was able to vary the voltage and modulate the speed so he could shape the effects like an animator. In addition to speeding up or slowing down, he could cut the power so that the metal coasted along under its own momentum, before being given another push.

A rod or strip of metal, as it struggles to absorb the energy being pumped into it by a motor, will respond by starting to move sideways or to rotate. As Lye said of *Rotating Harmonic*, 'You had a kind of drama going on, whether this metal could accept this energy . . . there seemed to be some kind of living business.'[11] He knew that kinetic sculpture was often regarded merely as a toy or a gimmick,

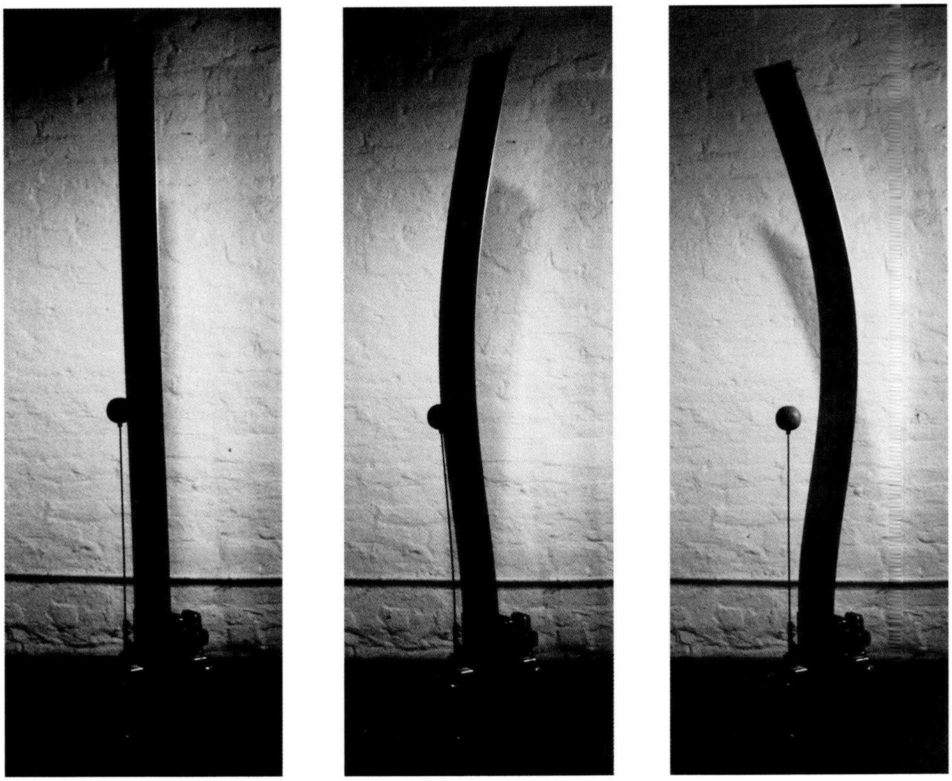

Two series of photographs of *Blade* in motion. The first shows it starting to oscillate and curve. In the second series, increased energy is causing the blade to strike the ball and to produce what Lye called 'double' and 'triple' harmonics. Courtesy Len Lye Foundation.

but a sense of 'drama' gave it an unmistakable seriousness. It also implied that the work was tapping into the old brain and its intuitive feeling for energy processes

As energy increases, the rod or strip will go through a series of harmonics. As Evan Webb explains:

> The first harmonic is a 'Y' shape where the standing metal sweeps from side to side like a wind-screen wiper. The second is one curve, 'C' shaped. The third, which Lye typically called a double, has two curves and is 'S' shaped. Increased energy superimposes other movements over the top of these basic patterns. The harmonics are not always in the same plane – for example, there is a stage at which *Blade* starts to twist (an action clearly visible from above), creating a fluttering effect.[12]

Lye said of *Blade*, 'As faster reciprocating action is applied . . . many harmonic curves are caused so that the blade of steel performs a constant rippling motion. This rippling action can be regulated from a slow undulating shimmer to a fast quiver.'[13] At high speed, the work became a 'pulsating, reflecting surface of

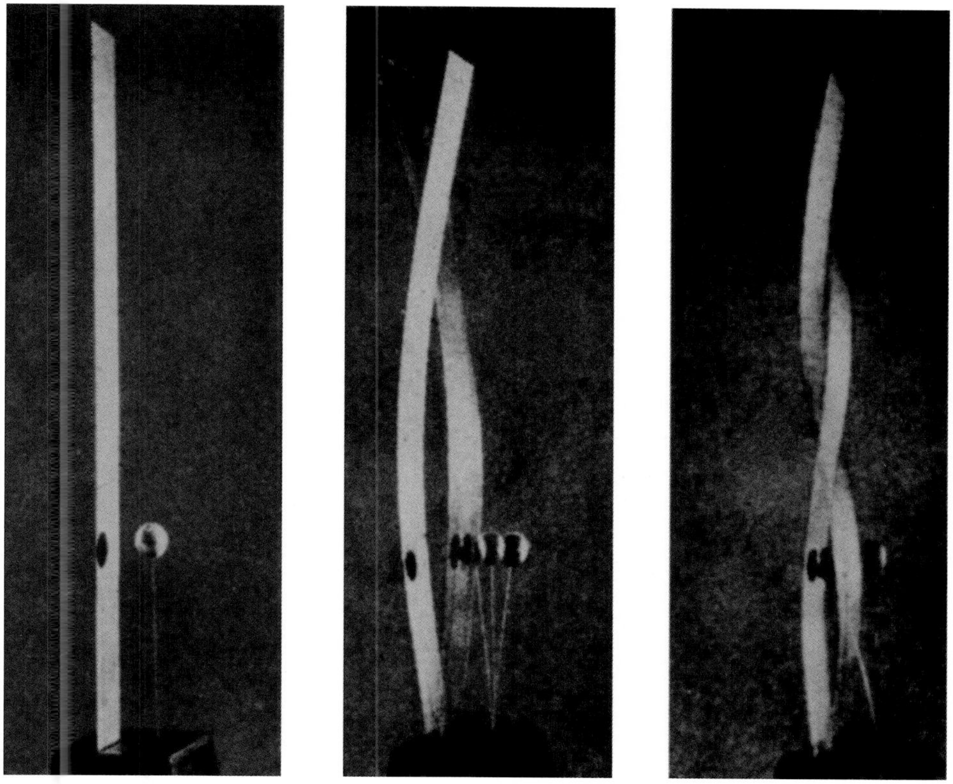

light with ‘an immensely strong vibrant type of shivering all up and down the blade’. Interesting effects could also be produced at lower speed, such as the first harmonic stage which he described as ‘a nice, lethargic or euphoric kind of sway, slowly oscillating’.[14]

Other possibilities included attaching the motor to the ceiling so that it fed energy down a hanging strip of metal (as in the case of the *Twisters*), rather than up from the floor. Springs were another source of movement, and a cam – a rotating wheel with an irregular shape that could activate another part each time it came round – helped to produce the rhythmic seesaw movement of *Grass*. Lye used other devices well-known to mechanics such as a universal joint (for *Rotating Harmonic* and *Dancing Atoms*). Whether the movement was fast or slow, rotated or reciprocated, he was ‘interested in the business of energy and getting a feeling of zizz in the thing’ – it had to encourage a sense of empathy.[15]

His technology was relatively simple, but the process by which he developed an idea was very demanding. He would (in his words) take his potential idea on ‘a journey’,[16] like a composer of music seeing how many variations he could create.

His quiet ('serene' or 'euphoric') sculptures tended to be based on a single figure of motion, but those sculptures look deceptively simple because a great deal of care has gone into presenting the figure to its best advantage. For example, the cycle of *Fountain* involves periodically switching off the motor, leaving the rods to coast to a stop. So there is great variety in their movement – swinging, rebounding, brushing against one another, slowing down and so on. There is a similar calculated subtlety to the movements of *Grass* or *Roundhead*. In the case of *Wind Wand*, the unusual curving movement ('*not* a droopy fishing rod') was extraordinarily difficult to achieve.[17] And for each sculpture he wanted some subtle differences to occur from one performance to the next – variation within a particular range.

The faster sculptures – which he called 'the wild kinetic stuff' – were taken on a more dramatic 'journey' or process of variation.[18] The shape of a work could be transformed by even a slight increase in voltage. At first, *Fire Bush* has a clear, orderly, unified shape like *Fountain*, but as it gathers speed it becomes wild and dishevelled – reminiscent of the unstable 'asterisk' shape in *Free Radicals*. In Lye's sculptures as in his films, form undergoes a constant process of metamorphosis. As he had written in his very first essay, the aim was 'to extricate movement from the static finalities or shapes which the mind imposes on living experience'.[19] The sculptures also matched the films in the way they played with depth, as fast spinning lines created an illusion of three-dimensional form (the effect known as 'virtual volume'), or objects lost their solidity as they dissolved into a flurry of motion.

In developing his original idea, he would sometimes add a second element, like a counter-theme in music. For example, *Singing Blade* is paired with a contrasting form known as *Thunder Sheet*. *Blade* consists of a different combination – a tall vertical strip in front of a shorter rod with a ball (like a drum stick). There are two motors and two kinds of movement: the base rotates while the strip oscillates. During one phase, a great sense of tension is produced by allowing the blade to vibrate close to the static rod but not quite touching. In such sculptures, the two 'protagonists' have a constantly changing relationship that runs the gamut from detachment, to a gentle caress, to violent percussion. Lye thought of each variation as another stage of the journey, and he wanted to present each one clearly before changing the speed again.

Although sound was secondary to the visual dimension, it was still important. Lye was willing to make an occasional visual tradeoff for the sake of the

Lye with *Fountain*, and a photograph of this sculpture in motion. Courtesy Len Lye Foundation.

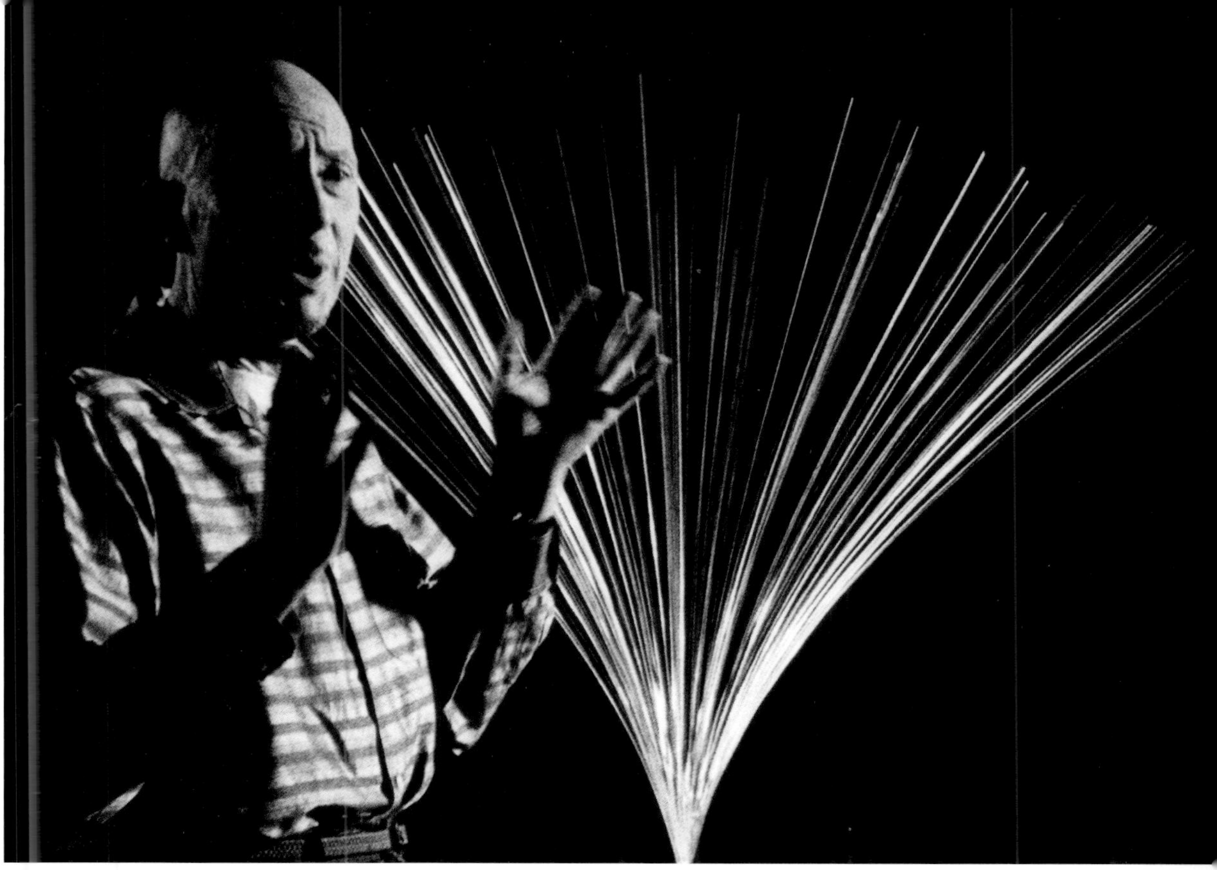

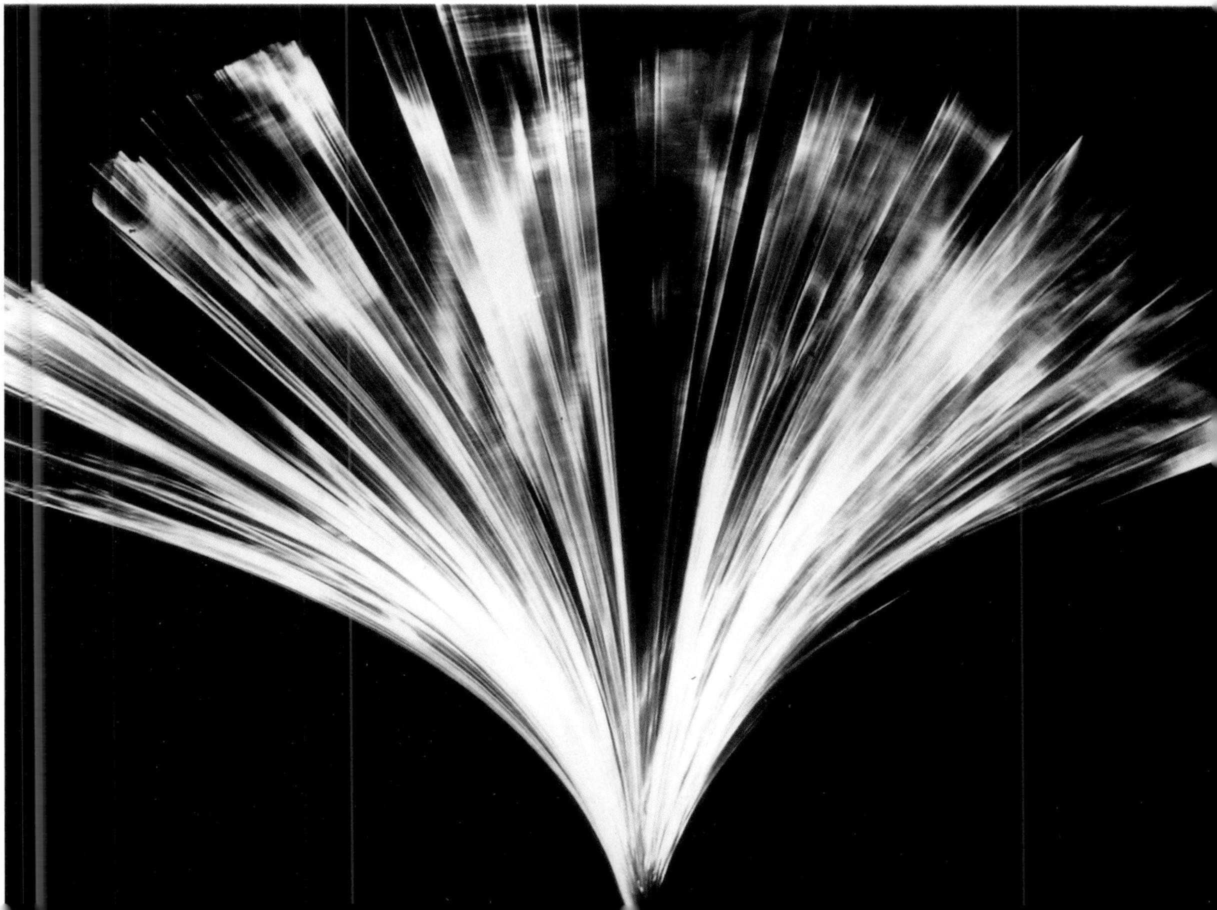

sound. He tried to ensure that the noise of the motor never overwhelmed other sounds (such as the swish of rods). He listened very carefully to the way the sound changed as he played with the speed. *Blade*, for example, 'starts to make a whipping sound, a very silky kind of sound . . . a cross between a whistle and a shriek'.[20] *Singing Blade* contrasts two sounds – the *Thunder Sheet* made of brass which is 'slow and rumbling' and the *Singing Blade* made of carbon steel which has 'a very shrill, high-pitched, piercing kind of sound, very angry . . . and yet in moving back slowly it makes a nice little crooning silky kind of whistling sound'.[21] Lye always hated 'cuteness' and he undertook a long search to find a type of ball that would create an appropriately serious sound for *Universe.* (His choice was compressed cork.) Similarly, he was adamant that he did not want the sound of *Bell Wand* to be 'too romantic' but rather 'vehement' and 'sonorous'. He attached 'clanker plates' to the bottom of the wand which clanked (or clanged) against each other as the sculpture moved, to dispel any sentimental 'sleigh bell' associations.[22]

At this stage in the fine-tuning process, Lye would arrange to have some metal cut exactly to size and he would decide on the most suitable coating. He selected a nickel finish for *Roundhead* because the stainless steel seemed 'a little cold'.[23] He liked the light effects created by the highly reflective surfaces of stainless steel, but he was also drawn to rougher finishes because he was afraid of his work developing a 'tinny, shiny, pseudo-elegance'.[24] For example, the two springs of *Thunderbolts* had to be 'very heavily sandblasted before nickling' to give them 'a rough surface with a good texture' and to 'stop them looking too shiny'.[25] The process of trial-and-error was slow because of Lye's perfectionism – he would go on worrying about the precise size, kind of metal, type of finish and motor setup that would most fully realise the potential of a particular figure of motion.

When he felt he had his 'composed theme of motion' under control, the next stage was 'choreography' – to design a sequence. The sculpture needed to 'start slow and gradually build up to give you a range of the patterns you can get out of the unfolding [by] putting in more energy'.[26] For example, the unfolding might involve a series of harmonic curves. The climax of the sequence usually came when the maximum level of energy was reached. It was desirable to push a particular effect 'to the absolute limit', but it was also important to understand how much punishment the sculpture could take without actually damaging it.[27]

The climax was not always a matter of high speed, as shown by the great tension we feel as we watch the painful, creaking slowness with which *Flip* strains to

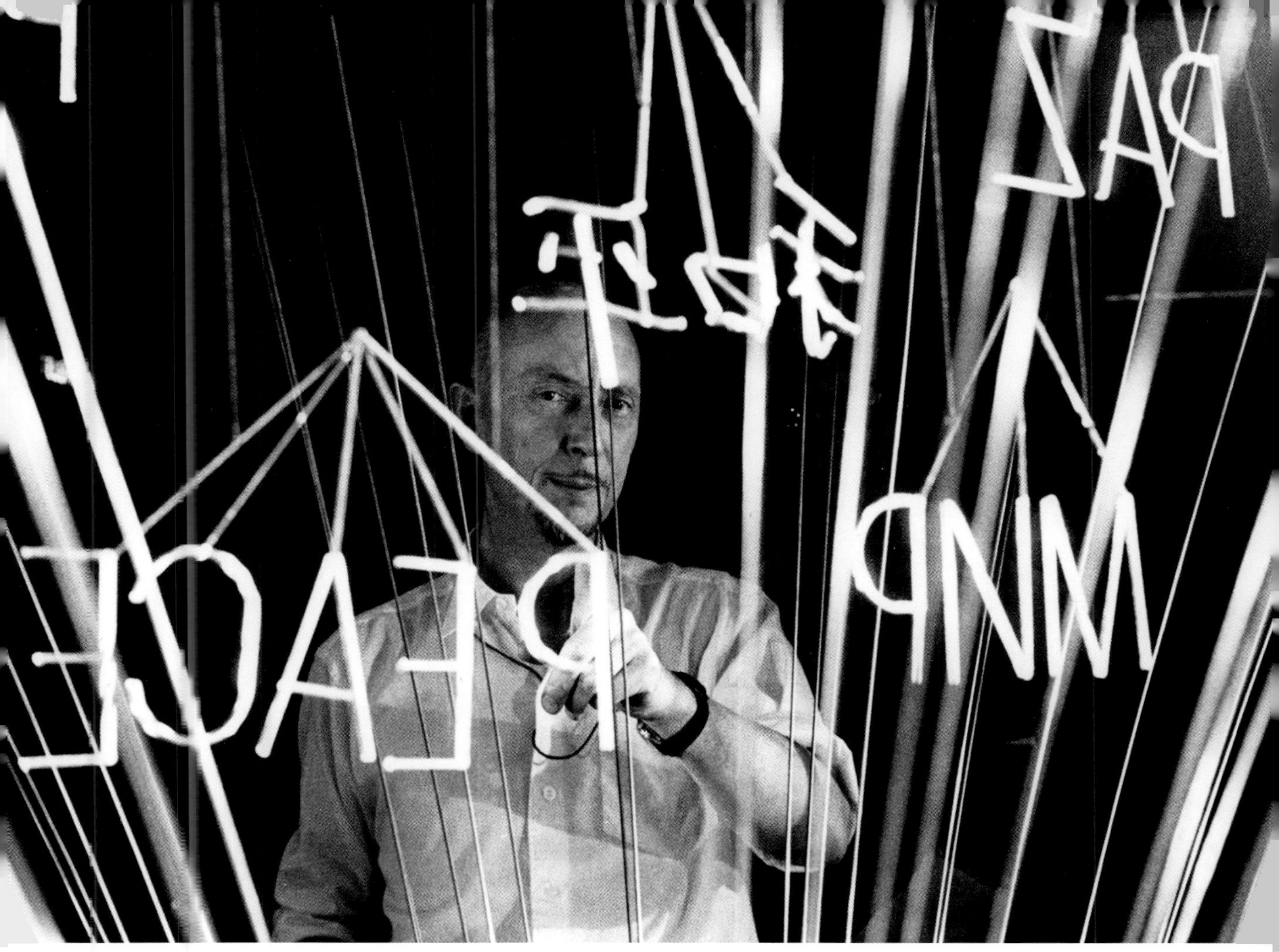

turn itself inside out. When it finally succeeds, the sense of relief is accompanied by an avalanche of sound. Once a work had reached its climax, Lye would bring the speed down, and he would not linger over the coda 'because you can't go backwards with these things . . . . you can't control the backwards unfolding.'[28]

The artist developed such sequences by hand, experimenting with the Variac; but once a routine had been planned precisely, he needed a system that could control the process automatically. In those pre-computer days, Lye often found it difficult to establish reliable methods. In preparing the sculpture for display, durability was another consideration. Every exhibition involved wear and tear, even when there were regular rest periods for the sculpture. A base was needed to conceal the motor and to muffle its noise because such details were likely to distract the viewer from the focus of the work, its figures of motion. When a

Lye making the film *Peace* for United Nations Day 1959. He is combining the word 'peace' in many languages with his kinetic sculpture *Fountain*. Courtesy Len Lye Foundation.

museum consulted Lye on the way his work was to be presented, he would have strong opinions about the background and the lighting. Now and then he would request coloured lighting to exploit the reflective, polished surfaces of the sculpture, and for a few works he even provided music as an accompaniment; but this was not a regular practice, and his first concern was always the movement. He urged curators to give the sculptures enough space so that the visual and auditory impressions of each work remained distinct. Every exhibition involved some technical challenges, such as the need for a sculpture like *Blade* to be attached to the floor without shaking the whole gallery.

INDIVIDUAL SCULPTURES

Kinetic art is often associated with noise and speed, but equally important in Lye's case are 'euphoric' sculptures such as *Grass*, *Fountain* and *Wind Wand*. The patterns of light and the rustling sounds of the rods are very important to the first two as elements that reinforce the movement. As Evan Webb sums up *Fountain*, 'Lye has managed to get light to come out of a bundle of rods' by highly polishing the rods, twisting them at the base and giving them a gentle push from the motor.[illegible] The

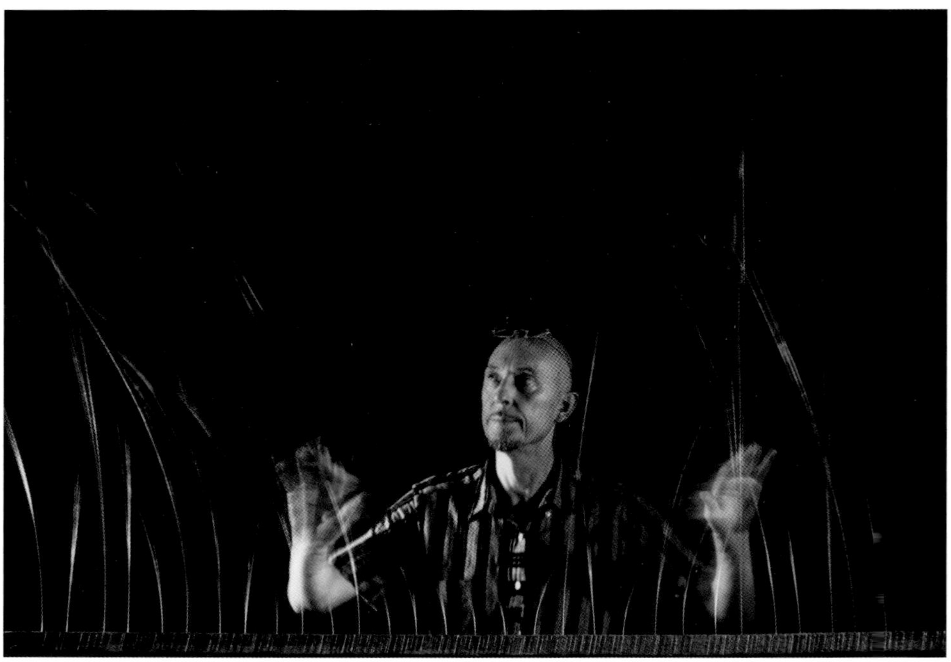

Lye in 1965 with *Grass*. Photo Albert Gruen. Courtesy Len Lye Foundation.

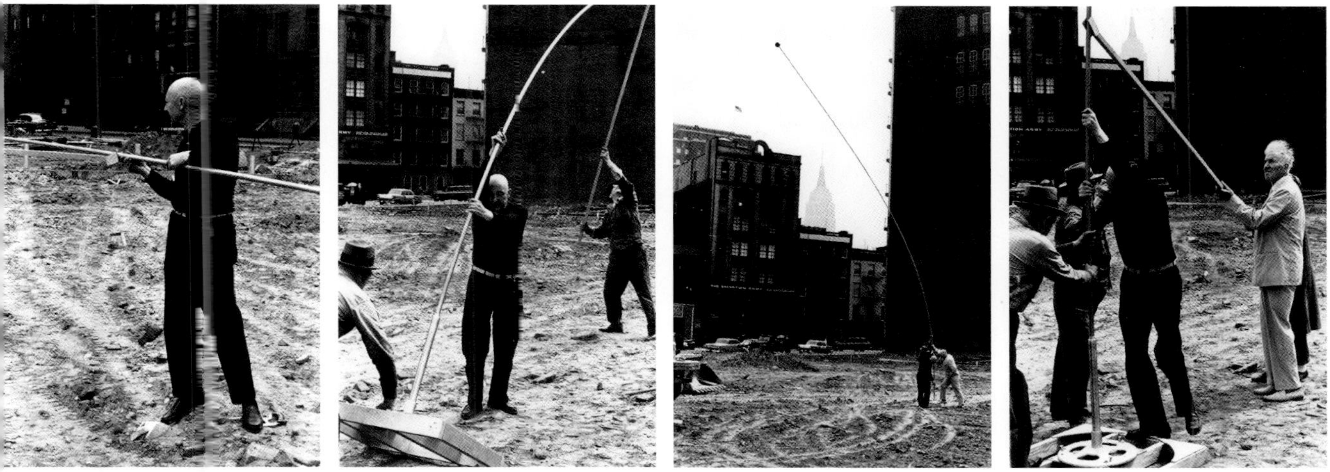

tensility of the rods is also important – they are strong enough to stand upright yet flexible enough to curve outwards and move with some freedom.

As noted above, these works are based on the repetition of a single figure of motion, but there are subtleties to this figure as it unfolds like a musical phrase – there is 'some kind of living business'. The movement of *Fountain* is reminiscent of rippling water or merging currents in a stream, but it can also suggest other natural rhythms such as wind in tree branches. The stop-start motion may remind us of human breathing. Watching the work is like listening to a quiet piece of Minimalist music – at first it seems repetitive in its slow, hypnotic rhythm, but as we pay close attention we become aware of subtle changes. Similarly, each of the 'stalks' of *Grass* has a measure of independence, so their overall pattern is never perfectly symmetrical, nor is it exactly the same each time the base lifts or lowers.

Wind Wand creates endless variations on a basic figure of motion – it does not simply sway back and forth but adds curving movements. One can watch it from many angles, including looking directly up from the base. It is easy to feel physical empathy for a shape that stands so tall, is sensitive to the wind, yet always carries its weight gracefully. The people of New Plymouth had mixed feelings about this 45-metre sculpture when it was built (to mark the 2000 Millennium), but many have come to feel a strong rapport and there are residents who visit the *Wand* after a storm to check it is safe.

Setting up a 40-foot (approx. 13-metre) aluminium version of *Wind Wand* in 1960 on a vacant lot in New York's West Village. Those helping Lye include mechanic Morris Gross and poet Robert Graves (in a light-coloured suit), who was visiting the Lyes at the time. Ann Lye is standing behind Graves. Courtesy Len Lye Foundation.

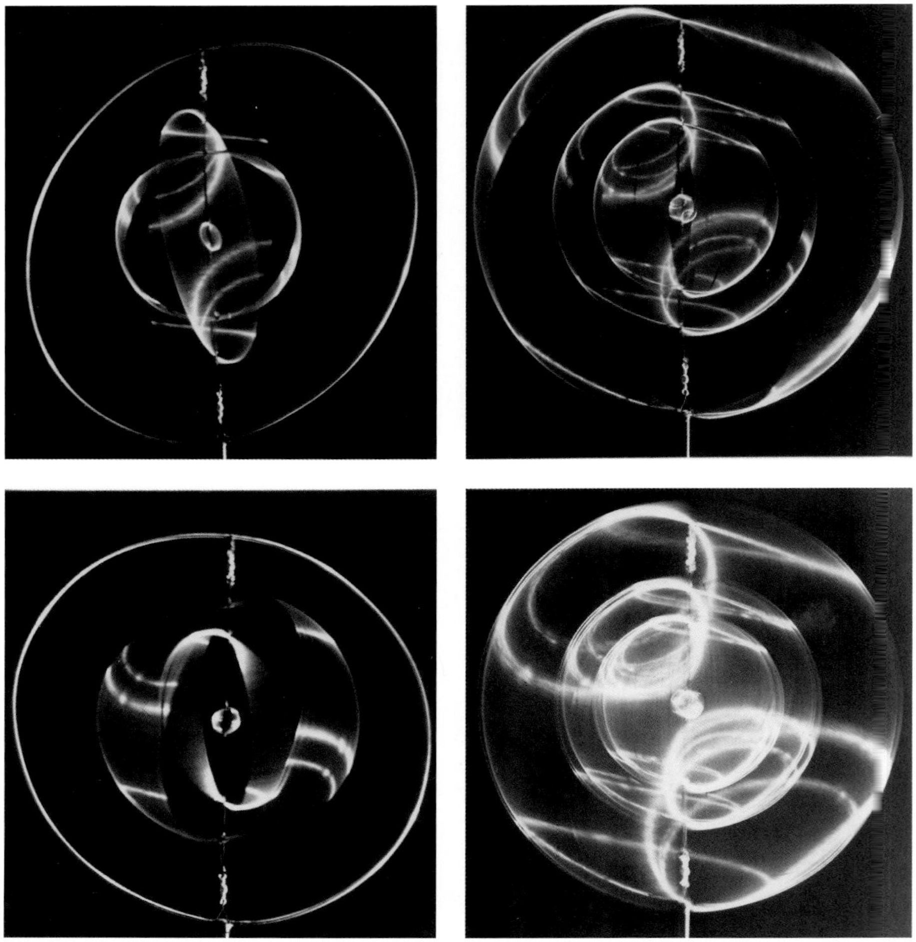

Successive time-lapse photographs of *Roundhead* in motion. Courtesy Len Lye Foundation.

Roundhead, another quiet work, was described to me by Ann Lye as offering the same pleasure to the viewer as the ever-changing shapes of flames in a fireplace on a winter's night.[30] It exploits the idea that movement is relative by combining four concentric rings which move independently yet act upon one another through the nylon threads connecting them. Our gestalt (or grasp of the form) of *Roundhead* is ever-changing, as individual rings can stop moving clockwise and be tugged in the opposite direction. The flashing highlights from the polished rings add to the shifting sense of depth. A music box accompanies the dancing rings, but its relationship to them is complex. The overall patterns of the work suggest musical forms such as canons and rounds. At first, this sculpture was called *Orrery* as a reference to old clockwork models of planets in their orbits round the sun (like the one in *Birth of the Robot*); but later Lye was so impressed

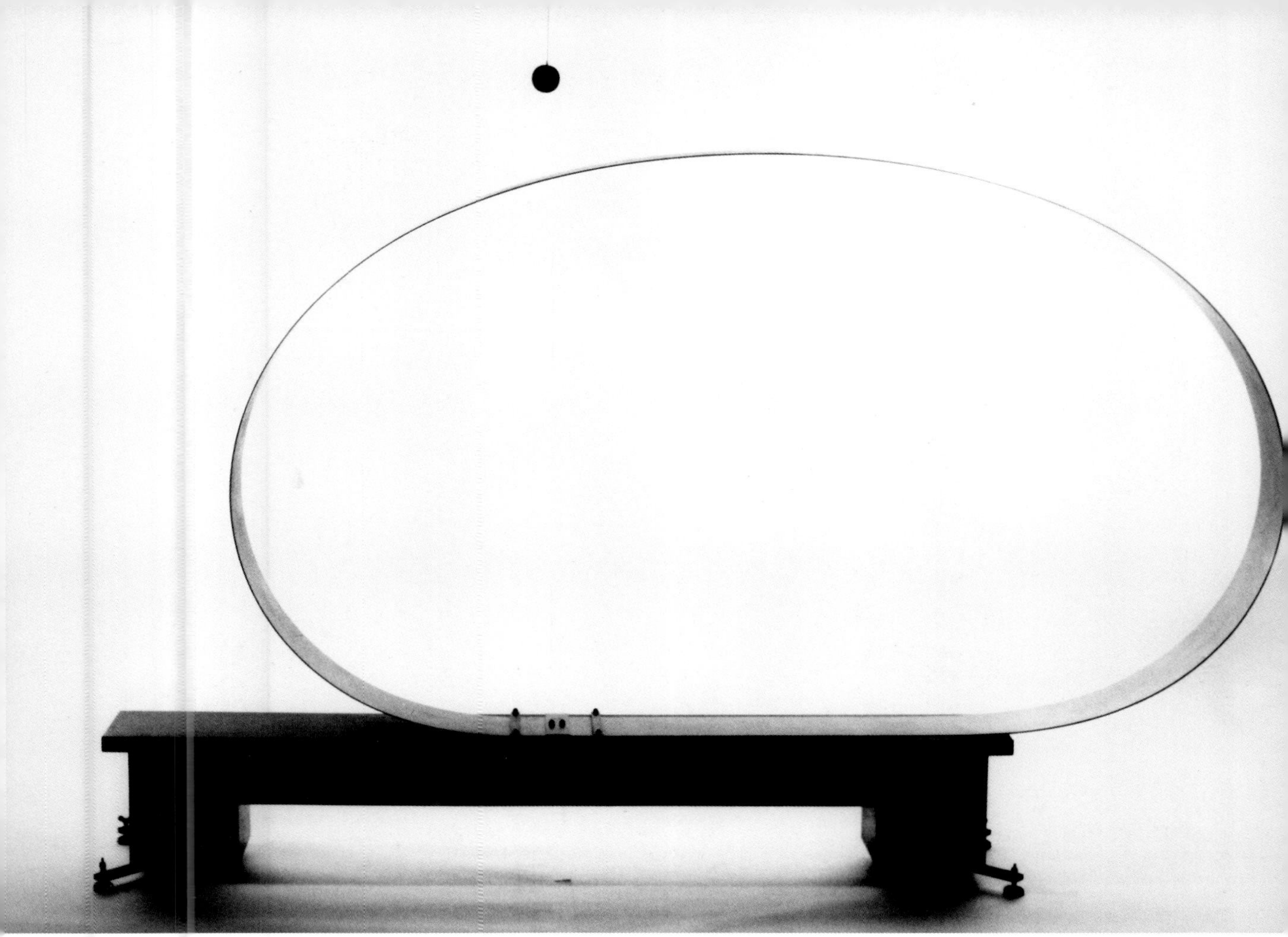

by an electron-microscope photograph of the 'roundhead' chromosome that he changed the title.[31]

The more vigorous *Universe* also has a single figure of motion but one that permits a wide range of variation. Its oval loop of polished steel rests on a flat base which conceals two electro-magnets. The magnets are timed to go on and off, so they tug at the loop then release it, which causes the steel band to lurch sideways first in one direction and then in the other. The band also tends to bounce upwards, causing it either to strike or narrowly to miss a cork ball suspended from the ceiling. Viewers wait expectantly for the loop to hit the ball, which produces a deep percussion sound. At first, the work looks simple – a loop and a ball – but it creates the most complex effects. Every cycle is subtly different. As the band teeters from side to side, it seems alive and charged with energy. At

The kinetic sculpture *Universe*. The striker ball is suspended above the steel loop, which has just rolled over to one side. Photo Brian Eastwood. Courtesy Len Lye Foundation.

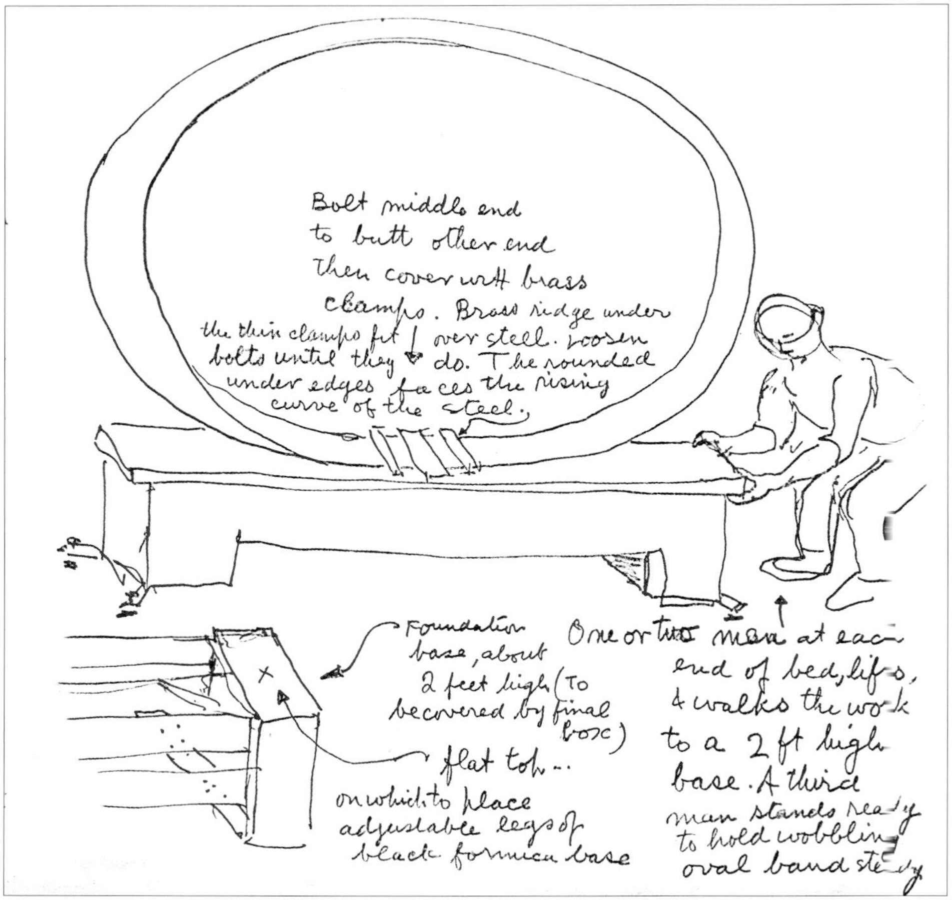

Lye made this diagram to explain how to assemble his sculpture *Universe*. Courtesy Len Lye Foundation.

times, it wobbles like a fat stomach. Photographs with a long exposure produce dramatic patterns.

Situated on the Wellington waterfront, *Water Whirler* starts its routine quietly but goes on to perform a wild, idiosyncratic dance. The slender pole has small nozzles on each side that shoot out water, as though drawing white lines The work is best seen at night when its spotlit sprays of water gleam in the dark. They are, however, also visible against a blue sky. As in the case of *Wind Wand*, the weather adds some unique nuances to each day's performance. The *Whirler* begins a slow, hip-swaying, rotating movement; and as this dance becomes more energetic, the jets of water are shaken into particles of light, or ripple like the banner shapes at the end of *Free Radicals*, with curves adding a sense of depth. At one stage, the *Whirler* seems to be surrounding itself with spirals of water. As the movement grows more hectic, the water patterns change constantly, creating after-images (like a sparkler in the dark).

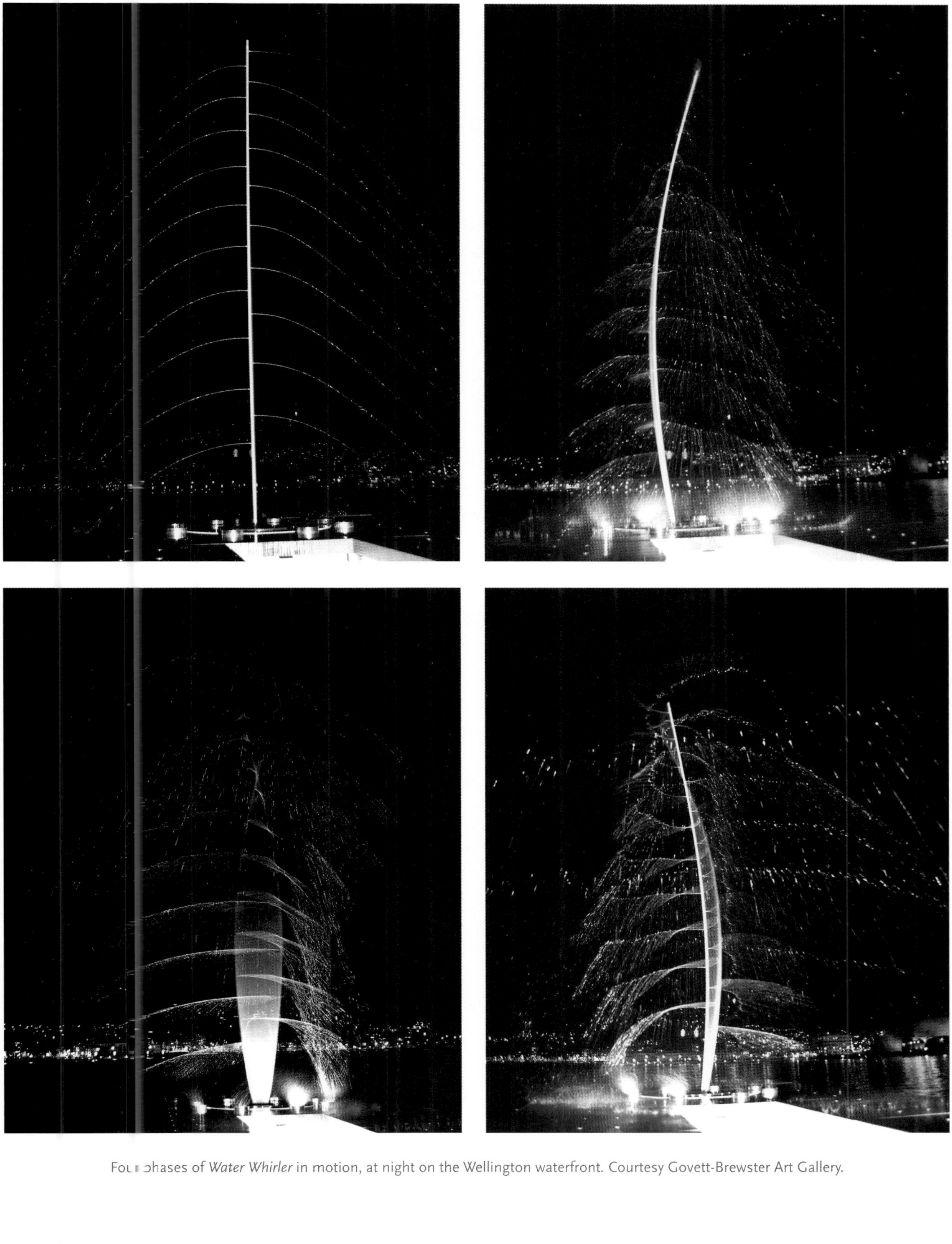

Four phases of *Water Whirler* in motion, at night on the Wellington waterfront. Courtesy Govett-Brewster Art Gallery.

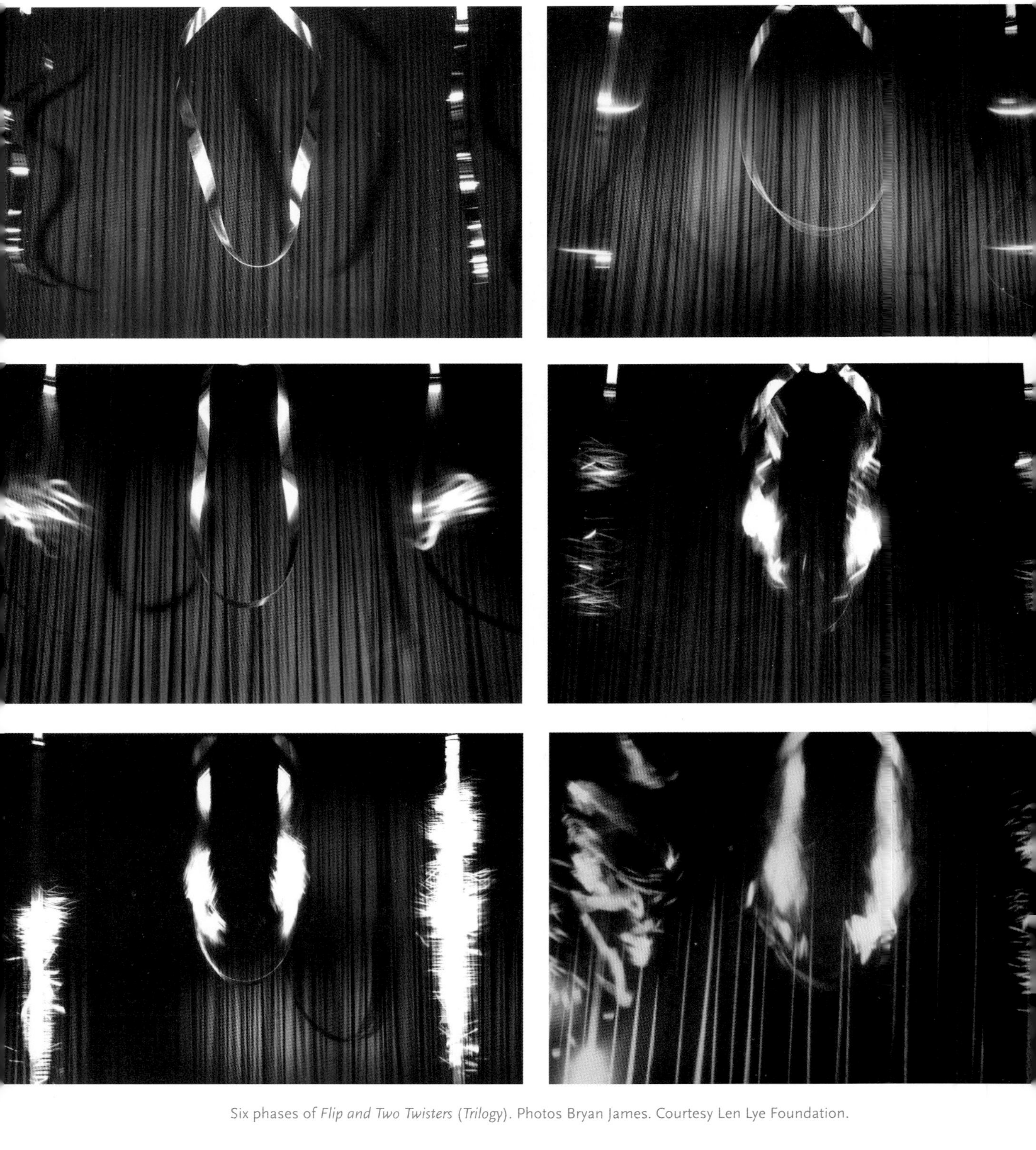

Six phases of *Flip and Two Twisters (Trilogy)*. Photos Bryan James. Courtesy Len Lye Foundation.

Lye's most rapid sculptures – such as *Fire Bush*, *Storm King*, *Blade* and *Flip and Two Twisters* – convey a dramatic sense of energy and danger. With oscillation creating strong rhythms, they are programmed to pass through a series of harmonics and a range of striking sound effects. The wildness of *Fire Bush* links it with sculptures such as *Witch Dance* and *Storm King* that reflect Lye's interest in ecstatic, ancient forms of dance.

In addition to the well-known sculptures above, the restoration of other works is introducing us to a fascinating new range of movements. For example, the droopy *Ribbon Snake* moves and metamorphoses as slowly as the amoeba-like creatures of *Tusalava*. As its two loose loops of plastic material (an off-white loop inside a fleshy pink one) slide gently through the rollers, they tremble, twitch, bulge and flop, and their contours slowly change. The loops travel in opposite directions as a counterpoint, reversing direction from time to time. Sometimes they touch and slide over one another, and the rubbing action creates a build-up of static electricity which produces a crackling sound. As Webb has noted, this sculpture is reminiscent not only of organic forms but also of the passage of film through a (very eccentric) projector.

Flip and Two Twisters (aka *Trilogy*) is arguably the most powerful of his sculptures especially in the large version to be seen at the Govett-Brewster Art Gallery. This building was once a cinema, and when the sculpture is put on display, it is located – appropriately for Lye – in the large space where the screen used to be. The two *Twisters* (long strips of metal) hang from the ceiling, as does *Flip* (the metal loop positioned between them). Surges of energy drive the *Twisters* through many transformations as they spin, including a wonderful moment when the brakes are applied and they stretch back out to their full length with a shudder and crash. The analogy with choreography is particularly relevant to this work as *Flip* and the *Twisters* react to each other in turn, building the dance gradually to a climax.

Flip's noisy climactic release as it turns inside out also has strong sexual associations. The duet of *Blade* has similarly caused viewers to think of love-making. Lye had no problems with such a suggestion if it helped the viewer to relate to a work. At the same time, he hoped we would go further and appreciate the sculptures as a kind of archetypal image. He shared Jung's notion of the archetypal as the deepest layer of human experience, though he saw the empathy that we feel for movement and energy as a more direct way to connect with the 'old brain' than by studying the imagery of dreams. *Flip and Two Twisters* would seem to provide a compelling example. Since 1977, the drama of watching this work has been shared by many thousands of New Plymouth residents, and some can recall their first encounter as a child, watching it accelerate with growing excitement or alarm.[32]

Artforum, the leading American art magazine of the 1960s, tended to see kinetic art as the 'dumb imitation of machines', as unfashionable as the 'dumb imitation of nature'. Philip Leider, one of the most scathing critics, viewed the 'movement movement' as a gimmick dressed up in pseudo-scientific rhetoric. But even he admitted, during his *Artforum* review of the 1966 survey exhibition 'Directions in Kinetic Sculpture', that *Flip and Two Twisters* was an exception:

> The single artist in Dr. [Peter] Selz's exhibition who seems to transcend all the confusion – esthetic, mechanical, rhetorical – of kinetic sculpture is Len Lye, whose work manages to compress so ferocious an energy that the viewer stands paralyzed, gripped by an emotion almost of terror. Lye's elements are supremely simple: hanging strips of stainless steel, six or seven feet long, are set to spinning around at very high speeds. The whiplash strain on the steel produces a series of frightening, unearthly sounds in perfect accord with the mood of barbaric energy that seems to have been released. Installed by itself in a black-painted room, the viewer comes upon Lye's *Trilogy* as he would upon a volcano. The effect is beautiful, frightening, utterly beyond the petty limitations of the other artists in the exhibition.[33]

This work provides strong support for the argument that Lye can be usefully regarded as the greatest exponent of an Abstract Expressionist aesthetic in sculpture as well as in film.[34] The counterpart of 'action painting' is 'action sculpture', with its similar emphasis on energy, on process and on the body. As noted earlier, Lye was also fascinated by the tradition of 'the sublime' in art, as were other Abstract Expressionists. In the words of Robert Motherwell, their ideal was to create 'an abstract picture as rich as nature'. He added, 'We replaced the nude girl and the French door with a modern Stonehenge, with a sense of the sublime.'[35] Not all of Lye's work aspired to this quality but it was one of the ways he sought to combat the assumption that kinetic art was merely a game. The sublime linked up with his interest in ancient cultures, their spiritual view of nature and the life-and-death importance of their dance rituals. He described a cluster of giant sculptures he planned to build as 'Steelhenge'.[36]

His focus on specific figures of motion shaped his sculptures as strongly as his films. Although he greatly enjoyed the anarchist spirit of sculptors such as

Tinguely he was a perfectionist when it came to his own practice, refining his work through a process of constant revision. In *Free Radicals* he had focused almost totally on the workings of energy, and he was able to explore this theme with similar drama and immediacy via the interaction of energy with steel. While a few pieces may stand out – *Flip and Two Twisters*, *Universe* and *Blade* are particularly memorable – his sculpture deserves to be seen as a whole because it represents such a rich and coherent body of work. And of course that coherence encompasses his films. While some other kinetic sculptors have also created moving images, it is hard to think of an artist who has produced equally important work in both media.[37]

In public debate, critics have sometimes rejected kinetic sculpture on the grounds that it embraces the mechanical and is therefore hostile to nature and the environment. (They may make an exception for Calder because his mobiles are driven by the wind.) This sweeping judgement fails to take account of Lye's intense interest in the dynamics of nature and his methods of relating art ultimately to the human body. What made his kinetic work so distinctive was the thoroughness with which he developed the physical dimension of movement, and from that came his special rapport with metal as though it too was a body engaged in 'living business'.

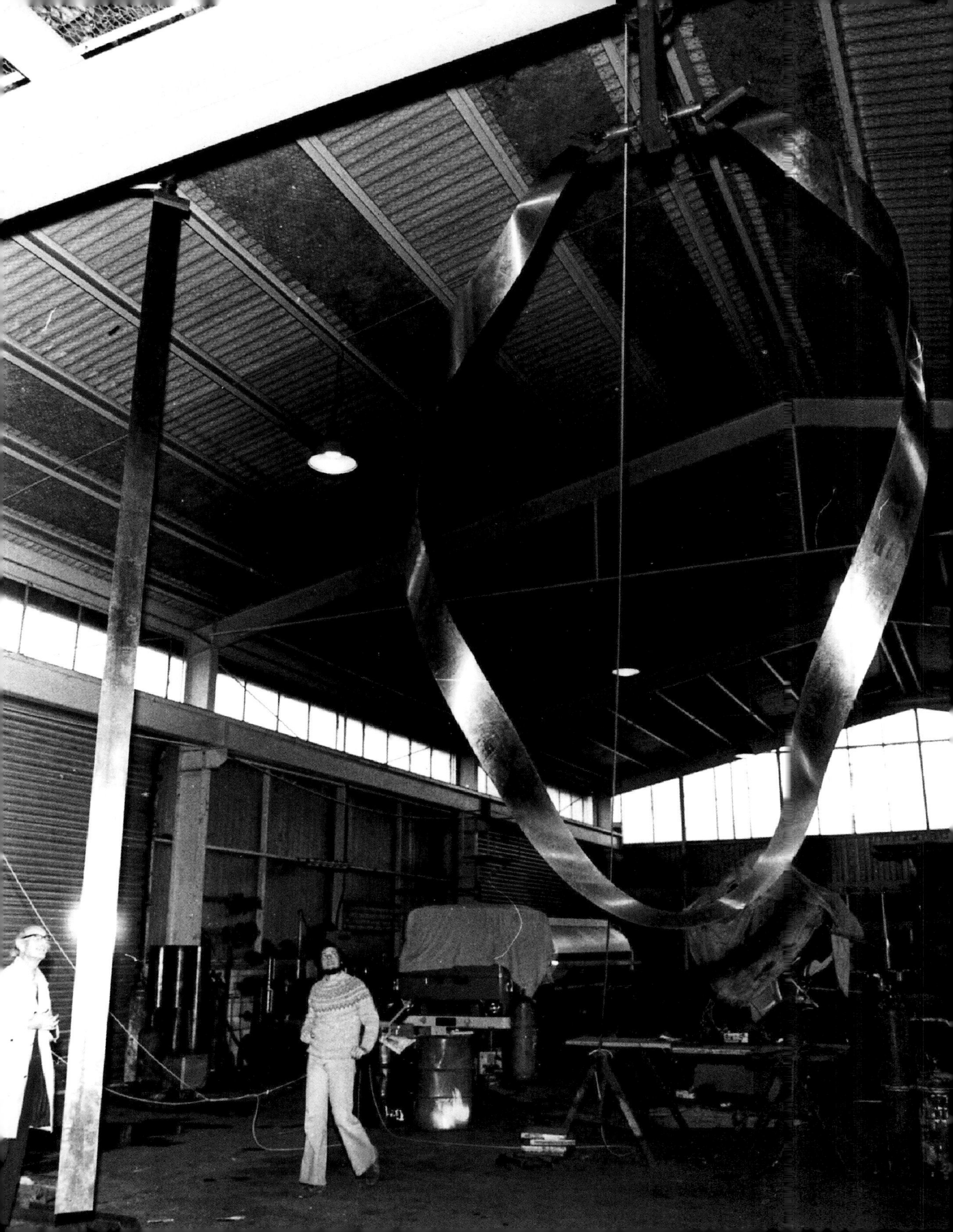

six Len Lye today

conserving, restoring and building kinetic art

MY WORK I THINK IS GOING TO BE PRETTY GOOD FOR THE 21ST century. Why the 21st? It's simply that there won't be the means until then . . . to have what I want, which is enlarged versions of my work, big scale jobs . . .'. Lye made this comment in 1968 when he was interviewed for the CBS documentary *The Walls Come Tumbling Down.*[1] Today, 28 years after his death, his prediction is gradually being realised – his 'big scale jobs' are in the process of being built.[2] His work also retains a contemporary feel thanks to its sheer energy and originality. Few films of the 1930s carry their years as lightly as Lye's, and new generations of viewers continue to discover them not only in archives and museums but also on YouTube and MTV.

So there are a number of continuing aspects to the Lye story, including the ongoing work involved in keeping his films and kinetic sculptures on the move. There are works that Lye planned but was never able to realise except in the form of small prototypes, and some of these have recently been built and exhibited for the first time. The instructions he left for creating 'enlarged versions' of his sculptures have presented his New Zealand team with huge technical challenges, but they have so far produced a 3-metre *Blade*, a 12-metre *Water Whirler*, and a 25-metre and a 45-metre *Wind Wand*. Through many years of work on Lye's sculpture, the team of John Matthews, Evan Webb and Stuart Robb has developed an

Flip and Two Twisters (Trilogy) under construction at Fitzroy Engineering, New Plymouth, in December 1976. Don O'Reilly is standing on the left next to a *Twister* (the vertical metal strip) while John Matthews is walking past *Flip* (the metal loop). Photo Bryan James. Courtesy Len Lye Foundation.

expertise in the conservation and building of kinetic sculpture that exists in few parts of the world. (The museum in Basel devoted to the work of Jean Tinguely is one of the few organisations with a similar fund of experience.)

I have not had any practical involvement with the sculpture-building, but, as a trustee of the Lye Foundation, I have had a front-row seat from which to observe this team's remarkable combination of art and engineering. Their work has helped Lye's reputation to grow steadily, particularly in New Zealand and Australia; but it has also generated some controversy because posthumous work raises complex questions of authenticity, and there is disagreement about the answers. This chapter will track these recent aspects of the Lye story, many of which have not previously been documented. The struggle to maintain his work offers additional insights into the nature of kinetic art. It is a case study with international implications because kinetic art confronts museums with conservation problems for which they do not have solutions, and as a consequence many sculptures of the 1950s and 1960s are no longer in working order and have been consigned to basements. Because the difficulties involved in conserving Lye's work are representative of problems associated with all mechanised sculpture, and with many other forms of modern art, I want to approach the subject from a broad perspective before focusing on his individual solutions.

CONSERVATION AND RESTORATION, FROM THE RENAISSANCE TO THE MODERN PERIOD

Works of art are often described rhetorically as timeless, but in fact all objects suffer the erosion of time, and it is important to be aware of the serious activities that are required to preserve art and the degrees of choice and chance involved in the success of these activities.

Some media have been around long enough for standard methods of conservation to have evolved specifically for them.[3] Oil painting as we know it goes back at least as far as the Middle Ages, and it emerged as a common technique in Europe in the 15th century. Sculpture tended to use a limited range of materials (such as wood, marble and bronze). Yet even for these media, the approach to restoration – the repair of a work that has become faded or damaged – has changed over the course of history, both in practical terms as new technologies have become available, and philosophically as conservators and art historians have become more aware of the differences between periods and styles.

A major change in ideas about conservation between the Renaissance and the modern period stems from differing attitudes towards the notion of *completion*. In the words of Hiltrud Schinzel, 'The Renaissance wanted to restore completeness to the work of art. When the [incomplete Greek sculpture] *Laocoön* was restored by Montorsoli in 1532, the urge for completion of the fragment stemmed from the respect for the skill of the artist who made the antique work of art.'[4] However, whereas during the Renaissance it was felt that its aesthetic values were coterminous with those of ancient Greece, the modern period developed a heightened sense of historical difference and was therefore nervous about imposing contemporary assumptions and techniques on an earlier work of art. Restoration became an increasingly cautious process, combined with the concept of *reversibility* – the belief that intervention should be limited to processes that are reversible, even if the work has to remain in a somewhat sorry state.

Nevertheless, there are many examples of visual works of art being completed posthumously, such as Alexander Calder's sculpture *Mountains and Clouds*, Joseph Beuys's *7000 Oaks Project*, Diane Arbus's series of photographs *Untitled*, several neon installations planned by Dan Flavin and Barnett Newman's sculpture *Zim Zum II*. The process of completion has also been applied to many movies and books,[5] and to the final plans of many famous architects.[6]

Outside of the visual arts, the issues of completion and reversibility are seen as unnecessarily purist. There are countless examples of work being finished posthumously on the assumption that it does honour to the artist, since something incomplete is much less likely to be seen, read or performed. Part of the reason for this may be the fact that whereas an oil painting or a carved sculpture is a unique object that stands alone and exists as a concrete entity, there are other forms of art in which performance or execution is a separate activity from the original score or plan. The experience of the audience must be considered. Reversibility is not compromised by completion since the original score or set of directions continues to reside safely in the archive. The main points to consider in completing such a work are: Would the artist have approved, and are there any legal constraints? Does the proxy artist have what it takes to do a good job? (Works are often finished by an artist's assistant or member of his family, or by a fellow artist who has done extensive research.) And will the fact that the resulting work is a posthumous completion be clearly acknowledged?

The many classical composers who have had works of music completed include: Wolfgang Amadeus Mozart (*Requiem*), Johann Sebastian Bach (*The Art of*

Fugue), Franz Schubert (some songs and piano works, and his *Eighth Symphony*), Jacques Offenbach (*The Tales of Hoffman*), Giacomo Puccini (*Turandot*), Alexander Borodin (*Prince Igor*), Gustav Mahler (*Tenth Symphony*), Edward Elgar (*Third Symphony*), Pyotr Tchaikovsky (*Cello Concerto* and *Seventh Symphony*), Anton Bruckner (*Tenth Symphony*), Manuel de Falla (*La Atlantida*), Béla Bartók (*Viola Concerto*), Dmitri Shostakovich (*The Gamblers*) and Alban Berg (*Lulu*). Much early music requires some form of completion (an area to which we shall return later). This is also a common practice in the world of popular music, such as the last albums of Johnny Cash and Bob Marley.

Changes in the nature and conception of art over the last 100 years have created many problems for what one might call a purist or conservative approach to conservation and restoration. The production of vanguard art has ceased to be primarily a matter of oil painting or sculpture in wood or marble. All materials are now possible, and this presents the museum or archive with complex unfamiliar problems of conservation. Painters have used new media such as acrylic, enamel, spray cans and the computer, and have incorporated (or collaged) many other materials, including the ephemera of contemporary life. Sculptors have employed such ingredients as plastic, perspex, cardboard, wire and metal, and have harnessed technologies such as electric motors, neon lighting and sound equipment. Photography, introduced in 1826, became prominent in the 20th century. During that century, art also came to include moving images (in film, video and digital form), 'multiples' (making use of mechanical types of reproduction), 'conceptual art' (such as Duchamp's ready-mades and the 'post-object' art of the 1960s), and performance art (such as Dada events and the happenings and body art of the 1960s and 1970s).

This is only a partial list as there have been many other forms of multi-media, appropriation, re-mixing and so on. In 1935, Walter Benjamin's famous essay on 'The Work of Art in the Age of Mechanical Reproduction' identified some of the new issues associated with printing and film-making, but visual artists had already introduced a number of other innovations. Every aspect of the common sense idea of the work of art as a unique, static, precious, lasting, tangible object, which bore the distinctive imprint of the individual artist, came under attack. Granted, there were historical precedents for some of these practices, as earlier forms of art had sometimes been made by teams of artists and intended for immediate social use rather than long-term preservation and investment; but museums were quite unprepared for the explosion in the range of media and materials. Today, in the 21st century, a growing proportion of the art of the 20th century – even work in the care of museums – is now showing signs of wear and tear. The preservation techniques developed over the centuries for canvas, oil paint, marble and bronze are not relevant to many 20th-century forms, and a conservative approach to restoration simply cannot cope with the problems.

The survey *Modern Art: Who Cares?* (2005) illustrates the debates occurring internationally among conservation experts. Dionne Sillé writes in the Introduction:

> Over the centuries, a structural approach to conservation and restoration has been developed for old masters' art. Practice, theory and training have resulted in clear guidelines. But what about modern and contemporary art? The materials used here are often far more fragile than those of traditional art . . . [and] when faced with the problem of conservation, many museums have to make it up as they go – sometimes with tragic results.[7]

Museums have a responsibility not only to preserve art but also to provide public access – work has to be exhibited to keep it alive in the culture. The diverse case studies in *Modern Art: Who Cares?* make it clear that sweeping, prescriptive guidelines for conservation and restoration are no longer possible.[8]

Art thought of as a performance rather than as an object represents a special case because the process of realising it remains separate from the original score or plan (kept in archival storage). This is clearly the case with music; and it is normal procedure in the world of films to continue to make prints from the 'master negative' after a film-maker has died. This model can also be applied to forms of kinetic sculpture, such as Lye's, where the artist conceived of his original model as the 'prototype' for an ongoing series. Reproduction may also be relevant to multiples, photographs, conceptual art and performance art – at least in the case of artists who accepted that kind of renewal as part of their aesthetic. Since Duchamp and Man Ray, artists have been more open to the idea of recreating work on the basis that what counts is the idea. Of course, even with the artist's approval, the reproduction of work is an activity that should be undertaken only with the greatest care and respect.

Although the idea of replacing parts or completely reproducing a work of art remains controversial, this possibility is raised by several contributors to *Modern Art: Who Cares?* such as D. H. van Wegen who writes, 'justice can be done to the theatrical nature of the visual experience of much contemporary art by creating exhibition copies in which the main concern is to communicate the artistic statement to the museum public . . . . The original material piece can then be preserved as an objective source of its *Kunstwollen* [artistic intentions] and also act as a score for each new execution.'[9] This approach encourages us to think about certain kinds of art as a 'score' rather than as a 'fetish'.[10] Some conservators regard this attitude as 'non-ethical', and believe that the 'physical death [of art works] has to be accepted';[11] but others feel that leaving works to 'die' is an excessively purist attitude, particularly in relation to artists who conceived of their work in performance terms. Lye fits that profile as an artist who accepted the practical necessity for replacement copies of his films and kinetic sculptures, and looked ahead to a time beyond his death when he saw his art works as still being exhibited, performed and built.

PRESERVING AND RESTORING FILMS

As Lye often pointed out, both films and kinetic sculptures have a 'theatrical nature' – when activated, they dance. Both art forms require a high level of maintenance and technical knowledge, as both prints and sculptures wear out and they must be kept in working condition if they are to continue to perform.

Although film prints become scratched, broken or faded, it is taken for granted that new copies should be made. The film's negative is preserved as the 'master' copy, stored at a lab or archive in a cool, dry environment and checked from time to time to ensure it does not become mouldy, sticky or brittle. The negative will itself be copied if that becomes necessary. In some respects, films are easier to preserve than kinetic sculptures because specialised archives have existed since 1919 when the first such archive was established in the Netherlands. Since the New Zealand Film Archive opened in 1981, it has looked after the conservation and restoration of Lye's films, in partnership with the Foundation. Technical expertise and protocols have been developed internationally, and there is cooperation between archives. But film restoration is a slow, complex and expensive business. Just as the materials and technologies associated with kinetic sculpture have kept changing, so film stocks have come and gone rapidly. This has created problems for film history, particularly in terms of colour. Lye used Dufaycolor, Gasparcolor and the colour-separation version of Technicolor for the films he made between 1935 and 1937, and those stocks eventually became obsolete. Because each stock

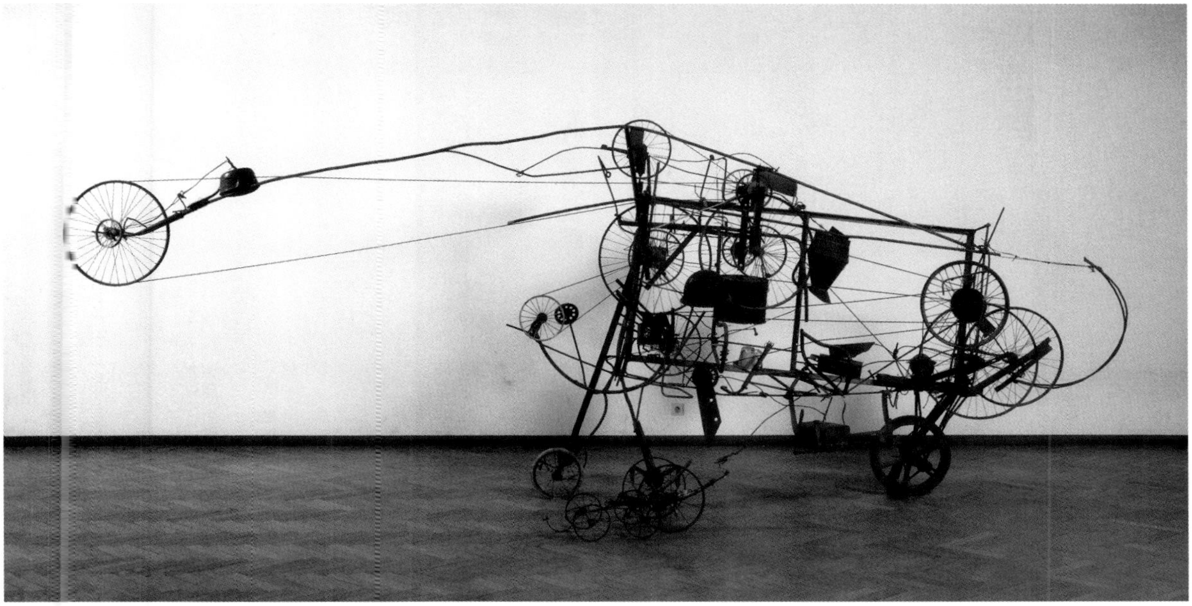

Jean Tinguely's *Gismo* (1960), composed of 'scrap iron, pots, pans, helmet, and a motorized transmission system of belts and cranks'. Collection Stedelijk Museum, Amsterdam. Licensed by Viscopy, Australia.

had a slightly different colour range and texture, it is difficult today to be sure that a new print has been correctly colour-graded. Colour was sometimes very important for Lye – as implied by titles such as *Colour Box*, *Color Cry* and *Rainbow Dance* – so making prints involves difficult decisions. But such work is at least informed by a long tradition of film archive expertise.

Lye always pushed the possibilities of film to the limit, and this created as many problems for black and white as it did for colour. Obtaining satisfactory new prints is not easy now that black and white film is almost obsolete. There is a widespread assumption that digital formats will provide the answer to any moving image problems. Digital has many advantages, particularly for ease of access, but the film medium has a very different basis. The light of a film projector shines through a transparent strip of celluloid, producing the rich colours of Lye's hand-painted films and the intense flashing forms of those he scratched. Digital projection has had difficulty (at least up to now) in reproducing the particular glow and translucence of these films, the grain structure of their emulsion, or the exact 'signature' of their hand-painted and scratched textures – in the same way that even a very fine digital reproduction cannot yet reproduce the exact look of a richly textured oil painting or engraving.

The worst reproductions are the low-definition copies of Lye's films that enthusiasts have posted (without permission) on the YouTube website. Yet while Lye would have been appalled by the quality, it is hard not to be impressed by the excited responses of a new generation of viewers seeing his work for the first time. This is a constant tension in the area of conservation – the first priority must be fidelity to the original, yet the contemporary demand for access and convenience cannot be totally ignored. Many museums want digital copies of films. Museums have tended to jump straight from paintings to digital art – a leap from the 19th to the 21st century, without having fully come to terms with the 20th-century medium of film. (Many archives and libraries have made a similar leap directly from books to computers.) A possible compromise is to permit museums and galleries to screen Lye's films in digital form in proximity to his sculptures, but to require them at some time during an exhibition to screen the films also in their original form. Today, however, it is difficult to find a museum, school or university still equipped with a film projector. But a few institutions such as the Museum of Modern Art and the Centre Pompidou have long-established film departments and cinemas.

A great deal of restoration work has been devoted to Lye's films. For example, after rediscovering his original hand-painted copy of *Colour Box*, the British Film Institute made a new negative more faithful to the original colours. The Lye Foundation, the New Zealand Film Archive and the Govett-Brewster Art Gallery in partnership have undertaken an international film search to identify the best 'master copies' of each of his films. With the assistance of the Museum of Modern Art, the search has led to the restoration of several films that have been out of circulation for over 50 years. An example, completed in 2007, was *All Souls Carnival* that Lye had screened twice in the 1950s. The film had been lost, but after locating a number of fragments in the collection of the Museum of Modern Art, I set out to reconstruct it with the help of Kurt Otzen of the New Zealand Film Archive and editor Annie Collins (who took time out from her work on *Lord of the Rings*). I could only guess at the order of the sections, but fortunately the relationship between the music and the images had never been precise. Our initial version ran for the full fifteen minutes of Brant's piece, but some of the footage was in such poor condition that I eventually decided to cut the film back to eleven minutes.[12] While this has left *All Souls* incomplete, audiences appear to find it interesting as the only sample of these unusual film-painting experiments. In 2008, the Govett-Brewster Art Gallery believed it had located a copy of the original version of *All Souls* in the United Kingdom, but alas, this proved to be a false sighting.

The restoration process has been simpler in the case of other short films. We have followed a traditional approach to restoration based on a small archival team familiar with the artist's work, extensive research, discussion with anyone who knew the original and a clear description of the status of the film (such as 'reconstruction').[13] When the film goes out into the world, there is always the hope that someone will come forward with new information.

PRESERVING AND RESTORING KINETIC SCULPTURE

The preservation and restoration of kinetic sculpture runs along similar lines but tends to involve more difficult decisions than film because this field lacks an archival infrastructure or tradition. Kinetic sculptures moved by hand or by the wind (such as Calder's mobiles or Lye's *Wind Wand*) have their own preservation problems, but I want to focus here on kinetic sculptures involving motors. The key issue in preserving such sculptures is sustaining the movement, the kinetic qualities, which are threatened by the fact that parts and motors wear out. Jean Tinguely was as troubled as Lye by the sight of one of his kinetic sculptures stationary in a museum. As Ad Petersen, the former curator at the Stedelijk Museum who often worked with the sculptor, has said of the current state of one of his sculptures, 'If Tinguely were still alive and saw *Gismo*, he would say, "We've got to do something about this . . . ." '[14] And 'He would have instantly fixed it, since it bothered him if things didn't work . . . . *Gismo* needs to live and not become a stuffed bird . . . .'[15]

A sculpture that can no longer move is like a dancer too tired or broken-limbed to dance, so either a major operation is required or the choreographer needs to find a new dancer. It is sometimes difficult to decide when to retire a sculpture, for as it grows old its speed and movement, its springiness and sound, will subtly change. When do the variations start to exceed the artist's intentions? Such questions involve tough judgement calls. In repairs, it is not easy to keep aesthetic and engineering priorities perfectly aligned. Mechanics or engineers may be called in to repair the sculpture, but in doing so they may unconsciously modify the artistic intentions, making its movement so regular that it loses its element of surprise. Also, the required part or type of metal may no longer be manufactured.[16]

While paintings and prints also throw up many problems, the art world is used to dealing with them. It seems clear that one of the reasons museums, dealers and private buyers lost interest in kinetic sculpture – despite the artistic vitality of the genre and the huge public response to it – was their reluctance to get into the business of mechanical repairs. Museums did not want to have to establish workshops and conservation staff were reluctant to have to develop engineering expertise. Hence, many of the sculptures of the 1960s, such as *Gismo*, are no longer in working order.

LYE'S TECHNICAL PROBLEMS

When Lye started seriously working on kinetic sculpture around 1958, it felt to him that he had hit the mother lode because his ideas came so thick and fast. They were the result of his lifetime study of movement. Building the works, he could not keep up with his flood of ideas because he was short of money, and he was not able to secure the continuous help of good engineers or assistants (essential for this kind of work). Minor problems multiplied and sculptures would often break down halfway through an exhibition. The problems were made more difficult by his desire for size. He was attempting not to be grandiose but to maximise the sense of empathy. He spent a huge amount of time trying to find sponsors; but in contrast to the support given to European kinetic sculptors by European corporations, governments, architects and patrons, their American counterparts tended to be suspicious of this genre of art.

When Lye did obtain sponsorship, it usually involved compromise. A classic example was the offer by the city of Toronto to sponsor a large *Wind Wand* in 1967. Lye was initially excited because of the scale and the opportunity to experiment with fibreglass. Unfortunately, behind the scenes the city decided to cut costs. When the Protective Plastics Company took the job, Lye gave them detailed drawings to scale. Ann Lye recalled that 'he had the whole thing absolutely down pat. But when we went round every day to inspect it, they would never let us see it. They made one excuse after another. When it finally arrived, it was all wrong.' In Lye's words, the stem was 'fabricated to their view of their concept, not mine'. To make it easier to manufacture, they had tapered it in three stages, and the top section was solid and inflexible. Angry as he was, the artist was persuaded there was now no alternative at this stage but to allow the wand to be erected. In Ann's words, 'Before we left Toronto I remember driving around there again, and Len wanted to knock it down.' At the beginning of May 1968, the wand developed cracks. City officials, in the midst of an embarrassing public argument with another sculptor, tried to hush up the problem. A Parks Department crew took down the wand and hauled it away. To a friend who sent his condolences, Lye wrote, 'It seems to me that art is the only hope we have of ever getting perfection but, to get it, we have to make a kind of war. If so, it's the only war worth fighting.'[17]

It was experiences of this kind that convinced him he had no choice but to leave some of his works to be produced posthumously. He spoke of his existing sculptures as small-scale 'working models' or 'prototypes'. Having belonged to one of the early generations of modernists, he had had the experience of seeing artists like Picasso progress from bohemian obscurity to international fame; hence, he was optimistic that today's avant-garde would set tomorrow's agenda. This helps to explain why he became so reluctant to sell work – he knew his collection would have more impact as a unified legacy. In his later interviews, he often talked about the projects that would be realised posthumously. In *Len Who?*, he said of his existing sculptures, 'You know, in my studio I make these types of models [as a] kind of a prototype, and they're really planned for the big scale image.'[18] In *Ray's Saga*, he said he was documenting his work 'to show the engineers what kinds of things they have to enlarge'.[19]

There was no guarantee that Lye was going to be successful in finding a future base for his art, but such a breakthrough occurred in the last decade of his life. The story of how New Plymouth became the home of his sculpture is one I have told previously in my biography of the artist, but it is important to summarise those events here because they were crucial in shaping his attitude to the conservation of kinetic art. Several artists in New Zealand, such as Ray Thorburn, were campaigning for a major Lye exhibition. Having no luck with the National Art Gallery in Wellington, Thorburn decided to look for a provincial gallery with 'less red tape, more imaginative thinking, younger people and a greater chance of a commitment'.[20] He found this in the Govett-Brewster Art Gallery, which had been exhibiting a wide range of contemporary art despite local pressure on the gallery to show more traditional and regional work. Its current director was a Californian, Bob Ballard, who had seen *Flip and Two Twisters* at the University Art Museum in Berkeley and was aware of Lye's reputation as a film-maker. Although the artist had not had any previous connection with New Plymouth, Ballard was intrigued by Thorburn's suggestion. He wrote to ask Lye if he had a

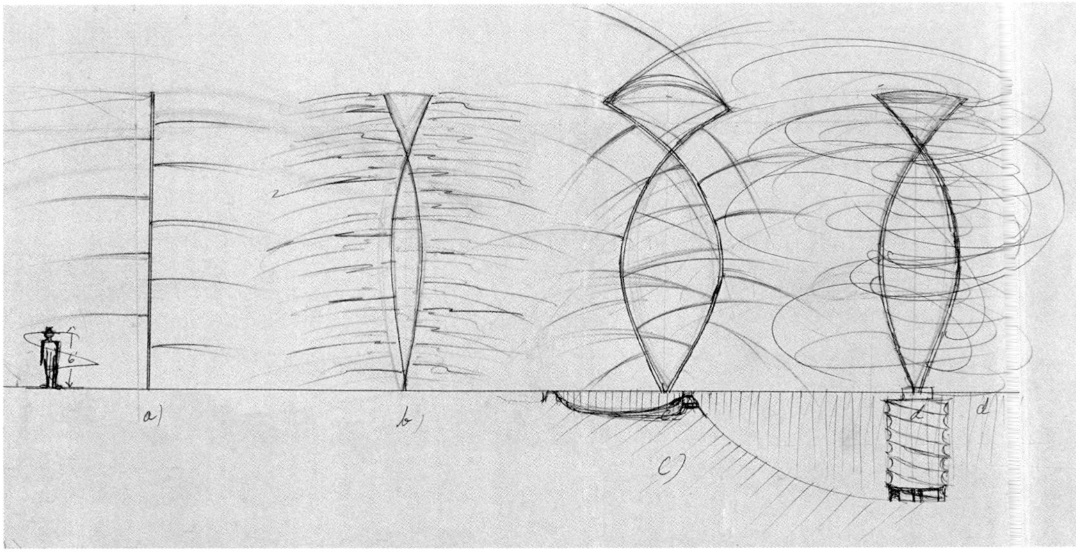

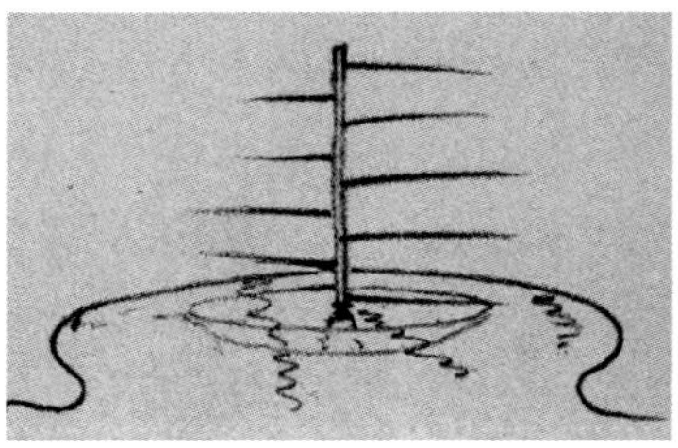

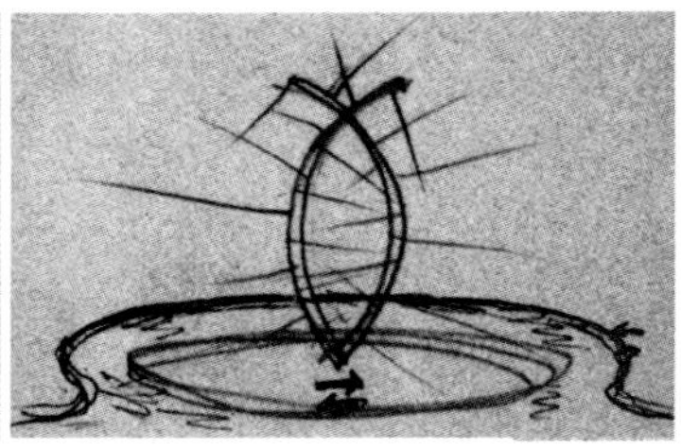

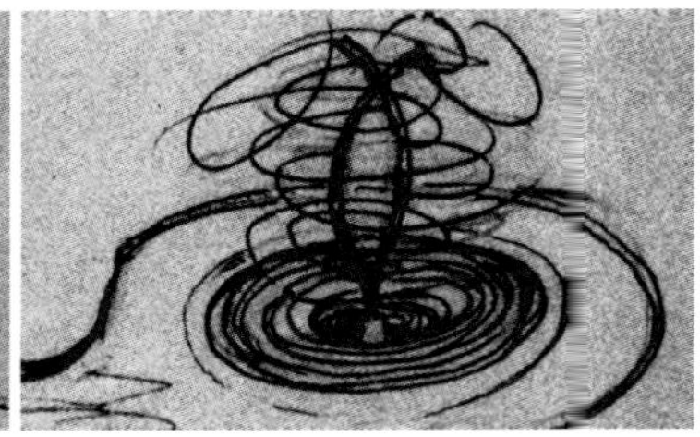

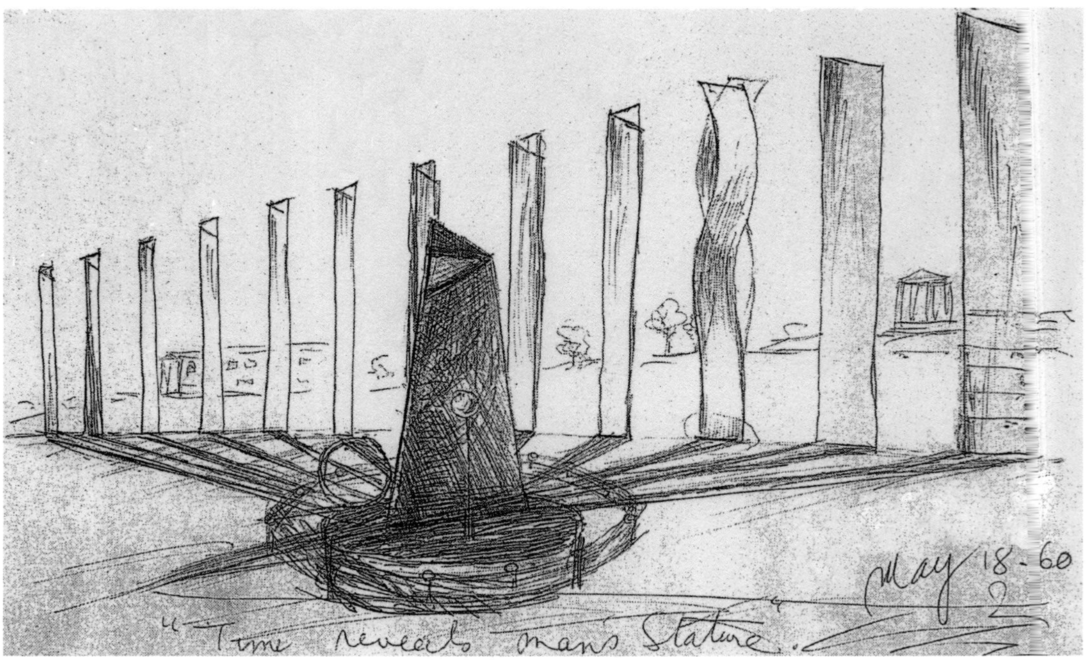

Examples of Lye's many plans and proposals for sculpture. They include drawings of *Water Whirler*, and a 1960 design for a kinetic clock sculpture, *Steelhenge*, with a *Blade* for each hour, accompanied by Frankin D. Roosevelt's comment 'Time reveals man's stature'. The illustration on the facing page describes *Wall Serpent* (which has affinities with Lye's sculpture *Ribbon Snake*). Courtesy Len Lye Foundation.

Wall

Serpent

(Timed with industrial timers)

The "Serpent would consist of a ribbon of thin high tempered stainless steel of any length from fourty to five hundred feet.

The continuous band of six-inch wide steel would be motivated by either rubber or toothed rollers. It would be held in convoluted shapes between thin roller-pins.

The "Serpent" would be held edgeways to the flat of an interior or exterior wall surface.

Some roller-pins would travel in wall channels to give the "Serpent" an undulating and bulging motion as it fed through the motivating rollers.

The action would occur in reverse when the rollers were reversed to take up the slack and tighten the bulging parts.

This "serpent" concept could serve as a motion sculpture mural or a motion sculpture freize.

I would make a large practical model of the "Serpent". It would consist of a free-standing fifty-foot band of six-inch Barret plastic. Rollers and pins would be set up between the stays of a frame to motivate and hold the shapes of the slowly undulating "Serpent".

The concept allows for a wide variety of applications to walls which might otherwise assume a blank two-dimensional quality. In this respect it would become a valuable aesthetic device for two-dimensional architectural planes.

Mural type Freize type

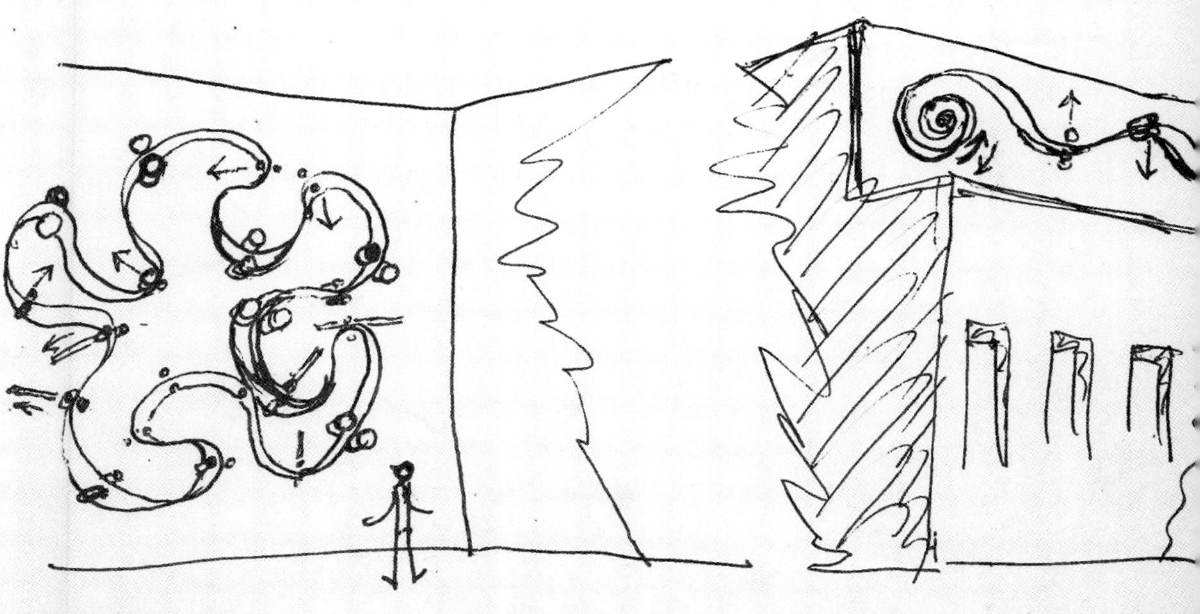

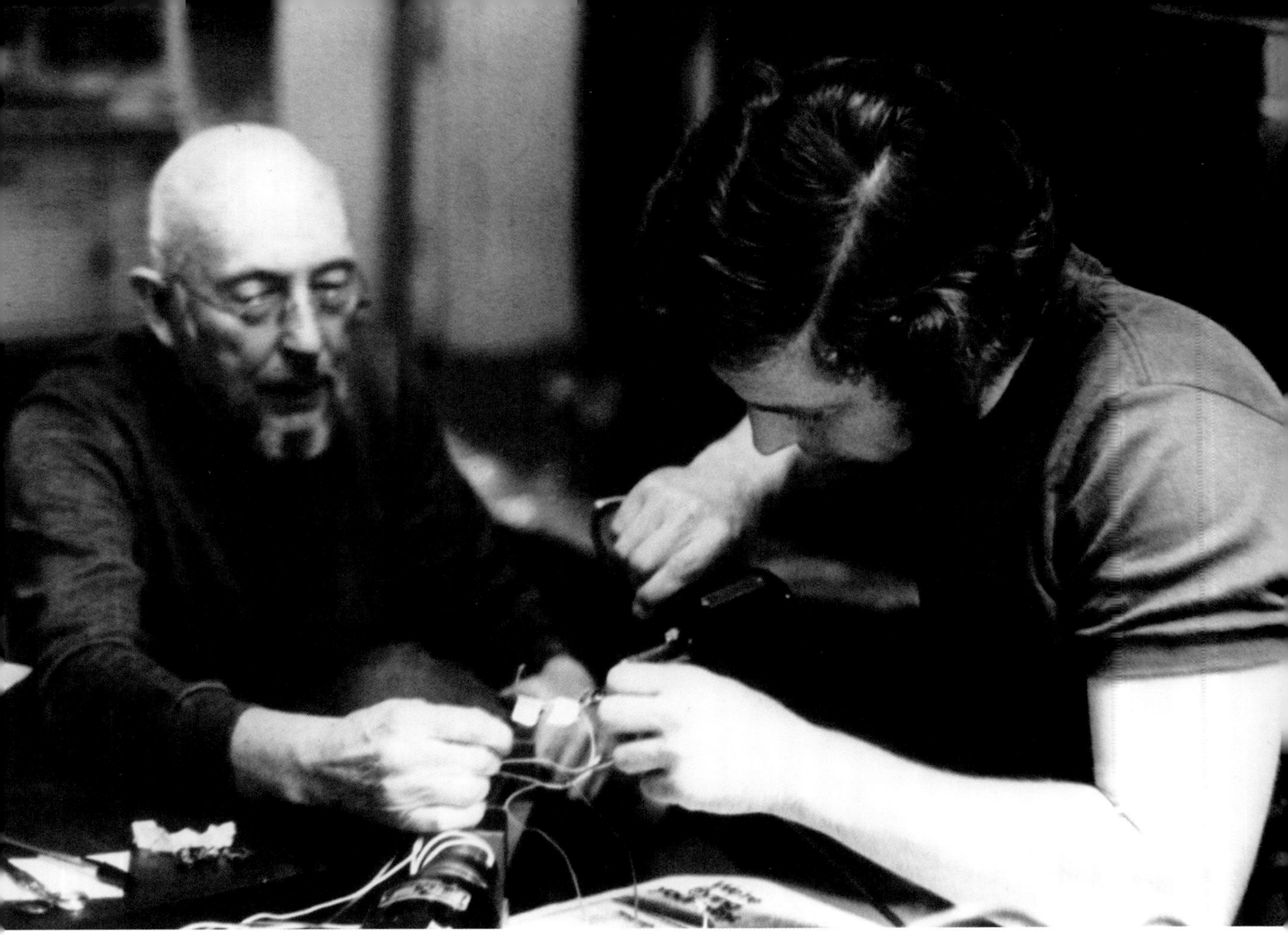

John Matthews working with Lye in his New York studio in 1974. Courtesy Len Lye Foundation.

project suitable for the Gallery. The artist replied, 'Yes, but I'll need a very clever engineer.' Tired of wrestling with technical problems, he was reluctant to get involved unless the Gallery could provide him with 'a genius engineering designer and technical motion programmer'.[21]

A member of the Gallery committee expressed interest – John Matthews, at that time the owner of Fitzroy Engineering Ltd, who remembered some years earlier seeing 'a colourful maverick named Len Lye shaking pieces of steel in *The Walls Came Tumbling Down*'. He found Lye's criteria daunting but felt that someone had to accept the challenge. He was excited by the idea of bringing such sculpture to the Govett-Brewster with its large space and good acoustics, and by the opportunity of working 'with such an artist outside the mundane concerns of conventional engineering'.[22]

In his next letter, Lye said he would like two works to be built, *Fountain* and *Flip and Two Twisters* (*Trilogy*), representing the two sides of his kinetic sculpture, the gentle and the vigorous. He was initially suspicious because he feared the New Zealand interest in his work was merely a nationalist reflex ('that snooky stuff of being . . . a native son of home grown chlorophyll', as he remarked to Robert Graves).[23] But when Matthews visited New York, Lye got on well with him – and here at last was an engineer with the knowledge and commitment he needed. Matthews for his part was impressed by the artist's energy and jaunty style. He returned to New Plymouth with the challenge of making *Trilogy* 8 feet (2.4 metres) high and *Fountain* 10 feet (3 metres) high. The former required Swedish surgical stainless steel and the latter involved 120 stainless steel rods of a special type. The engineer was very struck by the artist's approach to motors: 'The motivation force is a sophisticated little DC unit that uses fractional horsepower. The wonderful thing is that Len never mounts so much power that the motivation force dominates. The work goes through all its various harmonics and those sources of energy get controlled by the work – there's a lot of feedback. The art always dominates the motors, the motors only just cope.'[24] The budget of $18,250 (shared between the Gallery and the Arts Council) was tight, but various individuals and companies were prepared to donate their time, including Matthews and Fitzroy Engineering. The artist himself asked for only a nominal fee, thus making the sculpture virtually a gift. This was in striking contrast to his reputation for setting outrageously high prices when he was dealing with organisations he did not respect.

By November 1975, Matthews had been busy for nine months in the Fitzroy Engineering workshop in New Plymouth developing an 8-feet working model of *Trilogy*. Confident he had overcome the complex technical problems, he wrote to tell Lye he was returning to New York. But he was disturbed by the artist's reply: 'Terrific, John, bring me some plans for the art gallery so we can get the scale right.' Matthews recalls:

> I went to New York with photographs and sound recordings and I said to Len, 'Here it is'. And then I really got to know this man because he put me down in a chair, poured a stiff rum and orange juice – got me all relaxed, you see – and he said, 'Now John, now that we've mastered this, we're gonna build the real one'. And I looked at him with amazement. 'What do you mean?' He said, 'I want one twice the size'. And I thought, oh my god, here we go again, because I knew that he had a history

> of this sort of scaling up. I said, 'Well, Len, that's not the way we all agreed to do it'. But that didn't seem to matter. He didn't seem to hear, he just went on and on about the scale. That's really when the end of the fun came for me.[25]

Lye wanted *Fountain* to have 15-feet (4.6-metre) rods and *Trilogy* to be 25 feet (7.6 metres) high.[26] Matthews knew this involved a whole new set of engineering problems because making a kinetic sculpture twice as large is never simply a matter of doubling the size of the components. As the weight increases so does the energy required. There was no longer any certainty that the steel would hold together or that the *Twisters* would produce the desired shapes. Matthews, who was aware of the 1967 disaster in Toronto, began to have nightmares about the New Zealand venture ending as a heap of rusting metal.[27] Nevertheless, he returned to New Plymouth and said he was prepared to continue. One way to keep the cost down was to buy uncut steel. Because of its hardness, the metal was difficult to cut but he believed his workshop could handle it. The artist offered to buy the steel, and Matthews and many other individuals were prepared to donate their work to the project. The Arts Council agreed to increase its contribution to $12,500 and the Gallery matched this figure, which at the time was a large and potentially controversial amount for a provincial gallery to risk.

Matthews turned to his former university teacher, Cliff Stevenson, who was now Dean of the Engineering School at the University of Canterbury to help with the mathematical work required. Stevenson decided to make it an exam question. But even after some of the best students in the school had made a computer analysis, the problems appeared to be mathematically insoluble, and Matthews began to have serious doubts about the project. The artist might know what shapes and sounds he wanted and might display an intuitive understanding of metals, but he could not offer any help with the engineering problems. Matthews decided to keep experimenting. He imported all the materials – the motors and the steel – and enlisted the help of Colin Corcoran's engineering firm to plan the electronic control aspects. That was a challenging task as the artist required a very precise sequence of movements. Matthews and his team spent many nights and weekends in the engineering shop, running tests with ordinary stainless steel because of the high cost of the Swedish steel. Despite the small size of the motor, the movement would sometimes twist the metal horribly out of shape.[28] Finally, the work seemed to be performing satisfactorily, and Matthews again felt a deep respect for Lye and his intuitive sense of what was possible.[29]

By now, there were strong time pressures since the exhibition had already been delayed for a year, and the Lyes had booked to come to New Zealand. The critical moment arrived when the scarce Swedish steel had to be cut. Previously the team had proceeded by a lengthy process of trial and error, aware that a difference of half an inch, or even less, could make a huge difference to the way a strip of metal performed under speed. There were many variables associated with the motors, which was why the Engineering School had given up on the problem. Finally, Matthews took a deep breath and gave directions for the cutting of the *Flip* and the two *Twisters*. When the cut strips were set up on crane rails in the roof and the motors were turned on, the work went crazy, almost slicing off the workmen's heads. It was a moment of great drama and despair for Matthews who now realised that the Swedish steel behaved in a completely different fashion from the steel used to date. Again the team went through a long process of testing. Finally, by trial and error, they found the magic numbers and all three parts of the sculpture began to perform perfectly. Matthews' doubts were at last resolved – Lye was 'a bloody awful engineer but a genius when it came to handling steel'.[30]

Even the more gentle work, *Fountain*, presented its own technical challenges, such as how to polish 120 stainless steel rods to produce the glitter required. The team tried pumice, sandpaper, and polishing and buffing machines but nothing seemed to work. There was neither time nor money to get more rods shipped over. Finally, Tony Smale of Cambrian Engineering in New Plymouth pointed to a grinding machine under a dusty canvas in a corner of his workshop. In Matthews' words, 'It was an ancient cast-iron machine that looked as though it had come out with Captain Cook. We had one of those magical moments when we fed a rod into the machine and it came out the other end looking absolutely perfect.'

When *Trilogy* was mounted in the Gallery, its energy was so great that the main roof beam cracked and had to be braced.[31] Fortunately, the director at the time, Ron O'Reilly, remained supportive. And John Maynard, who had been the first director, did an outstanding job of designing the exhibition to ensure the art was seen to its best advantage. At last, early in 1977, everything was ready. When the artist arrived, he was very pleased with the engineering work, producing great sighs of relief all round. He also liked the Gallery for its 'temple' feeling. But he had enough suggestions to keep the team busy for several frantic days making adjustments. He wanted the sculptures at the Govett-Brewster to be dramatically spotlit against dark backgrounds, maximising the effects of light on their highly reflective metal surfaces.

Lye reported to his old friend Barbara Ker-Seymer, 'They [the gallery] happened to show my film and my steel cracker-jacks perfectly as if made for the job. Perfect is a word to write a hundred times and it was, I mean, perfect.'[32] Ann Lye wept at the sight of her husband's sculpture realised on a giant scale after so many years of frustration. Astonished by the resourcefulness and commitment of those who had worked on the project, she later commented, 'It's like we found New Zealanders to be still members of a tribal society where every man takes pride in his own work. It was very stimulating. With John Matthews supervising and with a local electrician . . . inventing electronic controls for the sculptures, it was the first time they'd ever worked all the way through a show – they never broke down and they're still running, it's magic!'[33] Those who saw the exhibition were astonished by the energy, sound and drama of *Flip and Two Twisters*.

LYE ORGANISES HIS LEGACY

For all artists who create mechanised sculptures, there is a strong risk that their art will cease to function once they are no longer on hand to supervise repairs. Accepting the inevitable loss of control, Lye sought to put in place the best possible support system for his sculpture. Granted, he had no other option because he was aware by this time that he was in the final stages of leukaemia; but arguably his plan has unfolded in such a successful way that it establishes a model for how kinetic sculptors can ensure a future for their work.

After the New Plymouth exhibition, and with increasing interest from the New Zealand art community, Lye met with Matthews, Thorburn and Hamish Keith to discuss the creation of a non-profit foundation in New Zealand to which he could bequeath his work – his paintings, films, manuscripts, sculptures, and plans and models for unfinished projects. Although Lye had a global rather than a nationalist perspective, he had come to trust the New Zealand group, and saw a pleasing symmetry in the fact that his art would return to his country of origin. He told Ker-Seymer about the idea, 'This is miraculous as it lets Ann off the hook when I peg out – maybe sooner maybe later – the sooner the better if there's plenty of gorgeous angels soaring round.'[34]

On 24 April 1980, Lye signed a 'Deed of Trust' with John Matthews as the chairman of a newly formed Len Lye Foundation. This transferred 'ownership' and 'copyright' of his work 'to the Foundation for the public benefit of the people of New Zealand', with the work to be housed at the Govett-Brewster Art

Gallery in New Plymouth. Those signing the Deed undertook to 'provide for the storage and display' of his art and to maintain it 'in good order and condition'. It was agreed that the details of the Deed might be reviewed after five years, but no changes could be made without the consent of the artist, or his 'designee' Max Gimblett (a fellow artist and old friend) or his heirs (his wife Ann and his children Bix and Yancy).

Lye died three weeks later, on 15 May. In August, at the inaugural meeting of the Foundation, it was noted that 'A copy of the [Foundation] Constitution . . . had received the approval of Mr. and Mrs. Len Lye, the New Plymouth City Council and the Minister of the Arts . . . .' (The government had an 'ex officio' involvement during the early years of the Foundation, having contributed to the cost of shipping Lye's work back to New Zealand.) The artist's widow was present at this first meeting and would remain an influential member of the board until her death in 2000 at the age of 90. The Constitution summed up the activities of the Foundation as 'the acquisition, conservation, reproduction and promotion' of Lye's works, adding that it was authorised 'to make such contracts as the Trustees shall from time to time think fit for the reproduction of works and the disposal of the reproductions by sale auction exchange or otherwise'. The term 'reproduction' left no doubt that Lye had accepted the need to make new copies of his kinetic sculpture, both to keep it on the move and to help finance the work of the Foundation.

Today, the Foundation has up to seven trustees, appointed for three-year terms, including ex officio positions for the director of the Govett-Brewster Art Gallery and a representative of the New Plymouth District Council. At least one of the trustees must be a professional artist. People have come and gone but Matthews is still the Chairman and Gimblett is still a trustee. There are two other trustees who knew Lye – Wystan Curnow and me. The board is completed by Greg Burke (director of Canada's Power Plant Contemporary Art Gallery), Rhana Devenport (director of the Govett-Brewster Art Gallery) and Tyler Cann (appointed by the Council as its representative). As usual with non-profit trusts, the board members contribute their time and are not allowed to derive any personal benefit from the Foundation's activities.

The first challenge accepted by the Foundation was to keep Lye's motorised sculptures in working order. The further tasks set by the artist were the dissemination of his ideas, the completion of sculptures he had planned but not fully realised, and the building of large-scale versions. He did not know how far along this road the Foundation would get, but he had made utopian plans for a 'temple' of art as an ultimate showcase for giant-size versions of his work. He was well aware that each of the above tasks would involve many financial and technical difficulties, but he was not inclined to compromise his vision. He ended an interview about his plans for the sculpture *Harmonic* with a comment that was typical in the way it combined a playful tone with a serious call for collaboration: 'I don't expect this sort of thing to be done in my life-time, but the directions are there, and when we're ready to get around to it – go ahead – don't let me stop you!' The use of 'we' suggested that Lye still hoped to be around to see it, but he knew he might be present only in spirit; and so, by the end of the sentence, he had turned the job over to 'you'.

This is a sharp departure from the traditional approach to conservation, but the Lye legacy has an exceptionally clear rationale. Motorised kinetic sculpture has special requirements, and the artist was explicit about the way he wanted his work treated and 'reconstructed'. He left a great deal of information via documents and interviews, and made sure the collection of work he gave to the Foundation was as complete as possible. Satisfied there was a capable team to look after his work, he organised a Foundation to serve as a support structure. This special combination of circumstances has made it possible for the Foundation to follow the active approach that Lye called for.

At the same time, the group has proceeded with fear and trembling because of the responsibility of remaining true to the artist's vision. The project calls for expertise in both art and engineering, and requires the closest possible partnership between those areas. Such specialists must also be prepared to put their egos to one side since they are devoting their skills to realising the artist's vision. The Foundation board seeks to act as an instrument of 'quality control' on behalf of the artist, a task assisted by the fact that four trustees knew Lye. Matthews has played a particularly important role because of his extended working relationship with the artist. Various experts have joined the team, including Tyler Cann (the Govett-Brewster's first Lye curator) and the sculptor Evan Webb (director of the Foundation, whose work will be discussed shortly).

THE PRINCIPLES OF THE LEGACY

All conservation or restoration, such as reviving the colour of a faded painting, relies on circumstantial evidence and careful interpretation. But what data are relevant to kinetic sculpture? How can we know the way a work should perform when so many variables are involved in creating patterns of movement?

All of Lye's 'prototypes' are held in the archive at the Govett-Brewster. Interviews were recorded in which Lye discussed technical nuances, such as a lengthy conversation with Matthews about how he wanted the Foundation to handle particular sculptures. Then there are the artist's plans, sketches and descriptions, and also the theoretical writings in which he discussed aesthetics.

Moving images – television items, documentaries and some amateur footage of exhibitions – are a particularly rich source of information. It is important, however, to know when and where the filming was done and the extent to which the artist was involved. Sculptures can have a bad day – and there were quite a few bad days for Lye, since he had to work with inadequate budgets and cut-price technology. Other useful information is provided by sound recordings since sound can play a significant part in Lye's sculpture. There are plenty of static photographs, including the slide-tape programmes that Lye made about his art for educational purposes. There are also his films, as another form of kinetic art; and there are reviews, news items, critical essays, and other publications about him and his work. Finally, we can interview those who worked with the artist or saw the sculptures in movement during his lifetime.

It is also helpful to know that Lye used a few generic types of small motor (sometimes adapted from sanding or sewing machines), and that his art conformed to basic engineering principles and natural properties (such as gravity and harmonics). An earlier chapter described his empirical approach, his respect for the qualities of the metal he used; so, for example, he would test a vertical strip of steel and cut it just at the point where it started to bend.[35] In building large-scale versions of his work the fabricators must similarly be guided by the inherent properties of the metal. They also need to produce a sense of tension and strain (which Lye sometimes called 'that tingling business') by using a motor that is only just strong enough for the job.[36]

Any motorised kinetic sculpture will eventually break or wear out, which is why a gallery should avoid running it continuously. Safety is also important. Worried about what would happen if *A Flip and Two Twisters* ever broke, the Foundation commissioned a report in 1989 from the Department of Mechanical Engineering at the University of Canterbury which arrived at the reassuring conclusion that there was no danger of a fragment flying out into the audience

– it would simply drop to the ground. A piece did break off two years later during an exhibition in Wellington, and, as predicted, it fell straight to the floor.

In such cases, there is no alternative but to replace the part. One must try to locate the original source, and it is wise to buy up extra parts if they are available. Industrial materials are sometimes difficult to replace since they can differ slightly from one batch to the next as a company keeps trying to improve its products.

A time comes when the whole of a kinetic work needs to be retired from exhibition, as the rods droop and the motor is so tired that continuing to run it not only produces the wrong figures of motion but also risks seriously damaging the sculpture. It should then be archived, preserved as an historical record, particularly if it is the artist's prototype, and a new copy should be created for exhibition use. Lye conceived of his sculptures in somewhat the same way as his films – as prototypes or 'masters' that could be copied, enlarged (like the 35mm 'blow-up' of a film) or made to last longer with the help of improved materials.

Changing the technology – 'migration', to use the film term – is not a step to be taken lightly since there is a danger it may change the type of motion. We have to identify which features are essential. Lye believed that ultimately his art consisted not of the object but of the figures of motion it produced. Of course, the two were closely related, but there was often some scope for substitution. If a new material or mechanism looked the same and functioned in basically the same manner but was going to be more durable, then that was a desirable change. In the case of *Wind Wand*, Lye began by using titanium but changed for practical reasons to fibreglass. He kept searching not only for better materials but also for better technology. The kind of small sanding machine he used as an 'animating, reciprocating device' was cheap and convenient but not always reliable: 'There are all sorts of little quirky problems in the silly thing. To me it's really a mock-up prototype, where the next step would be to perfect this, that, and the other part of it.'[37] In a 1962 television interview, he said he was looking forward to the future development of 'electronic programming'.[38] He was hungry for the computer age, and urged his New Zealand team to take advantage of new developments to facilitate his 'controlled composition in motion'. Using state-of-the-art technology has in fact been the only possible way to create the large-scale sculptural versions he called for, but the Foundation has remained mindful of the danger that what seems a simple improvement may subtly alter the aesthetics of a work.

Museums are eager for sculptures to last longer, work harder and be more consistent; and when engineers assess the condition of kinetic sculptures, they tend to look for ways 'to produce versions that yield repeatable (or near-identical) performances – rather than trying to emulate the randomness . . . of the originals'.[39] Instead, the Foundation has sought to preserve an element of unpredictability in Lye's work. A sculpture should follow the same basic pattern from one performance to the next but there may be slight variations due to the temperature in the room or to pure accident such as the angle at which one part makes contact with another – small variations of the kind described by chaos theory. This is a deliberate feature of Lye's aesthetic, similar to the differences between live performances of any piece of music or choreography. In the case of *Universe*, when the loop makes its distinctive lateral movement, it does not always hit the ball. As Evan Webb puts it, 'Sometimes half a performance can go by without the distinctive "bonging" sound; then, in the next performance, *Universe* will go to town. This is pure theatre – Lye at his best. It would be possible to set up *Universe* so that the loop was more vigorous and made contact more consistently, but the sense of strain and surprise would be lost. Conservation must take such aspects into account.'

Lye wanted works to be sited outdoors as well as indoors, and this introduces other variables such as wind. *Water Whirler* has a cut-off switch when the speed of the wind reaches 20 knots (approximately 35 km per hour). Clearly, Lye welcomed a certain amount of variation and saw this as part of the potential of a sculpture – one of the reasons for returning to see it at different times – but this was variation within sensible limits because he was also mindful of the safety of the work and of the bystanders. His art was not as open-ended as some 'chance' or 'aleatory' work of the 1950s and 1960s. Indeed, if Lye's sculptures were to operate more randomly, some (such as *Blade*) could become dangerous.

As one might expect of a film-maker, he was very interested in light. To make the most of the highly reflective surfaces of his metal sculpture, he experimented with various kinds of gallery lighting, including coloured and strobe lights. At other times, he presented his sculptures in a purist fashion with black walls as a background and no colour to distract. These complex aspects of light and reflection were part of the 'performance' and thus need to be considered when exhibiting his work. The fact that this innovative artist tried out a range of possibilities leaves room for different curatorial approaches to the display of his sculpture.

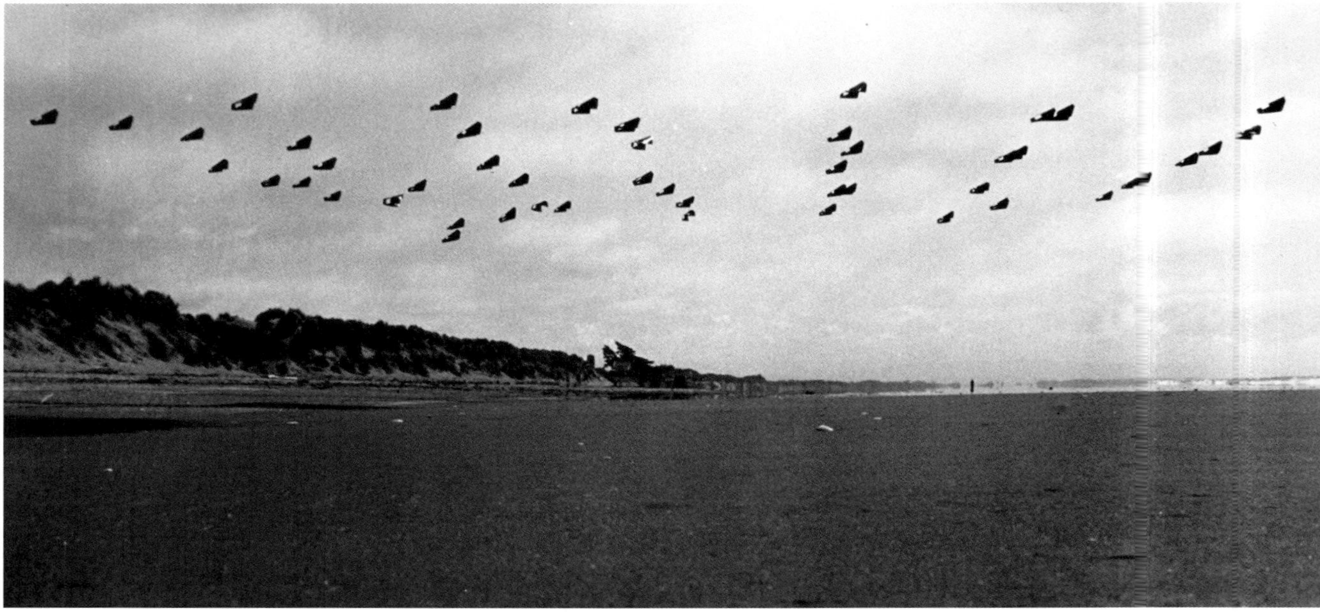

GRAPPLING WITH THE LEGACY: THE WORK OF EVAN WEBB, JOHN MATTHEWS AND THE FOUNDATION

Although Lye has left a large archive of information (expertly managed by Tyler Cann at the Govett-Brewster Art Gallery), the handling of his sculptures still involves complex decisions, as I have already indicated. Two people have spent many years grappling with the problems – John Matthews, an engineer with a fascination for sculpture, and Evan Webb, a sculptor with a fascination for engineering. Matthews, whose story was told earlier in this chapter, is well-known for his role in bringing Lye's work to New Plymouth. Webb, working quietly behind the scenes, remains relatively unknown though he too has made a key contribution. Arguably, he is New Zealand's most important kinetic artist but for much of the last 20 years he has dedicated his skills to the realisation of Lye projects.

Webb combines an artist's eye with a strong practical bent, qualities he regards as a legacy from his parents who were trained sign-writers and commercial artists. He attended Ilam, the University of Canterbury's art school, and graduated in 1983 with a Diploma in Fine Arts with Honours. His sculptures display a strong conceptual element, a diverse use of materials and a sharp sense of humour – interests that are perhaps more typical of Webb's generation than of Lye's. What the two artists share is an intense involvement with movement and

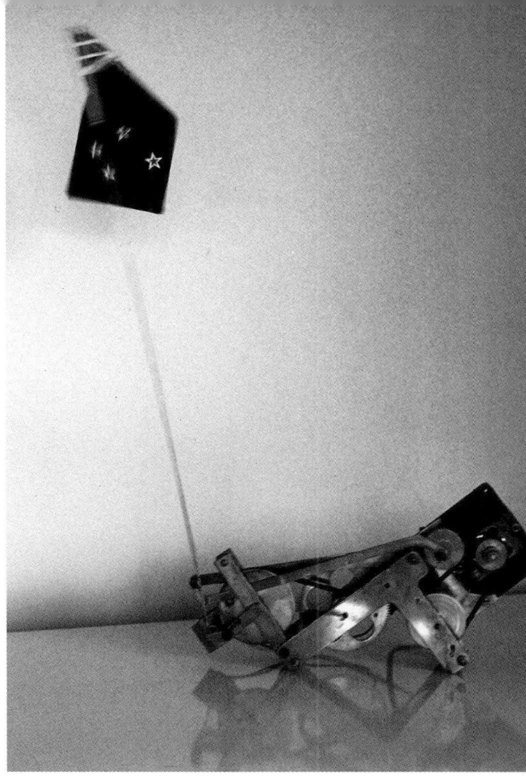

energy. Webb's work *Kites* created a pixellated image in the sky using hundreds of identical kites. The kites were of the 'sled' type, made from black polythene, and under the right conditions they could be tethered to the ground to fly unassisted. The artist focused on what happened to the image after mapping it out on the ground then transferring it to the sky where it was redrawn by the vagaries of the wind, with subtle differences occurring to each kite.[40] *Store Below Zero* (exhibited at the Robert McDougall Art Gallery) involved loaded mouse traps in an ice installation. As the ice melted, the traps fell to the gallery floor and were triggered off. Other Webb sculptures have satirised nationalism, such as *Flying the Flag*, in which an electric motor powers a series of brass clock wheels which raise a small flag pole. When fully erect, the pole does a vibrating dance and its flag vigorously flaps before collapsing in spent ecstasy. Perhaps most reminiscent of Lye is *A-Trophy*, which has so far been realised only as a working model and is designed to be enlarged to a monumental scale. It comprises two large electrodes made from copper, modelled on gazelle horns. A large electrical discharge known as a 'Jacob's Ladder' is generated between the horns, a display of lightning even more intense and primordial than what is known as the Tesla effect.

Two sculptures by Evan Webb: *Kites* (opposite) which creates a pixellated image in the sky using hundreds of identical kites; and *Flying the Flag* (above) in which an electric motor powers a series of brass clock wheels to raise a New Zealand flag that goes on to perform an ironic, vibrating dance. Courtesy Evan Webb.

As a student, Webb had travelled from Christchurch to New Plymouth in 1977 to attend Lye's exhibition. He recalls, 'I saw Len and listened to him but never met him. At the time, I was fascinated by the formality (abstract form) of his art and its energy. I was also intrigued by how it worked – especially *Universe*.' Webb was also impressed by the 1967 book *Constructivism: Origins and Evolution* by another kinetic sculptor, George Rickey, which talked about Lye. After graduation, Webb went on to various art teaching and gallery jobs. Then, in 1987, Matthews phoned him to ask if he was interested in a job restoring Lye's sculpture. Intrigued by the challenge, Webb began his connection with the Foundation in 1988 as a project consultant and curator of the Lye collection, then as acting director from 1993 and director from 1997. In addition to his work on the sculpture, Webb has looked after much of the day-to-day work of the organisation – applying for grants, responding to requests for the use of films and sculptures, and other administrative work of the kind that Lye himself always had trouble keeping up with.

Maintaining Lye's sculpture in working order has called for much patience and resourcefulness. In Webb's words:

> Many of the technical problems arise because Lye's work relies upon vibration, and bits of steel and machines don't like being vibrated for long periods of time – they shake apart, wear out or finally break. Most engineers avoid designing machines that deliberately run at frequencies that cause them to vibrate. Or, if it's unavoidable, they dampen (cushion) the effects of the vibration with rubber mounts and springs and shock absorbers. (A spin-dry washing machine and a car engine are examples of dampened vibrators.) Lye celebrated vibration, and harnessed the 'natural' vibration in the wires and strips he shook and spun. Although *Water Whirler* is an elegant work, its mechanism takes a pounding and it has caused us much head-scratching as we continue to modify various parts to absorb the loads and yet allow the 'good vibrations'.

Webb has had to spend a large part of his time installing exhibitions. In his words, 'Some of the challenges of working overseas are peculiar to kinetic sculpture, but they're not unexpected – securing works like *Blade* to the floor for example. In Cologne I was not allowed to drill into the floor so I had to cast a large block of concrete on which to secure the work. Sorting out technical matters in another language can sometimes be intriguing.'

Replacing a part is difficult when the artist has not left any information about it. For example, when Lye created *Roundhead*, whose visual patterns suggest musical forms, he decided to heighten the effect by incorporating an old-fashioned music box in the base which played a quirky sequence of sounds. The sight and sound relationships were meant to 'engender both harmony and counterpoint depending on whether they [were] in or out of phase'.[41] When the music box wore out, Webb had to work hard to identify the manufacturer (Reuge of Switzerland). This was followed by another challenge – identifying the melody. Finally, a musician friend realised that the original tune had been *Silent Night*, which Lye had modified so that only some of the notes remained.[42] Fortunately, the manufacturer still produced *Silent Night* music boxes, and Webb was able to stock up.

A delicate work like *Roundhead* is always in danger of being damaged by the curious hands of the public, and the Foundation decided to start displaying it within a plastic transparent case. The sculpture still looked good but the sound of the music box was muffled. Webb did much research on possible ways of amplifying the sound or using a digital recording. Synchronising sound and image proved extremely difficult; and any recording lacked the touches of unpredictability that went with a music box. The Foundation has therefore gone back to exhibiting *Roundhead* uncovered.

Security remains an important consideration for outdoor sculptures because deliberate damage is common In the case of *Water Whirler*, vandals have climbed up the pole and shaken it violently off its springs. Protecting a sculpture involves difficult tradeoffs because a more secure base may compromise the aesthetics. Sponsors may add their own requirements for the base since the art will usually be commissioned as part of a larger landscaping or architectural development. Matthews and Webb have always struggled to obtain artistic results, but in the matter of bases some compromises with political, financial and security demands are simply unavoidable.[43] After running into similar problems, Lye would reassure himself with the thought that the moving parts of a kinetic sculpture were what mattered most. This attitude informed a 1978 recorded interview with Matthews in which he said, 'I'm not much good at devising foundation mounts. You've got enough aesthetic to do it yourself.'[44]

The Foundation's most challenging projects have been the building of large-scale sculptures. *Blade*, which can shake a gallery, stands 4.5 metres high. The blade itself is made from titanium and is 3.5 metres long, 400 mm wide and 5 mm thick. Webb, who was in charge of this project, turned to the Department of Mechanical Engineering at the University of Canterbury for help in determining the exact specifications.[45] The research was carried out by Shayne Gooch, who earned a PhD for it. Another student, Zane Meredith, has investigated the scaling up of *Universe*. Together with their supervisor Professor John Raine, Gooch and Meredith have published reports on their research in international engineering journals.[46]

Enlarging *Blade* was not simply a matter of increasing size proportionally because so many factors were involved – such as height, width, thickness, the buckling point of the metal and the sound resonance. In scaling up sculptures, it is crucial to be clear about all the factors that may be essential to the figures of motion and sound required, and the exact size of the sculpture may need to be modified accordingly. In selecting material, the relevant aesthetic properties must come first – flexibility, reflective surface and ability to transmit sound – though safety and durability also need to be taken into account. Safety is obviously a

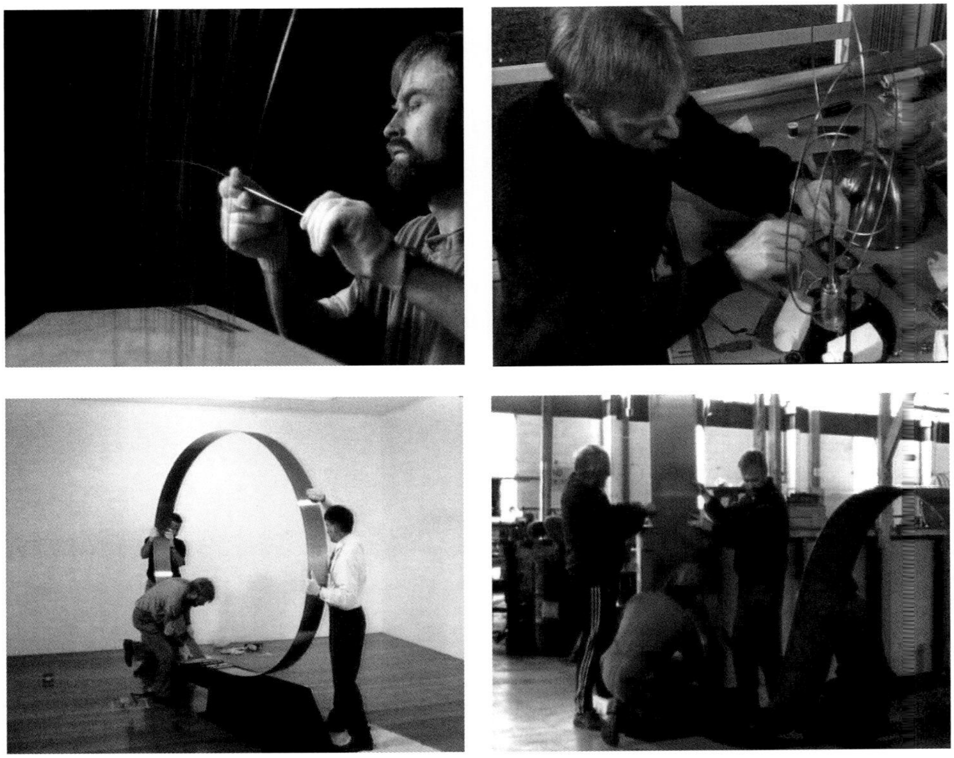

Evan Webb doing maintenance work on *Grass* and *Roundhead;* assembling *Universe* at the Gow Langsford Gallery in Auckland (with John Matthews); and deciding on the correct height to cut a new sheet of steel for *Blade*. Courtesy Point of View Productions.

concern for a large, wild sculpture like *Blade*. Lye liked the energy level of some of his sculptures to verge on the terrifying, but contemporary technology makes it possible to set definite limits. Durability is also an issue for a work that vibrates fiercely. Lye had used cold rolled carbon steel for the smaller *Blade*, but that material would have disintegrated under the increased strain, so the larger version required titanium. Webb comments:

> It is usual engineering practice to think of permanence or at least lifetime use as 'one million performances' – that is the magic number. During the 1950s and '60s, few works of kinetic sculpture could aspire to that longevity, and this discouraged many dealers and museums from getting involved with the genre. It was a risk for artist or dealer to have to guarantee on-going performance. Although it is not possible to eliminate the risk entirely, the Lye sculptures being built today can – with the help of improved technology – aim for the symbolic figure of a million performances.

The challenge of scaling up *Wind Wand* was how to realise the artist's unorthodox and seemingly impossible demands. As Webb wrote in *Art New Zealand* in

199[illegible], 'There are no precedents in design engineering for very tall, slender fibreglass poles that wave about in the breeze. Most research is towards producing stiff and inflexible structures. To compound the problem, designing a wand flexible enough to wave about yet strong enough to withstand strong and even gale force winds was a *tall* assignment.'[47] He initially commissioned a design for the wand from another university's engineering school, but in the end the school told Webb it seemed impossible to get a pole to flex in the way Lye required. One day, reading a boating magazine, Webb came across an article about Dave Marks and his unique method of building yacht masts. He and Matthews then flew to Auckland and signed up Marks and his assistant Chris Raynes to tackle the problem. It was necessary to draw upon state-of-the-art research on yacht masts developed for the Americas Cup. There was much trial and error – the first 25-metre wand bent all the way to the ground and never stood up – but Marks and Raynes finally achieved the impossible, and a wand was produced without the need for stepping. A minuscule amount of tapering was required, but the basic figure of motion was achieved – described by Webb as 'the wand shooting upwards like a drawn line that rockets away from the base, *not* a droopy fishing rod'. Some very fine calculations were required to achieve the right balance between too much and not enough bend, such as the fact that the bottom of the wand bends more than the top. Interestingly, potential buyers of this sculpture have asked for it to be modified to allow the top to bend more dramatically, but that was never the artist's intention.

Webb was in charge of the realisation of the 25- and 45-metre versions of *Wind Wand*, though he had many discussions with Matthews on technical matters. For the larger *Wand*, he took on the engineer Stuart Robb as an assistant. Robb has since become increasingly important in the engineering design and construction of Lye sculptures. Like Matthews, he combines a professional knowledge of engineering with an interest in the arts. Another major project by Webb and Robb was the 10-metre *Water Whirler* which required several years of research to resolve the engineering problems and create the right movement. Initially, Webb worried that the *Whirler* might be 'too beautiful and not wild enough', but the end result was a dancer as energetic as a whirling dervish.

A research report in April 2006 identified thirteen other small Lye sculptures existing in prototype form that still need to be restored. As previously noted, Webb has already completed the first – *Fire Bush* – which has an extremely physical vibrating dance like a wild hula, which also resembles the vigorous phase of

Water Whirler. Although other experts such as Dave Marks and Shayne Gooch have made important contributions, and the Govett-Brewster Art Gallery has provided essential archival and exhibition support, the development of Lye's sculpture over the past two decades has been mostly the work of three people – Webb, Robb and Matthews. The artist seems lucky indeed to have had such a team looking after his legacy. Though busy managing an engineering company (Technix Group), Matthews has continued to maintain an overview of the projects and to contribute engineering suggestions and insights from having worked with the artist. Webb's relationship to Lye can perhaps be likened to that of an outstanding director of photography working in close partnership with a great film director, putting his technical and aesthetic skills at the service of the director's vision. Another analogy would be the musical virtuoso who premieres the compositions of a great composer, although a performer of that kind is rewarded by more applause and public recognition than a sculpture specialist working quietly behind the scenes.

THE LEGACY UNDER FIRE

Although Lye's decision to concentrate his collection in one place has had many advantages, the remoteness of New Zealand has meant that most art historians and curators in other countries are simply not aware of the scope of his work. A few sculptures have reached overseas exhibitions, but it costs a great deal to transport such heavy work.[48] The situation is a vicious circle, since a large exhibition of Lye's sculpture would give a great boost to his international reputation, but such an event is not yet possible because museums will only sponsor a big off-shore exhibition if the artist is already well-known and/or fashionable.

Wider exposure of the work would also contribute to the debate in Europe about the conservation of kinetic sculpture. Meanwhile, this debate has flared up occasionally in New Zealand as several critics and artists have challenged the idea of reproducing Lye's work posthumously. This happened in August 2004 during a visit by Dr Britta Schmitz, Chief Curator of the Hamburger Banhof (National Galerie) in Berlin, who had come to explore the possibility of a Lye show. When she spoke to an art audience in Christchurch, sculptor Stuart Griffiths asked Schmitz if she knew that the Lye works were reproductions. He then went on to compare her interest in these works with past visits by German curators who had came to New Zealand to purchase inauthentic shrunken Maori heads.[49] Griffiths later said that his comment was designed 'to liven up . . . an otherwise dull presentation', but it also deeply shocked the curator.

In April 2006, the Wellington Sculpture Trust organised an event in the City Gallery to discuss Lye and 'the general issue of posthumous works'. Andrew Drummond, former head of sculpture at the University of Canterbury's School of Fine Arts, took a negative view: 'Len said, "I want my work to be made". But how do you know that the decisions made are the decisions the artist would have made? It's a moral issue as much as an aesthetic issue – it's about the morality of someone making someone else's work.'[50] Drummond added that he would never want a foundation established to look after his own sculptures.

Three months later in 'Whose Lye Is It Anyway?' – Sally Blundell's *Listener* article on the debate – art critic Ian Wedde added his concerns:

> Lye did express a vision of works upscaled and located in particular conditions. He may even have anticipated the engineering and metallurgic progress that would make this happen, but this doesn't answer the critical question of when an artist's concepts, preliminary drawings and sometimes doodles are actually indications of final intention. Lye was a compulsive and highly creative doodler and dreamer-on-paper, and much of this material should perhaps be left in that condition. Without the artist being present to advance concepts or critically test the ways in which they are installed, it's not easy to benchmark the moments when Lye's vision stops and institutional ambitions take over.[51]

Wedde's phrase 'institutional ambitions' alludes to a suspicion that economic temptations may be involved. He added:

> There have been frequent examples of posthumous art-work materializations whose drivers were largely commercial. In Lye's case, the production of editioned work may or may not constitute a self-serving economic loop in which work is made to generate funds for the production of work – or for the prolongation of opportunity generated by the institutionalization of Lye as a brand, asset or article of cultural capital.[52]

This 'commercial' suspicion will elicit a wry smile from those involved with the Lye project who have known it not as a money-spinner but as an endless struggle to raise funds. The Foundation is more accurately described as a small band of dedicated workers than as an 'institution'. As a non-profit trust, it is powered by unpaid labour and personal donations from trustees, together with occasional donations from private patrons and from public organisations (such as the New Plymouth District Council, the Govett-Brewster Art Gallery, the Stout Trust and Creative New Zealand). Those individuals and companies who have been paid for their work have often contributed to the cause by accepting a modest level of payment. A handful of sculptures have been sold but the market for kinetic art is still very limited. The idea of 'editions' came from Lye himself, and has so far meant only a few copies of a few sculptures, with the return from sales covering only part of the Foundation's expenses. In short, to think of the Lye project as having a 'commercial' motivation is as fanciful as talk of 'shrunken Maori heads'.

Most of the debate has been thoughtful and moderate, and the critics mentioned above are respected members of the art scene so they deserve a serious response. They accept the evidence that Lye did urge the Foundation to continue building his work, but they appear to regard such an activity as inherently wrong ('a moral issue'), and to imply that trustees should have known better than to get involved. I want to offer two counter-arguments.

First, I think it is important to identify the black and white assumptions involved in this perspective and to remind critics of the complexities. Reference to 'someone making someone else's art' is based on the concept of the unique creative individual, the auteur or master artist, valued because of the distinctiveness of his or her style and vision. The very notion of posthumous work seems impossible to reconcile with that concept. Yet there are many aspects of art that cannot be fitted into the idea of unique authorship. In earlier periods of painting, it was not unusual for artists to be surrounded by assistants and students. The term 'School of Rembrandt' (or Caravaggio, or Tintoretto, etc.) is used to describe paintings in the style of the master artist, or paintings whose authorship cannot be established. There are many instances in the history of art – or music – where a work attributed for many years to a particular master has later been re-attributed to a colleague or 'school'. The mystique of 'individuality' in art only developed with the Romantic movement in Europe from the end of the 18th century. In practice, art-making at the studio level has continued to be a complex business. Although the art market today talks up the uniqueness of an artist in order to increase his or her dollar value as a brand, a number of modern sculptors and painters have had teams of assistants – Auguste Rodin, Andy Warhol, Julian Schnabel, Jeff Koons and Damien Hirst, for example – and most kinetic sculptors have needed technical support.

It is true that individuality was a central concept in Lye's own theorising. But in practice, he needed technical help in making films and sculptures. His 'direct' method did bring the film medium closer than ever before to 'authorship' (the concept of filmic individuality) since a single artist could create all the images – but even he required a music editor, and sometimes he also depended upon lab technicians with specialised skills. On the occasions when he used a camera, he needed to work with a film crew. And *Particles in Space* included images drawn by assistants. At the same time, he never saw this teamwork as compromising the role of the director (or sculptor) as the central creative force – the two things co-existed in his thinking. We all share a more or less complex view of individuality when we talk about feature-films as the work of individual directors ('a Fellini film', 'a Scorsese film', etc.). We assume from the credits that the work of hundreds of people has been unified by the director's vision, but that is clearly not a simple process. In his last years, Lye embraced a similar complexity when he accepted the need for a team to take over from the artist as the best (and indeed only) way to keep his sculptures in working order, and to realise his plans for large-scale sculptures. He wanted his name to remain on posthumous work, and even left a signature to be copied for the express purpose of signing it off. While he appears never to have written an essay about the problems of attribution, he clearly assumed that a sophisticated audience would understand the complex nature of posthumous work, and he hoped it would concentrate on what the art had to offer.

The Foundation is careful to acknowledge the posthumous status of the sculptures it has built with a plaque such as this:

> *Water Whirler* is a posthumously realized work built by the Len Lye Foundation in accordance with drawings and descriptions left by the artist.[53]

Denis Dutton has suggested alternative phrases such as 'in the manner of' or 'completions of the artist's work'.[54] One might also use the term 'School of Lye'. But those phrases do not go far enough, since the aim is not merely to imitate or complete, but also to interpret as faithfully as possible the artist's intentions, a struggle that puts the work into a different category.[55] Further, such phrases do not recognise Lye's own wish for the completion of some of his works after his death, completion that was expected to occur posthumously as technology made the realisation of his vision possible.

Problems arise from the tendency of PR people, journalists or members of the public to ignore these nuances. The Foundation has not succumbed to that temptation, and it is to the credit of sponsors that the term 'posthumous' has not scared them off. Also, the sculptures produced have, in general, been not only popular but well-received critically.

A second counter-argument can be based on the idea that Lye's kinetic sculpture should be understood as a kind of musical score. His plans and / or his kinetic 'prototype' provide the basis for a posthumous performance. Classical music offers useful comparisons because music is the time-based art from which he derived his concept of 'figures of motion'. Audiences *want* to hear a musical score brought to life in performance, and composers are usually not present when their music is played. We know and accept the fact that musicians contribute something of their own, and even a less than perfect rendition will not prevent us from gaining a strong sense of the music and its 'figures'.

A particularly useful analogy is the 'early music' or 'historically informed performance' movement, since this is driven by a strong desire for historical accuracy. Total 'authenticity' may be an impossible goal, but taking that challenge seriously over the past half century has inspired a great wave of research and attempts to revive old instruments and performance practices. This has led to many musical rediscoveries. Virtually all music prior to the 18th century (and much subsequent music) involves an element of posthumous reconstruction or speculation about how to interpret or complete the score, but experienced listeners take that for granted – often there is no mention of it in the programme, though a musicologist associated with the group may discuss the issues for those interested. Basically the performers proceed confidently, as though to say, 'We've spent years studying this kind of work and we've reached some conclusions about the composer's intentions and how the work sounds best. So sit back and listen and we'll do our best to convince you!' Today's early music audiences understand the rules of this game.

The alternative approach would be to avoid any attempt at performance, leaving the music in the form of a score because a perfect realisation is never going to be possible without the composer 'being present to critically test the results' (to borrow some of Wedde's words). Musicians would see that as an odd attitude; and when they do perform a piece of music, they know it is best to be confident rather than tentative or half-hearted. The most valued early music performances are not timidly purist but strive to recapture the original vigour and excitement of the music. Similarly, a *Wind Wand* has to stand tall and confident – either you build it proudly or you leave it at the planning stage. Both the musicians and the *Wand*-builders are saying: 'Ultimately we will never know if this is entirely true to the artist's intentions but we are giving it our best shot. We've devoted our lives to researching and building (or performing) this kind of work. We have a great deal of evidence to back up everything we've done – but in any case, even if you remain sceptical, we hope you will at least find it an interesting piece of work.'

As for the listener, he or she may have to overcome an initial scepticism. We can use a well-known music example and ask, 'How can they possibly know what a score by a twelfth-century composer like Hildegard of Bingen is supposed to sound like?' A willing suspension of disbelief allows the listener to say, 'Reconstructing this work must involve a certain amount of speculation, but it's giving me a chance to experience something unfamiliar – an interesting artistic idiom and perhaps a piece of musical history.' In the case of Hildegard, it is probably hoped by the performers that listeners will go on to seek more information about the composer, and such research will quickly help them to identify which recordings are based on serious historical research (by Gothic Voices, for example, led by musicologist Christopher Page) and which ones impose a fashionable modern idiom (New Age versions of Hildegard's music such as are presented on the album *Vision*).

The audience at an early music concert is free to judge the success of the realisation. Since no musical period is monolithic, it is possible to have well-researched but competing interpretations and performances of (say) 'musica ficta' in 16th-century choral music.[56] Unfortunately, to build large Lye sculptures is such a complex and expensive business that we do not have the luxury of competing versions. (There are actually three large *Wind Wands* – one of 25 metres and two of 45 metres – but they were made by the same team and rely upon the same basic interpretation of Lye's directions.) Perhaps one day there will be a different 45-metre *Wand* inspired by the discovery of alternative plans or a different prototype.

In classical music, there is a spectrum of possible approaches that range from 'very free modern interpretation' to – at the other extreme – 'historically informed performance' based on thorough research. The Lye team operates as close to the latter end of the scale as it can. (Compare my earlier comment that 'the aim is not merely to imitate or complete, but also to interpret as faithfully as possible the artist's intentions'.) If Drummond and Wedde's points of view were applied to music, it would seem to require musicians to fall silent, and listeners would have to confine themselves to reading scores.[57] Granted, this may be a consistent position, and Drummond has every right to decide personally that he does not want a foundation to look after his own kinetic work.

Less serious are the kinds of public criticism based on superficial research – like the critic who came across a photograph of the artist's 'real' *Wand* and complained how different the New Plymouth version was. His evidence was in fact a photo of the rejected Toronto *Wand*. Criticisms based merely on gut instinct ('This sculpture doesn't look right to me') are reminiscent of the sweeping criticisms of the early music movement often heard in the 1970s and 1980s ('It sounds too dry, it can't be correct!'). The early music specialists persevered and eventually won their case (at least with the majority of listeners) simply by giving audiences time to get used to the sound, and by putting so much remarkable music out into the public domain. The initial opposition to *Wind Wand* has similarly given way to enthusiasm and a sense of ownership.

Although the Foundation is a coherent group in terms of its commitment to Lye's work, there is sometimes internal debate about priorities, as one would expect in any team that takes its responsibilities seriously. A proposal to build or enlarge a sculpture has to persuade trustees that enough is known about the artist's intentions to give it integrity, and trustees must also approve the work once it has been built. Solving the practical problems is another matter which depends, to some extent, upon a process of trial and error, which makes every project challenging from a financial point of view. The Foundation lost money on the building of *Wind Wand* and *Water Whirler*, despite generous sponsorship. But it hopes to continue its activities for as long as it can. Keeping Lye's existing sculptures in working order must go on, but the realisation of plans or the building of larger versions may no longer seem appropriate once the present team ceases to be involved and the last personal links with the artist have been lost.

CONCLUSIONS

Ian Wedde has recently made the useful suggestion that all sides in the debate should avoid 'essentialist' or 'determinist' assumptions and instead engage in a careful 'scrutiny' of each sculpture: 'I think the argument about whether Lye's more speculative graphic-think items could or should be made is an interesting one to have. It's also an ethical one to have in that it asks for intelligent scrutiny of intentions, modes and economies of production, and (not least) of historicity.'

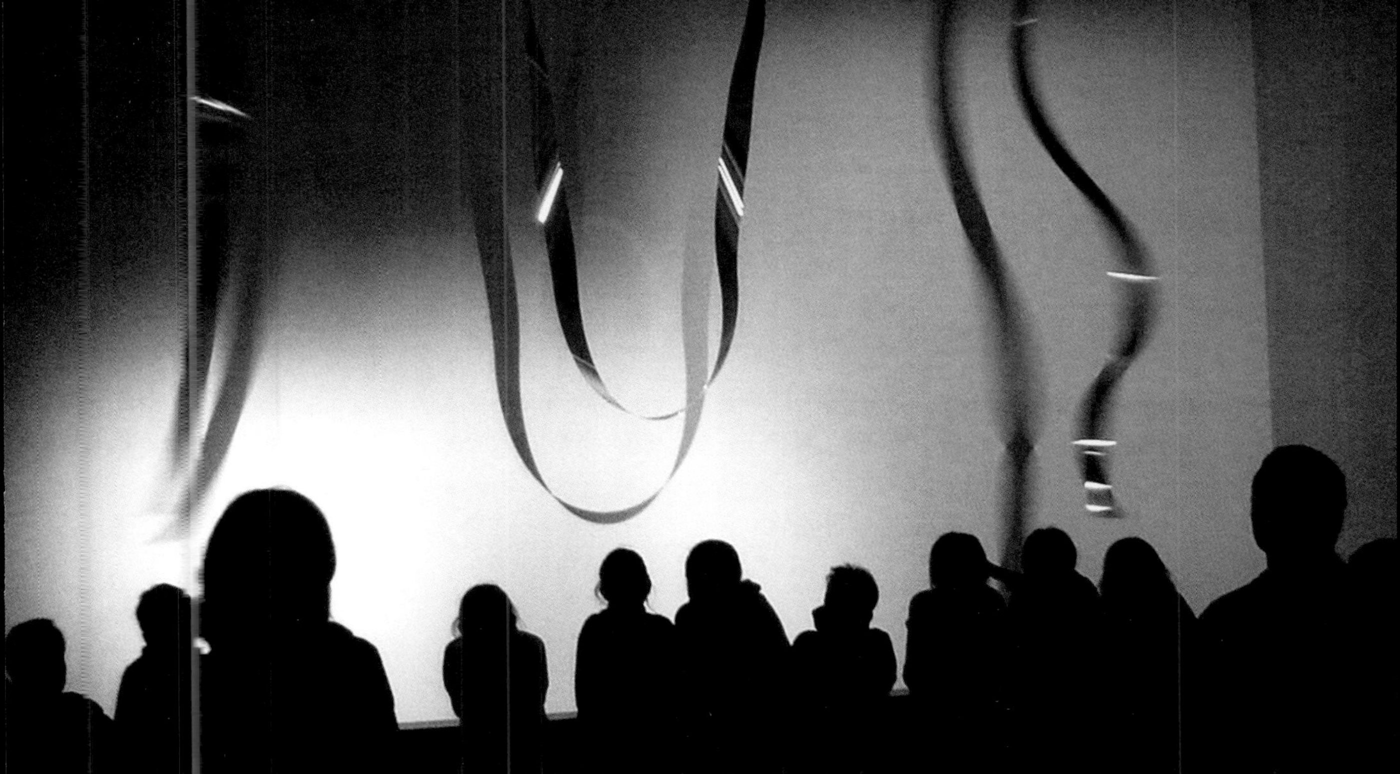

Visitors to the Govett-Brewster Art Gallery watching *Flip and Two Twisters* in action. Courtesy Govett-Brewster Art Gallery.

And: 'Whatever the case, it needs to be argued vigorously and intelligently. The moment where an artist's unrealized plans are given material form should generate critical heat, not either essentialist prohibitions or varieties of subaltern determinism, the tendency to obedient orthodoxy.'[58]

Debate would certainly benefit in this way from being less dogmatic and more focused on specifics, and that links up with the suggestion put forward by a workshop of conservation experts in *Modern Art: Who Cares?*, that 'so-called ethical guidelines are more properly considered as guiding principles. They can not be applied prescriptively . . . . Each [work] requires an individual balance' and many factors 'will all have a bearing'.[59]

At the same time, I believe some generalisations can be made about the overall Lye project over the past 20 years. Above all, I think the Lye reconstructions deserve to be seen as an unusual, ambitious achievement. Ultimately, whether one thinks of them as sculptures by Lye, or by 'the school of Lye', they articulate a particular idiom, a vision of what kinetic art can be (including some examples on an unusually large scale).

The history of Lye's work after his death has unfolded as an exceptionally detailed model of how a kinetic artist can handle the problems of succession. He was very explicit about the way he wanted his legacy handled. Not every artist will be attracted to this arrangement, but it does represent a clear option. It illustrates a new way of thinking about conservation – making exhibition copies, while keeping the prototype safely preserved. This 'reproduction' may challenge traditional thinking, but forms of modern art such as kinetic sculpture simply do not fit the old assumptions. While the comparison between kinetic sculpture and music does not work in every respect, it reminds us that it is important to look beyond traditional painting and sculpture for possible models. Like conceptual art, performance art and other modern genres of art, kineticism requires a different context.

The above aspects will no doubt continue to be accompanied by debate and controversy. And the full international response to Lye's legacy is yet to come.

acknowledgements

Evan Webb was always patient and thoughtful in supplying expert answers to my many questions about the sculpture – not that he should be held responsible for my interpretations or any errors that may have crept in to this book.

Tyler Cann at the Govett-Brewster Art Gallery was extremely helpful in providing images and manuscripts from the Lye collection. Thanks also to Rhana Devenport (director of the Govett-Brewster) and again to Tyler for facilitating our filming of *Fire Bush* at the Gallery.

The Len Lye Foundation kindly granted me permission to use Lye images, texts and films. The book would not have been possible without its cooperation.

When I was negotiating permission to use other illustrations, I was grateful to those rights-holders who understood the value of historical research and generously took my limited budget into account.

I should add that reasonable attempts have been made to seek permission from and to acknowledge all rights-holders. The author and publisher apologise for any omission that may have occurred, and invite any rights-holder not credited to contact them.

Over the years I have valued my discussions about Lye with friends such as Wystan Curnow, Max Gimblett, John Matthews, Stuart Robb and many others. And I am grateful for my memories of earlier conversations with Len, Ann and Jane Lye, and Jack and Doris Ellitt.

So many pages of this book were written at the café Occam that I want to thank its friendly staff.

My film *Art that Moves* was funded in part by a grant from the Screen Innovation Production Fund, a partnership between Creative New Zealand and the Film Commission. The film could not have been made without this support. I would also like to thank all those who worked on the film. Because of their respect for Lye, they did so either gratis or at mate's rates. A special thanks to the members of my family who were involved (Dylan, Oscar, Richard, Steve and Tony).

Auckland University Press has, as always, done a painstaking and thoroughly professional job. Special thanks to director Sam Elworthy, Katrina Duncan, Anna Hodge and Christine O'Brien.

I must end with two particularly important acknowledgements. Lani-rain Feltham lent her expertise to many aspects of the book, including the sourcing and preparation of images.

My wife, Shirley (who also knew Len, Ann and Jane Lye), has always played a central role in my research. She has made a particularly significant contribution to the present project by directing the superb footage of Lye's sculptures, producing the film *Art that Moves*, and preparing the DVD.

notes

INTRODUCTION

1 Len Lye, 'The Art that Moves', in Wystan Curnow and Roger Horrocks (eds), *Figures of Motion: Len Lye Selected Writings*, Auckland University Press / Oxford University Press, Auckland, 1984, p. 78. Lye used the words 'movement' and 'motion' interchangeably. Both words are derived from the same Latin verb. Obviously there are idioms that make use of one word or the other (such as 'slow motion'); and 'movement' is a more appropriate word to describe a single action, whereas 'motion' tends to imply ongoing activity. Some writers contrast implied 'motion' with literal 'movement' (as in op art). But for Lye, 'the art that moves' and 'the art of motion' simply referred to the same thing – 'kinetic art'.
2 From a letter by Lye to Albert Bush Brown, 20 May 1960.
3 The phrase is from 'A Kinetic Biography', unpublished manuscript (written for the exhibition 'Röreise Konsten' at the Moderna Museum in Stockholm in 1961).
4 Roger Horrocks, *Len Lye: A Biography*, Auckland University Press, Auckland, 2001.
5 Of course, 'the human experience of motion' focuses on a particular range. Human beings cannot immediately and directly perceive movement that is as rapid as (say) the speed of light or as slow as the growth of plants.
6 Len Lye, 'No Trouble', in Curnow and Horrocks (eds), *Figures of Motion*, p. 112.
7 Len Lye, 'The Art that Moves', in Curnow and Horrocks (eds), *Figures of Motion*, p. 81.
8 Pontus Hultén, 'Preface', *Territorium Artis*, Kunst und Ausstellungshalle der Bundesrepublik Deutschland, Bonn, 1992, pp. 19–[illegible].
9 Hultén, 'Tangible Motion Sculpture', *Territorium Artis*, p. 190.
10 Jack Burnham, *Beyond Modern Sculpture*, Allen Lane / The Penguin Press, London, 1968, p. 226. Lye remarked in an (unpublished) 1965 essay, 'Notes on Programmed Sculpture': 'As it is, judgements on the aesthetic value of mechanically-timed figures of motion . . . have to wait until . . . a practiced body of kinetic art lovers and critics . . . sift them out . . . . No such body of criticism exists in relation to kinetic art.'
11 Lye's comment is from the CBS documentary, *The Walls Come Tumbling Down* (1968), also known as *Art of the Sixties*.

ONE PRECEDENTS

1 Len Lye, 'No Trouble', in Wystan Curnow and Roger Horrocks (eds), *Figures of Motion: Len Lye Selected Writings*, Auckland University Press / Oxford University Press, Auckland, 1984, p. 105.
2 Herbert Spencer, *First Principles*, Williams and Norgate, London, vol. 1 (sixth edition), 1910, p. 160.
3 Mark Francis, *Herbert Spencer and the Invention of Modern Life*, Cornell University Press, Ithaca, 2007, p. 155.
4 Spencer, *First Principles*, p. 140.
5 *Ibid.*, p. [illegible]00.
6 *Ibid.*, p. [illegible]09.
7 *Ibid.*, p. [illegible]02 (footnote), and pp. 202–3.
8 See E. M. W. Tillyard, 'The Cosmic Dance', in Roger Copeland and Marshall Cohen (eds), *What is Dance?: Readings in Theory and Criticism*, Oxford University Press, Oxford, 1983, pp. 497–502.
9 Francis, *Herbert Spencer and the Invention of Modern Life*, p. 242.
10 Compare George Rickey's description of the way a kinetic artist sees the world: 'The artist finds waiting for him, as subject, not the trees, not the flowers, not the landscape, but the *waving* of branches and the *trembling* of stems, the piling up or scudding of clouds, the rising and setting and waxing and waning of heavenly bodies . . . [and] the repertory of the sea – from ripple and wavelet to tide and torrent . . .' (quoted in Jack Burnham's *Beyond Modern Sculpture*, Allen Lane / The Penguin Press, London, 1968, p. 267).
11 Arthur Mitchell (trans.), *Creative Evolution*, Macmillan, London, 1919, p. 134.
12 *Ibid.*, p. 385 (on Spencer).
13 *Ibid.*, p. 390.
14 *Ibid.*, p. 321.
15 *Ibid.*, p. 335.
16 *Ibid.*, p. 174.
17 *Ibid.*, p. 322.
18 Granted, early films were inclined to flicker. In Lye's time, viewing was thought to be based on 'the persistence of vision' but today the effect of continuity is explained differently. (See, for example, Joseph and Barbara Anderson, 'The Myth of Persistence of Vision Revisited', *Journal of Film and Video*, vol. 45, no. 1, Spring 1993, pp. 3–12.)
19 Robert Vischer, *Über das optische Formgefühl: Ein Beitrag zur Aesthetik*, Hermann Credner, Leipzig, 1873. It was translated as 'empathy' by American psychologist Edward Titchener in *Lectures on the Experimental Psychology of Thought Processes*, Macmillan, New York, 1909.
20 A particularly valuable collection is Harry Francis Mallgrave and Eleftherios Ikonomou (trans.), *Empathy, Form and Space: Problems in German Aesthetics, 1873–1893*, Getty Center, Santa Monica, 1994.
21 Len Lye, 'A Note on Dance and Film', in Curnow and Horrocks (eds), *Figures of Motion*, p. 56.
22 For the anticipation of Freud, see (for example) Mallgrave and Ikonomou's discussion of Karl Albert Scherner in Mallgrave and Ikonomou (trans.), *Empathy, Form and Space*, p. 24.
23 Quoted in 'Empathy', *Dictionary of the History of Ideas*, vol. 2, p. 86 (accessed 17 October 2007 at: http: / / etext.virginia.edu / cgi-local / DHI / dhi.cgi?id=dv2-09).
24 August Schmarsow, 'The Essence of Architectural Creation', in Mallgrave and Ikonomou (trans.), *Empathy, Form and Space*, p. 286.
25 'The word "kinetics" comes from the vocabulary of science and was first used in the middle of the 19th century to denote the branch of dynamics concerned with the motions of bodies and the forces acting upon them, as opposed to "statics". "Kinetic" entered the artistic lexicon in 1920 . . .' ('Kinetic Art', in Michael Clarke, *The Concise Oxford Dictionary of Art Terms*, Oxford University Press, Oxford, 2001).
26 Mallgrave and Ikonomou (trans.), *Empathy, Form and Space*, p. 121.
27 Bernard Berenson, *The Florentine Painters of the Renaissance*, G. P. Putnam's Sons, New York (third edition), 1909, p. 5.
28 *Ibid.*, p. 18.
29 'Foreword to the New Impression, 1948', in Michael Bullock (trans.), *Abstraction and Empathy*, Routledge and Kegan Paul, London, 1953, p. vii. (This was the first publication of Worringer's book in English, but his ideas had long had an influence in English artistic circles.)
30 *Ibid.*, p. 123 and p. 130.
31 Mallgrave and Ikonomou (trans.), *Empathy, Form and Space*, p. 153.
32 Herbert Langfeld, *The Aesthetic Attitude*, Harcourt Brace, New York, 1920, p. 136 [accessed via Questia].
33 *Ibid.*, p. 128.
34 Vernon Lee, *The Beautiful: An Introduction to Psychological Aesthetics*, Cambridge University Press, Cambridge, 1913, p. 72. It is interesting to note that in the final chapter of the book, Lee also linked art and empathy with evolution.
35 See John Willett (ed.), *Brecht on Theatre*, Eyre Methuen, London, 1964, especially the essay 'Alienation Effects in Chinese Acting'.
36 From *The New York Nation*, 1887, quoted in Brian Clegg, *The Man Who Stopped Time*, Joseph Henry Press, Washington DC, 2007, p. 211.
37 From the catalogue of the Duchamp Retrospective at the Palazzo Grassi in 1993, quoted in Semir Zeki and Mathew Lamb's essay, 'The Neurology of Kinetic Art', *Brain*, vol. 117, 1994, p. 618.
38 X. J. Kennedy, 'Nude Descending a Staircase', *In a Prominent Bar in Secaucus: New and Selected Poems, 1955–2007*, Johns Hopkins University Press, Baltimore, 2007, p. 7.

39 *The Sydney Mail*, 3 September 1913, quoted in John Frank's *The Quarantined Culture: Australian Reactions to Modernism*, Cambridge University Press, Cambridge, 1995, p. 73.
40 Len Lye, 'Experiment in Colour', in Curnow and Horrocks (eds), *Figures of Motion*, p. 49.
41 See Anson Rabinbach, *The Human Motor: Energy, Fatigue, and the Origins of Modernity*, University of California Press, Berkeley, 1992.
42 Étienne-Jules Marey, *Le Movement*, Éditions Jacqueline Chambon, Nimes, 2002 (facsimile edition), pp. 44–49. The book was translated into English and published as *Movement* by W. Heinemann in London in 1895. Unfortunately, we do not know whether Lye ever saw this remarkable book.
43 For example, Ottomar Anschütz (1846–1907) and Albert Londe (1858–1917).
44 Curnow and Horrocks (eds), *Figures of Motion*, p. 40.
45 The term 'modernism' carries different meanings in different contexts. I am using it here in an art historical sense to refer to the wave of innovation in art that occurred during the first decades of the 20th century and was associated with various overlapping 'movements' in art (such as Cubism and Futurism). The popular term is 'modern art', though that term is losing its relevance now that so many years have elapsed.
46 See newspaper story facing p. 105 in Roger Horrocks, *Len Lye: A Biography*, Auckland University Press, Auckland, 2001.
47 Umberto Boccioni, Carlo Carra, Luigi Russolo, Giacomo Balla and Gino Severini, 'The Exhibitors to the Public' (1912), in Umbro Apollonio (ed.), *Futurist Manifestoes*, The Viking Press, New York (Documents of 20th Century Art series), 1973, p. 50.
48 F. T. Marinetti, 'The Founding and Manifesto of Futurism', in Apollonio (ed.), *Futurist Manifestoes*, p. 21.
49 Umberto Boccioni, 'Technical Manifesto of Futurist Sculpture', in Apollonio (ed.), *Futurist Manifestoes*, p. 64.
50 F. T. Marinetti, 'Destruction of Syntax – Imagination Without Strings – Words-in-freedom' (1913), in Apollonio (ed.), *Futurist Manifestoes*, p. 96.
51 Anton Giulio Bragaglia, 'Futurist Photodynamism', in Apollonio (ed.), *Futurist Manifestoes*, p. 39.
52 Bragaglia, in Apollonio (ed.), *Futurist Manifestoes*, p. 28.
53 The sets were designed by Enrico Prampolini.
54 *Ibid.*, p. 28.
55 Giacomo Balla, Umberto Boccioni, Carlo Carra, Luigi Russolo and Gino Severini, 'The Exhibitors to the Public', in Apollonio (ed.), *Futurist Manifestoes*, p. 46.
56 *Ibid.*, p. 49 ('chaotic excitement'); and Umberto Boccioni, 'Futurist Dynamism and French Painting', in Apollonio (ed.), *Futurist Manifestoes*, p. 109 ('fast and fragmented').
57 Balla, Boccioni, Carra, Russolo and Severini, 'The Exhibitors to the Public', in Apollonio (ed.), *Futurist Manifestoes*, p. 49.
58 Boccioni, 'Technical Manifesto of Futurist Sculpture', in Apollonio (ed.), *Futurist Manifestoes*, p. 51.
59 Umberto Boccioni, 'Plastic Dynamism', in Apollonio (ed.), *Futurist Manifestoes*, p. 93.
60 *Ibid.*
61 Umberto Boccioni, 'Absolute Motion + Relative Motion = Dynamism', in Apollonio (ed.), *Futurist Manifestoes*, p. 152.
62 *Ibid.*, p. 153 ('The concept of motion'), and p. 151 ('The search to find a new form').
63 Giacomo Balla and Fortunato Depero, 'Futurist Reconstruction of the Universe' (1915), in Apollonio (ed.), *Futurist Manifestoes*, p. 197.
64 Giannalberto Bendazzi's interesting account in *Cartoons: One Hundred Years of Cinema Animation* (John Libbey, London, 1994, p. 13) notes that the brothers' original surname was Corradini.
65 Bruno Corra, 'Abstract Cinema – Chromatic Music', in Apollonio (ed.), *Futurist Manifestoes*, p. 69.
66 See, for example, two essays: Stephen Jay Gould, 'Boats and Deckchairs: Marcel Duchamp's Optical Illusions', *Natural History*, December 1999; and Rhonda Roland Shearer, 'Of Two Minds and One Nature', *Science*, vol. 286, no. 5442, 5 November 1999.
67 George Rickey, 'The Morphology of Movement: A Study of Kinetic Art', *Art Journal*, vol. 22, no. 4, 1963 (Summer), p. 221.
68 Len Lye, 'The Art that Moves', in Curnow and Horrocks (eds), *Figures of Motion*, p. 83.
69 See John E. Bowlt (ed.), *Russian Art of the Avant-garde: Theory and Criticism 1902–1934*, Thames and Hudson, London (revised and enlarged edition), 1988, p. 209.
70 *Ibid.*
71 See Martin Hammer and Christina Lodder, *Constructing Modernity: The Art and Career of Naum Gabo*, Yale University Press, New Haven, 2000, p. 65. See also endnote 25 of this chapter.
72 *Ibid.*, pp. 68–69 (on Bergson). And Bowlt (ed.), *Russian Art of the Avant-garde*, pp. 213–14 ('We renounce . . .').
73 Bowlt (ed.), *Russian Art of the Avant-garde*, p. 211.
74 Curnow and Horrocks (eds), *Figures of Motion*, p. 83.
75 Quoted in Hammer and Lodder, *Constructing Modernity*, p. 70.
76 *Ibid.*, p. 152.
77 *Ibid.*, p. 112.
78 *Ibid.*
79 Lye's phrase in Curnow and Horrocks (eds), *Figures of Motion*, p. 83.
80 Quoted in Hammer and Lodder, *Constructing Modernity*, p. 172.
81 *Ibid.*, p. 175.
82 *Ibid.*, p. 173.
83 Robert Russett and Cecile Starr, *Experimental Animation: Origins of a New Art*, Da Capo Press, New York, 1976, p. 36.
84 This sense of time in paintings was sometimes related to Medieval paintings that incorporated different phases of an event on the same canvas. And sophisticated comic books and graphic novels also play with space and time.
85 Hammer and Lodder, *Constructing Modernity*, p. 250.
86 It may be argued that Ginna and Corra made the first, but since their films have not survived it is hard to know whether colour or movement was central to them.
87 Walter Schobert, 'Art and the Cinema', in Angelika Leitner and Uwe Nitschke (eds), *The German Avant-garde Film of the 1920s*, Goethe-Institut, München, 1989, p. 6.
88 *Ibid.*, p. 8.
89 Walther Ruttmann, 'Painting with the Medium of Time', *ibid.*, p. 104.
90 At the time of writing, a restored, coloured version of this film is available on YouTube, complete with Butting's music (http://www.youtube.com/watch?v=LvjFvosgmVw). It does not, however, include the wave sequence, which Ruttmann may have decided to separate. A review of the first public screening of the film in 1921 clearly describes the waves, which are included in some other versions. See Russett and Starr, *Experimental Animation*, pp. 40–43.
91 Leitner and Nitschke (eds), *The German Avant-garde Film of the 1920s*, pp. 106–8.
92 In his essay 'Absolute Film', William Moritz (http://www.iotacenter.org/visualmusic/articles/moritz/absolute) argues that Hans Richter withdrew his 30-second *Film is Rhythm* from the programme once he had seen the scope and complexity of Ruttmann and Eggeling's films. See also: http://www.centerforvisualmusic.org/library/WMAbsoluteFilm.htm. Other sources (such as Leitner and Nitschke [eds], *The German Avant-garde Film of the 1920s*) assume that Richter's film was screened.
93 Christine Noll Brinckmann, 'Collective Movements and Solitary Thrusts: German Experimental Film 1920–1990', *Millennium Film Journal*, no. 30–31, Fall 1997 (from the *Millennium Film Journal* website).
94 See Walter Schobert's comments in Leitner and Nitschke (eds), *The German Avant-garde Film of the 1920s*, p. 14.
95 See William Moritz, 'The Films of Oskar Fischinger', *Film Culture*, no. 58–60, 1974, pp. 37–188.
96 I would include modern forms of classical music, such as the composers associated with the Bauhaus.
97 Laszlo Moholy-Nagy, *Vision in Motion*, Paul Theobold, Chicago, 1947. Moholy-Nagy taught at the Bauhaus in the 1920s, as did Gabo. His other writings include a 1922 manifesto with Alfred Kemény, 'The Kinetic-Constructive System of Force', and his book *The New Vision* (the English translation of *Von Material zu Architekture*, 1929). He attempted to establish an American Bauhaus. There is a very interesting 1992 essay by Yann Beauvais, 'Rapports entre Laszlo Moholy-Nagy et Len Lye', MA DAI and Fonction Cinéma, Geneva

(at http://manou16.phpnet.org/article_us.php3?id_article=43).

98 Moholy-Nagy independently developed his own version of the method in the same year.

99 Man Ray, quoted in David Curtis and Richard Francis (eds), *Film as Film: Formal Experiment in Film 1910–1975*, Hayward Gallery, London, 1979, p. 26.

TWO LEN LYE: A KINETIC BIOGRAPHY

1 The term 'imprint' comes from Lye's 'Slow but Sure', in Andrew Bogle (ed.), *Len Lye: A Personal Mythology*, Auckland City Art Gallery, Auckland, 1980, p. 90.

2 Roger Horrocks (ed.), *Happy Moments*, The Holloway Press, Auckland, 2002, p. 4.

3 Cecile Starr, letter to Stan Brakhage and Roger Horrocks, 27 December 1980.

4 See 'The Watch', in Horrocks (ed.), *Happy Moments*, p. 19. His brother Philip Lye told me similar stories.

5 Wystan Curnow, 'An Interview with Len Lye', *Art New Zealand*, no. 17, 1980, p. 59.

6 The painting is the 'celebration of a fleeting moment' according to Seymour Slive, *Frans Hals*, Phaidon, London, 1970, vol. 1, p. 92.

7 'Two Grand Illuminations / Illuminated Turn Ons / My Best Ideas', unpublished ms.

8 'Ray Thorburn Interviews Len Lye', *Art International*, vol. 19, April 1975, p. [illegible].

9 'Inspiration', unpublished ms. It is not possible to determine an exact date for Lye's epiphany but my guess is 1920. (He himself sometimes gave an earlier year, but his memory for dates was highly unreliable.)

10 For example, his fellow student Gordon Tovey was quoted as saying, 'What a spark he was! We used to talk for hours about movement and the clouds moving across the skies of Wellington!' (See Roger Horrocks, *Len Lye: A Biography*, Auckland University Press, Auckland, 2001, p. 27, and the related footnotes 31 and 32 on p. 394.)

11 Horrocks, *Len Lye: A Biography*, p. 28.

12 'My Model', unpublished ms.

13 'The New Muses – Aesthetic Kinesthesia', unpublished ms; and 'My Model' (a variant version).

14 'A Kinetic Biography', unpublished ms.

15 Robert Russett and Cecile Starr, *Experimental Animation: Origins of a New Art*, Da Capo Press, New York, 1976.

16 *Ibid.*

17 'My Model', unpublished ms.

18 [My italics]. From Anne Kirker's unpublished interview with Len Lye, 19 August 1979. Compare Lye's comments in Robert Del Tredici, 'Lye Lye Interview', *The Cinema News* (San Francisco), nos. 2–4, 1979, p. 35.

19 Ezra Pound, *Gaudier-Brzeska: A Memoir*, John Lane / The Bodley Head, London, 1916.

20 Lye quoted by Anne Kirker in her essay 'The Early Years in London', *Art New Zealand*, no. 17, 1980, p. 50.

21 A famous haiku by Arakida Moritake.

22 Curnow, 'An Interview with Len Lye', p. 55.

23 One of his sketchbooks features machine shapes, and his early contributions to the Seven and Five Society were described as 'mechanical art' – yet he liked to relate even these images to the totem objects of tribal art.

24 Curnow, 'An Interview with Len Lye', p. 57.

25 Note 'For S.A., re: my old brain imagery', unpublished ms.

26 For an example, see Bogle (ed.), *Len Lye: A Personal Mythology*, p. 74. (NB: The catalogue has printed the photo of the carving upside down.)

27 See Horrocks, *Len Lye: A Biography*, pp. 344–45 for an example of Lye criticising a museum display.

28 Edwin J. Kempf, *Psychopathology*, C.V. Mosby, St. Louis (Missouri), 1920, pp. [illegible]3–26.

29 *Ibid.*, p. [illegible]

30 For a more detailed description, see Horrocks, *Len Lye: A Biography*, p. 53.

31 *Ibid.*, p. 55.

32 See Roger Horrocks, 'Len Lye: Origins of his Art', in Jean-Michel Bouhours and Roger Horrocks (eds), *Len Lye*, Centre Pompidou, Paris, 2000; or Horrocks, *Len Lye: A Biography*, Chapter 12.

33 Letter, 26 March 1981.

34 Laura Riding, *Len Lye and the Problem of Popular Films*, Seizin Press, London, 1938, p. 39.

35 It would be possible to look at Lye's paintings in some of the ways suggested by Gaston Bachelard in his book *Air and Dreams: An Essay on the Imagination of Movement*, The Dallas Institute of Humanities and Culture, Dallas, 2002. (Bachelard's themes include rivers, flight, evolution, etc.)

36 Lye's later version of this painting was called *God of Light (The Big Bang Man)*.

37 'No Trouble' suggests that Lye photographed each drawing twice, a common animation practice. Hence, eight drawings per day yielded one second of film (at the silent speed of 16 fps). See Len Lye, 'Light Returns', in Wystan Curnow and Roger Horrocks (eds), *Figures of Motion: Len Lye Selected Writings*, Auckland University Press / Oxford University Press, Auckland, 1984, pp. 102–3. See also Chapter Four, footnote 17.

38 Roger Horrocks, 'Jack Ellitt: The Early Years', *Cantrills Filmnotes*, no. 93–100, December 1999–January 2000, pp. 20–26.

39 Tredici, 'Len Lye Interview', p. 37.

40 See Dorothy Knowles, *The Censor, the Drama and the Film 1900–1934*, George Allen and Unwin, London, 1934, p. 237; and Ivor Montagu, *Film as Art*, Penguin, Harmondsworth, 1964, p. 260.

41 See later chapters for their comments.

42 This account draws upon Len Lye, *Tusalava*, in Curnow and Horrocks (eds), *Figures of Motion*; and Anne Kirker's interview with Lye. See also Horrocks, *Len Lye: A Biography*, p. 128; and Oswell Blakeston, 'Len Lye's Visuals', *Architectural Review*, vol. 72, July 1932, p. 25.

43 Blakeston, 'Len Lye's Visuals', *ibid.*

44 The Company had a month-long season at Covent Garden in 1929, including Igor Stravinsky's *Rite of Spring*. Diaghilev himself died in August 1929 but the company continued.

45 Horrocks, *Len Lye: A Biography*, p. 130.

46 Riding, *Len Lye and the Problems of Popular Films*, p. 39.

47 Len Lye and Laura Riding, 'Film-making', in Curnow and Horrocks (eds), *Figures of Motion*, p. 40.

48 Bogle (ed.), *Len Lye: A Personal Mythology*, p. 70.

49 From 'The Practice' section of 'The Art that Moves', in Curnow and Horrocks (eds), *Figures of Motion*, p. 83.

50 No. 8 was the standard gauge of farm fencing wire – a material that lent itself to lateral thinking and unexpected uses.

51 See Lye and Riding, 'Film-making', in Curnow and Horrocks (eds), *Figures of Motion*, pp. 39–42.

52 Strictly speaking, auteurship as a 'theory' did not emerge until many years after *A Colour Box*. François Truffaut wrote about 'la politique des auteurs' in 1954, and Andrew Sarris coined the phrase 'auteur theory' in 1962 – but the central idea had emerged much earlier.

53 Reported by Basil Wright in G. Roy Levin, *Documentary Explorations*, Anchor, New York, 1971, p. 39.

54 In fact, *A Colour Box* is the one direct film Lye seems to have made rapidly and on long strips of film. Presumably this was thanks to a year of preparation and trial runs. Regardless of how it was made, its rapid changes create the effect of editing.

55 See Horrocks, *Len Lye: A Biography*, pp. 138–39.

56 Anthony Vessolo, '"The Colour Box"', *Sight and Sound*, vol. 4, no. 15, Autumn 1935, p. 117.

57 *Daily Herald*, 20 September 1935.

58 See 'The Len Lye Lists' (*Bulletin of New Zealand Art History*, vol. 8, 1980) for 1936–38 reports of European screenings. The film was later 'chosen as a culminating point in the cavalcade of films at the Paris Exposition' ('The First Swing Film', *Melody Maker*, 18 September 1937).

59 *Film Kurier*, 16 August 1936 – quoted by William Moritz in his essay, 'Lye Lye's Films in the Context of International Abstract Cinema', in Bouhours and Horrocks (eds), *Len Lye*, p. 194.

60 There are interesting discussions of the history of direct film by

William Moritz in *Film as Film*, p. 59, and by Jean-Michel Bouhours, in Bouhours and Horrocks (eds), *Len Lye*, pp. 202–20. Moritz says that Stoltenberg describes a direct film experiment, made in 1911 or 1912, in his book *Reine Farbkunst in Raum und Zeit und ihr Verhältnis zur Tonkunst* (Unesma, Leipzig, 1920 – reprinted 1937).

61 Horrocks, *Len Lye: A Biography*, pp. 144–45.
62 *Focus*, no. 4, December 1935, pp. 60–61.
63 Like Lye, Jennings did important work in several media. He was a painter, writer and film-maker.
64 Curnow and Horrocks (eds), *Figures of Motion*, pp. 39–42. The essay was originally published in *Epilogue* 1, 1938, pp. 231–35.
65 See Horrocks, *Len Lye: A Biography* pp. 172–73.
66 The other two are 'Is Film Art?' (1959) and 'The Art that Moves' (1964), to be discussed below.
67 MacLeish's famous line appears in his 1926 poem 'Ars Poetica.'
68 His life provides an interesting parallel to Lye's since he died in 1976 (four years before Lye).
69 Alexander Calder, 'Mobiles', written for Myfanwy Evans (ed.), *The Painter's Object*, Gerald Howe, London, 1937 (viewed June 2008 at http://home.etu.unige.ch/~said8/Texts.html).
70 Statement by Alexander Calder for an exhibition at the Berkshire Museum, 12–27 August 1933 (viewed June 2008 at http://home.etu.unige.ch/~said8/Texts.html).
71 Calder, 'Mobiles'. The name 'mobile' was suggested to Calder by Duchamp.
72 One of the harshest criticisms of Calder is a 1943 review by Clement Greenberg who pounces on the emphasis on static (or nearly static) shapes in Calder's work as revealing a lack of originality as they feed off modern abstract art: 'It becomes apparent . . . that the fundamental aesthetic concept setting Calder in motion is good taste – a good taste already established by others, since his shapes and especially his colour stem entirely from the works of Picasso, Miró and Arp.' (Review in *The Nation*, 23 October 1943, reprinted in Clement Greenberg, *The Collected Essays and Criticism*, University of Chicago Press, Chicago, 1986, p. 159.)
73 Text on the cover of Time Records S/8007 (music by Morton Feldman and Earle Brown). The text has been published elsewhere as 'Transformations and Developments of a Radical Aesthetic' (for example, passages from it appear in Christoph Cox and Daniel Warner [eds], *Audio Culture: Readings in Modern Music*, Continuum, London, 2004, pp. 189 ff). Calder made a playable mobile for Feldman, called *Chef d'Orchestre*.
74 Cf. Jean Mitry, *Le Cinéma Expérimental: Histoire et Perspectives*, Editions Seghers, Paris, 1971, p. 182. The Calder analogy was suggested by Jim Hoberman in the *Village Voice*, 31 December 1980, p. 40.
75 Calder was also very interested at this time in the orrery genre.
76 Len Lye, 'Voice and Colour', in Curnow and Horrocks (eds), *Figures in Motion*, p. 45.
77 Len Lye, 'The Man who was Colourblind', *Sight and Sound*, vol. 9, Spring 1940, p. 6.
78 Len Lye, 'Television: New Axes to Grind', *Sight and Sound*, vol. 8, Summer 1939, p. 65.
79 His essays on the subject include 'Television: New Axes to Grind', *ibid.*, pp. 65–70; 'A Case for More News in Television', *Life and Letters Today*, vol. 22, 1939, pp. 238–45; and 'In Search of a Technique for Television', *The Journal of the Television Society*, vol. 3, no. 4, 1940.
80 This was Laura Riding's phrase but she was evidently quoting Lye (*Len Lye and the Problem of Popular Films*, p. 39).
81 Lye saw individualism at work even in ancient and tribal art. A possible gap in his aesthetics is the fact that it has very little to say about communal or collaborative aspects of art.
82 *Time*, pp. 50–51.
83 See, for example, *Documentary News Letter*, March 1940, p. 6.
84 *Ibid.*
85 Wendell Willkie, *One World*, Simon and Schuster, New York, 1943.
86 Newman was quoted in *Artforum*, November 1973, p. 38. Also see Lawrence Alloway, 'The Biomorphic Forties', *Artforum*, September 1965.
87 Harold Rosenberg, 'The American Action Painters', *ARTnews*, vol. 51, no. 8, December 1952, pp. 48–50 (reprinted in *The Tradition of the New*, Thames and Hudson, London, 1962).
88 Letter from Len to Ann Lye ('Dearest of all leaves'), undated. And see Horrocks, *Len Lye: A Biography*, pp. 230–33.
89 Larry Rivers, 'The Cedar Bar', *New York*, 5 November 19[illegible]. The present Cedar Tavern is a few blocks north of the original location.
90 Letter to Wystan Curnow, 1 June 1981.
91 Len obtained a divorce from Jane in 1948. He and Ann always regarded each other as the most important person in their lives, but they shocked some of their friends when they both agreed, from the beginning, to have an open marriage. (See Horrocks, *Len Lye: A Biography*, pp. 316–17 and p. 369.)
92 Some of Lye's unsuccessful 'promos' or 'pilot films' have survived: *Life's Musical Moment* (aimed at *Life* magazine), *Station Prime Time* and *Pictures for Percussion* (aimed at television channels).
93 As a trial run, Lye made a new version of *Full Fathom Five*, drawing and painting Shakespeare's poem from *The Tempest* onto black film to accompany the recording John Gielgud had made for him in 1935. This short film has recently been restored.
94 I do not know the origin of the phrase, but it is often linked with phenomenology. For example: Hubert L. Dreyfus and Mark A. Wrathall (eds), *A Companion to Phenomenology and Existentialism*, Blackwell Publishing, Malden (Massachusetts), 2006, p. [illegible]; or Ram Adhar Mall, *Experience and Reason: The Phenomenology of Husserl and Its Relation to Hume's Philosophy*, Springer, New York, 1973, p. 131. Lye himself used it in his unpublished essay on 'Empathy (Concerning Coloured Hearing' where he writes: 'It's the awareness of the experience of experience that matters to the subject-matter of "I".'
95 All the writing described here is as yet unpublished.
96 Amos Vogel's Cinema 16 series and the Museum of Modern Art were the most important regular outlets for avant-garde films in New York in the early 1950s. Lye was a member of Cinema 16's 'Committee of Sponsors' (*Wide Angle*, vol. 19, no. 2, 19[illegible], p. 170).
97 Interview with Francis Lee, 1980.
98 Adrienne Mancia and Willard Van Dyke, 'The Artist as Film-maker: Len Lye', *Art in America*, vol. 54, 1966, p. 105. *Dom* was made by Walerian Borowszyk and Jan Lenica. Other American film-makers praised by the jury included Stan Brakhage, Kenneth Anger and Hilary Harris. Of the 400 films entered, 133 were screened at Brussels.
99 Len Lye, 'Is Film Art?', in Curnow and Horrocks (eds), *Figures of Motion*, p. 52. The essay does not appear to have been published until 1963 when it appeared in the Summer issue of *Film Culture* (no. 29, pp. 38–39). In that context, Lye was unfortunately preaching to a relatively small audience of the converted.
100 Len Lye, 'Is Film Art?', in Curnow and Horrocks (eds), *Figures of Motion*, p. 54.
101 *Ibid.*, p. 53.
102 'Len Lye Speaks at the Film-makers' Cinematheque', *Film Culture*, no. 44, Spring 1967, p. 49 (reprinted as 'Getting Out of the Griffith Technique', in Curnow and Horrocks [eds], *Figures of Motion*).
103 Interview with Ann Lye, 1980.
104 There is a useful 'Chronology', in *Force Fields: Phases of the Kinetic*, Hayward Gallery, London, 2000, pp. 179–223.
105 See, for example, Peter Selz, 'The Berkeley Symposium of Kinetic Sculpture', *Art and Artists*, vol. 1, no. 11, February 1967, p. 26ff (a panel discussion between Lye, Rickey, Takis and others); and 'The Berkeley Symposium (Part II)' in the following issue (March 1967), pp. 46 ff.
106 'Voyeurama Voyeurama', *East Village Other*, issue of 1[illegible] June–1 July 1966.
107 On Lye and drugs, see Horrocks, *Len Lye: A Biography*, pp. 315–16.
108 Horrocks (ed.), *Happy Moments*.
109 Horrocks, *Len Lye: A Biography*, p. 338.
110 *Ibid.*, p. 344.
111 Hamish Keith, *The Big Picture: The History of New Zealand Art from 1642*, Random House, Auckland, 2007.
112 Held in Auckland on 3–4 September 2005. Organised by Miriam Harris and Eu Jin Chua, and sponsored by Unitec New Zealand and the Moving Image Centre.
113 At the Museu d'Art Contemporani de Barcelona and at the Hayward Gallery in London.

THREE THE ART OF MOTION

1 Gilles Deleuze, *Cinema 1: The Movement-Image*, Hugh Tomlinson and Barbara Habberjam (trans.), The Athlone Press, London, 1983, p. 55.

2 Nicholas Schöffer, *Perturbation et Chronocratie*, Editions Denoël-Gonthier, Paris, 1978; and George Rickey, *Constructivism: Origins and Evolution*, George Braziller, New York, 1995. Also see Rickey's essay 'The Morphology of Movement: A Study of Kinetic Art', *Art Journal*, vol. 22, no. 4, Summer 1963, pp. 220–31. Compare Lye's comment in his (unpublished) 1965 essay 'Notes on Programmed Sculpture': 'My work does not fit into either the constructivist or the "mobile" category of kinetic art .... I would much rather consider myself an "heir" of the Australian Aboriginal with his boomerang and bullroarer than an "heir to constructivism".'

3 Len Lye, 'Tangible Motion Sculpture', in Wystan Curnow and Roger Horrocks (eds), *Figures of Motion: Len Lye Selected Writings*, Auckland University Press / Oxford University Press, Auckland, 1984, p. 75.

4 Len Lye, 'The Art that Moves', in Curnow and Horrocks (eds), *Figures of Motion*, p. 78.

5 For example, 'Optical and Kinetic Art' in 1967 at the Tate Gallery, or 'Force Fields: Phases of the Kinetic' in 2000 at the Hayward Gallery – both important exhibitions but Lye would have considered them too wide-ranging.

6 Letter to Lye, 3 December 1929.

7 David Judd, 'New York Notes', *Art International*, vol. 9, May 1965, p. 65.

8 Len Lye, 'The Art that Moves', in Curnow and Horrocks (eds), *Figures of Motion*, p. 79.

9 R. E. Allen (ed.), *The Concise Oxford Dictionary of Current English*, Clarendon Press, Oxford, eighth edition, 1990, p. 436.

10 Paul Klee, *Pedagogical Sketchbook*, Frederick A. Praeger, New York, 1969, p. 16. (First published in 1925.)

11 Wassily Kandinsky, *Point and Line to Plane*, Dover, New York, 1979, p. 57. (First published in 1926.)

12 Len Lye, 'Tangible Motion Sculpture', in Curnow and Horrocks (eds), *Figures of Motion*, p. 75.

13 Len Lye, 'The Art that Moves', in Curnow and Horrocks (eds), *Figures of Motion*, p. 81.

14 Len Lye, 'Voice and Colour', in Curnow and Horrocks (eds), *Figures of Motion*, p. 43.

15 Len Lye, 'The Art that Moves', in Curnow and Horrocks (eds), *Figures of Motion*, p. 83.

16 Lye talking with John Matthews and Paul Fiondella, New York, 9 November 1978 (tape recording).

17 *Ibid.*

18 Letter to Wystan Curnow and the author, September 1979.

19 Len Lye, 'Voice and Colour', in Curnow and Horrocks (eds), *Figures of Motion*, p. 43.

20 The films include *Colour Flight* and *Swinging the Lambeth Walk.* The sculpture *Wave* is described by Len Lye, 'Considering a Temple', in Curnow and Horrocks (eds), *Figures of Motion*, pp. 88–89, and in the section on *Wave* on the tape of Lye talking with John Matthews and Paul Fiondella, New York, 9 November 1978.

21 From Lye's NYU lecture notes.

22 Lye talking with John Matthews and Paul Fiondella, New York, 9 November 1978 (description of 'Rotating Harmonic').

23 Len Lye, 'A Note on Dance and Film', in Curnow and Horrocks (eds), *Figures of Motion*, p. 56.

24 Author's interview with Steve Jones, 1980.

25 *Focus*, no. 4, December 1935, p. 60. (A magazine published by Laura Riding and Robert Graves.)

26 Len Lye, 'Voice and Colour', in Curnow and Horrocks (eds), *Figures of Motion*, p. 45.

27 I wonder if Lye read a 1957 *Art News* essay by Harold Rosenberg on Hans Hofmann which included, 'in painting, the primary agency of physical motion (as distinct from illusionary representation of motion, as with the Futurists) is the line, conceived not as ... edge, contour or connective but as a stroke or figure (in the sense of "figure skating")'. This passage was quoted in Rosenberg's *The Tradition of the New*, Paladin, London, 1970, footnote p. 38.

28 The games come from Horrocks (ed.), *Happy Moments*; and 'Somewhat Autobiographically' (unpublished ms).

29 From Lye's lecture notes, 17 May 1967.

30 Horrocks (ed.), *Happy Moments*, pp. 39–40.

31 A hand-written comment by Lye on Gerald Holton's essay, 'Science and the Deallegorization of Motion', in Gyorgy Kepes (ed.), *The Nature and Art of Motion*, Braziller, New York, 1965, p. 24. Here Lye sees the 'brain' as equivalent to the 'intellect', whereas today it would be more usual to speak of the brain as a physical site for receiving 'sensory, neuro-motor' information *as well as* for performing intellectual processes.

32 From Lye's New York University lecture notes, 13 October 1966.

33 This is the title of a 1932 composition by Duke Ellington with lyrics by Irving Mills.

34 *Webster's New Twentieth Century Dictionary of the English Language*, William Collins / Simon and Schuster, second edition (unabridged), 1980, p. 1002

35 From 'The 'I-Me' and the Atom in the Age of Freedom' (unpublished ms).

36 Lye knew these terms from the work of psychologist Nina Bull.

37 See, for example, Barbara Montero's paper 'Proprioception as an Aesthetic Sense', *Journal of Aesthetics and Art Criticism*, vol. 64, no. 2, Spring 2006, pp. 231–42 (the quotation is from pp. 231–32); and Jonathan Cole and Barbara Montero, 'Affective Proprioception', *Janus Head*, vol. 9, no. 2, 2007, pp. 299–317.

38 Montero, 'Proprioception as an Aesthetic Sense', p. 240.

39 Len Lye, 'The Art that Moves', in Curnow and Horrocks (eds), *Figures of Motion*, p. 82.

40 'Somewhat Autobiographically' (unpublished ms), 1975 version, p. 57.

41 This was a variation on the sexual embrace represented by his sculpture *Unit* which started out as a more explicit version of Brancusi's *Kiss* (Andrew Bogle [ed.], *Len Lye: A Personal Mythology*, Auckland City Art Gallery, Auckland, 1980, p. 74).

42 *Ibid.*

43 Len Lye, 'Film That Needs No Camera ...', *The Australian*, 21 December 1968. Lye's idea is remarkably similar to the scientific concept of body maps, as described in *The Body has a Mind of its Own* by Sandra and Matthew Blakeslee (Random House, New York, 2007), pp. 21–22.

44 Compare Rosalind E. Krauss's description of Brancusi's *The Beginning of the World*: 'the smooth shape of the top half is contorted by myriad and changing visual incidents .... It is this differential [between the upper and lower halves] that gives to the geometry of the form something of the kinesthetic quality that recalls the feeling of the back of one's head, resting heavily on a pillow, while the face floats, weightless and unencumbered, toward sleep', *Passages in Modern Sculpture*, MIT Press, Cambridge (Mass.), 1994, pp. 86–87.

45 Dore Ashton, 'Vision and Sound: Today's Art at Buffalo', *Studio International*, vol. 169, May 1965, pp. 211–12.

46 Emily Genauer, 'Sensation and Sensibility', *Herald Tribune*, March 1965 (day of month not known).

47 *Len Lye: Two Studios*, documentary, 1980.

48 Len Lye, 'Somewhat Autobiographically', unpublished ms, p. 63. Drew Leder's *The Absent Body* (University of Chicago Press, Chicago, 1990) comments on some aspects of this tradition.

49 See Charles Olson's *Collected Prose*, Donald Allen and Benjamin Friedlander (eds), University of California Press, Berkeley, 1997, p. 179 ('Proprioception') and p. 239 ('Projective Verse').

50 Olson did become aware of Merleau-Ponty's work in the 1960s.

51 'The Berkeley Symposium (Part II)', *Art and Artists*, vol. 1, March 1967, p. 46.

52 'Somewhat Autobiographically', p. 3. Also see Roger Horrocks, 'Len Lye: Reading with the Body', in David A. Gerstner and Janet Staiger (eds), *Authorship and Film*, Routledge, New York, pp. 175–92.

53 Semir Zeki and Mathew Lamb, 'The Neurology of Kinetic Art', *Brain*, vol. 117, 1994, p. 611. Zeki discussed the subject more fully in his important book *Inner Vision: An Exploration of Art and the Brain*, Oxford University Press, Oxford, 1999 (especially pp. 133–64), where he argues that kinetic art is 'perhaps the best example of how art can be, and is, tailored to the physiology of a visual

area' (p. 153). It is interesting that Zeki, who seems to associate 'form' with static shape, speaks of 'motion that devours and destroys form' (p. 159), in contrast to Lye who sought to theorise form *within* motion.

54 *Ibid.*, p. 628 and p. 630.
55 *Ibid.*, p. 608.
56 *Ibid.*, p. 632.
57 *Ibid.*, cf. p. 616 ('other routes').
58 Zeki, *Inner Vision*, p. 10.
59 Vilayanur S. Ramachandran, 'Mirror Neurons and Imitation Learning as the Driving Force Behind 'the great leap forward" in Human Evolution', *Edge* (website: www.edge.org posted 2006).
60 See, for example, Raymond Tallis's critique, 'Licence my Roving Hands', *The Times Literary Supplement*, no. 5480, 11 April 2008, pp. 13–15. For a more sympathetic view, see John Onians, *Neuroparthistory: From Aristotle and Pliny to Baxandall and Zeki*, Yale University Press, New Haven, 2007.
61 'Notes 2 (Empathy)', unpublished note.
62 David Freedberg and Vittorio Gallese, 'Motion, Emotion and Empathy in Esthetic Experience', *Trends in Cognitive Sciences*, vol. 11, no. 5, 2007, p. 198.
63 A psychoanalytical example is the work of Harry Stack Sullivan. See his posthumously published *The Interpersonal Theory of Psychiatry* (1953). Rudolf Arnheim in his reconsideration of Herbert S. Langfeld's *The Aesthetic Attitude* notes that 'Freud, who had read [Theodor] Lipps with much attention, developed in his early papers the concept of projection as a defense mechanism – a direct parallel with, and perhaps an offshoot of, the theory of empathy' (*The Journal of Aesthetics and Art Criticism*, vol. 38, no. 2, Winter 1980, p. 201).
64 From 'You Be Me: Image, Empathy and Experience', an unpublished Lye essay written circa July 1946.
65 E. G. Boring, H. S. Langfeld, H. P. Weld and collaborators, *Introduction to Psychology*, John Wiley, New York, 1939, pp. 274–76. The 'Empathy' section was by Langfeld. It is interesting that this section also referred to Herbert Spencer.
66 Quoted in Dorothy Seckler's 'Can Painting be Taught?', *Art News*, vol. 50, no. 1, March 1951, p. 63.
67 See, for example, Carl Rogers, *Client-Centred Therapy: Its Current Practice, Implications and Theory*, Constable, London, 1951.
68 W. H. Sheldon, with the collaboration of S. S. Stevens, *The Varieties of Temperament: A Psychology of Constitutional Differences*, Harper, New York, 1942.
69 Nina Bull, *The Body and its Mind: An Introduction to Attitude Psychology*, Las Americas Publishing Company, New York, 1962. (This tradition in American psychology had begun with William James and Carl Lange and the so-called 'James-Lange hypothesis'. Bull discussed her relationship with this tradition in the paper 'Towards a Clarification of the Concept of Emotion', *Psychosomatic Medicine*, vol. 7, no. 4, July 1945, pp. 210–14.)
70 From the section on 'Empathy' in the unpublished ms 'You Be Me'.
71 'Notes 2 (Empathy)', unpublished note.
72 Lipps wrote in 1903, 'When I am watching an acrobat walking on a suspended wire, I feel myself so inside of him.' Quoted by Björn Vickhoff in 'H-speech: The Musical Self: A Phenomenological Approach to Music & Emotion', *Kapten Mnemos Kolumbarium: A festschrift for Helge Malmgrens*, Umea University (on-line publication), 2005, p. 246 (http://www.phil.gu.se/posters/festskrift2/mnemo_vickhoff.pdf). Compare the Langfeld quotation in Chapter 1; and in *Introduction to Psychology* he wrote, 'when spectators watch an acrobat climb to the top of a pole balanced on the head of a colleague and swing back and forth with the tottering pole, the whole crowd sways in unison' (p. 273).
73 'The Sedentaries' [Les Assis], in *Selected Verse Poems of Arthur Rimbaud*, trans. Norman Cameron, Hogarth Press, London, 1942, p. 18. The translator was Lye's friend, and this volume of Rimbaud's poetry was one of Lye's favourite books. To quote the original French version of this stanza:

Ils ont greffé dans des amours épileptiques
Leur fantasque ossature aux grands squelettes noirs
De leurs chaises ; leurs pieds aux barreaux rachitiques
S'entrelacent pour les matins et pour les soirs !

74 Len Lye, 'The Art that Moves', in Curnow and Horrocks (eds), *Figures of Motion*, pp. 82–83.
75 Curnow and Horrocks (eds), *Figures of Motion*, pp. 82–84.
76 Lecture notes, 1 April 1968. Hiroshige's image is discussed in this chapter under the heading 'The Experience of Stillness'.
77 Curnow and Horrocks (eds), *Figures of Motion*, p. 83.
78 Len Lye, 'Considering a Temple', in Curnow and Horrocks (eds), *Figures of Motion*, p. 88; and Len Lye, 'The Art that Moves', in Curnow and Horrocks (eds), *Figures of Motion*, p. 80.
79 Lye talking with John Matthews and Paul Fiondella, New York, 9 November 1978.
80 Curnow and Horrocks (eds), *Figures of Motion*, p. 51.
81 From Len Lye, 'Self at the Prow in Waters of Lard' in 'Song Time Stuff', *Figures of Motion*, p. 116.
82 Some similar aspects of instinct have been explored in a recent bestseller – Malcolm Gladwell's *Blink: The Power of Thinking without Thinking*, Little, Brown and Co., New York, 2005.
83 Ted Hughes, 'Thrushes', *New Selected Poems 1957–1994*, Faber and Faber, London, 1995, pp. 39–40.
84 Curnow and Horrocks (eds), *Figures of Motion*, p. 123 and p. 125. Hughes had been influenced by D. H. Lawrence, another writer with a strong interest in non-human and intuitive forms of consciousness.
85 P. D. MacLean, 'Man and his Animal Brains', *Modern Medicine*, 3 February 1964, pp. 95–106.
86 For a detailed presentation of MacLean's theory, see his book *The Triune Brain in Evolution: Role in Paleocerebral Functions*, Plenum Press, New York, 1990.
87 See Lye's essay 'Gene-Deep Myth', in Curnow and Horrocks (eds), *Figures of Motion*, pp. 90–94.
88 MacLean had mixed feelings about this shift of focus. He suggested to Kelly G. Lambert during an interview in 2002 that 'the most unfortunate event that ever occurred in the history of biological psychiatry was [the] discovery of a new technique to stain neurons because neuroscientists tackled the microstructure questions and abandoned their curiosity concerning the systems of the brain' (Kelly G. Lambert, 'The Life and Career of Paul MacLean: A Journey toward Neurobiological and Social Harmony', *Physiology and Behavior*, vol. 79, no. 3, August 2003). MacLean died in 2007.
89 Len Lye, 'Considering a Temple', in Curnow and Horrocks (eds), *Figures of Motion*, pp. 87–88. Lye, playing with a saw, demonstrated the process to Hamish Keith in the 1980 TVNZ *Kaleidoscope* documentary about Lye.
90 Lye talking with John Matthews and Paul Fiondella, New York, 9 November 1978.
91 *Ibid.*
92 *Ibid.*
93 Author's interview with Hilary Harris, 1980.
94 Marina Estela Graça, 'Cinematic Motion by Hand', in *Animation Studies* [on-line journal], vol. 1, 2006 (viewed May 2008 at http://journal.animationstudies.org/2006/06/26/marina-estela-graca-cinematic-motion-by-hand). Graça also writes: 'By overwhelming the cinematic technical workings with the gesture of the hand, "cameraless" authors exposed its technical scheme to contingency, thus opening the production process to new unpredictable expressive and communicative possibilities. This corresponds to a renewed way of comprehending technology by, simultaneously, revealing the human reality it contains and physiologically incorporating it.'
95 Norman McLaren, 'Animated Films', *Documentary Film News*, May 1948, pp. 52–53 (quoted by Graça in 'Cinematic Motion by Hand').
96 Len Lye, 'No Trouble', in Curnow and Horrocks (eds), *Figures of Motion*, p. 112.
97 See David Bodanis's book *$e=mc^2$: A Biography of the World's Most Famous Equation*, Macmillan, London, 2000, p. 11 ff.
98 Email to the author, 15 May 2008.
99 Len Lye, 'No Trouble', in Curnow and Horrocks (eds), *Figures of Motion*, p. 83.
100 *Ibid.*, p. 85.

101 See 'The Absolute Truth of the Happiness Acid', unpublished essay, 1968.
102 *Ibid.*
103 Len Lye, 'The Art that Moves', in Curnow and Horrocks (eds), *Figures of Motion*, p. 85. Of course, this was not a static 'image'. (The term 'image' could carry the same meaning for him as 'figure of motion'.)
104 *Ibid.*, p. 86.
105 Email to the author, 15 May 2008.
106 Charles Olson's *Collected Prose*, Donald Allen and Benjamin Friedlander (eds), University of California Press, Berkeley, 1997, p. 239 ('Projective Verse').
107 For example, Lye said of kinetic art, 'We have arrived at a general idea of energy . . . [such as] its enactment in terms of visual motion which bore the impress of the individuality of its creator, in the creation of a kinetic work of art' (Len Lye, 'The Art that Moves', in Curnow and Horrocks (eds), *Figures of Motion*, p. 87).
108 Len Lye, 'The Art that Moves', in Curnow and Horrocks (eds), *Figures of Motion*, pp. 80–81.
109 Len Lye, 'Is Film Art?', in Curnow and Horrocks (eds), *Figures of Motion*, p. 52.
110 Len Lye, 'Tangible Motion Sculpture', in Curnow and Horrocks (eds), *Figures of Motion*, p. 78.
111 Len Lye, 'The Art that Moves', in Curnow and Horrocks (eds), *Figures of Motion*, p. 81.
112 Len Lye, 'Is Film Art?', in Curnow and Horrocks (eds), *Figures of Motion*, p. 52.
113 'My Model', unpublished ms. Cf. Horrocks, *Len Lye: A Biography*, pp. 30– ; and 'Chair in your Hair' in the sequence 'Song Time Stuff' (in Curnow and Horrocks [eds], *Figures of Motion*, p. 114).
114 See Len Lye, 'The Art that Moves', in Curnow and Horrocks (eds), *Figures of Motion*, p. 81.
115 Horrocks (ed.), *Happy Moments*, p. 42.
116 Len Lye, 'The Art that Moves', in Curnow and Horrocks (eds), *Figures of Motion*, p. 81
117 See 'Living Energy', in *Len Lye Talks about Art*, a DVD produced by the Len Lye Foundation and the Govett-Brewster Art Gallery in 2003.
118 See Len Lye, 'No Trouble', in Curnow and Horrocks (eds), *Figures of Motion*, p. 105.
119 Attachment to letter from Lye to Ernest Smith, 16 February 1979.
120 Len Lye, 'Night Tree', in *A Brief Description of the Whole World*, no. 3, June 1996, p. 9.
121 *Ibid.*, pp. 6–7.
122 See Len Lye, 'Considering a Temple', in Curnow and Horrocks (eds), *Figures of Motion*, p. 87 ff; or 'Temple of Lightning', in *Len Lye Talks about Art*.
123 Len Lye, 'The Art that Moves', in Curnow and Horrocks (eds), *Figures of Motion*, p. 81.
124 See, for example, Roger Copeland and Marshall Cohen (eds), *What is Dance?: Readings in Theory and Criticism*, Oxford University Press, Oxford, 1983, pp. 473–502.
125 Among Hindu gods, Shiva, the lord of yoga, performed Anandatandava or the dance of bliss, which symbolised 'the cosmic cycles of creation and destruction, the rhythms of birth and death and the perennial movements of the cosmos' (Yana Zafiri, 'Chorus and Dance in the Ancient World', in Marianne McDonald and J. Michael Walton [eds], *Cambridge Companion to Greek and Roman Theatre*, Cambridge University Press, Cambridge, 2007, p. 47).
126 Copeland and Cohen (eds), *What is Dance?*, p. 473.
127 Horrocks, *Len Lye: A Biography*, pp. 54–55.
128 *Ibid.*
129 'The Fire', unpublished ms. For more context, see Horrocks, *Len Lye: A Biography*, p. 88.
130 Len Lye, 'Notes on a Short Colour Film', in Curnow and Horrocks (eds), *Figures of Motion*, p. 51.
131 Curnow and Horrocks (eds), *Figures of Motion*, p. 56.
132 From Selma Jeanne Cohen, 'Next Week, *Swan Lake*: Reflections on Dance and Dancers', in Copeland and Cohen (eds), *What is Dance?* p. 345.
133 *Ibid.*, p. 349.
134 Selma Jeanne Cohen, 'Dance as an Art of Imitation', in Copeland and Cohen (eds), *What is Dance?*, p. 21.
135 Curnow and Horrocks (eds), *Figures of Motion*, p. 55. Merce Cunningham is widely recognised as one of the most innovative figures in modern choreography.
136 Wayne Laird recorded the sounds they produced for his remarkable CD, *Len Lye: Composing Motion* (Atoll ACD305).
137 As presented in the exhibition 'Five Fountains and a Firebush', curated by Tyler Cann at the Govett-Brewster Art Gallery, December 2007–February 2008.
138 See Lye's essay 'Tangible Motion Sculpture', in Curnow and Horrocks (eds), *Figures of Motion* (for example, p. 76).
139 Roger Copeland, 'Merce Cunningham and the Politics of Perception', in Copeland and Cohen (eds), *What is Dance?*, p. 308 [Copeland's italics].
140 Interview with the author, 1980. See Horrocks, *Len Lye: A Biography*, p. 374.
141 Len Lye, 'The Art that Moves', in Curnow and Horrocks (eds), *Figures of Motion*, p. 84.

FOUR THE FILMS

1 Letter from John Taylor on tape, 1981.
2 Alberto Cavalcanti, 'Presenting Len Lye' (a lecture originally given to the Netherlands Historisch Filmarchief), *Sight and Sound*, vol. 16, Winter 1947/48, pp. 135.
3 Gretchen Weinberg, 'Interview with Len Lye', *Film Culture*, no. 29, Summer 1963, p. 42.
4 For example, Harold A. Albert, 'Diary of a Young Man', *Sunday Mercury* (Birmingham), 8 December 1935. Compare Cavalcanti's comment, 'Perhaps the greatest of Len Lye's experiments were with colour' ('Presenting Len Lye', p. 135).
5 David Curtis, *Experimental Cinema*, Studio Vista, London, 1971, p. 36.
6 Jeffrey Richards and Dorothy Sheridan (eds), *Mass Observation at the Movies*, Routledge, London, 1987, pp. 445 ff. The film most favoured by the report was 'the least cinematographic' (p. 454).
7 Cavalcanti, 'Presenting Len Lye', p. 135.
8 Reported by Basil Wright in G. Roy Levin, *Documentary Explorations*, Anchor Press, Garden City (New York), 1971, p. 39.
9 'Made a Film without a Camera', *Daily Express*, September 1935 (precise date unknown).
10 Ernest Betts, 'Coloured Novelty', *Daily Express*, 22 September 1935.
11 Weinberg, 'Interview with Len Lye', p. 44.
12 *London Film Society*, programme notes no. 33, 1929.
13 Len Lye, 'The Tusalava Model', in Robert Russett and Cecile Starr, *Experimental Animation: Origins of a New Art*, Da Capo Press, New York, 1976, p. 70.
14 Wystan Curnow, 'An Interview with Len Lye', *Art New Zealand*, no. 17, 1980, p. 54. There were other awkward aspects to *Tusalava* such as the way Lye drew the upwards flow of dots (or single-celled creatures) at the beginning by repeating the same stencil pattern, half-a-dozen times per frame.
15 Len Lye, 'No Trouble', in Wystan Curnow and Roger Horrocks (eds), *Figures of Motion: Len Lye Selected Writings*, Auckland University Press/Oxford University Press, Auckland, 1984, p. 105. Any unattributed quotations in this account of *Tusalava* are from the same source (pp. 103–7).
16 Lye's account is in 'No Trouble', in Curnow and Horrocks (eds), *Figures of Motion*. NB: The BFI's prints have the embryo on the left, and Tyler Cann has found some preparatory drawings that support that orientation, so the question remains open.
17 In Len Lye, 'No Trouble', in Curnow and Horrocks (eds), *Figures of Motion*, Lye says '8 [drawings] a day is the going and that equals one second of projection' (p. 103). It was not unusual for animators to film each drawing twice. This would suggest a speed of sixteen frames per second. Granted, *Tusalava* was screened after the arrival of sound, by which time the projector may have been running at 24 frames per second. There was a letter from Ellitt to Lye urging him to screen the film at 16 fps to allow more time for his music.
18 Len Lye, 'No Trouble', in Curnow and Horrocks (eds), *Figures of Motion*, p. 103.

19 He described his plans in 'No Trouble' and in Oswell Blakeston's essay, 'Len Lye's Visuals', *Architectural Review*, vol. 72, July 1932, p. 25.

20 He would have read this in F. J. Gillen and Baldwin Spencer's *The Native Tribes of Central Australia* (1899) with its striking illustrations of Aboriginal art, one of which he copied into his notebook. I also suspect that what I have called the embryo shape was influenced by the Maori tiki, which he had used as the motif for a carving. This suggested influence has, however, been challenged.

21 *Close Up*, February 1930, p. 155.

22 Ellitt had written a two-piano accompaniment for *Tusalava*. Unfortunately, he and Lye were unable to afford to have this music added to the film, and subsequently the score was lost. Later Lye suggested Eugene Goosens' *Rhythmic Dance* for two pianos as a replacement. For a more detailed account of what happened, see Roger Horrocks, *Len Lye: A Biography*, Auckland University Press, Auckland, 2001, pp. 93–94. In recent years, many composers have written their own music for *Tusalava*.

23 Joseph Kennedy, 'Len Lye – Composer of Motion', *Millimeter*, vol. 5, 1977, p. 20.

24 I am not absolutely certain that Lye made such a film, but Jack Ellitt spoke of it, and there was a review in *Life and Letters Today*. (See Horrocks, *Len Lye: A Biography*, pp. 134–35; or *Life and Letters Today*, vol. 17, no. 9, Autumn 1937, p. 152.)

25 The group recorded the track in August 1938 during a visit to England.

26 According to Wikipedia, the dance is 'beguine' but the music is spelled 'biguine'.

27 Len Lye, 'A Note on Dance and Film', in Curnow and Horrocks (eds), *Figures of Motion*, p. 56. Lye's post-1958 kinetic sculptures also have a very fluid sense of space. At rest, they are three-dimensional objects but when set in rapid motion they produce various illusions of 'virtual volume'.

28 This may have been one of the reasons he began exhibiting strips of film (see Horrocks, *Len Lye: A Biography*, p. 411, footnote 19). This remained very much a second priority for him, though he came to attach more importance to individual frames in the 1960s when he began to speculate about 'old brain' information unconsciously encoded within some of the frames.

29 All time indications are approximate. They were worked out via DVDs, so there may be a few seconds' difference if one is watching a film version projected at 24 fps.

30 Ray Thorburn in his 'Len Lye Film Notes' (unpublished, dated June/July 1978). For a more detailed analysis of the film, see my essay 'Swinging the Lambeth Walk: The Hand of the Filmmaker', in Tyler Cann and Wystan Curnow (eds), *Len Lye*, Govett-Brewster Art Gallery/Len Lye Foundation, New Plymouth, 2009.

31 'Len Lye Speaks at the Film-makers' Cinematheque', *Film Culture*, no. 44, Spring 1967, pp. 49–51 (reprinted as 'Getting Out of the Griffith Technique', in Curnow and Horrocks [eds], *Figures of Motion*, pp. 50–51).

32 Len Lye, letter to Roger Horrocks and Wystan Curnow, 28 February 1979 (unpublished).

33 Len Lye, 'Song Time', *London Bulletin*, nos. 18–20, June 1940, p. 30.

34 Lye pointed out this connection in an early newspaper interview ('Len Lye The English Disney', *Sunday Referee*, 10 November 1935); and Cavalcanti noted it in *Sight and Sound*, Winter 1947–48, p. 135. Subsequently, this connection seems to have been forgotten.

35 Letter from Jack Ellitt, 12 September 1981.

36 See Len Lye, 'Voice and Colour', 'Experiment in Colour' and 'Notes on a Short Colour Film', in Curnow and Horrocks (eds), *Figures of Motion*, pp. 42–51.

37 Len Lye, 'Experiment in Colour', in Curnow and Horrocks (eds), *Figures of Motion*, p. 49.

38 *Ibid.*, p. 48.

39 Len Lye, 'Voice and Colour', in Curnow and Horrocks (eds), *Figures of Motion*, p. 44.

40 The three positives had a gelatin relief contoured surface because of the use of an 'imbibition' printing process. (The film strip 'imbibed' colour from the three dye-soaked strips.)

41 See Len Lye, 'Experiment in Colour', p. 46, and 'Voice and Colour', p. 49, in Curnow and Horrocks (eds), *Figures of Motion*.

42 Adrian Klein, *Coloured Light: An Art Medium*, Technical Press, London, third edition, 1937, p. xxxix. NB: Another Gasparcolor project that Lye began around this time (October 1936) but did not complete was 'Fireworks' (of which a few frames have survived).

43 Len Lye, 'Experiment in Colour', in Curnow and Horrocks (eds), *Figures of Motion*, p. 47. 'Film-ballet' is how its producer Cavalcanti described *Rainbow Dance* in 'Presenting Len Lye', p. 135. In 'Voice and Colour', Lye used the phrase 'sensory ballet' (Curnow and Horrocks [eds], *Figures of Motion*, p. 45).

44 The clarinet player Filiberto Rico was among the first to bring Cuban music to Paris. Recorded in 1934, *Tony's Wife* is available on the CD *Rico's Creole Band Vol. 2* (Harlequin HQ CD41), where it runs for 2m 44s. Lye and Ellitt edited out the vocal and extended the remaining music by repeating certain passages. The film begins with an (uncredited) piece of orchestral music.

45 See Ian Christie's essay, 'Colour, Music, Dance, Motion: Len Lye in England, 1927–44', in Jean-Michel Bouhours and Roger Horrocks (eds), *Len Lye*, Centre Pompidou, Paris, 2000, p. 189. The Group Theatre produced plays by T. S. Eliot and W. H. Auden. Doone sought to revive theatre as 'an art of the body', an approach reminiscent (as Christie observes) of Meyerhold's bio-mechanics.

46 Len Lye, 'Voice and Colour', in Curnow and Horrocks (eds), *Figures in Motion*, p. 45.

47 See McLaren's comments, quoted by Russett and Starr, *Experimental Animation*, p. 117.

48 Letter, 25 March 1981. As another response, a blogger interested in graphic design recently came across *Rainbow Dance* for the first time on YouTube, saw that it was an extraordinary film and commented: 'A great animation. In technical terms it would be quite easy to do this nowadays with After Effects and other programmes. But this is not driven by software. It is the product of Lye's imagination' (http://digitalscribbling.blogspot.com/, 7 January 2008 post, 'Len Lye').

49 Letter from Lye to John Halas, 15 January 1958.

50 The recordings were: 'Anacaona', 'La Havane à Paris', 'Conga dans la Nuit', 'Pour Toi Madonne' and 'Adieu Mon Amour' (letter from Barbara Ker-Seymer, 29 June 1981). The group was then playing in England on the variety circuit.

51 Film-makers such as Eisenstein had attempted to present such titles rhythmically, but it could be argued that their use in *Trade Tattoo* was even more kinetic.

52 The GPO film sources included the recently completed *Night Mail* (1936).

53 Malcolm LeGrice, *Abstract Film and Beyond*, Studio Vista, London, 1977, p. 71.

54 Keith Griffiths interview with Jack Ellitt, 1987.

55 See the letter from John Halas to Len Lye, 2 January 195[illegible] and Happé's memories of the film in John Halas and Roger Manvell's *The Technique of Film Animation*, Focal Press, London, 19[illegible]6, pp. 87–88. For Lye's comment, see his letter to John Halas, 15 January 1958.

56 Len Lye, 'Experiment in Colour', in Curnow and Horrocks (eds), *Figures of Motion*, p. 48.

57 On screen, the title of *N or NW* does not have any periods.

58 See Len Lye's articles, 'Television – New Axes to Grind', *Sight and Sound*, vol. 8, 1939, pp. 238–45; and 'Len Lye Speaks at the Film-makers' Cinematheque', *Film Culture*, no. 44, Spring 196[illegible], pp. 49–51 (reprinted as 'Getting Out of the Griffith Technique', in Curnow and Horrocks [eds], *Figures of Motion*, p. 55). Lye's other films contain examples of the kind of transition he had in mind – for example, the shift from tennis court to bed in *Rainbow Dance*, and the abbreviated car assembly in *Rhythm*. One wonders if Lye knew the sequence in *Sunrise* (1927), directed by F. W. Murnau, where the development of a relationship is conveyed by changing backgrounds as a couple walks along.

59 Cavalcanti, 'Presenting Len Lye', p. 135. Other British film-makers of the period who liked the film included Basil Wright ('The Cinema', *The Spectator*, 25 February 1938) and Paul Rotha (*Documentary Diary*, p. 221).

60 Griffiths interview of Jack Ellitt, 1987.

61 Robert Herring, *Life and Letters Today*, vol. 17, no. 9, Autumn 1937, p. 152.

62 Len Lye, 'Song Time Stuff', in Curnow and Horrocks (eds), *Figures of Motion*, p. 120.
63 Curnow and Horrocks (eds), *Figures of Motion*, especially p. 42 and p. 44
64 *Ibid.*, p. 44. Another Lye essay of this period that looks at the possibilities of 'subjective' film-making was 'The Man who was Colour-Blind' in *Sight and Sound*, vol. 9, Spring 1940, pp. 6–7. Like 'Voice and Colour', the essay focused particularly on the subjective use of colour.
65 The critic who liked Corbett's voice was Tom Driberg, 'Wide-eyed Starlet', *Daily Express*, 18 January 1938.
66 On the downturn, see (for example) C. A. Lejeune, 'How High is the Public', *Observer*, 28 February 1937.
67 Letter from Lye to Graves, late 1942. The film runs for around 17m 20s.
68 Letter, September 1979.
69 McIntyre's voice was dubbed in for Chisholm's, while the thoughts of the German soldier were spoken by Marius Goring (who had played Hitler in the BBC series *In The Shadow of the Swastika*).
70 Interview, 1988.
71 Cavalcanti, 'Presenting Len Lye', p. 134.
72 *Documentary News Letter*, January 1943, p. 165. (There is some evidence that the film was screened in British cinemas.)
73 Interview, 1983.
74 See *Filmestra* (Amsterdam), nos. 6–7, 1948, p. 155.
75 'Sight Sound Consanguinity', unpublished ms. Terry recorded a number of different versions of this piece (some entitled 'Hound Dog Holler' or 'Silver Fox Chase') and it became something of a signature tune for him. One of the musicians inspired by it was Eric Clapton (who first heard it when he was ten). Paul Oliver in *The Story of the Blues* celebrates Terry's 'skill at combining voice and harmonica with falsetto whoops and hollers, alternating with the wails of the instrument played "crossed" . . .' (Northeastern University Press, Boston, 1998, p. 149). Some versions included verbal cries (such as 'Catch him!'). Lye chose a long version without words, recorded by Alan and Bess Lomax. This is still available on *Afro-American Blues and Game Songs* in The Library of Congress Archive of Folk Culture series (Rounder CD 1513).
76 Brent Cashmere in a thoughtful commentary ('Len Lye' at www.sensesofcinema.com) also sees 'a palpable social subtext' in such images as 'saw blades and string, which, when enlarged, resembles rope' – but I think Lye would have avoided such explicit symbolism, and instead he would have selected images for their general 'feel'.
77 'Sight Sound Consanguinity', unpublished ms.
78 Len Lye, letter, September 1979.
79 Unpublished note.
80 Incidentally, Newman, whose paintings were still considered highly controversial, was writing for *The Tiger's Eye* at the same time as Lye.
81 Brant's dates are 1913 to 2008 (see http://www.jaffe.com/brant.html).
82 See 'Lye Horn is Blown at Bowery Jazz House', *Village Voice*, 30 August 1962, p. 3 and p. 13. The Basie collaboration was described in a letter from Barbara Ker-Seymer, 29 June 1981. *All Souls Carnival* has had to be reconstructed (see Chapter 6 for an account of the process).
83 Interview with Henry Brant, 1989.
84 Quoted in P. Adams Sitney (ed.), *Film Culture Reader*, Praeger, New York, 1970, p. 293. (Kubelka replied that he had seen the film in 1958.)
85 P. Adams Sitney, *Visionary Film*, Oxford University Press, New York, 1974, p. 269.
86 Letter to the author, 2 September 1980.
87 John Adams, 'Free Radicals', *Film Quarterly*, vol. 12, no. 3, 1959 (Spring), p. 58. To mention another critical response, in a discussion of abstract films Jonas Mekas drew a useful contrast between Lye's approach and that of film-makers with a more intellectual orientation: '*Free Radicals*, though highly formal and pure, is charged with emotion. The drawings and scratches have a spontaneous quality of powerful impact upon the viewer' (Jonas Mekas, 'Movie Journal', *Village Voice*, 15 April 1959, p. 6).
88 'Somewhat Autobiographically', unpublished ms.
89 Letter, September 1979.
90 See Horrocks, *Len Lye: A Biography*, p. 55. NB: Leader may be transparent or (in this case) black film.
91 Yann Beauvais said of the images of *Free Radicals*, 'These are lines of force, and not lines of figuration, as in . . . *Blinkety Blank*' ('Free Radical', in Bouhours and Horrocks (eds), *Len Lye*, p. 212). I strongly recommend Beauvais's essay which offers many insights into Lye's film.
92 Len Lye, letter to John Halas, 15 January 1958.
93 Lye, quoted in Russett and Starr, *Experimental Animation*, p. 68.
94 See comments by Paul Barnes and Steve Jones, who worked as Lye's assistants on later projects, in Horrocks, *Len Lye: A Biography*, pp. 373–74.
95 Russett and Starr, *Experimental Animation*, p. 68.
96 Quoted in Adrienne Mancia and Willard Van Dyke, 'The Artist as Film-maker: Len Lye', *Art in America*, vol. 54, no. 4, July–August 1966, p. 105.
97 The best bits were made into loops and run through the projector over and over.
98 'Sight Sound Consanguinity', unpublished ms.
99 Russett and Starr, *Experimental Animation*, p. 69. The Bagirmi people are spread through West and Central Africa, today being most closely associated with Chad. Also see Lye's description of the process of selecting music for *Particles in Space* in 'A Note on Dance and Music', in Curnow and Horrocks (eds), *Figures of Motion*.
100 Thanks to Eve de Castro-Robinson and Wayne Laird for commenting on the music. They noted its similarity to some of the Cuban rhythms used by Lye in earlier films.
101 Len Lye, 'A Note on Dance and Film', in Curnow and Horrocks (eds), *Figures of Motion*.
102 For example, Lye's *Serpent* (or *Sea Serpent*).
103 The film was never made, though one of the experiments (*Full Fathom Five*) has survived.
104 When some random frame enlargements were made, the Lyes were delighted to discover the initials of their first names – 'L' and 'A' – not only visible but also linked together. This image was an accident because at the time the film-maker was thinking of his marks purely as shapes, not letters.
105 Interview with Paul Barnes, 1980, quoted in Horrocks, *Len Lye: A Biography*, p. 372.
106 *Ibid.*
107 Steve Jones remembers him 'taking out images that could be dispensed with not because they were necessarily bad but because the body of the film would have been just as good without those parts – it would keep the film shorter and sweeter' (Interview with the author, 1980).
108 The title, which was removed in 1978, is evidence that Lye was thinking in utopian terms as early as 1958. Compare 'When the Venutians Sing "Auld Lang Syne"', his contribution to Robert Hughes (ed.), *Film: Book 2*, Grove Press, New York, 1962.
109 Parker Tyler, *Underground Film: A Critical History*, Penguin, Harmondsworth, 1974, p. 146.
110 Lye joined the English branch of the Surrealist movement and his work was represented (for example) in the 1936 International Surrealist Exhibition in London.
111 Relevant 1930s paintings by Lye include *Helium*, *Snow Birds Making Snow* and *The King of Plants Meets the First Man*. See also his woodcuts for the Surrealist magazine *London Bulletin* (illustrated in Horrocks, *Len Lye: A Biography*, among the pictures following p. 264).
112 See Wystan Curnow's essay, 'Lye and Abstract Expressionism', in Bouhours and Horrocks, *Len Lye*, pp. 205–12.
113 Yann Beauvais, 'Free Radicals', in Bouhours and Horrocks, *Len Lye*, p. 212. (My italics.)
114 'Somewhat Autobiographically', unpublished ms.
115 The news item appears on a slide of the 'Art & the Genes, II' programme.
116 In 1963, Lye reported to Alastair Reid that the film was 'more than half done'. He described it as 'particles in space that spin and change momentum and speed and go "thrang thrup" between

galaxies' (Letter, 11 February 1963). Money was needed to carry the film through to completion and so Lye applied in 1963 to the Ford Foundation which was offering fifteen grants of $15,000 to finance non-commercial projects. In the application, the film was now called 'Rays' and he described it as conveying a 'feeling of the nature of energy and the vastness of space'. The application was unsuccessful. In 1964, he told his friend Jacques Ledoux of the Royal Cinemathèque of Belgium that he 'would rather not have copies of *Free Radicals* on the loose' because he was thinking of expanding it to include the *Particles* material. But in the following year, he was again talking about it as a separate film; and when he was invited to Berkeley, he tried unsuccessfully to persuade Peter Selz's museum to fund the completion of a film that he now described as 'Kinetic Particles In Space'. He screened a five-minute version of *Particles in Space* as part of the 'Absolute Truth of the Happiness Acid' programme which he presented at various venues in 1968. He also showed it as part of 'The Creative Imagination' lecture he gave at the Albright-Knox Gallery in Buffalo in February 1968. In 1971–72, he made a new version that ran for six minutes.

117 I suspect that other sound edits were also made within these nine sections.

118 'Art and the Genes, II' (slide-tape programme), circa 1971.

119 In relation to New Zealand art, it is interesting to compare the use of words and numbers by Colin McCahon (a calligraphy that at first seems rough but is in fact highly skilful).

120 Interview with the author, 1980.

121 See Lye's slide-tape programme, 'Polymer and Callagen'.

FIVE THE SCULPTURES

1 Semir Zeki and Mathew Lamb, 'The Neurology of Kinetic Art', *Brain*, vol. 117, 1994, pp. 607–36. The quotation is from p. 618.

2 To mention some exceptions, Lye gave *Roundhead* a built-in music box, *Singing Blade* is blue, *Wind Wand* is topped by a red lamp and *Ribbon Snake* has a fleshy pink loop. He also experimented at times with coloured lighting.

3 There is, of course, an important trend in modernism towards specialisation, with some artists becoming famous for their in-depth exploration of a single area of visual possibility.

4 Lye talking with John Matthews and Paul Fiondella, New York, 9 November 1978.

5 From 'Art, Happiness and Value', unpublished essay, circa 1964.

6 See Len Lye, 'Considering a Temple', in Wystan Curnow and Roger Horrocks (eds), *Figures of Motion: Len Lye Selected Writings*, Auckland University Press / Oxford University Press, Auckland, 1984, pp. 87 ff.

7 'Somewhat Autobiographically', unpublished ms.

8 Interview with Paul Barnes, 1980. Helpful engineers and machinists mentioned in Lye's notes include Lou Adler, Maurice Gross, Maury Logue, Carl Schulmann, Harvey Sleighton and Bert Stanleigh. (This is how Lye spelled the names.) Rufus Stillman and the staff of his engineering company also helped Lye. No doubt there were others.

9 Lye demonstrated his doodling with metal in two documentaries, *Len Who?: Into an Unknown* (1973) and *Kaleidoscope: Len Lye* (1980).

10 Peter Selz, 'The Berkeley Symposium of Kinetic Art', *Art and Artists*, vol. 1, February 1967, p. 31.

11 Lye talking with John Matthews and Paul Fiondella, New York, 9 November 1978.

12 Email to the author, 25 July 2008.

13 'Tanges' (an unpublished ms that describes *Steel Blade*).

14 Lye talking with John Matthews and Paul Fiondella, New York, 9 November 1978.

15 *Ibid.*

16 *Ibid.*

17 This phrase is Evan Webb's vivid summary of Lye's requirements.

18 Lye's phrase 'the wild kinetic stuff' comes from his conversation with John Matthews and Paul Fiondella, New York, 9 November 1978.

19 Len Lye, 'Film-making', in Curnow and Horrocks (eds), *Figures of Motion*, p. 41.

20 Lye talking with John Matthews and Paul Fiondella, New York, 9 November 1978.

21 *Ibid.*

22 *Ibid.*

23 *Ibid.*

24 *Ibid.*

25 *Ibid.*

26 *Ibid.*

27 *Ibid.*

28 *Ibid.*

29 Webb's comment occurs in the documentary *Flip and Two Twisters.*

30 Ann Lye makes a similar comment in the documentary *Len Lye: Two Studios* ('*Roundhead* is what we think of looking at in our house when it's too hot to have a fire').

31 In his words, it was 'a magnified picture of a male hormone with its concentric circles'. By 'hormone' I assume that Lye meant chromosome since 'roundhead' refers to the Y (or male) chromosome.

32 See Rachel Buchanan's 'Len Lye and Me' in *Meanjin Quarterly*, pp. 20–27, vol. 68, no. 2, Winter 2009.

33 Philip Leider, 'Kinetic Sculpture at Berkeley', *Artforum*, May 1966, pp. 40–42. (The 'dumb imitation' comments are also taken from this review.)

34 Wystan Curnow and I have both made this case on various occasions, with Curnow's essay 'Lye and Abstract Expressionism' as the most detailed presentation (in Jean-Michel Bouhours and Roger Horrocks [eds], *Len Lye*, Centre Pompidou, Paris, 2000, pp. 205–13).

35 Robert Motherwell, quoted in *Artforum*, September 1965, p. 46.

36 See Roger Horrocks, *Len Lye: A Biography*, Auckland University Press, Auckland, 2001, p. 327.

37 The artists who have worked in both media include Duchamp, Moholy-Nagy, Robert Breer and Kenneth Snelson.

SIX LEN LYE TODAY

1 This 1968 documentary is also known as *Art of the Sixties.*

2 For the history up to 2001, see Roger Horrocks, 'In and Out of History: A Century of Len Lye', *Art New Zealand*, no. 101, Summer 2001–2, pp. 52–61

3 In this chapter, 'preservation' refers to the general attempt to help historical material to survive. The activity of 'conservation' has the same aim but the term is applied specifically to the care of collections in museums or art galleries, which usually have a department devoted to conservation.

4 Hiltrud Schinzel, *Touching Vision: Essays on Restoration Theory and the Perception of Art*, Ghent University / Brussels University Press, Brussels, 2004, pp. 136–37.

5 Movies include Bruce Lee's *The Game of Death*, Mario Bava's *Kidnapped*, Maya Deren's *Divine Horsemen* and Stanley Kubrick's *AI*. Books include Ferdinand de Saussure's hugely influential *Course in General Linguistics* and novels by J. R. R. Tolkein, Charles Dickens, Ralph Ellison and many others.

6 Including those of Frank Lloyd Wright, Eero Saarinen, Gerrit Rietveld, Aldo Rossi and Louis I. Kahn. And Antoni Gaudi's *La Sagrada Familia* has had several additions.

7 Dionne Sillé, 'Introduction to the Project', in Usbrand Hummelen and Dionne Sillé (eds), *Modern Art: Who Cares?*, Archetype (in association with the Foundation for the Conservation of Modern Art and the Netherlands Institute for Cultural Heritage), London, 1999, p. 14.

8 See, for example, Marie Louise Sauerberg, 'Proceedings', in Hummelen and Sillé (eds), *Modern Art: Who Cares?*, p. 3[illegible]; and Renée van de Vall, 'Painful Decisions: Philosophical Considerations on a Decision-making Model', *ibid.*, p. 1[illegible].

9 D. H. van Wegen, 'Between Fetish and Score: The Position of the Curator of Contemporary Art', in Hummelen and Sillé (eds), *Modern Art: Who Cares?*, p. 209

10 Compare Jack Burnham's far-sighted comment in 1968 that 'the kinetic construction is not an *objet d'art* in the conventional sense, but a *systeme d'art*' (*Beyond Modern Sculpture*, Allen Lane The Penguin Press, London, p. 263).

11 *Ibid.*

12 Related film material was labelled as 'Carnegie Abstracts' and 'Henry's Paint'. Incidentally, Lye worked on other films in this lyrical style such as *Colour Clouds*. None appears to have been completed to his satisfaction but various sequences have survived. This is dazzling footage with brilliant colours and extremely rich, varied textures, though some of it has unfortunately faded or deteriorated in other ways.

13 The archival team includes Kurt Otzen and Sarah Davy.

14 Dionne Sillé and Marjan Zijlmans, 'The Playful World of Jean Tinguely: An Interview with Ad Petersdon', in Hummelen and Sillé (eds), *Modern Art: Who Cares?*, p. 37.

15 *Ibid.*, p. 41. It is true that Tinguely created works such as *Homage to New York* (1960) that were consciously designed to self-deconstruct, but this was only an occasional impulse. Tinguely worked to ensure the longevity of many of his sculptures.

16 Many small problems also crop up such as the fact that electrical systems differ from country to country, so that when a sculpture is sent to an overseas exhibition its motor may run at a different speed.

17 Letter from Lye to Yusing Jung, 11 October 1967.

18 *Len Who?: Into an Unknown*, NZBC, 1973.

19 From *Fay's Saga*, one of Lye's slide-tape programmes.

20 Letter from Ray Thorburn, 10 August 1981.

21 John Matthews, 'The New Zealand Collection', *Art New Zealand*, no. 17, 1980, p. 32.

22 *Ibid.*

23 'June the Merry Something 1974ish', unpublished note.

24 John Matthews interviewed by the author, 1994.

25 Matthews interviewed by Shirley Horrocks, 1994

26 Matthews, 'The New Zealand Collection', *ibid.*

27 John Matthews interviewed by the author, 1994.

28 See *The Press* (Christchurch), 31 March 1977. This was a one-twentieth of a horsepower motor.

29 John Matthews interviewed by the author, 1994.

30 *Ibid.*

31 *The Press*, *op. cit.*

32 Letter from Lye, 23 April 1978.

33 Ann Lye interviewed by the author, 1980.

34 Letter from Lye, 23 April 1978.

35 Shayne Gooch has established a formula for the ratio between the 'buckling' length and the shorter 'Lye' length. The film *Flip and Two Twisters* shows the making of a *Blade*.

36 See Roger Horrocks, *Len Lye: A Biography*, Auckland University Press, Auckland, 2001, p. 358.

37 Lye talking with John Matthews and Paul Fiondella, New York, 9 November 1978 (tape recording).

38 Lye interviewed by James Macandrew for *Camera Three*, WCBS-TV New York, 1962.

39 From a 2004 report by Stuart Robb for the Govett-Brewster Art Gallery and the Len Lye Foundation, p. 5.

40 Webb writes: 'I first attempted this on the polder lands in Holland because there the sky is clear and large – a clean canvas, so to speak. More recently I have attempted the project on New Brighton Beach, Christchurch, where the easterly is steady and not too strong, and as part of Scape, an Art and Industry project.' (This and other comments by Webb in this chapter are his answers to my questions via an exchange of emails in March 2008.)

41 Wystan Curnow and Roger Horrocks (eds), *Figures of Motion: Len Lye Selected Writings*, Auckland University Press / Oxford University Press, Auckland, 1984, p. 77.

42 In the music box, 'a drum with pins, driven by an electric motor, revolves so that the pins strike or pluck the steel reeds of an 18-reed tuned comb. Len had extracted striking pins from the drum leaving only eight which in turn plucked or struck five separate notes from the tuned comb' (Evan Webb, letter to the author, 23 September 2000).

43 Cf. Jennifer King's letter to the *Dominion Post*, 15 March 2004, p. B4: 'I love the new Len Lye water sculpture on Wellington's waterfront, but wonder if he really meant it to have that large and rather brutal concrete base?'

44 Lye talking with John Matthews and Paul Fiondella, New York, 9 November 1978.

45 The Foundation trustees (including Matthews as chairman) have the ultimate responsibility for approving projects, but Webb is in charge of the process of design and production. As he would be the first to acknowledge, he consults widely along the way with other experts.

46 For example: S. D. Gooch and J. K. Raine, 'The Engineering Design of a Vibrating Kinetic Sculpture', *Spectrum* (The Journal of the Vibrations Association of New Zealand), no. 41, Spring 2003; S. D. Gooch and J. K. Raine, 'The Dynamics and Limits on the Scaling of a Flexible Kinetic Sculpture', *Journal of Mechanical Engineering Science* (Proceedings of the Institution of Mechanical Engineers), vol. 214, no. 4, 2000, pp. 537–48; J. K. Raine and S. D. Gooch, 'Dynamic Analysis and Engineering Design of Kinetic Sculptures', *IPENZ Transactions*, vol. 25, no. 1 / Gen., 1998; J. K. Raine, J. J. Harrington, E. A. Webb and Z. A. Meredith, 'Expanding Universe: Design Study for Scaling Up a Kinetic Sculpture', *Journal of Engineering Design*, vol. 7, no. 4, 1996, pp. 397–410; J. K. Raine, S. D. Gooch and E. A. Webb, 'Artistic Dreams: Engineering Limitations', *New Zealand Science Monthly*, October 1997, pp. 11 ff.

47 Evan Webb, 'Wind Wand: The Magic of Len Lye and the Toronto Affair', *Art New Zealand*, no. 78, 1996. Webb has just published another essay about his work on Lye's sculptures, 'Planting at Night', Cann and Curnow (eds), *Len Lye*, Govett-Brewster Art Gallery / Len Lye Foundation, New Plymouth, 2009.

48 Webb has been working on the logistics, including the design of a different kind of base for *Large Blade* that would make it easier to tour the sculpture.

49 The exchange was reported in 'Reproducing Len Lye's Art', a talk by Evan Webb at the Wellington City Art Gallery, 30 April 2006.

50 Sally Blundell, 'Whose Lye Is It Anyway?', *The Listener*, 22 July 2006, p. 38.

51 *Ibid.*, p. 37.

52 Email to the author, 2 April 2008.

53 Another example is the plaque for *Wind Wand*: 'Conceived by New Zealand born artist Len Lye, this sculpture was commissioned by the New Plymouth District Council and made by the Len Lye Foundation . . . . Lye produced several smaller versions of *Wind Wand* during his lifetime but hoped that one day a 45 metre *Wand* could be built. This posthumous version realizes the artist's intention through the use of glass and carbon fibres . . . .'

54 Reported from a debate about the completion and reproduction of Lye's sculpture at the University of Canterbury School of Fine Arts, 7 October 2004.

55 The agreement for the building of *Wind Wand* said: 'Every endeavour will be made by the Foundation to interpret as faithfully as possible the designs and drawings for the *Wind Wand* in accordance with the late artist's wishes . . . .'

56 The musica ficta controversy refers to notes sung in European choral music prior to about 1600 that were not part of the score but added by performers who understood the conventions of the day. Information about those conventions is contradictory, so that when singers added notes, we cannot be certain whether they avoided combinations that a modern listener would regard as dissonant, or accepted them as normal. Some modern performers of the music take care to avoid any harshness of sound, whereas others relish it on the grounds that early composers are likely to have had a different sense of harmony.

57 Wedde says of *Water Whirler*, 'For me, it's far more interesting, graceful, weightless and intelligent in its conceptual form' (email to the author, 2 April 2008).

58 Email to the author, 2 April 2008.

59 Sauerberg, 'Proceedings', in Hummelen and Sillé (eds), *Modern Art: Who Cares?*, p. 367.

Len Lye resources

This selected bibliography has been brought up to date for the 2015 reprint of this book. Some items are now out of print but may still be available in libraries. A number of other relevant titles appear in the footnotes to this book.

LYE'S WRITINGS

Curnow, Wystan and Roger Horrocks (eds), *Figures of Motion: Len Lye Selected Writings*, Auckland University Press / Oxford University Press, Auckland, 1984.
Horrocks, Roger (ed.), *Body English: Texts and Images by Len Lye*, The Holloway Press, Auckland, 2009.
Horrocks, Roger (ed.), *Happy Moments: Texts and Images by Len Lye*, The Holloway Press, Auckland, 2002.
Horrocks, Roger (ed.), *Zizz!: The Life and Art of Len Lye, in his Own Words*, Awa Press, Wellington, 2015.

BOOKS ABOUT LYE

Bouhours, Jean-Michel and Roger Horrocks (eds), *Len Lye*, Cinéma Quinze Vingt et Un, Centre Pompidou, Paris, 2000. [This collection of essays, by a range of international art and film scholars, is printed in both French and English. The book includes an extensive bibliography and filmography.]
Curnow, Wystan and Tyler Cann (eds), *Len Lye*, Govett-Brewster Art Gallery / Len Lye Foundation, New Plymouth, 2009. [An edition of this book has been co-published by ACMI in Melbourne].
Horrocks, Roger, *Len Lye: A Biography*, Auckland University Press, Auckland, 2001.

GALLERY CATALOGUES

Annear, Judy, *Len Lye*, Art Gallery of NSW, Sydney, 2002.
Batchen, Geoffrey *et al*, *Shadowgraphs: Photographic Portraits by Len Lye*, Adam Art Gallery, Wellington, 2011.
Bogle, Andrew, *Len Lye: A Personal Mythology*, Auckland City Art Gallery, Auckland, 1980.
Brobbel, Paul, *Len Lye: The New Yorker*, Govett-Brewster Art Gallery, New Plymouth, 2012.
Brobbel, Paul, *Len Lye: Kaleidoscope*, City Gallery, Wellington, 2013.
Brobbel, Paul and James Pinker, *Len Lye: Agiagiā*, Mangere Arts Centre, Auckland, 2013.
Burke, Greg, *The Long Dream of Waking: Len Lye Centenary 1901–2001* (2001) and *Trilogy: A Flip & 2 Twisters* (2003), Govett-Brewster Art Gallery, New Plymouth.
Burke, Greg and Tyler Cann, *Len Lye: Motion Sketch (Drawing Papers No.115)*, The Drawing Center, New York, 2014.
Cann, Tyler, *Len Lye's Trilogy: A Flip and 2 Twisters* (2003), *Len Lye: Individual Happiness Now!* (2006), *Double Harmonic: Len Lye and Tony Nicholls* (2007), *Len Lye: Five Fountains and a Firebush* (2007), *Len Lye: Chronosome* (2008), *Len Lye: All Souls Carnival* (2011) and *Old Genes: Artists Reading Len Lye* (2013), Govett-Brewster Art Gallery, New Plymouth.
Cann, Tyler, *The Body Electric*, Ikon Gallery, Birmingham, 2010.
Curtis, David, *Len Lye*, Watershed, Bristol, 1987.
Davy, Sarah, *A Work in Progress: Archiving Len Lye*, The Film Archive, Wellington, 2001.
Horrocks, Roger, *Composing Motion: Len Lye and Experimental Film-making*, National Art Gallery, Wellington, 1992.
Horrocks, Roger, *Art that Moves: The Work of Len Lye*, Gus Fisher Gallery, Auckland, 2009.
Menzies, Michelle, *Cinema and Painting*, Adam Art Gallery, Wellington, 2015.
Scott, Hanna and John Hurrell, *The Long Dream of Waking: Len Lye 1901–2001*, Govett-Brewster Art Gallery, New Plymouth, 2001.

SECTIONS OF BOOKS

Harris, Miriam, 'Literary Len: *Trade Tattoo* and Len Lye's Link with the Literary Avant-Garde', in Suzanne Buchan (ed.), *Animated Worlds*, John Libbey Publishing, Eastleigh, 2006.
Horrocks, Roger, 'Free Radicals', in Geoff Mayer and Keith Beattie (eds), *The Cinema of Australia and New Zealand*, Wallflower Press, London, 2007, pp. 73–82.
Horrocks, Roger, 'Len Lye', in Ian Conrich and Stuart Murray (eds), *New Zealand Filmmakers*, Wayne State University Press, Detroit, 2007, pp. 18–34.
Horrocks, Roger, 'Len Lye: Reading with the Body', in D. A. Gerstner and J. Staiger (eds), *Authorship and Film*, Routledge (AFI Film Readers series), New York, 2003, pp. 175–92.
Thorpe, Jo, *Len and Other Poems*, Steele Roberts, Wellington, 2003.

PERIODICALS

Art New Zealand, no. 17, 1980. [An issue devoted to Len Lye, edited by Wystan Curnow]
Horrocks, Roger, 'In and Out of History: A Century of Len Lye', *Art New Zealand*, no. 101, Summer 2001–2, pp. 52–61.
Horrocks, Roger, '"My Word My World": Len Lye's Poetry', *Landfall*, no. 205, May 2003, pp. 179–85.
Lye, Len, 'Night Tree' [a sequence of poems], *A Brief Description of the Whole World*, no. 3, June 1996, pp. 6–10.
'The Len Lye Lists', *Bulletin of New Zealand Art History*, vol. 8, 1980. [This bibliography includes hundreds of items about Lye published during his lifetime.]

AUDIO-VISUAL RESOURCES

Addressing the Nation: The GPO Film Unit Collection Vol. 1, BFI, London, 2008. [A set of two DVDs, with a booklet, which includes Lye's film *A Colour Box*. Volume 2 in the series, *We Live in Two Worlds*, includes Lye's films *N or NW*, *Rainbow Dance* and *Trade Tattoo*.]
Doodlin': Impressions of Len Lye, VHS. [A documentary directed by Keith Griffiths of Koninck Studios in 1987.]
Flip and Two Twisters. [A documentary about Lye directed by Shirley Horrocks, produced in 1995. Available on DVD. See: www.pointofview.co.nz]
Free Radicals: Len Lye's Films Vol. 1, New Plymouth, 1997. [A VHS video collection of eight films, produced by the Len Lye Foundation. Some copies of this and other items on this list are still available from the Govett-Brewster Art Gallery bookshop. The Len Lye Foundation, in association with Ngā Taonga and the Len Lye Centre, will soon be releasing a DVD collection of nineteen Lye films entitled *Colour Box*.]
History of the Avant-Garde: Britain in the Twenties, BFI, London, 2000. [A VHS video that includes Lye's film *Tusalava*.]
Le Mouvement des Images, Centre Pompidou, Paris, 2006. [A DVD that includes Lye's film *Rhythm*.]
Len Lye: Rhythms, Re:Voir, Paris, 2001. [A VHS video collection of twelve of Lye's films, with a booklet.]
Len Lye Talks about Art, New Plymouth, 2004. [A DVD containing seven of Lye's slide-tape lectures about art, with a booklet, co-published by the Govett-Brewster Art Gallery and the Len Lye Foundation.]

MUSIC/SOUND/THEATRE

Len Lye: Composing Motion: The Sound of Tangible Motion Sculpture, Atoll ACD 305. [This remarkable CD by Wayne Laird is based on the sound patterns of Lye's kinetic sculptures. With booklet.]
Bob, C. L. *The Great Flash*. Yellow Eye 023. [Jazz music dedicated to Lye.]
Others who have composed music influenced by Lye include Harry Harrison and Thrashing Marlin (whose 'All You've Got Somebody' on the *Wit's End* CD incorporates a vocal sample by the artist).
Zig Zag. [This music and visual event, inspired by Len Lye and designed by Tim Gruchy, has been performed at the Taranaki and Auckland arts festivals. It is available on DVD.]
Hannan, Brian, *Len*. [A play.]
Composer Eve de Castro-Robinson has written these works of music associated with Lye: *Len Dances* (premiered in 2003 by the Auckland Philharmonia), *Len Songs* (premiered at the Wellington Festival in 2004 by Helen Medlyn), *Knife Apple Sheer Brush* (premiered by Mette Leroy and the Karlheinz Company in 2006) and *Pearls of the Sea* (premiered in 2005 by the chamber group Flight, and included on Atoll CD 709 *Flight*). Eve also collaborated with Roger Horrocks on *Len Lye: The Opera*, which was premiered in Auckland at the Maidment Theatre in 2012. Samples of de Castro-Robinson's music are available on YouTube.

INTERNET

The Len Lye Foundation's website is: www.lenlyefoundation.com/
The Govett-Brewster Art Gallery/Len Lye Centre website is: http://govettbrewster.com/len-lye/
There is a Len Lye entry in *The Dictionary of New Zealand Biography*, on-line at: www.dnzb.govt.nz/dnzb/default.asp
The New Zealand Electronic Poetry Centre website includes a number of examples of Lye's creative writing: www.nzepc.auckland.ac.nz/
The NZ On Screen website (www.nzonscreen.com) includes a ten-minute clip from *Flip and Two Twisters*, Shirley Horrocks's documentary about Lye.
The Point of View Productions website has Lye links: www.pointofview.co.nz/Flip.htm
www.screenonline.org.uk/ (under 'Lye') offers a British perspective.
Flickr has photos of Lye sculptures, posted by members of the public.
The *Art New Zealand* website contains essays from the magazine's two Lye issues (No. 17 and No. 101): www.art-newzealand.com/
An Internet search will reveal hundreds of other items, including a Wikipedia entry on Lye. Some of his films are also available on the net, but the copies are unauthorised and are of poor quality.

EXHIBITIONS

There are exhibitions of Lye's work in art galleries, museums and film archives. For New Zealanders, the most important venue is the Len Lye Centre in Queen Street, New Plymouth. There are also public sculptures in New Plymouth (*Wind Wand*) and Wellington (*Water Whirler*).

index

art that moves the work of len lye dvd

The attached DVD will play continuously, but also includes a menu that makes it possible to play directly any of the following numbered items.

About Len Lye:

1. ART THAT MOVES

Director and writer: Roger Horrocks. Producer: Shirley Horrocks. Camera: Leon Narbey. Music: Eve de Castro-Robinson. Point of View Productions, 2009. This dramatised short film imagines the world through the eyes of the young Len Lye as he develops his ideas about motion. It was made with the assistance of the Screen Innovation Fund of Creative New Zealand.

Films by Len Lye:

2. SWINGING THE LAMBETH WALK
3. TRADE TATTOO
4. COLOR CRY
5. FREE RADICALS

Sculpture by Len Lye:

6. FOUNTAIN
7. ROUNDHEAD
8. BLADE
9. FIRE BUSH
10. UNIVERSE

Note: The footage of *Fire Bush* was directed by Shirley Horrocks and filmed by David Paul for Point of View Productions (2008). The other sculpture footage was directed by Shirley Horrocks and filmed by Leon Narbey for *Flip and Two Twisters* (1995), a documentary about Len Lye. For more information about this documentary, see the Point of View Productions website: www.pointofview.co.nz

Lye's films are included on this DVD by permission of the Len Lye Foundation and are provided for home use only. To contact the Len Lye Foundation or to enquire about public screenings of Lye's films, write to Evan Webb at: e.webb@ext.canterbury.ac.nz

The principal archive in charge of Lye's films is Ngā Taonga Sound & Vision (www.ngataonga.org.nz).

Other material on this DVD is also provided for home use only. Any enquiries about public or institutional screenings of *Art that Moves* should be addressed to info@pointofview.co.nz